Teaching
CITY
KIDS

Studies in the
Postmodern Theory of Education

Joe L. Kincheloe and Shirley R. Steinberg
General Editors

Vol. 306

PETER LANG
New York • Washington, D.C./Baltimore • Bern
Frankfurt am Main • Berlin • Brussels • Vienna • Oxford

Teaching

CITY

KIDS

Understanding and Appreciating Them

Joe L. Kincheloe
& kecia hayes, Editors

PETER LANG
New York • Washington, D.C./Baltimore • Bern
Frankfurt am Main • Berlin • Brussels • Vienna • Oxford

KH

Library of Congress Cataloging-in-Publication Data

Teaching city kids: understanding and appreciating them /
edited by Joe L. Kincheloe, Kecia Hayes.
p. cm. — (Counterpoints: studies in the postmodern theory of education; v. 306)
Includes bibliographical references and index.
1. Education, Urban—United States.
2. Pluralism (Social sciences)—United States.
I. Hayes, Kecia. II. Title.
LC5131.K56   371.009173'2—dc22   2006022715
ISBN-13: 978-0-8204-8603-1
ISBN-10: 0-8204-8603-5
ISSN 1058-1634

Bibliographic information published by **Die Deutsche Bibliothek**.
Die Deutsche Bibliothek lists this publication in the "Deutsche
Nationalbibliografie"; detailed bibliographic data is available
on the Internet at http://dnb.ddb.de/.

Cover design by Lisa Barfield

The paper in this book meets the guidelines for permanence and durability
of the Committee on Production Guidelines for Book Longevity
of the Council of Library Resources.

© 2007 Peter Lang Publishing, Inc., New York
29 Broadway, 18th floor, New York, NY 10006
www.peterlang.com

Printed in the United States of America

8/25/08

Table of Contents

1.

INTRODUCTION

1. City Kids–Not the Kind of Students You'd Want to Teach

JOE L. KINCHELOE

One of the most important themes that I have developed in my work on urban education involves the complexity and diversity of the enterprise. In *19 Urban Questions: Teaching in the City* in which Shirley Steinberg and I attempt to provide a general overview of city teaching, I write about the co-existence of extremes under the urban education umbrella. From the richest of the rich to the poorest of the poor, from the most well-equipped to the most ill-equipped schools, from the highest achieving to the lowest achieving classrooms—one can find it all in urban education. In this book with its focus on city students, the same is true—in urban education we can find children and young people with vastly diverse experiences and needs. The types and levels of diversity of urban students are at times overwhelming. Take, for example, the demographics of all the second-grade classes in a public school in Ozone Park in Queens, New York. Consider the educational implications of the following statistics. Out of 425 total students in the second grade, the following nationalities (and their numbers) are represented on the next page.

Diversity and complexity reside in these second-grade classrooms and the thousands like them in various cities around the country and the world.

Demographics for Second-Grade Classes in Ozone Park School

Puerto Rico	66 students	Venezuela	3 students
Guyana	63 students	Vietnam	2 students
Dominican Republic	52 students	Germany	2 students
Ecuador	47 students	Honduras	2 students
Bangladesh	25 students	England	2 students
Italy	23 students	Indonesia	2 students
Colombia	20 students	Jamaica	2 students
Trinidad	19 students	Brazil	1 student
China	12 students	Canada	1 student
Philippines	9 students	Lebanon	1 student
Mexico	8 students	Greece	1 student
Peru	8 students	Ukraine	1 student
Yemen	8 students	Hong Kong	1 student
Poland	7 students	Albania	1 student
India	7 students	Korea	1 student
Ireland	6 students	Costa Rica	1 student
Egypt	4 students	Argentina	1 student
Guatemala	4 students	Russia	1 student
Spain	3 students		

Getting to Know You:
The Necessity of Knowing Our Urban Students

The emphasis of this book is on the complexities surrounding urban students—especially the ones most marginalized by race, class, gender, religion, and language. All of the authors in this book are very concerned with the ways opportunity and mobility are undermined for these diverse students. They are interested in who these students are and the multitude of creative ways educators can use their knowledge of such students to create curricula that speak to and motivate them. While the book is grounded on a critical pedagogical foundation that is concerned with power and justice, it takes its first insight from John Dewey's progressive tenet that pedagogy should begin with an understanding of the learner—who she is and what interests and concerns her.[1] This enables teachers to help urban students cultivate the academic skills, information, dispositions, and research proficiencies they need to pursue their curiosities. Indeed, teachers in a critical context become the mediators of urban students' confrontations with the world. Critical urban teachers use their knowledge of students and the contexts in which they operate to help them interpret, make sense of, and reconceptualize the world around them and their relation to it.

These teachers as mediators are empowered through their knowledge of their students and the contextual forces that shape them to understand their students as learners in all the diverse ways learning can take place. Such teachers are experts at developing curricula that account for the ways of learning and the contexts in which such processes transpire. Thus, critical urban teachers become explorers of the worlds of their students, their social and cultural contexts as well as the mindspaces produced by operating in such locales. Here individual identities are recognized, problems faced are understood, hopes and dreams are carefully taken into account in a larger effort to provide positive academic and social experiences. In this context, individual experiences are addressed and many times moral and emotional support is provided. The ultimate point of such a critical urban pedagogy, however, is not only to validate identities but also to challenge students to cultivate their intellects and engage in civic acts of courage for social improvement. This is a lot to ask of marginalized urban students, but to do otherwise is to fail to respect their amazing abilities, their great potentials.

When urban teachers fail to develop profound insights into the lives of their students, all kinds of nasty things begin to happen. The title of this chapter comes from a conversation I heard several years ago between two white teachers taking graduate courses at the university where I was teaching. One had a chance to leave a bad situation with a principal who was giving her a hard time and go to another school in a poor African American section of the city.

First teacher: "I have to leave my school. The principal is torturing me. I've got an offer over at Opal Gardens. I don't know what to do. Should I take it?"

Second teacher: " Oh God, no. Have you ever been over there? It's horrible. Those kids there, they're not the kind of students you'd want to teach. It's better to stay where you are than go to Opal Gardens."

Such a statement, of course, is based on crass stereotypes and simple prejudice. Because such perspectives on economically challenged urban students of color are so prevalent and powerful, it becomes even more important to know about city kids. Who are these students that are allegedly so dangerous and unteachable? What is important to them? What worries them? What are their dreams? What are their goals? What role does school play in their lives? When urban teachers can answer questions such as these, they are better able to engage in one of the most important and most difficult of pedagogical acts: the construction of teaching and learning experiences that meet the needs of particular students and in the process move them to a new domain of understanding, insight, and scholarly skills. In this context critical urban teachers understand the interactions of students and contexts, studying the ways poverty and racism, for example, shape the lives of students.

Here, critical teachers trace the micro-impact of such macro-forces on the relationship between student and school, tracing even the affective dimensions of the experience of growing up and living in marginalized circumstances. Such affective factors might include the ways everyday anxieties coming from living in poverty and tough neighborhoods can affect one's ability to concentrate on abstract concepts. The level of hope and optimism that a student brings to school exerts a profound impact on how one engages in schoolwork.[1] Understanding this, critical urban teachers make sure that they work with urban students to lessen anxiety by creating safe and emotionally supportive classrooms and by working to increase the reasons a student might have to be hopeful and optimistic.

Thus, critical urban teachers not only need to know various subject matters and the various contexts in which their students live, but they also need to understand the affective/emotional effects of these contexts on their students and ways of dealing with such powerful dynamics in their teaching. In his autobiography Bob Dylan writes of struggling in his teens as a young musician in Minnesota.[2] One day his band was playing as the most famous wrestler of the 1950s, Gorgeous George walked by. Dylan thought he heard the golden haired wrestler say to him in reference to his music: "you're making it come alive" (p. 44). This was all the encouragement Dylan would need for years to come. The same is true for many marginalized urban students. Recognition by a teacher that one has a special talent can help counter some of the negative emotional effects of having to live in poverty. What a difference such an acknowledgment can make in a young person's life! Understanding this power of recognizing and "calling out" ability, whenever I see a young person exhibiting a particular talent I go out of my way to let her know how much I appreciate her talent.

In a larger context where we work for socio-political and economic justice for marginalized peoples in urban contexts, these affective dimensions of urban education are very important. Alone they are not sufficient, but when combined with a larger understanding of the way power operates to undermine achievement and success of individuals in low-status situations, they are an integral aspect of a critical urban pedagogy. In this larger context, we can begin to make sure that urban students marginalized by race, class, language, and immigration status develop a sense of belongingness in a tough urban cosmos. A central aspect of a critical urban education that promotes personal and social transformation involves creating this sense of belongingness to the classroom, the school, the community, and larger social commitments such as justice and fairness for everyone despite their racial, class, gender, or national origins.

The only way, the editors and authors of this book argue, to accomplish such goals is for teachers and educators to deal with the lived realities of students. Here we move to the critical ontological—the branch of philosophy that deals with being—level. In this context we understand our students' being in the world, the forces that shape them, the larger processes of which they are a part, and the contexts in which they operate. The critical dimension of our critical ontology moves us to think about the ways dominant power attempts to shape the consciousness, the identity, the subjectivity of our students.[3]

Such ways of thinking about and getting to know our students not only help us teach them better, but also help us resist the ways dominant corporate power operates to standardize the curriculum in a way that rolls students off the assembly line so they can become replaceable, low-paid employees in the free market-driven workplace of the globalized economy. Not only are such educational policies ethically and politically regressive, but they also alienate economically and racially marginalized students from schools that have little respect for them as human beings or that value the unique experiences they bring to the classroom.[4] Efforts to connect marginalized urban student experience to the curriculum in the standardized right-wing curriculum are viewed as threats to the established social order with its unequal power relations.

Persistent Perceptions of Non-White Inferiority: The Social Construction of Ability

It is amazing in the twenty-first century that white perceptions of non-white peoples continue to be deficit laden and inscribed by fear. Not only do many whites believe that black people, Latinos, and Native Americans/indigenous peoples are cognitively deficient, but also that urban "ethnic" street culture contradicts dominant white values such as the work ethic, generational improvement, socio-economic mobility, self-sufficiency, family values, and sobriety. While there is debate over whether or not non-white culture is genetically inferior or environmentally inferior, numerous social and educational policies continue to be made on the assumption of white superiority. In the twenty-first century, urban educational policies and curriculum development is grounded on a set of tacit social assumptions that:

- take for granted non-white deficiency
- ignore various modes of racial and class-based oppression
- accept the pathologization of African American, Latino, Muslim/Arab, and indigenous peoples for opting not to choose "good values"
- and never challenge the justice and fairness of the larger social order.[5]

In this hidden—don't ask, don't tell—dominant racial ideology of the contemporary era, many white people believe that we are devoting too many resources to teach the "wrong students." In this construction urban students of color are deemed to be not good enough for such monetary resources. As Richard Herrnstein and Charles Murray wrote in their best selling book *The Bell Curve* we should be diverting educational funds from those poor and non-white students who are beyond help and focus our funding on education for the gifted and talented. Operating in this ideological climate, many teachers simply do not expect their urban students from poor neighborhoods and urban students of color to be good students. And teacher expectation profoundly influences student performance. Critical urban teachers realize that they must understand the insidious and complex ways that teacher expectations of urban students are constructed. The prevailing politics of knowledge in the twenty-first century creates an information climate that supports deficit views of minority students.[6]

When we watch movies, for example, that ascribe predatory, animal-like characteristics to young black males from the inner city, we begin to gain insight into where these deficit views come from and how they are inserted into the public consciousness. This racial consciousness penetrates the walls of the school and helps shape policies, curricula, programs, and pedagogies grounded on perceptions of students' racial and cultural identities. In such a context the abilities and talents that marginalized urban students bring to school are ignored, the complexity of the identities of urban youth is disregarded. What makes these dynamics especially hurtful for urban students marginalized by race and class involves the tendency of students to accept the school's debased view of them and their academic abilities. Over and over again I speak with urban students who tell me that they do not possess academic ability. They have learned a key lesson often taught in concealed ways and sometimes inculcated in a more overt manner.

The covert ways such lessons are taught may be more effective, as they subconsciously plant seeds of inferiority into the psyches of urban students. A linguistic example of this insidious dimension of the pathologization process involves the frequent use of the term, "immature," to characterize urban students of color and justify their retention in the same grade or relegation to a lower track. When marginalized urban students are held back a grade or placed in a low academic track, they become extremely frustrated and depressed in regard to academic matters. They lose faith in their ability to perform in school and come to see themselves as failures. These are the wages of larger social constructions of inferiority. Thus, a vicious cycle is created that eventuates in large numbers of African American and Latino students being labeled emotionally disturbed and cognitively disabled.

Once such labels are ascribed to urban students, they never get "unlabeled." Some studies indicate that school psychologists believe that about 16% of all urban students are "abnormal." Of course, such inferior and deviant students cannot be expected to respond to a rigorous academic curriculum. Ensnared by dominant cultural attributions of inadequacy and malformation, educational and political leaders ignore the demographic patterns surrounding those students relegated to special education. Too often they turn their heads the other way as tens of thousands of poor, non-white, and English-as-second-language speakers are filtered into low tracks and special education.

Of course, African Americans, especially African American males, are over-represented in special education—particularly so in programs for the mentally retarded and severely emotionally disturbed. Concurrently, these same students are under-represented in gifted and high academic tracks. Most of the urban students that are relegated to special education are not "severely handicapped" or suffering from severe disabilities. Most of these students have exhibited mild behavior and academic problems, and are hard to distinguish from students in "regular" classrooms. Public Law 94–142, designed to provide for the needs of students with disabilities, has been co-opted by politicos with profoundly different goals. Such operatives have promoted the use of special education as a holding pen for economically and racially oppressed students who are deemed undesirable by the larger society and the schools. So-called objective science grounded on these assumptions of inferiority, comfort educational and political leaders, assuring them that such students cannot operate in normal frameworks.[7] A critical urban pedagogy concerned with the best interests of city kids challenges these assumptions and the authority of the psychological science that "validates" them. It challenges the social construction of ability/inability.

In light of these insights, it is important to note that middle/upper-middle class white teachers often have difficulty understanding the social construction of ability and its effects on students of color. Do not take this as an attack on white people—it is not. Instead, it is a recognition of the need for many white teachers to work hard to grasp the racial dimensions of teaching in an urban school. In the present ideological climate this is often a difficult recognition for white teachers to make because of the bombardment of the racial imagery previously referenced. In this information climate, it is very hard to work with students who are racially and culturally different from oneself. It is especially difficult when status differences enter the picture. Status differences often provoke anger and resentment from those in the lower-status group. Teachers must be acutely aware of such dynamics and be ready to address them whenever they occur. If such situations are not addressed, they can undermine all the efforts an urban teacher makes to be a good educator.

When studying urban students in relation to questions of race, class, gender, and language, these issues of power are omnipresent. Power always works best when it is hidden, when it is flying under the radar. Thus, in this context, well-intentioned white middle/upper-middle class teachers can publicly condemn racism and class bias while unconsciously engaging in behaviors that perpetuate structural forms of these social pathologies. By acting upon tacit white norms and privileges, such teachers can assume particular deficiencies of poor and non-white students—deficits that such students are likely to reflect in their construction of self-images and the behaviors in which they engage. I have watched this process far too often for comfort. Too often when such teachers are confronted about their racist and class-biased behavior, they do not react very positively.

In most non-elite urban schools, teachers have much more formal education than the parents of their students.[8] In these contexts everyone is aware of this disparity, but it is not something that is typically discussed. On occasion I have heard it mentioned by parents of poor or non-white urban students who are angry about the way their son or daughter is being treated at school. I have heard many of these parents say something such as: " I don't care how educated that teacher is, she hates black people and treats them like shit." At the same time I have heard white middle/upper-middle class teachers say in private after a conversation with an angry parent of color from a poor neighborhood: "She has a bad attitude. She sees everything as a racial issue—she doesn't know what she's talking about." Many white teachers who unwittingly hold some of the tacit prejudices discussed above speak approvingly of parental involvement in education in the abstract, but when examined more closely one begins to discern a distinction in their attitudes involving the backgrounds of the parents involved. Some poor parents of color in this context have little business making suggestions to such teachers about the education of their children.

While there are many personal, psychological, and individualistic dimensions to these behaviors, they can only be deeply understood when viewed both in these micro- and macro-social contexts. Thus, the critical ontological dimension emerges again, as critical pedagogical researchers encourage all urban educators to understand the ways that larger social forces, dominant power discourses, and hegemonic processes shape the ways they view themselves, the world, and their students. Specifically, how have these larger forces shaped their racial and class consciousness? How do such dynamics help construct the ways they view the cognitive abilities of their urban students? Do they dismiss many of their students' abilities that might be classified under the category of "street smarts," as if such capacities had nothing to do with issues of cognitive ability in general? Such dismissal usually results in brilliant urban kids being viewed as incapable or slow. Such perceptions profoundly shape the quality of such students' lives.

As I observe many marginalized urban students, I am often amazed by the cognitive sophistication they demonstrate in their daily struggles to survive in challenging environments. In such circumstances I ask myself how would I have dealt with a similar situation. My answer too often for my own comfort is: not as well as the student I am observing. Contemporary socio-cognitive theory focuses more attention on an individual's ability to deal with and negotiate the obstacles found in one's environment than it does on one's talent for solving abstract, decontextualized problems on a standardized test. Yet, contemporary educational policy continues to put more and more emphasis on test performance than anything else. I challenge anyone to observe many of our economically poor and racially marginalized urban students negotiate everyday life in tough neighborhoods and then tell me that such actions do not constitute smart, sometimes brilliant, cognitive activity. From my perspective such actions illustrate forms of intelligence that I believe are far more sophisticated than some of the skills needed to excel in, even *design* existing intelligence tests.

I watch these young people engage in potentially dangerous social interactions and interpret the meaning and the possible hazards of such encounters. Concurrently, I watch them design effective behaviors to deal with the demands of the circumstance. The ability to discern the affective status, meanings, motivations, and intentions of others in quick meetings and confrontations is a key cognitive skill when one operates on dangerous streets. I believe that such cognitive skills can be identified, analyzed, and transferred to academic tasks by discerning and well-informed urban educators. Thus, if we abandon narrow, race and class-inscribed cognitive theories that automatically dismiss the sophistication of such skills, we can develop more multidimensional and complex cognitive insights that alert us to the wisdom of marginalized urban students. Only when this happens will educators begin to understand the academic potential of city kids.[9] This is how power works best—in this case through cognitive theories that become ideological tools to retard the progress of economically poor and/or urban students of color.

The Great Fear: White People's Fear of Blacks and Other Non-Whites and Urban Education

Lurking behind every conversation about race is what W.E.B. DuBois called decades ago—the Great Fear. DuBois's term refers to white people's discomfort with what he called "the darker races." Deal carefully with these dark peoples, the Great Fear whispers into the ears of white people:

> Put their rights in the background; emphasize their duties—say little of ambition or aspiration; and above all, watch and ward against the first appearance of arrogance or self-assertion or consciousness of great power. Take the eyes of these millions off the stars and fasten them in the soil; and if their young men will dream dreams, let them be dreams of corn bread and molasses.[10]

While times have changed in many ways since DuBois first wrote these words—a more industrial/post-industrial society does not look as much to the soil, to agriculture, for non-white employment—the idea of low-level jobs for social regulation still operates today. As I watch economically poor African American and Latino students in the city struggle through school with its standardized tests and vocational placement, I understand the power of DuBois's words in a new era. When I observe white reaction to confident and assertive people of color, I see a contemporary reflection of the Great Fear.

This white fear leads to calls, often encoded, for greater control of the black and *de colores* population. We see clearly the results of such positions in the ever-climbing incarceration statistics for non-white peoples.[11] At the same time, we can observe this quest for order and control of urban students of color in the educational reforms of the late twentieth and first decade of the twenty-first centuries. Such policies promote a needless waste of the talents of city students of color, as they value gratuitous forms of social control over efforts to motivate and involve such students in a critical curriculum. In many urban areas, for example, young black men are twice as likely to end up in prison than at a university—and the cost of incarcerating is higher than that of a college education.

In the last half of the first decade of the twenty-first century, it is merely the common wisdom among white people that they have much more to fear from people of color than vice versa. Of course, from the perspective of Blacks and Latinos this comfortable belief seems quite odd. For generations African Americans have had much to fear from whites, white police, white juries, and racial hate groups. In the contemporary era many urban people of color sense that with their awkward relationship with the police that they are not legally well protected in their homes and neighborhoods. Yet, none of this seems to affect the dominant white public consciousness of the twenty-first century. One does not hear presidential candidates assuring their audiences that when they are elected, black people will be safer. Such promises are directed at white groups who fear black crime and violence toward Caucasians. This inversion of racial trepidation rests on the established image of the dark-skinned male as a hypersexual predator. This construction of men of color as dire threats operates to rationalize increasingly severe modes of regulation.[12]

Given this pervasive representation of black male violence, many members of the general public as well as many individuals in the education community ask why anyone would want to teach around these "sadistic" young people. Critical urban educators' explanations of their commitment to such students is in this context often met with blank stares. It is fascinating to watch young African American and Latino males react to these predatory, brutal pictures of them many white people carry around in their imagination. Over the past several decades numerous scholars have reported the ways that men of color have insolently elevated such hypersexual, violent representations into a celebration of white people's fear of them.[13] As a male from the southern Appalachian Mountains, I can understand the feelings that low-status groups might possess in such circumstances. Many times I watched men that I knew let people that looked down on them as inferiors know: "You may not think I'm as good as you, but I can kick your ass like it's never been kicked." In such cases the greatest power one might possess in his relationships with others higher on the socio-economic ladder involve his ability to evoke fear in them.

One does not have to be an adept sociologist to understand how these efforts to frighten middle/upper-middle class white people can morph into an even more virulent form of white racism. A vicious circle of race hatred is set into motion here that adds fuel to the flames of racial distrust and violence. Until racial minorities came to be viewed as violent menaces to society, white people viewed as "ethnics" did not feel the need to form groups to celebrate their European legacy. In other work I have referred to this as the crisis of whiteness that emerged after the Civil Rights Movement and the urban riots of the late 1960s.[14] In the crisis, white people sense that white supremacy is being lost, white power is being diluted, and the white portion of the economic pie is being reduced. In the crisis of whiteness white people see themselves as the real victims of racism and must fight to retain what is justly their birthright.

In a society operating within a crisis of whiteness the city kids that we are concerned with here are placed at a profound disadvantage. On many levels the education of urban students of color from low socio-economic backgrounds may be seen as a threat to many white people. As previously referenced, these students are often perceived as the wrong students, young people unworthy of the resources needed to meet their educational requirements, graduates who will get the jobs white people and their children rightfully deserve. These are profoundly important issues in contemporary urban education, but they are the very matters that are too infrequently discussed in schools. While significant exceptions to this tendency exist, one would be hard pressed at many urban schools to hear an open dialog about race and socio-economic class between members of different racial groups. In the crisis of whiteness marked by a movement on the part of many conservative white people to "recover" what they perceived to have lost during the Civil Rights Movement and policies such as affirmative action, there is a desperate need to address the educational issues raised by such perspectives.[15]

As the concierge to the allotment of the society's assets, education is situated in the middle of these racial and class dynamics. DuBois's Great Fear rears its head in such a pedagogical context, as many white people are apprehensive of the very idea of African Americans, Latinos, and Native Americans gaining open access to educational resources. Buoyed and emboldened by their knowledge, such students might issue a stinging evaluation of social institutions and the historic and contemporary actions of white people. Over the past three decades, I have had many white students who when faced with my analysis of the role of race and class in shaping educational institutions reacted in response to the Great Fear dominating their consciousness. "We can't teach black people the things you're talking about in here," they proclaim. When asked why not, they respond clearly and directly: "If black people know about all the racism of schooling and society, there's no telling what they'd do to us." What is the alternative, I ask such students. Should white people withhold knowledge about racism from students of color? "Yes," they respond. This anti-racist education, this critical multiculturalism can ruin our country, some white students tell me.

Whites ensnared in the crisis of whiteness find little capacity for empathy with the struggles of students of color. They refuse to ponder the desperate onus of responsibility that African American and Latino students carry to prove to the white world that they are capable and trustworthy. Such a burden evokes feelings of degradation and resentment that contemporary white people often dismiss and ridicule. Traditional psychology and other academic disciplines often support white students in this context with their normalization of white ways of thinking and being. The humiliation and resentment experienced by many students of color in these traditional discourses are often viewed as abnormal behaviors. Indeed, African American language patterns are often viewed as not simply deficient academically but as hostile and threatening. When an African American or Latino student's language is viewed in this way, teachers are quick to refer students to special education or a lower track curriculum. Here the regulation of behavior takes precedence over academic and cognitive growth.

One views the Great Fear at work in urban classrooms with the effort to control the so-called non-submissive black males. Researchers have found that urban teachers devote an inordinate amount of time attempting to restrain and manage the energy and bodies of black male students.[16] In this context, we observe male students of color castigated for their speech patterns, gestures, eye contact or lack of eye contact, dress, and non-verbal interactions. The point here is not that male students of color do not engage in behaviors that must be addressed, they do. The salient aspect of this issue involves the comparative number of school expulsions and suspensions between male students of color and white males. It is also important in this context to understand the way educators punish behaviors of male students of color that they extol with other students. One can view the same tendencies at work in the penal system. Society's concern with the Great Fear and its pernicious educational effects is not on the public radar in the last half of the first decade of the twenty-first century.[17]

The other side of the Great Fear is the white teacher as the savior of urban students of color. In this model, heroic white teachers come to the ghetto to save African American and Latino young people from their unconcerned families, the gangs that are taking over their neighborhoods, and most of all, from their own demons. Here teachers come to rescue their students, bringing them the civilizing influences that white people have provided people of color for centuries. In this historic construct, civilizing influences involve inculcating students with the dominant culture's code of behavior and ways of seeing the world. What we are talking about here is the attempt to "whiten" urban students of color as much as is possible. The optimism of the white savior teacher rests on his or her belief that these students can be whitened. They differ from the Herrnsteins and Murrays of the world who believe that such effort is useless—students of color just do not have the genetic capability to get it. The saviors have hope—African Americans, Latinos, and indigenous peoples can become more like white people if we just do not give up on them.[18]

In this whitening framework, Philip Anderson and Judith Summerfield write of this salvation motif in the context of educational reforms that replace the urban with the rural idealized (white) past.[19] As the urban becomes more and more a signifier of the non-white, immigrant, non-English speaking, globalized diasporic world's intrusion on "the West," the more the need for Disney's nineteenth century middle-American (white) Celebration community, small schools, and rigorous academic standards to save the day. As Anderson and Summerfield argue, the rural has come to signify the "lost America"—the urban represents what destroyed it and is, thus, a problem to be solved. Rural whiteness is the antidote to urban "coloredness." This colored urban is marked by mayhem and unrest, and is concurrently exoticized and feared.

From Fear to Hope: The Challenges Urban Students Face

To study urban students is to study power and its complex workings in the twenty-first century. A variety of power dynamics including discourse and ideology are constantly at work interacting with urban student consciousness to produce particular perspectives and activities. Two quick definitions: discourse involves a constellation of hidden historical rules that govern what can be and cannot be said, and who can speak and who must listen—discourses shape how we operate in the world as human agents. Ideology involves forms of meaning making that support dominant power interests. Dominant ideology does not determine student consciousness, as students interact with such a form of power in complicated and sometimes convoluted ways. Indeed, the way the power of ideology and discourse work is often unconscious. The study of how dominant ideology and discourse shape us, help make us who we are, is a central dimension of a critical urban education.

Such an undertaking demands that urban educators who accept this critical charge must be profoundly adept at tracing the footprints of power in its macro-social productive stage, at its meso-institutional stage at school, and its micro-individual stage at the level of student and teacher consciousness construction. These are very complex processes—but committed teachers and students are certainly capable of learning how they operate and how they can be interrupted. In this delicate critical pedagogical process, teachers and students work together to identify the nature and origins of their worldviews, their sense of selfhood, and their interpretations of their experiences. In this process they analyze the political (power-related) dimensions of these existing worldviews, self-images, and understandings of experience. How has power shaped my ways of seeing? What are the discursive and ideological implications of these ways of viewing world and self? How can I change these dynamics so they benefit my interests and the needs of my community rather than the interests of those who wield the most power? This pedagogical process operates at every level of the curriculum in a critical urban education.

Critical teachers working in this context carefully study the interaction of their and their students' old ways of understanding a situation, an aspect of the world in relation to the new critical perspective. How do they interact? What unique insights do they produce? What internal conflicts, if any, do they generate? What behaviors, or change in behaviors do they elicit? Does the interaction have affective and emotional consequences? Again, the types of educational reform that are reshaping the face of urban education in the twenty-first century completely ignore these crucial questions as to the impact of the teaching and learning process on our students. In the reductionism, the emphasis of simple-minded standardized test scores, these profound dimensions of the educational process are removed from consideration. When these dynamics are ignored in urban classrooms, the psychic problems marginalized students may bring to learning situations may simply crush teachers in ways that subvert positive teacher–learner interactions. All teachers must study student consciousness in relation to the learning process, but the conditions in which marginalized urban students operate make such analysis unavoidable. Without it teachers have little idea what is happening with their students.[20]

To get from fear to hope, teachers must understand city kids in profound ways that account for the multiple identities of contemporary urban children and youth. Such insight most definitely takes into consideration the race, class, and gender aspects of urban student identity, but concurrently appreciates the complexity of and the multiple forces that shape the subjectivity of city kids. To outside onlookers—even to inside observers who are uninformed—the reactions of marginalized urban students to the everyday life of school, to particular requests that may seem innocuous, can appear baffling. The traumatic events students may have suffered at home, on the way to school, or at school in the bathroom or other places hidden from public view, may make it extremely difficult for them to concentrate on the lesson *du jour*. Indeed, such experiences and the hurt that often accompanies everyday life in these circumstances can make customary reactions to everyday events hard to provide.

Sometimes sociopathic conditions produce sociopathic behaviors—amazingly many times they do not. When young people have to face difficult conditions, I am always amazed at what many of them do—they construct social organizations such as gangs or produce compelling poetry, literature, or music to help in their efforts to survive. Such cultural and aesthetic productions provide teachers profound insight into the lives and the consciousness of their students. It is absolutely necessary for teachers to pay attention to these creations, this popular culture of the young people they teach. It provides us insight into their dreams, joy, pain, and anger. Like the blues men and women of old, contemporary urban youth are able to laugh in the middle of the fiefdom of fear and despair. They are able to celebrate in the midst of their "soulache" and anger.

Just as the world tells urban kids that they are not smart or industrious, some of them organize themselves into drug and prostitution cartels that generate amazing income. Of course, my point here is not to celebrate selling drugs and sex. Instead, it is to point out the acumen of cognitively maligned, poverty-stricken urban kids. When all other pathways to socio-economic mobility were blocked, these shrewd young people created their own corridor to financial opportunity. As scholars began to study inner-city youth gangs, they were many times shocked by the levels of structure, the discipline, the systems of emotional support and mutual respect that existed within them. Feeling so scorned, knowing that many teachers and potential employers thought of you as unteachable and uncontrollable, gangs have offered affective and emotional support often not found in the everyday of such young people. Add the fear that urban students sometimes harbor when at school or between home and school, and the immediate security that gangs offer becomes more understandable. In particularly vulnerable moments that doo rag can become worth its weight in gold.

No matter how much many middle/upper-middle class adults might not like to admit it, there is a libidinal aspect to gang membership. Just like the "rush" a young man gets from scaring a person who has socially looked down on him with his badass countenance, a gang member gains pleasure from the solidarity found in the group and the respect/deference the gang elicits. Indeed, gang membership taps into a warrior energy that welcomes the dangerous expedition through the minefields of gang activity. Critical urban educators are not afraid of this warrior energy, and instead of trying to conquer it, they seek to cultivate and direct it. In this context they help young people move it to a new level of insight and intelligence where urban kids begin to understand the forces that have shaped them, appreciate both the oppressive and liberating nature of these powers, develop productive modes of resisting their negative effects and accentuating their positive consequences, and deploy their energy in ways that are exciting yet socially transformative.

There is no reason that such young people can become warriors for liberation, warrior intellectuals. I use this term in a non-violent and gender inclusive manner, understanding that urban youth need something to live for, goals in which to invest their libidinal energy, and outlets for the adolescent rage that burns in their guts. A socially just, emancipatory education based on the objectives of individual and social transformation can rearrange the map of urban education. It can change city kids in profound and electrifying ways. It is critical in the sense that it is grounded on a detailed understanding of power and its effects; it is rigorously pedagogical in its belief in the need for warrior intellectuals to cultivate their intellects. In the critical domain it studies the way power:

- molds behavior, and those who possess power shape the form of this behavior;
- is hidden from everyday awareness—the behaviors power shapes appear to be free from power, natural modes of "good behavior" that are universally respected:
- constructs what passes as essential knowledge, basic learning, and academic success;
- is harder to attain by those marginalized in low-status situations than by those privileged in high-status situations;
- is a dynamic whose presence as a force in the world is denied most vociferously by those who benefit the most from it;
- produces without most of us knowing it, the nature of our identities/consciousness.

Thus, one can understand why critical urban educators are so dedicated to helping marginalized urban students learn about the nature of power. Critical urban education is grounded on a literacy of power that is always ready to take what has occurred in the local neighborhood around the school or in school itself as fodder for curriculum development. The problems that arise in these local domains can help students realize in very concrete ways the manner in which power operates. Here warrior intellectuals in training come to understand that the issues that a critical education deals with are omnipresent and timely. Unlike more traditional forms of education, critical learning is for now—not some distant time in a fuzzy future when "you'll need to know this." Critical urban educators are always thinking of ways of moving students from fear and despair to hope, in this process understanding that dispositional factors are profoundly important.

Grounded on an appreciation of the political economic dimensions of marginalized urban students' lives, critical teachers appreciate the need in all education—especially contemporary urban education—to engage the emotions of learners. Such teachers have to "sell" students on the usefulness of critical insights about power and the value of cultivating the intellect. "Scoring higher on a standardized test" is not a compelling justification for learning. Critical educators must get marginalized urban students to a mindspace where the learning process produces pleasure, where what the learning process empowers one to do evokes even more pleasure for more people. In the critical context this mindspace involves developing a compelling worldview that is constantly self-monitored and refined and which helps students make sense of the data and the life experiences they encounter. In the socio-affective context, critical urban educators work to graduate warrior intellectuals with a searing passion to learn and apply that learning to personal and social change. Student involvement in such a process is the most powerful expression I can imagine that hope in the inner city is alive.[21]

City Kids and the Culture of Power

Our urban students have a hell of a time dealing with the contemporary destruction of a sense of place and community. Twenty-first century right-wing, market-driven politics does not operate on the assumption that community has a value. Thus, the idea that social policies designed to help rebuild a sense of place and community are valuable not only intrinsically but are also key to improving urban education is dismissed as leftist drivel. Contemporary cities are decentralized, sprawling megalopolises with too few lively neighborhoods with indissoluble social connections. Industrial jobs with union protections are long gone in the twenty-first century post-Fordist service economy. Class-and race-based segregation has actually grown much worse in the decades following the Civil Rights Movement of the 1960s. In this setting, community is quashed, as these larger socio-economic processes insidiously sever the social bonds that connect individuals to one another.

Since the Reagan Administration the federal government and the judicial system have worked to undo the legal protections gained by urban people of color and poor people. Efforts to keep this class- and race-based segregation of communities, and their schools from intensifying have failed. What makes this re-segregation so disturbing is the separate-and-unequal dimension of urban schooling that has followed in its wake—a factor that exacerbates the loss of community and of hope in the inner city. In the twenty-first century, a resident of the South Bronx, East Saint Louis, Roxbury, or South Central Los Angeles would be hard-pressed to tell of a time she heard a group of residents express optimism about the future of their communities and schools. Those who live in such urban communities in the twenty-first century have never seen a national politician come to their neighborhood and say: we are going to make this community and these schools less separate from and unequal to those in surrounding districts. Where does hope reside in these conditions? The fact that students in urban education in the second and third decades of the twenty-first century will become even more multicultural and poor makes our efforts to keep hope alive in the existing culture of power even more difficult.[22] The task of producing a better, more rigorous, more useful education for urban students is daunting.

The lack of hope that comes out of these understandings affects everyone involved with urban education. The way people conduct themselves is profoundly affected by their analyses of the socio-cultural and political conditions surrounding them. Urban students growing up in neighborhoods where there is little chance of gaining access to economic, social, and vocational tools necessary to mobility might fall victim to hopelessness. Urban teachers need to understand that such students' behavior in class often reflects this despair. Too often such material factors are overlooked when disciplining a student. A young person who is suffering from an understandable sense of hopelessness and despair is not simply a "bad kid." When I observe such a student suffering from the effects of hopelessness, I have found that an expression of understanding about what he or she is going through, a little empathy, goes a long way in cultivating both a sense of connection to the school and a disposition to learn. This is how the culture of power operates—by creating an absence of opportunity for displaying their talents, dominant power creates hopeless situations where an individual's depression and anger often make their lack of mobility appear to be the result of their own inadequacy.

Walk into any classroom populated by a lower academic track group of students in an urban school. As one observes such a collection of young people, he or she will be overwhelmed by every student's sense of rejection and denunciation by the school and its teachers. Such students have no hesitation to tell you how they have taken to heart the academic culture's view of them. One student at a New York City high school recently told me: "They think I'm an idiot. I never have done well in school and I guess they're right. But damn, when I'm away from this shit hole, there're a lot of things I can do well. Sometimes I don't know what to think." I had the feeling that a great teacher who was able to explain the way the culture of power had positioned this young man could spend a little time with him, he could develop a very different view of his academic abilities and his life prospects. This is not some naive comment based on a false sense of hope. I have watched many great urban teachers do exactly this with particular students floundering in a similar mindspace. They were able to find the talent of such students, connect such abilities to academic tasks, and engage these learners in the joy and power of reading, writing, and researching.

Of course, there is nothing easy about doing what these teachers do. There are many students they do not reach, who opt out of learning altogether, who sleep through class. Teachers have to learn to negotiate such a terrain, to figure out how to deal with students who react to their socio-cultural situations, their relation to the culture of power in diverse ways. One thing that does seem apparent in this context is that simply demanding that students memorize a particular amount of designated data for standardized tests will never work. Such pedagogies will never engage students in the life of the mind and the uses to which particular academic skills and knowledge can be put in larger struggles for justice and social change. Successful urban pedagogies must help students understand their existential situations and the forces that construct them. In this context students begin to learn that they are "relational beings"—that who they are cannot be separated from the context in which they operate.

Hope emerges when students begin to appreciate the forces that shape them, for this implies that they are shapeable. Such a realization means that they, like all human beings, can be reshaped. They can change their zone of proximal development (ZPD), as psychologist Lev Vygotsky put it in the 1930s. That is, they can change the nature of their relationships to the world in ways that create learning opportunities. Thus, in this educational context, critical urban educators help students make connections with historical traditions of various sorts in the community and otherwise—DuBoisian insights, critical theory, critical pedagogy, Nuyorican poets, contemporary hip hop intellectuals, etc.—that help construct a unique voice and gain a sense of belonging. In this context, students gain detailed insights into the culture of dominant power and the way it subjugates and weakens those in marginalized positions. Here they begin to construct their identities as transformative intellectuals.

Such urban scholars, as previously referenced, work with their critical teachers to construct worldviews that facilitate their efforts to make sense of their lived experiences and the oppression of their urban community. Such scholars, warrior intellectuals, fuse their critical insights and transformative activities with a sense of play. Here they expand, elaborate, develop, and refine what they are doing intellectually in an aesthetic manner that creates desire and affective engagement. The blues did exactly this, and today, hip hop does it again. When such elaborations and extensions are performed well, a sense of elegance emerges that imprints style and grace on the most practical of exploits. While social transformation takes place, participants find the process itself creative, humorous, self-effacing, transgressive, and entertaining. The warrior intellectuals who engage in this critical action develop amazing abilities that can be deployed to challenge the status quo and the culture of power that supports it. Such warrior intellectuals:

- treasure the creative process and the role it plays in personal and social transformation,
- appreciate the possibility embedded in individuals who have attained a critical con-

sciousness,

- develop the ability to think critically and analytically,
- cultivate their intellects,
- understand the world as it is in relation to what it could be,
- interpret and make sense of the world around them by understanding the invisible forces at work in the culture of power and the way they shape particular situations,
- employ their aesthetic ability to get beyond ritualized but failed practices in school and society,
- use their imagination to transcend the trap of traditional gender, racial, sexual, and class-based stereotypes and the harm they can cause in their individual lives and in the larger society,
- reconceptualize the role of "good citizen" in a way that speaks and acts in relation to dominant power and the ways it oppresses those around them,
- develop the ability to teach themselves what they need to know to take on a particular task,
- cultivate a humility that allows them to be both good leaders and good members of diverse learning communities,
- devote themselves to never-ending, life-long growth as citizens, parents, workers, teachers, scholars, researchers, and lovers.

These skills of the warrior intellectual help urban kids make tough choices and life-changing decisions, in the process providing them with the fortitude to follow these courses of action to completion. Such qualities facilitate their struggle to challenge the stark environmental realities that undermine their quest for success. How difficult it is to face hunger, anticipate danger, confront scores of forces that undermine self-esteem, manage stress, and still pursue learning. Such realities take us back to the title of our book—*City Kids: Understanding and Appreciating Them*. No one can go into urban schools to teach successfully without understanding and appreciating the everyday challenges many city students endure and the creative responses they construct. Some are overwhelmed by the challenges, swallowed up in the abyss of violence, drugs, and capitulation to short-term needs. Many others persevere, develop amazing coping strategies, construct methods of concentration amidst the chaos, and even delay gratification in the pursuit of long-term goals. I am humble in the presence of such young people. On an individual basis they conquer the culture of power that oppresses and destroys.

These warrior intellectuals in the critical pedagogical context take these amazing powers and abilities to the social domain, employing them to bring about macro-, meso-, and micro-level transformation. They work to change a dominant culture that allows power wielders to perpetuate the inequitable status quo, they help change institutions such as schools so educators will aggressively address the ways inequality and oppression are reproduced, and they facilitate other young people's struggle to gather the strength to make decisions that help them escape the worst dimensions of the urban life of poverty. Warrior intellectuals work to control the anxieties that come out of this life of poverty, so that hope can survive in less than optimum circumstances.[23] The culture of dominant power is overwhelming in its ability to subvert the dreams of marginalized urban students. Warrior intellectuals understand that it takes a sensible, well-planned, pragmatic, and radical set of long-term actions to fight such power.

Understanding the Pain of Marginalized Urban Students

The pain of many urban students of color from lower socio-economic backgrounds is palpable. In my studies of urban education I do not see a lot of effort on the part of policymakers and educational and political leaders to understand this hurt. In this context, neither do I see a great deal of effort to humanize African American and Latino kids from poor urban neighborhoods. Such conditions hold ominous consequences for these young people and their relationship to education. Human beings express their pain in ways that are not always rational or in their own best interests. We have all known or known of particular men who express the pain in their lives by beating and humiliating the women who are emotionally close to them. The aggressive ways that many urban students of color express their emotional pain often fans the flames of white racism, as white people point to their actions as examples of the criminal and violent tendencies of Blacks and Latinos.

It is hard for white people to understand being non-white. Indeed, many white people find it difficult to comprehend the black or Latino experience, while they concurrently experience great trouble getting beyond blackness or Latinoness as the exclusive marker of a non-white person's identity. Because of this racial dynamic it is profoundly important that white people who want to be teachers attain a detailed understanding of their own selfhood vis-à-vis racial others. Without such ontological knowledge they may find too late that they should not have become urban educators. In the way that whiteness often erases itself as a culture, white people sometimes assume that cultural matters have to do with people "of color" and not themselves and their cultural perspectives. Culture shapes how all of us, regardless of our ethnicity, make sense of the world, other people, and ourselves. With this concept in mind it should not surprise us that whiteness, coming from a particular social location in the web of reality, can often warp people's perceptions of the world. Indeed, it may undermine a person's ability to discern the way white racism operates to sustain the unequal power relations of the status quo.

A critical urban education that is sensitive to understanding, appreciating, and teaching city kids is dedicated to an understanding of whiteness and its effect on teaching and learning. When urban teachers do not understand the impact of whiteness on constructing the norms and standards by which students are judged, serious damage to African American, Latino, and Native American students can take place. One of the ways that a white person learns about whiteness is by listening carefully to people of color. African Americans, for example, are generally very aware that they live in a white-dominated society and are surrounded by manifestations of white privilege and power. To non-white people, whiteness is ubiquitous. Most of the time when Whites learn of this we-are-surrounded sense of African Americans, Latinos, and Native Americans, they are shocked. Most white people want to believe that they are invisible to minorities.

The irony of this is that for decades and decades black people felt they were better off if they were invisible to Whites. One important dimension of this dynamic was that Blacks often acted literally as if they did not see white people. As African Americans walked by Whites on the street, they looked the other way. They knew that they could be severely punished for looking, for putting Whites under surveillance. As part of white power the "gaze" of African Americans had to be controlled. Thus, in a strange way for the racist system to work well, both races had to in a sense be invisible to one another. While many dimensions of race relations have changed—not all for the better—many Whites continue to believe they are invisible to people of color, that there is no pervasive image of whiteness in the black, Latino, and indigenous consciousness. Indeed, often times in the educational realm, white students and teachers believe that they appear simply as they simply want to appear to people of color. The mask of whiteness, uninformed white people believe, presents white people to non-whites as a kindly and safe presence.[24]

When I am teaching about whiteness and white power I have absolutely shocked many white students with my analysis of the historical representation of whiteness as menace, as source of pain in the black, Latino, and Native American psyche. With this in mind white urban teachers can begin to appreciate how their students of color might perceive them as they walk into their classrooms. This may especially be the case when white teachers display their higher socio-economic standing. In this racialized and class-inscribed context, many African American, Latino, and Native American students will assume that such teachers support the unequal status quo represented by the school and the educational system. A critical urban pedagogy believes that racial/class-based issues such as these and the pain they cause students of color must be addressed in the urban curriculum. Teaching city kids demands the courage to address what hurts them.

I understand how young white teachers and teacher education students may be shocked by the revelation that their pedagogy and their interpersonal intentions will not be perceived by their students and colleagues of color in the way they intended. I sympathize with well-intentioned white teachers who are discouraged when parents of color treat them with suspicion, assuming that they are mere representatives of racially unjust elementary or secondary schools. Of course, I understand why such parents would be apprehensive. They have often been made to feel unwelcome in schools, have been spoken down to by teachers and administrators, have had their concerns ignored, and have seen their children stigmatized by their social characteristics.[25] In this context the parents are often angry when they first meet a white teacher—she's just one more unknowing cog in the racial and class-based sorting machine called school.

In a critical urban pedagogy such teachers and teacher education students cannot just sit around and lament the misinterpretation of their objectives—they must take action to prevent such misunderstanding. The best way to begin such a process is to understand these painful race and class forces, and one's place in the complex social web they weave. With this appreciation well established, one can begin to shape one's curriculum, motivational strategies, interpersonal interactions, and pedagogical methods in ways that reflect this insight. Teachers will be amazed at the ways most people of color, African American, and Latino students in particular, will reach out to a white person who makes these efforts to grasp racial pain and its effects. Understanding that they have much to learn about these matters, critical white teachers are very humble as they pursue their pedagogy of justice.

The Recovery of Whiteness, Urban Education, and Students of Color

Because of all the pain, many people, both white and of color, feel extremely uncomfortable discussing these issues—as a society we have to overcome this fear of race and class. I am still amazed to visit teacher education programs, even ones designated to serve the needs of urban teacher education, that do not talk about race, racism, and whiteness, and their impact on what goes on in the process of education. As a society, we have not come to terms with the fact that the Civil Rights Movement evoked great hatred among many Whites toward African Americans, Latinos, and Native Americans. Aaron Gresson conceptualizes this anger as part of a larger socio-political construct he calls the recovery movement.[26] In this recovery movement emerging during the Civil Rights Movement of the 1960s and continuing into the contemporary era, Whites began to lament what they perceived to have lost in the effort to address the ravages of racism. In this context many white people began to work to recover the wages of whiteness undermined by these anti-racist efforts.

In the discursive construction of the recovery movement inferior black, Latino, and indigenous ways of doing things were replacing the superior norms and standards—as in, for example, quality education—established by white culture. White people could not let this slide toward mediocrity continue. The recovery movement would put an end to such a destructive cultural process. The larger society's refusal to adequately fund urban education and its support of cuts for educational programs designed to help students of color from economically poor backgrounds is in part explained by the recovery movement. White people who support the recovery of white supremacy have let it be known that they will not divert funds to help people who have already received too much special treatment. Meanwhile urban schools with large African American and Latino populations continue to suffer for lack of funding.

In this recovery movement white people have experienced great pain, as they have from their perspectives watched the benefits of white supremacy melt away. Ironically, just as these white people were perceiving this pain of white loss, urban people of color were facing increasing alienation coming from material deprivation, the mortification of increasing charges of racial inferiority, and the decreasing opportunity for socio-economic mobility resulting from the deterioration of their neighborhood schools. The recovery movement throws a match on the gasoline of African American, Latino, and Native American pain. As advocates of racial recovery fan the flames of the Great Fear, they call for tough responses to the violence, crime, and defiance of young people of color.

Many of the teachers who end up in urban schools are profoundly affected by the social climate created by recovery. The movement's re-vilification of youth of color and its demand for zero toleration of their trespasses shapes many teachers' perception of African American, Latino, and Native American students and how they need to deal with them. The race of a student is the most important factor in shaping a teacher's perception of him or her. In the "recovered" twenty-first century teachers behave very differently toward different students. Depending on the race of students, many teachers hold differing behavioral and academic expectations. Students often act in ways that meet the expectations of their teachers. They sometimes act out the violent stereotypes perpetuated by the white racism of the recovery movement. The cycle is perpetuated—the human damage is exacerbated.

City kids stand at the nexus of all these social, cultural, political, and economic forces. And because of this, teachers of urban students have to know a lot more than those standing outside of this complex process think they do. Indeed, since urban students live their lives at the intersection of all these dynamics, a book on understanding, appreciating, and teaching them has to deal with a wide variety of complicated topics. All of these complex knowledges and insights mean very little, however, if we do not connect them to the way we engage and treat urban students.[27] Caring for such students is necessary, but it is not sufficient to accomplish the educational goals we pursue. The complex understandings referenced here help teach us *how to care* about marginalized urban students.

Our race and class insights, for example, allow us to become more understanding, more empathetic, more helpful, more thoughtful, and more respectful in relation to our often hurting students. Here we begin to understand the tensions and burdens they carry with them to the classroom. With this knowledge of our students, we are better able to act intelligently and productively when they display destructive behaviors. As a teacher, I know that I approach a student whom I know to be under great stress very differently from one who is not. The same principle applies in urban education: when teachers are aware of the causes of student stress and its effects, they are better equipped to serve their needs and help them get an education. Caring for students without a wide range of knowledges to accompany it is a hollow approach to urban teaching. A critical urban pedagogy moves beyond emotional protestations of how much we care about the students. Concurrently, this critical urban pedagogy based on understanding is far more effective than a pedagogy based on the recovery project's machismo educational politics of fear. Any form of education that hates and fears its students is predestined for failure—the students', the teachers', and the system's.

Aggressive Students: Problems and Possibilities

If one is going to teach in urban schools she has to understand—and even appreciate—

the hostility of marginalized urban students. This does not mean glorifying or romanticizing them in ways that lead to coddling them as students. We must demand that they work hard, that they understand and overcome the obstacles dominant power places in their paths. What I am discussing here is the ability of urban teachers to deal with what often seems to be, and many times is, unprovoked hostility. By the phrase "deal with", I am referring to the capacity to handle both pedagogically and emotionally such student reactions. Too many urban teachers instead of attempting to understand such unprovoked hostility, simply get mad and base their teaching around "getting back" at particular students. Obviously, such a strategy is doomed from the outset.

Racial and class hostility are central factors not only in understanding urban students but also in understanding the larger societies in which we live. Thus, individuals in any occupation are remiss in not attempting to make sense of such hostility and the way it operates in their civic, vocational, and personal lives. The economically poor and racially marginalized students we encounter in urban classrooms have more often than not faced disgrace and humiliation, disillusionment and loss, sorrow and rejection, not to mention the stress previously discussed. Poor kids always have to deal with some of these feelings, wherever they live. I remember as an elementary student growing up in the poverty-stricken rural mountains of Tennessee, how much some of the poorest children among us suffered. I was so touched by the pain of the rejection they expressed to me that I could never simply recover from the experience. I know that many of my life choices have been made in response to the way poverty warped Jacob Ketron's and Ray White's lives and so emotionally wounded them. I see their faces so often in the urban kids I observe in the South Bronx of today.

Young people do not react well to be constantly mistrusted. Sometimes such perspectives evoke such anger and resentment that students feel that their only recourse is to act in a manner that substantiates the misgivings people hold about them. Their rage boils over from the embarrassment they feel when confronted by the recent actions of their father, the rats that live in their house, the incarceration of their aunt, or their family's inability to rent a better apartment. Of course, this public exhibition of rage simply redoubles the mistrust of their teachers and other important figures in their lives. African Americans, Latinos, and Native Americans face forms of humiliation that white people have never imagined.[28]

Middle/upper-middle class and even working-class Whites rarely have to deal with "slips of the tongue" dealing with race. These so-called slips of the tongue provide insight into the socio-psychological racial turbulence churning just under the surface of everyday interactions. I remember in high school the racial tension that was caused by one of these white slips of the tongue. While talking about contemporary social problems, a working class white student inadvertently made reference to the "problems we're having around here with the niggers." Recognizing his faux pas, he immediately added "I mean the colored people." I looked at my black friends in the class, as they muttered "that son of a bitch" under their breath. Nothing was said "out loud" about the comment, but all of us knew that the black students had experienced a clear sense of racial indignity. Indeed, the racial tensions were so intense that the teacher chose not to overtly address the issue. All he said, with his voice trembling from tension, was "let's all be calm, let's all be calm." Nobody was surprised when racially motivated fights and violence erupted in the following months. The white student's slip of the tongue revealed a poisonous racial climate that would spawn disastrous consequences for the school.

One way to deal with such racial humiliation, no doubt, is to become what is often called a "bad motherfucker." Many times I have been around urban students who after many indignities told and showed those around them that they were not going to take it any more. Consider this: when one assumes the persona of a bad motherfucker, the degradation, hurt, and apprehension that all marginalized urban students feel is successfully covered up. When one is dealing with a bad motherfucker in a dark alley, his (or sometimes her) hurt is not the first picture one sees. Unlike the benefits of mainstream education that are projected to accrue far out in a distant future, the benefits derived from being a bad motherfucker are short term. For example, bad motherfuckers derive a good deal of respect from those around them. I have heard it hundreds of times, "don't mess with Tre, he's a bad motherfucker."

"Did you hear about Tre?" one student asks his classmates.
"No, what'd he do this time?" they respond.
"That crazy Tre beat Rasheed Parker and Don Kincade half to death."
"Wow, he's a bad motherfucker," the classmates respond in unison.

As I listen to such conversations, I understand that Tre and all the other kids who fit in the category in question are eliciting awe, fear, and, most importantly, respect from their classmates. In addition to gaining a higher status persona in his peer group, Tre has internalized a prevalent stereotype of black violence, advanced so successfully by TV and movies. In Tre's case he has transformed this damaging stereotype into a heroic image in the microcosm of his urban neighborhood. He is a self- and peer-proclaimed heroic nigger/nigga. Tre and his classmates with the aid of hip hop artists of various stripes have taken the most reviled racial epithet of all time and transformed it into a word that champions a particularly aggressive form of blackness—all the while offending anyone who challenges their use of the term. This transgressive, self-conscious revisionist use of the term (nigga in lieu of nigger) is very controversial and evokes powerful emotions from individuals from different races. Even discussing it here may be offensive to some people. My intent, certainly, is not to offend but to frankly discuss a phenomenon that is central to the lives of city kids. My position as a white male, I clearly understand, induces me to approach the topic respectfully and humbly.

Young black males have often explained to me the epic dimensions of the nigga persona they embrace. Niggas, they tell me are:

- sly like a fox and can engage in covert, often illegal, operations when necessary;
- style setters, know how to dress, how to "carry themselves" in public;
- fearless and know how to fight and protect themselves;
- better lovers than their counterparts from other races;
- uncompromising in their refusal to buy into the system, accept mainstream (i.e.,

white) values;

- aesthetically more discerning, more talented;
- physically more capable than males from other races;
- street wise, able to negotiate their way in dangerous and complex situations.

While the term has a vile history and is offensive to many, many people for good reasons, I find that the transgressive actions of these young African Americans offer critical educators an emancipatory opening, a possibility for intellectual and ethical growth. As much of the world provided young black men and women little opportunity to enhance their self-esteem and self-efficacy, they took it on themselves to create their own. What they constructed is controversial, volatile, contradictory in its effects, and highly creative. In this context I bring back the previously referenced notion of the warrior intellectual. The libidinal energy inscribed in the concept of the bad motherfucker and the nigga persona, I believe, can be adapted to the warrior intellectual's goals of social and personal transformation. When the term, intellectual, can be stripped of its hegemonic, geekish, status quo-supporting meanings—as it is among many prisoners—a new world of learning emerges. Imagine what can happen when all this youthful genius, creativity, aesthetic sensibility, anger at injustice, emotional energy, and capacity for solidarity is focused on socially, culturally, politically, intellectually liberatory ends.

While critical educators cannot and should not dictate the nature of such ends, they can, however, raise issues, ask questions, and provide socio-historical context to induce more complex thinking about such activities. Such considerations would involve the examination of the glorification, even aestheticization of violence, the fetishization of wealth, the exaltation of dominant masculinity and the misogyny and homophobia that often accompany it, etc. The ironic use of the term, nigga, illustrates the complexity of all of these dynamics—indeed, in this context rests a signifier of the complications of contemporary urban education. The self-conscious revisionist inversion of African American imagery can work in profoundly divergent ways: (1) it can reinforce negative stereotypes of aggressive and dangerous blackness and exacerbate existing racism; or (2) it can be used as an assertion of self-efficacy that lays a foundation for an exciting new fortitude and chutzpah among urban youth that serves to change the world in an emancipatory manner.

This is a paradoxical moment in urban education, propitious yet ominous, promising yet discouraging, creatively charged yet beset by a self-destructive rage. And all of these contradictory dynamics are understandable to those immersed in the context. Do critical urban educators have the wisdom and the courage to make sure that in the midst of the Bush era, a time of overt hostility toward city kids, great good can come from the libidinal power of urban youth? This may be one of the greatest tests of the power of our ideas. Is our rhetoric more than just empty talk? Does our theorizing about power and justice have practical consequences? Do our ideas have meaning for those who have grown up in a time different than our own? Can Tre and I form a synergistic partnership that makes us both more than we presently are? I passionately believe the answer to all of these questions *can be* yes. There is much work to be done.

A Critical Curriculum of Self-Study

In the era of Bush, literally the last thing that right-wing educational policy values is the implementation of critical curricula. In the ideological world of right-wing education the construction of a rigorous academic curriculum that carefully studies the social, cultural, political, and economic forces that shape the lives of inner-city youth and the emotional damage such dynamics can leave in their wake is absurd. The only reasonable response to Tre and the urban kids under study here involves better forms of control, more jail space. To such right-wing ideologues, the idea that these students have something powerful to offer the world is ludicrous. Even urban schools deemed to be doing well on standardized tests can be hellish places for marginalized students to be. Few understand and fewer address the issues we are concerned with here—the social and emotional context of life in the inner city. When these factors are ignored, schooling can be profoundly damaging to the self-esteem of marginalized students. As educators such as Jerome Bruner and Paulo Freire have pointed out, schools should be places where students experience fewer esteem-damaging episodes than in the outside world. When we limit such harmful experiences, educators are better able to motivate students to experiment, to try to do things that they have never attempted before.[29] This is, of course, how we learn.

The right-wing pedagogical logic so pervasive in the twenty-first century scoffs at our concern with protecting and nurturing the self-esteem of marginalized urban students. Conservative critics often characterize scholarship such as *City Kids* as soft-pedagogy, lacking in rigor, concerned not with subject matter but with how students feel. This is such a cowardly misrepresentation of what critical educators are attempting in that it fails to account for the emotional/affective dimensions of marginalized students' lives and the complex process of learning. Even for a group of privileged students in elite institutions such right-wing pedagogies are unproductive, but for marginalized urban kids they are the kiss of academic death. I use the adverb, cowardly, in reference to the position because it is allows teachers to keep their distance from aggressive urban students. Instead of getting down and dirty with such students, understanding what hurts them, appreciating what they are feeling, gaining insight into what excites and motivates them, it basically says: "learn this data or get the hell out of school."

Since no justification is given for investing the time to learn such information and there is so little respect for marginalized students trying to find their way into academic institutions, the chances are pretty good that we will not have to see too much of these "undesirable" students. After all, these are not the students you would want to teach. Indeed, right-wing pedagogies seem to miss the important point that the very aggressive behaviors that help them endure the brutality that often surrounds them, typically put them into conflict with the conventions and protocols of school. "You don't fight here at school, Tre. There's no need for that behavior," teachers tell him. But Tre is thinking in response to such admonitions, "they must be crazy, no one will ever leave me alone if I don't show them that I'm ready to fight anytime, anyplace." The only way I can talk to Tre about fighting at school that will matter to him must begin with my acknowledgment that I understand his predicament.

I might, for instance, tell him about a principal who paddled me for fighting on my way home from school. When I explained to him that I had been attacked by two kids bigger than me, he told me it did not matter. Fighting was not allowed in or on the way to or from school. The circumstances I had faced and the fact that I was the decided loser in the struggle had no bearing on his dealing with me. My attitudes toward school authority and adult rules were forever altered. The Tres I have dealt with in urban settings always "get" that story and it never fails to open a dialog about the issues operating here. The students and I realize that many schools do not understand that if students follow the rules they have created, it puts particular students at great risk. Invariably, we begin a dialog about how schools might maintain safety and yet not put students who follow the rules at risk. Developing realistic policies in this context necessitates student participation and school officials who take student concerns seriously.

All of these issues become part of the critical curriculum of self-study. This definitely does not mean that all we do in a critical context in urban education is sit around and discuss incidents of violence and disciplinary responses to them. We deal with these issues as ways into an analysis of who we are and how our identities and consciousnesses shape our relation to academic material. Then we examine in a meta-analytical way the academic material in question. We learn the official curriculum and then move to the next crucial step, we examine its ideological inscriptions and the intended regulatory effects of such marks of power. In the step that follows we research and discern what knowledge is erased in the dominant power-driven curriculum and we begin to discern what might be learned when we explore alternate sources of information. The curriculum of self-study is not an end in itself, as the right-wing commentators mischaracterize it. It is the first step in a long-term rigorous educational process that, if successful, continues for the rest of our students' lives.

In this process trust between all parties is cultivated. It is amazing what happens when there is trust among students, parents, and teachers. Pain is acknowledged, vulnerability is exposed, tough gazes are softened, and learning takes place in ways previously unimagined. In such contexts the origins of misogyny and homophobia are explored and the purposes of education in general and for individual students in particular are analyzed. These educational purposes are always viewed in multiple contexts, in light of the various forces that shape urban neighborhoods and the students who emerge from them.[30] In this process the reasons for aggressive poses are understood in ways that many times produce a profound rethinking of the value and uses of academic work. The possibilities emerging from these encounters are endless.

Urban Kids and the Learning Process

As students in a critical urban pedagogy learn about the macro-, meso-, and micro-social structures that have shaped their lives, they come to understand that their identity is always connected to the learning in which they engage. There are thousands of examples of how diverse individuals stylize their actions in relation to particular learning experiences. I think of the curriculum of youth culture from the swing kids of the 1930s and 1940s, to punk rockers of the 1970s, to more contemporary hip hop kids. In this context psychologists talk about kids trying on identities. The same is true in an academic context—depending on what one is learning, the experience changes one's identity. Of course, such a process can be very damaging and even obnoxious, as particular academic learning experiences can produce arrogant behavior and feelings of superiority over those who do not possess the same experience. A critical urban pedagogy that understands the inseparability of learning and identity encourages learners to move toward humility—not the inflated self-importance of intellectual snobbery.

Because of this connection between learning and identity, it becomes even more important for urban teachers to know their students if they are ever going to teach them anything that matters. Of course, what we are dealing with here is the key issue of *City Kids, Understanding and Appreciating Them*. A central notion of any progressive pedagogy involves knowing a student well enough to know when she is ready to learn a particular skill or idea. In a critical urban pedagogy that understands and appreciates urban students, teachers have the ability, the knowledge, and the professional prerogative to make such curricular and pedagogical decisions. I have heard myself on many occasions say to students something like: "o.k. you are all obviously ready to learn the concept of hegemony and apply it to this situation." Such an assessment was not made without a wide range of insights into who my students were, where they came from socially and culturally, the nature of their conceptual development, and a sense of the curriculum they needed.

Such a critical pedagogy also rests on a knowledge of students' dispositions toward learning and what dispositions might need to be cultivated. For example, how willing is a student (or a teacher) to throw one's efforts into intellectually taxing undertakings? Does the student enjoy such activities? Can she cultivate a sense of pleasure and accomplishment from such tasks? How might a teacher facilitate such dispositional development? Such a weighty pedagogical maneuver is not possible unless we know and appreciate our students. And whether a teacher knows her students well enough to engage in such nuanced operations often decides whether or not students fail or succeed. There is so much a great urban teacher needs to know—hell, it is such a difficult job to do well. To serve our urban students in the manner they deserve, teachers much understand the nature of racism, its economic basis, its intersection with class bias, the complexity of racial inequality, the way the recovery movement has undermined opportunity for marginalized urban students, ad infinitum.

In the micro-sense critical urban teachers have to understand how these macro-factors shape their students' lives away from school. I have talked to urban teachers who had no idea how hard particular students had to work on a daily basis to protect themselves and their families. Such students have to use their physical toughness and their verbal savvy to keep diverse types of wolves from their door. Once teachers understood these aspects of a particular student's life, they could appreciate why he fell asleep in math class, or why he was so defensive in his interactions with other students in the English class, or why he carried a weapon onto the school bus last week. In these contexts it begins to become apparent why the lack of such knowledge about city kids eventuates in scenarios where teachers and administrators simply blame problems on students' and their parents' lack of character and ability. Once again, this is why many urban students fail in school. Without such understandings it is easy for educators to retreat into a hurtful deficit view of marginalized urban students. This deficitism is the bane of urban education.

Such deficitism makes, for instance, the multiple ethnicities and diverse languages spoken in urban schools a liability rather than a great resource and benefit to all students. The presence of students from all over the world and their knowledge of numerous languages could be used to help educators and their fellow students prepare for the globalized world of commerce, diplomacy, politics, health, art/aesthetics, knowledge production, ethics, etc. that now faces us. Indeed, such linguistic and cultural diversity is an intellectual and vocational goldmine in our urban backyard, yet the deficitism that shapes current educational thinking makes it seem an obstacle that is destroying our schools. Particular ideological frames(e.g., white supremacy, socio-economic class elitism, Eurocentrism, etc.)shape dispositions toward a variety of urban educational issues including, of course, linguistic diversity. Like everything else in the social universe, dispositions are political and exert profound consequences on how we deal with the world around us. These ideological dispositions shape not only the learning process of our city students but also our own ways of making sense of the urban educational cosmos.

School and society teach these dominant-ideology inscribed dispositions to those who are victimized by them. In my own life I quickly learned the dishonor of being viewed as a hillbilly from the poor southern Appalachian Mountains. I have seen many of my colleagues and students suffer as the result of being identified as ghetto blacks or inner city "Hispanics." Thus, these dispositions not only affect the way we are seen in the world but the way we see ourselves. Placing these socio-cultural teachings in an urban educational context, our students are taught to view themselves as bad students, low academic ability learners, and troublemakers. These factors may be far more important in shaping what has been viewed in the field of psychology and the academic world as intelligence than any form of genetic capacity. In this context the unconscious ways we deal with these ascriptions of low-ability and status are key dimensions of our larger attempt to understand and appreciate our urban students.

These unconscious dynamics are always at work, shaping and framing our relationship to academic work. Is it any surprise that most of my elementary school friends from a poor community in the mountains of Tennessee got away from formal educational institutions as soon as they could? Why would they want to stay in an institution that was so hard on their unconscious view of themselves? In the same way, why would many urban African American and Latino students want to pursue a career in a domain that wounded them at so many unconscious levels? Every time an urban teacher walks into a classroom he or she should remember that the learning process is an act of constructing identity and selfhood in relation to the unconscious forces at work in the process. And there is no doubt that much is occurring in this unconscious realm in domains where hurt and disdain are palpable. In addition to the previously mentioned understandable aversions to learning, modes of resistance to particular forms of learning emerge that are not explicable even to the learners themselves. Yet again, the obvious point emerges—we need to understand and appreciate our urban students in order to teach them.

What I am analyzing here is the complex internal construction of meaning and its relation to the formation of identity that is central to the teaching and learning process. Educators cannot look at this one-dimensionally but must study it from multiple perspectives—the social, cultural, political, historical, philosophical, cognitive, and psychoanalytical. This knowledge is central in the cognitive development of students and is equally important in the process of curriculum development.[31] Obviously, a curriculum that takes into account the contexts in which students live and their interests and needs, is superior to the externally mandated standardized ones distorting urban education in the twenty-first century. A rigorous urban teacher education makes sure practitioners have the ability to develop curricula that tie these dynamics to academic knowledges, cognitive skills, the ability to conduct research, and the capacity to teach oneself.

To accomplish these pedagogical tasks teachers must become researchers of their students. Teacher as researchers of students and their social contexts is a key characteristic of a critical urban education. Urban educator Betsy Quintero uses student personal narratives in her teaching to help her learn about the experiences that shape them and their struggles to assert their agency and transform their lives.[32] Researching students may be as simple as listening to students' concerns, taking seriously their ideas about the curriculum, or as complex as studying the socio-economic dynamics of the neighborhood surrounding the school and connecting such information to the development of job opportunities for students and their families. The more a teacher knows about students' experiences, contexts, dreams, passions, and hurts, the better equipped she will be to engage them in a meaningful educational experience. An adept urban teacher as researcher employs her students to teach her about their lives in ways that let both them and her know that they are important, unique, and precious beings in the world.

John Dewey put it so well almost a century ago when he argued that all educational approaches should be constructed around the purposes of the student.[33] By this assertion Dewey did not mean—as he has often been accused—that in a student centered curriculum that the child or the young person does whatever she wants. Instead, Dewey was concerned with teachers working with the interests of children so that they might want to learn valuable and civically useful things. When a brilliant urban teacher weaves together student interests with academic knowledges and civic issues in a way that catalyzes cognitive development and improves academic skills, it is a work of art. Here rests an important secret to the process of becoming a great urban teacher—yet, in No Child Left Behind and other contemporary conservative educational reforms, such a pedagogical process is not even mentioned. In these contemporary reforms teaching becomes a lost art.

Identity Change: No Chicken Intellectuals Here

A critical urban pedagogy is obsessed with this dispositional aspect of learning, with helping students develop into warrior intellectuals who pursue learning in their struggles for personal and social transformation. A word of caution for urban educators may be necessary in this context. A brief anecdote illustrates the danger of using the concept of warrior intellectual. I recently tried out my concept of warrior intellectual during a graduation speech I delivered in an inner-city high school in New York City. When I came to part where I challenged the students to be tough scholars, to become warrior intellectuals who were unafraid to develop academic skills for use in the larger struggles urban kids have to face, I sensed that many of the students were inspired by these words. But before I could take any satisfaction that the concept of warrior intellectual might be a powerful motivational device, several older men in the audience began to heckle me. The basic message they were conveying was that they had no respect for intellectuals. Both the students and I were taken aback at the depth of their feelings and their willingness to express them in this particular context.

I took a chance and answered them from the podium, saying that the word, intellectual, is not a dirty term. I argued that if an intellectual is humble and civic-minded, he or she can make heroic changes in the community. I asked my hecklers to reconsider their feelings about the word, intellectual, in light of how I was defining it in my speech. I am sure my effect was minimal on the hecklers, but it may have been more persuasive for some of the students. A few of them stopped me on the way out of the school and told me how much the speech had meant to them. "I'd never heard anybody put it that way," one young man told me. "I like that warrior intellectual concept." My point here is that in the last half of the first decade of the twenty-first century, the fact that the term, intellectual, can draw loud disapproval from a graduation audience reveals something profound about the spirit of our era. It tells us something about the ideological dispositions circulating in contemporary schools and communities and how they might exert an impact on our educational efforts. There are insights to be gleaned here for critical urban educators that have direct implications for the identity issues I am so concerned with in this book.

Thus, we are dealing with a complicated, complex, and controversial notion when we employ the warrior intellectual concept. As we push our talented urban students to work for personal and social transformation, we connect a rigorous academic curriculum with dispositions such as compassion, ethical behavior, social justice, egalitarianism, curiosity, and critical insight. Critical urban educators ask what these concepts might mean when we think of them within a critical pedagogical context concerned with issues of power and its fair dis-

tribution, and what they might look like when put into practice in poor urban neighborhoods and the city in general. To many these issues of putting intellectual work into practice in a way that is unafraid to challenge the status quo is highly controversial, if not
undesirable. I would ask such critics: why bother with academic work if we are not going
to use it to make our lives, our communities, and our world better? What then is the purpose of academic work—to show a test designer that we are capable of doing it? I guess this
is why many people want to keep academics removed from the lived world—if it is clois-
tered then it will not offend anyone with power. Warrior intellectuals do not accept such
chicken intellectualism.

Chicken intellectuals are like chicken hawks who start and support wars but want to
send other people—especially their social and economic "inferiors"—to go fight them.
Warrior intellectuals develop the above dispositions for compassion, ethical behavior, social
justice, egalitarianism, curiosity, and critical insight not as ideas that they work with in the
classroom, but as ways of living their lives. Chicken intellectuals separate academic work
from the lived world. The critical scholars, the warrior intellectuals we graduate from urban
schools do not blindly learn what they are told to learn. They question its social value and
its consequence in helping them accomplish their individual, collective, and larger sociopolitical goals. Their disposition for committing themselves to learning is connected to the
value of what it is they are exploring. Competition with their peers is not a sufficient motivation for such a commitment—warrior intellectuals are motivated by the intrinsic worth
of the material in question. When such students encounter things worthy of knowing—in
both a "knowing that" and a "knowing how" sense—they learn to teach themselves and those
around them. In this context they create learning communities of warrior intellectuals—
they learn about and construct their own zones of proximal development (ZPD)—where they
set goals, develop plans for learning, and then evaluate their progress.[34]

Warrior intellectuals understand that the right-wing pedagogies pushed by the Bush
Administration and many corporate leaders represent the antithesis of the critically
grounded, engaged scholarship described here. They have been victimized by skill and
drill, test-driven pedagogies and understand their limitations better than most people.
They know that such rote based, indoctrinating forms of education breed intellectual pas-
sivity and contempt for learning. Top down, standards-driven modes of education suck the
joy and the soul right out of learning and spit them into hegemonic latrine. The idea that
rigorous, meaningful learning can take place in a playful circumstance is lost on chicken intellectuals. They are afraid of joy, soul, and play—my god, students will get out of control if
there is a hint of liveliness and *jouissance* in the classroom. Warrior intellectuals and their
critical teachers want to uncover aesthetic facets to the most serious of pursuits. Education
in the critical urban school should if nothing else but a celebration of life, of the genius of
students, and the talented individuals within the local community.

In my *Critical Constructivism Primer* I write about "blue knowledge," based on the blues
aesthetic of African American bluesmen and women. Here despite all the pain and anguish
they had to face, they were able to write music that told of such suffering but in a way that

still celebrated how good life could be. The great blues singer and guitarist Howlin' Wolf could sing about being on death row in his classic blues song, *Killing Floor*, in a way that rocked everyone in the house. Everyone was sensitive to the plight of black men sitting on death row and the song reminded them of the need to fight against the racism that led to inordinate numbers of African Americans being unjustly put to death on these killing floors. But tonight, the Wolf told us, we could accompany such knowledge with some kick-ass dancing and hot sensuality that lets us all know how good it can feel to be alive.

The juxtaposition of the *jouissance* and the tragedy of the society's horrific racism was synergistic, not contradictory. The blues aesthetic told us that we have to get our love, our passion, and our thrills while we can—there may be sorrow waiting around the next bend in the road. Critical educators/warrior intellectuals learn a great lesson from this blue knowledge, as they work to create an education that is as coldly aware of the world's injustice as possible. At the same time, however, they work toward such a goal while indulging in joy, laughter, and sensuality whenever the possibility arises. Joy, laughter, and sensuality are central to the critical learning and the creative process. Play is not something here to be feared and punished but a phenomenon to be nurtured and put to pedagogical use.

Picking up on the work of Sigmund Freud, the great critical theorist Herbert Marcuse wrote about eros (the life impulse) and thanatos (the death impulse) and the way they circulate within both the larger social order and the individual subconscious.[35] The right-wing standardized curriculum is a thanocentric form of education that fears eros and the sensuality it implies. This thanocentric curriculum not only kills the motivation of our urban students to learn, it kills the desire of teachers to teach. We now "enjoy" the lowest retention rate for teachers in history.[36] The critical urban curriculum engages warrior intellectuals in a curriculum of intimacy with the world around them, their fellow learners, knowledges that are often considered dangerous because of their kinetic power to inspire, and the inherent eros of such an attitude toward learning.

Our urban education celebrates warrior intellectuals with an attitude (WIWA's)—an attitude grounded on love, courage, civic-mindedness, justice, diversity, and inclusion. Such an attitude can change urban education, the lives of city kids, and the world itself. Critical urban pedagogy and its WIWA's move to a new domain far from the fearful thanocentric world of the chicken intellectual. In this domain city kids are understood and appreciated. Here they get on with the business of building a new world. These are exactly the types of students we want to teach.

NOTES

1   J. Dewey, *Democracy and Education* (New York: The Free Press, 1916); K. Tobin, *The Practice of Constructivism in Science Education* (Washington, DC: AAAS Press, 1993); P. Taylor, B. Fraser, and L. White, *CLES: An Instrument for Monitoring the Development of Constructivist Learning Environments.* 1994. Paper Presented to the Annual Meeting of the American Educational Research Association. New Orleans. http://surveylearning.com/cles/papers/cles_aera94-award.htm; W. Schubert, *Toward Constructivist Teacher Education for Elementary Schools in the Twenty-first Century: A Framework for*

Decision-Making. 1998. my.netian.com/~yhhknue/coned19.htm; R. Shepherd, D. Fasko, F. Osborne, "Intrapersonal intelligence: Affective factors in thinking," *Education, 119(4)* (1999); M. Cochran-Smith, The Outcomes Question in Teacher Education. Paper Presented at AERA, 2000, New Orleans; R. Meyer, "Captives of the script: killing us softly with phonics," *Rethinking Schools*, 2003.http://www.rethinkingschools.org/special_reports/ bushplan/capt174.shtml.

2   B. Dylan, *Chronicles: Volume 1* (New York: Simon and Schuster, 2004).

3   J. Kincheloe, "Critical ontology: Visions of selfhood and curriculum," *JCT: Journal of Curriculum Theorizing, 19(1)* (2003): 47–64.

4   P. Parmar, "Rap music: The critical pedagogy of KRS-One," in J. Kincheloe, and D. Weil, eds. *Critical Thinking and Learning: An Encyclopedia for Parents and Teachers* (Westport, CT: Greenwood, 2004).

5   S. Haymes, "Educational reform: What have been the effects of the attempts to improve education over the last decade?" in J. Kincheloe, and S. Steinberg, eds. *Thirteen Questions: Reframing Education's Conversation* (New York: Peter Lang, 1995). J. Ng, "Multicultural education in teacher training programs and its implications on preparedness for effective work in urban settings," in G. Lopez, and L. Parker, eds. *Interrogating Racism in Qualitative Research Methodology* (New York: Peter Lang, 2003).

6.   J. Bamburg, *Raising Expectations to Improve Student Learning*, 1994, http://www.ncrel.org/sdrs/areas/issues/ educatrs/leadrshp/ie0bam.htm; D. Hurley, *Developing Students as Change Agents: Urban Education and Reform*. 2003, http://www.eastern.edu/publications/emme/2003spring/hurley.html.

7   S. Ginwright, "Identity for sale: The limits of racial reform in urban schools," *The Urban Review, 32(1)* (2000); P. McDermott and J. Rothenberg, "Why urban parents resist involvement in their children's elementary education," *The Qualitative Report, 5* (2000):3–4.http://www.nova.edu/ssss/qr/qr5–3/ mcdermott.html; G. Duncan, "School violence, black masculinities, and a mother's love: Reflections on (in)formal urban pedagogies," in M. Brown II and J. Davis, eds. *Black Sons to Mothers: Compliments, Critiques, and Challenges for Cultural Workers in Education* (New York: Peter Lang, 2000); M. Haberman, "Achieving 'high quality' in the selection, preparation and retention of teachers," *EducationNews.org*, 2002, http://www.educationnews.org; J. Valentin, "Is special education working in urban schools?" in S. Steinberg and J. Kincheloe, eds. *19 Urban Questions: Teaching in the City* (New York: Peter Lang, 2004).

8   L. Weiner, *Urban Teaching: The Essentials* (New York: Teachers College Press, 1999); S. Henke, *Representations of Secondary Urban Education: Infusing Cultural Studies into Teacher Education*. Dissertation, Miami University, 2000.

9   F. Shephard and Osborne, *Intrapersonal Intelligence: Affective Factors in Thinking*; K. Kelly and S. Moon, "Personal and social talents." *Phi Delta Kappan, 79(10)*; R. Carter, "Can aesthetics be taught in urban education?" in S. Steinberg, and J. Kincheloe, eds. *19 Urban Questions: Teaching in the City* (New York: Peter Lang, 2004).

10   W. DuBois, H. Aptheker (Ed.), *The Education of Black People: Ten Critiques, 1906<\#150>1960* (New York: Monthly Review Press, 1973), pp. 8–9.

11   *And Justice for Some*. 2005,http://www.buildingblocksforyouth.org/justiceforsome/jfs.html

12   A. Hacker, *Two Nations: Black and White, Separate, Hostile, Unequal* (New York: Ballantine Books, 1992); R. Frankenberg, *White Women, Race Matters: The Social Construction of Whiteness* (Minneapolis: University of Minnesota Press, 1993); L. Rubin, *Families on the Faultline: America's Working Class Speaks about the Family, the Economy, Race, and Ethnicity* (New York: HarperCollins, 1994); J. King and C. Mitchell, *Black Mothers to Sons* (New York: Peter Lang, 1996); J. Kincheloe, S. Steinberg, N. Rodriguez and R. Chennault, *White Reign: Deploying Whiteness in America* (New York: St. Martin's, 1998).

13   C. Nightingale, *On the Edge: A History of Poor Black Children and Their American Dreams* (New York: Basic Books).

14   J. Kincheloe and S. Steinberg, *Changing Multiculturalism* (London: Open University Press, 1997); Ibid., See Note 12.{AQ}

15   Rubin, *Families on the Faultline: America's Working Class Speaks about the Family, the Economy, Race, and Ethnicity*; A. Gresson, *The Recovery of Race in America* (Minneapolis: University of Minnesota Press, 1995); A. Gresson, *America's Atonement: Racial Pain, Recovery Rhetoric, and the Pedagogy of Healing* (New York: Peter Lang, 2004).

16   Ibid., see Note 7.

17   Duncan, Ibid.; J. Kincheloe, S. Steinberg, N. Rodriguez and R. Chennault, Ibid., see Note 12.

18   Henke, *Representations of Secondary Urban Education: Infusing Cultural Studies into Teacher Education*.

19   P. Anderson and J. Summerfield, "Why is urban education different than rural and suburban education?" in S. Steinberg, and J. Kincheloe, eds. *19 Urban Questions: Teaching in the City* (New York: Peter Lang, 2004).

20   D. Geeland, "Learning to Communicate: Developing as a Science Teacher," 1996, http://bravus.port5.com/learn.htm; K. Louis and B. Smith, "Teacher engagement and real reform in urban schools," in B. Williams, ed. *Closing the Achievement Gap: A Vision for Changing Beliefs and Practices* (Alexandria, VA: ASCD, 1996).

21   Ginwright, *Identity for Sale: The Limits of Racial Reform in Urban Schools*; D. Gaines, *Teenage Wasteland: Suburbia's Dead End Kids* (New York: Harper Perennial, 1990); L. Rodriguez, "Rekindling the warrior," *Utne Reader*, 64, (July/August, 1994): 58–59; USSR (Urban Schools Symposium Report), *Relationship, Community, and Positive Reframing: Addressing the Needs*. 1998, http://www.inclusiveschools.org/procsho.htm; A. Barton and K. Yang, "The culture of power and science education: Learning from Miguel." *Journal of Research in Science Education*, 37(8) (2000): 871–89; H. Kharem, "What do urban educators need to know about gangs?" in S. Steinberg, and J. Kincheloe, eds. *19 Urban Questions* (New York: Peter Lang, 2004); M. Haberman, "Urban education: The state of urban schooling at the start of the Twenty-First century," *EducationNews.org*, 2004, http://www.educationnews.org.

22   M. Wang and J. Kovach, "Bridging the achievement gap in urban schools: Reducing educational segregation and advancing resilience-promoting strategies," in B. Williams, ed. *Closing the Achievement Gap: A Vision for Changing Beliefs and Practices* (Alexandria, VA: ASCD, 1996); Louis and Smith, *Teacher Engagement and Real Reform in Urban Schools*; E. O'Sullivan, *Transformative Learning: Educational Vision for the Twenty-First Century* (New York: Zed, 1999); Education World, *Ordinary Resurrections: An e-Interview with Jonathan Kozol*. 2001, http://www.education-world.com/a_issues/issues164.shtml

23   USSR, ; F. Shephard, and Osborne, *Intrapersonal Intelligence: Affective Factors in Thinking*.

24   b. hooks, *Black Looks: Race and Representation* (Boston: South End Press, 1992); Hacker, *Two Nations: Black and White, Separate, Hostile, Unequal*; Louis and Smith, *Teacher Engagement and Real Reform in Urban Schools*; USSR, "Relationship, Community, and Positive Reframing: Addressing the Needs."

25   Weiner, *Urban Teaching: The Essentials*; McDermott and Rothenberg, *Why Urban Parents Resist Involvement in Their Children's Elementary Education*;

26   A. Gresson, *The Recovery of Race in America* (Minneapolis: University of Minnesota Press, 1995); A. Gresson, *America's Atonement: Racial Pain, Recovery Rhetoric, and the Pedagogy of Healing* (New York: Peter Lang, 2004).

27   M. Carvan, A. Nolen and R. Yinger. *Power through Partnership: The Urban Network for the Improvement of Teacher Education* 2002. http://www.urbannetworks.net/documents/tacte%20article, %20final%20revision%201–14–02.pdf; P. Noguera, *City Schools and the American Dream: Reclaiming the Promise of Public Education* (New York: Teachers College Press, 2003).

28   R. Zweigenhaft and G. Domhoff, *Blacks in the White Establishment* (New Haven, CT: Yale University Press, 1991); J. Kincheloe, *How Do We Tell the Workers: The Socio-Economic Foundations of Work and Vocational Education* (Boulder, CO: Westview, 1999).

29   J. Bruner, *The Culture of Education* (Cambridge, MA: Harvard University Press, 1996); P. Freire, *Pedagogy of the Oppressed* (New York: Herder and Herder, 1970); P. Freire, *The Politics of Education: Culture, Power, and Liberation* (South Hadley, MA: Bergin & Garvey, 1985).

30   D. Perkins and S. Tishman, *Dispositional Aspects of Intelligence.* 1998, http://learnweb.arvard.edu/alps/thinking/docs/plymouth.htm; D. Slaughter-Defoe, *Introduction: The Clayton Lectures* 2002, http://www.urbanedjournal.org/archive/issue%201/homepage/huest.html; Kharem, *What Do Urban Educators Need to Know about Gangs?*

31   F. Shephard and Osborne, *Intrapersonal Intelligence: Affective Factors in Thinking;* T., Fenwick, *Experiential Learning in Adult Education: A Comparative Framework.* 2000, http://www.ualberta.ca/~tfenwick/ext/aeq.htm.

32   E. Quintero, "How can literacy be taught successfully in urban schools?" in S. Steinberg, and J. Kincheloe, eds. *19 Urban Questions: Teaching in the City* (New York: Peter Lang, 2004).

33   Ibid., See Note 1.

34   F. Shephard and Osborne, W. Crebbin, *The Critically Reflective Practitioner.* 2001, http://www.ballarat.edu.au/~wcrebbin/TB780/Critreflect.html.

35   H. Marcuse, *Eros and Civilization* (Boston: Beacon Press, 1955).

36.   S. Ohanian, *One Size Fits Few: The Folly of Educational Standards* (Portsmouth, NH: Heinemann, 1999).

II.

UNDERSTANDING CITY KIDS

2. Latinas in Single-Sex Schools

An Historical Overview

ROSALINA DIAZ

In 1493, Christopher Columbus wrote to Queen Isabella of a group of women he had encountered while sailing in Caribbean waters. He referred to these women as Amazons, "These are the women who alone inhabit the island of Mateunin (or Matinino). These women, moreover, perform no kind of work of their sex, for they use bows and darts, like those I have described; they protect themselves with sheets of copper, of which there is a great abundance among them." The native men were said to avoid these women at all costs. For it was said that if any approached them *outside the agreed upon time*, or dared to follow them, they would "defend themselves with well-aimed arrows—believed to be shot with an expert eye." Columbus had learned of these women from the natives, but he had ample reason to believe their stories. There are several historical accounts of attacks on Columbus and his crew. Fernando Colon writes of one attack in which "the arrow, shot with such force and dexterity as to pass right through the shield was fired by . . . a woman." And in another account it was reported that these warrior "women so fiercely held off the landing parties that cannons were fired to frighten them off." Columbus searched in vain for the island of Matinino with no success. Later, historians would claim that the island never existed and that the story of the Amazon of Matinino was a myth. But then what of the attacks?

Several members of Columbus' crew, including Michel de Cuneo, Dr. Chanca, and Fernando Colon corroborated the accounts.

Based on the combined accounts of Bartolome de las Casas, Gonzalo Oviedo de Fernandez, and Ramon Pane, we know that young girls in the Caribbean were isolated from their villages during their liminal phase of development, beginning around the ages of 12 and 13, right after first menstruation, and lasting for approximately two years. These young women were "off limits" to all men during that period of time. It is quite possible that the 'Amazons' that Columbus encountered were actually Native adolescent girls undergoing their rites of passage. Once the predetermined period of isolation and gender role socialization was completed, the girls were reintroduced into their society with a ritual celebration, but were restricted from all sexual activity until they were to be married. One of these celebrations is described by Oviedo in his *Historia General y Natural de las Indias*, "More than 300 unmarried maidens danced, all god-daughters of Anacaona (female Taíno Chieftain), and she did not allow any woman or man who was sexually experienced to participate in the dance."[1] The period of European colonization in the Caribbean was perforce one of chaos and cultural disruption. Many traditions and cultural practices were irrevocably lost. Fortunately, as a result of Spain's assimilationist colonizing practices, concubinage with native women was widespread. It was through these women that aspects of the indigenous culture survived and were passed down from generation to generation. One aspect of indigenous culture that survived up to the twentieth century was single-sex education for girls.

The Spanish church implemented formal education in Puerto Rico in the early sixteenth century. These early schools were for boys only. There were no educational resources for girls until the nineteenth century. And then, only those families, who could afford it, sent their daughters to same-sex private or parochial schools, "Lessons for girls usually included sewing and embroidery. Boys and girls were taught separately by teachers of the same sex."[2] By 1897, the 551 public schools on the island were still very poorly funded by the colonial government, and were likewise segregated by gender. Of these schools, "nearly three-quarters (403) were attended by boys and the remaining (148) were used to teach girls. As a result of the Spanish American War, Puerto Rico was ceded to the United States in 1898. One might have reasonably expected the United States to immediately implement a coeducational system, such as was the norm on the mainland. This however was not the case. Instead the United States opened 34 new single-sex vocational schools, which continued the training in the traditional skills of embroidery and needlework that Puerto Rican girls learned in the home. The needlework industry soon became the second most important industry on the island, with American-owned businesses profiting from the labor of Puerto Rican women.[3] This delayed the introduction of coeducation in Puerto Rico until well into the twenty-first century.

Transnational Feminisms:
Expanding Our Notions of Feminist Identity

In the majority of Latino homes, family care-giving responsibilities fall primarily on girls. It is understood that a woman's obligation to her family is central to her identity as a Latina woman, and it supercedes any educational and/or career plans. Today, post-revolutionary Cuba has the highest literacy rate (96.8%) of any Latin American country and one of the highest in the world. Education is mandatory and free. Over 50% of college graduates and 60% of all doctors in Cuba are women.[4] Havana even boasts a Museum of Education. But in spite of high educational levels and a socialist political system which promotes more egalitarian and stable gender relations, Cuban women still perceive their fundamental role as mother and housewife. Teen pregnancy rates are high today, as they have always been. The average Cuban girl becomes sexually active at 13, and has her first baby by the age of 18. The rate of illiteracy in Santo Domingo is the highest in the Spanish speaking Caribbean. The literacy rate in 2001 was 84% for both men and women. Less than half of all Dominican children go beyond elementary school. Secondary schools begin at age 13, and only 40.8% of the population attends.[5] Most institutions are religious and many are still gender segregated. Public secondary education suffers from poor facilities and inadequate funding. The Dominican Republic is still largely a male-oriented society based on the values of paternalism and machismo. Female children are closely chaperoned and their lives are heavily circumscribed. Brothers and male cousins are expected to protect them and their reputations, and those middle-class and elite parents, who can, prefer to send their daughters to private or parochial same-sex schools. The average Dominican girl sets up her first home by the age of 14 or 15, many while they are pregnant or already have children. However, Dominican women still tend to attain higher educational levels than men. In 1997 (most recent available data), 27.1% of females attended college, as opposed to 19.2% of males.[6]

Puerto Rico, Cuba, and the Dominican Republic share a common cultural heritage rooted in Spanish colonialism, Catholicism, and a plantation economy. All were subjects of US hegemony, but followed quite different patterns of industrialization after World War II. In spite of differences in economic and political structures and ideologies, all have experienced significant increases in women's education and employment rates since the 1960s, in most cases surpassing that of the male population. Researcher and anthropologist Helen Safa identifies a common thread which differentiates Latin women's participation in the labor force from that of American women. She explains, "families provide women with a social identity that proletarianization as wageworkers has not diminished. Despite women's increasing incorporation into the labor force, they still define gender roles differently . . . Women view themselves as wives and mothers with economic responsibilities; . . . In fact, most women in our sample now consider paid employment part of their domestic role, because they are working to contribute to the household economy rather than for their own self-esteem or personal autonomy." Whereas for American women, "The decreasing importance placed by society on the family and housework undermined their value for women . . . women demanded a greater presence in the public sphere and began to claim individual rights based on equality with men and not simply on the basis of protecting women's separate domestic sphere."[7]

One reason for this difference is the importance attributed to the role of the mother in Latin American society. The Spanish-speaking Caribbean has historically been based on a matrifocal system, with an emphasis on complementary gender relations. Taking care of the family is seen as a sacred trust, and the status and respect afforded women in this role can be highly rewarding and satisfying. The mother is the acknowledged and unchallenged authority within the home, and her labor contributions in this sphere are considered of far greater importance than that of her male partner. For Latinas, contemporary attempts at gender equality have largely been an effort to expand on this role and extend it into the public sphere. Latinas, like their African American counterparts in the states, see little need to compete with male partners who have been even more disenfranchised by the dominant society than they themselves have. The persistence of elopement and consensual unions, especially in the lower classes, reflect resistance to interference from patriarchal/colonialist Church and State institutions into the private realm of conjugal relations.[8] These more indigenous marriage patterns have benefited women in that they allow them to maintain control over the home and children in the event of dissolution of the relationship. Ignorance, regarding the historical and social structures of the Spanish-speaking Caribbean, has contributed to a general belief that these women are passive/submissive victims of a misogynist Macho society, and completely disregards the fact that Machismo and Marianismo are European imports. Single-sex education in the Spanish-speaking Caribbean was grounded in a legacy of female empowerment and strength, and though it has gone through several transmutations, it continues to be a source of both feminine empowerment and respect for cultural tradition. To ignore the history of the development of single-sex education in the Caribbean is to omit information vital to a true understanding of how and why single-sex education works for Caribbean Latinas.

Caribbean Latinas living in the United States today are considered among the most educationally disadvantaged groups in the United States. According to The Urban Institute Education Policy Center, the graduation rates for Latinas in New York City were just above 30% in 2002 as opposed to 94.6% in Puerto Rico. Sadly, these statistics are neither new nor surprising. Latino students have had the lowest graduation rates in the United States for almost 30 years. Clearly, American schools have not been meeting the needs of the majority of Latino students. In light of these dismal statistics, concerned Latino parents consistently seek out a more culturally familiar option for their adolescent daughters—schools that offer the structure, discipline, and safety more typical of the Latino single-sex schools back in their native lands.

Latinas in American Single-Sex Schools: A Matter of Class

Single-sex education in the United States has always been segregated by race/ethnicity and class. The Life Adjustment movement of the 1940s and 1950s encouraged the tracking of many Latino students into single-sex vocational schools. Schools like Eli Whitney, Norman Thomas, Sarah J. Hale, Clara Barton, Mabel Dean Bacon, Washington Irving, and Fashion Industries High School offered Latina girls and their parents the option of a career oriented school in a single-sex environment. These schools reflected the traditional single-sex manual training programs (i.e., needlepoint and dress-making) that had been an integral part of the educational system in Latin America for girls over the age of 13 for centuries.[9] The New York City High School Division reports that in June of 1962, 24.7% of single-sex vocational school graduates were Puerto Rican as opposed to only 4.5% in academic high schools. New York City vocational high schools were coeducationalized by the 1980s, as a result of Title IX and increasing pressure from the Office of Civil Rights to "provide an educational environment that mirrored the diversity of modern society."[10] Washington Irving High School was the last to convert (1986), in spite of an excellent academic record (85%–90% of its graduates went on to post-secondary education) and vehement protests by parents and students. The tracking of Latinas into low-wage manual labor encouraged by these schools was problematic, but the loss of these single-sex institutions has been strongly felt by the Latino community, and has not resulted in superior or more equitable options. Today many Latino parents opt to send their daughters to single-sex private or parochial schools. However, given the socio-economic status of most Latinos, these numbers are in the minority and most Latino parents have no choice but to enroll their daughters in coeducational public high schools. With the closing of large numbers of New York City Catholic schools in 2005, the choices are now even more limited.

Four years ago, a new option for Latinas emerged in the midst of Spanish Harlem, The Young Women's Leadership School (TYWLS), a public school that offers Latino parents the best of all worlds—academic rigor, a single-sex environment, in a public school setting. The school was founded in 1996 by Ann Rubenstein Tisch (a noted journalist and philanthropist). According to an article in the *Daily News* by Diane Ravitch, "Ms. Ann Tisch wanted an all-girls school because she knew that the dropout rate among Hispanic and African American students was high and that many minority girls left school because they became pregnant. She wanted to create a girl's school because she believed that minority girls would focus on their academic work more if they were not distracted by the presence of boys." Even though her statements reflect a limited and essentialist understanding of the complex socio-economic factors that underscore the dropout problem, her solution seems to have been right on target. The Young Women's Leadership Academy has apparently been very successful and is now considered a role model for other same-sex institutions. The 2002 graduating class numbered 232, over 91% of its original cohort. Of these girls a total of 97% went on to college, in comparison to the City's average of 65%.[11] The success of this school has prompted the opening of several single-sex schools in New York City. It has also prompted rigorous debate and discussion. Proponents of same-sex education include such philosophically opposed parties as Diane Ravitch and Hillary Rodham Clinton. Opponents are equally powerful, and include the National Organization for Women, the American Association of University Women, and the American Civil Liberties Union Part of the reason for the controversy is that many of the benefits of Single-sex education, increased self-esteem, development of leadership qualities, increased opportunity for same-sex bonding, are very difficult to measure quantitatively. In addition, because the students in single-sex schools are a self-selected population, it is difficult to ascertain whether the benefits are attributed to a same-sex education or simply to the quality of the students. " . . . Researchers do not know for certain whether the benefits derive from factors unique to single-sex programs, or whether these factors also exist or can be reproduced in coeducational settings. Studies or anecdotes suggesting a correlation between same-sex programs and positive educational outcomes have no meaning unless an effort was made to control for variables such as socioeconomic status of the students, selectivity of admissions, greater resources invested in the program, and smaller class size. Indeed, without controlling for those variables, one could make the case for separating students based on any identity characteristic."[12] In response to this challenge, there has been extensive research on the academic benefits of a single-sex education for the general population,[13] but the research on the benefits of single-sex education for specific ethnic/racial groups, such as Latinas, is practically non-existent. The study of single-sex education for Latinas is very complex, as it must take into account gender, race/ethnicity, and socio-economic and cultural factors as these intersect in an educational setting.

Latinas in Single-Sex Schools: What Does the Research Say?

There has been a growing body of literature which addresses the cultural conflicts encountered by adolescent Latinas in traditional American public high schools and their possible correlation to increased dropout rates.[14] Most deal with the conflicts and problems encountered by first and second generation immigrant Latinas, but the reality is that newly arrived immigrants fare far better in the public school system than do later generation Latinos. In fact Puerto Ricans and Mexicans, who have the longest history of residence in the United States, also have the highest dropout rates among Latino groups. Although these works specifically address the cultural conflicts Latinas face in Public High Schools, most hesitate to take the logical next step of suggesting solutions in the form of culturally sensitive community-based models of education. They acknowledge the problem but place the onus for change (adaptation, acculturation, or assimilation) on the student or cultural group and not on the school system. Based on this existing literature, I have identified the following causal factors as those most often used to explain the high dropout rate among Latinas (all refer to cultural factors). Of these only Sonia Nieto (2000) clearly places the fault on the school system itself.

- High pregnancy rates—Latina girls have the highest birth rate in the nation (US Department of Health and Human Services). In 2001, the birth rate (per thousand) for Hispanic girls aged 15–19 was 92.4, compared to 73.1 for black girls, and 41.7 for white, and are much more likely to leave school as a result. "Latinas in this country come from areas where teenagers often marry and bear children as their primary (or only) rite of passage to adulthood, and the status associated with these events is highly rewarding."[15] Latina girls are less likely to return to school after giving birth than African American or White girls. Latin tradition dictates that they marry and take on the responsibility of raising their families regardless of age, and abortion is rarely an option. In all Latino homes, family care-giving responsibilities fall primarily on girls. It is understood that a woman's obligation to her family is central to her identity as a Latina woman, and supercedes any educational and/or career plans.[16]

- Conflicting cultural messages regarding appropriate behavior, values, and morals from the family/home culture and the school culture.[17] Traditional coeducational schools do not make the psychological/emotional connections with students that Latino students are accustomed to. "Though inclusive of formal academic training, 'educacion' additionally refers to competence in the social world, wherein one respects the dignity and individuality of others."[18] Traditional Latino teachers' expectations of students tend to focus strongly on the notion of respect, discipline, and social responsibility, which are often lacking in traditional coeducational public high schools.

- On average, Latina girls come from homes with lower socioeconomic status (SES). Overall, New York Latino families have lower household incomes than either African American or white families and consequently suffer higher poverty rates . . . well over one-third of Puerto Rican and Dominican families, live in poverty."[19] This translates into greater responsibilities in the home from household duties to child-care to possible part-time employment outside the home, which may interfere with schooling, and girls "charged with the maintenance of family ties" tend to shoulder more of these responsibilities.[20]

- Internalization of negative societal stereotypes regarding inborn-intelligence, and incapacity to succeed.[21] In spite of the fact that statistics have consistently found that quality education is a top priority for Latino families and youth,[22] the stereotype of educationally unmotivated Latinos has taken firm hold in the American imagination. Suarez-Orozco in the book, *Children of Immigration*, blames "misrecognition," a process by which children internalize negative societal stereotypes, for the poor academic performance of Latinos. She explains, "The hopelessness and self-deprecation that this resignation causes may in turn result in low aspirations and self-defeating behaviors," such as dropping out.

- School policies and practices that alienate Latino students. Latino students in the United States struggle to maintain their identity in the face of on-going pressures to assimilate and abandon their cultural diversity. A "1976 report by the US Commission on Civil Rights found that a primary reason for dropping out of school as identified by young people themselves was school's unresponsiveness to their cultural backgrounds."[23]

To date only a handful of scholars/researchers have looked to a single-sex education as a possible solution to the problem of Latina and African American "dropoutism." In the 1980s, Cornelius Riordan of Rhode Island College, and Valerie Lee of the University of Michigan, conducted research studies on single-sex education. As a result of the dearth of public single-sex schools, these studies focused on Catholic School populations. Both studies showed that there were definite benefits to single-sex education for girls, which included "higher educational aspirations, plans for post-secondary and graduate school education, and entry into less stereotypically female fields."[24] Several years later, Lee conducted similar research focusing on independent private schools. The results perplexed her, as they were not consistent with the results of her first study. In fact this research seemed to indicate that there were no substantial benefits to be gained from single-sex schools either for boys or girls. As a result of this new data, Lee apparently abandoned her advocacy of single-sex schools. She has instead focused her research on identifying those characteristics of Catholic single-sex schools responsible for the initial success rates she encountered, with the end goal of replicating these characteristics in coeducational settings. Cornelius Riordan, on the other hand was not dismayed by the results of this second study. Riordan analyzed the data and explained that the results were actually predictable. Catholic School students, he explains, tend to come from working class minority families, whereas private school students tend to be elite whites. This difference accounts for the skewed results. Riordan went on to explain that single-sex schools only worked for historically disadvantaged groups. "They work for girls and boys, women and men, whites and non-white, but this effect is limited to students of lower socioeconomic status and/or students who are disadvantaged historically—females and racial/ethnic/religious minorities. The major factor that conditions the strength of single-sex effects is social class, and since class and race are inextricably linked, the effects are also conditioned by race and gender."[25] Unlike Lee, Riordan does not believe that the success of single-sex schools can be replicated in coeducational school settings. He explains that the "organizational differences" that Lee describes in her research, "more successful same-sex teacher and student role models, more leadership opportunities, greater order and discipline, and fewer distractions from academic matters," are set into motion because of an independent variable, which is single-sex education. He adds, "Single-sex schools provide an *atmosphere* that 'empowers' African and Hispanic American students." These words echo those of Elizabeth Tidball, who in her 1970s study on women's colleges suggested that it was the "wholeness of the environment" which accounted for the success of same-sex institutions.[26] Riordan's work has been immensely important to the study of single-sex schooling. However, by positing that same-sex education benefits Latinas mainly because of their low SES, he implicitly denies the role of culture. Riordan never once references the long history of single-sex education in Latin America and the obvious correlation that this history would have on present-day educational practices. Riordan's oversight is typical of the decontextualized research practices prevalent among quantitative scholars. This decontextualizd type of study can only lead to the further essentializing of already stigmatized groups.

Building on the work of Riordan, Karen Stabiner, a journalist, writes a moving comparative ethnography of two single-sex schools in her book, *All Girls: Single-Sex Education and Why It Matters*. The book, clearly written for a mainstream audience, follows two separate groups of students for a year—one from TYWLS and the other from Marlborough, an elite prep school in Los Angeles. Stabiner attempts to take us into the minds of these students, their struggles, and their triumphs, as well as the critical role that economics plays in determining the future destinies of these girls. It is also evident from her descriptions that she perceives single-sex education (SSE) for both groups to be a positive and viable educational option. However, like Riordan, Stabiner dances around the issue of race/ethnicity and culture without ever directly addressing it. A lexical analysis of her word choices reveals cultural biases. She includes her own perception that the girls at TYWLS "were *embarrassed* by what they saw as their cultural heritage." And she quotes one teacher who explains to the students "culture is a group of people's unique way of life." She adds as an aside to this, "It was not, as some girls assumed, their *destiny*." The then principal of the school Celenia Chevere is quoted repeatedly and excessively. "It was part of Celenia Chevere's plan to *separate* her girls from the people they pass on the way to school. The girl at the coffee cart and her boyfriend represented to her a *pervasive threat* . . . She made it clear from the start that *escape* demanded something more than the obvious attributes of dedication and academic excellence. A successful young woman made TWYLS her community, and *left the temptations* of her neighborhood behind." The implication here is that success for minority girls can only be attained at the cost of culture and community, but this is not the case at Marlborough where the family and community are considered important social capital. "Most of the girls at Marlborough considered a good education their birthright; their parents, and many of their grandparents, were college graduates. It was one of the perquisites of a comfortable existence, along with travel, access to cultural events, lessons, and sports." She presents the school experiences and outcomes of both sets of students in a completely de-contextualized fashion, without ever confronting the social, historical, and political reasons behind the apparent inequalities in their lives. This process of de-contextualization and mystification leaves one with the feeling that this is just the way things are, and may, in many cases, lead the public to believe that it is just a matter of individual or group merit. She ends the book with the following quote. "Why should Diana Perez miss what the Rich girls had? No reason at all." Really?

In this same vein, Rosemary Salomone of St. John's Law school (legal advisor to Rubinstein Tisch—founder of TYWLS) also advocates for single-sex schools for minority groups in a book entitled *Same, Different, Equal*. She presents a reasoned well thought-out legal and historical analysis of single-sex education in which she is careful to point out the dangers of essentialism. Unfortunately her own seemingly unbiased narrative falls apart in her revealing descriptions of the social issues affecting Latinas.

> Viewing life through the lens of *few available options*, they (Latinas) perceive their economic and social situations as *hopeless* and resort to *early and repeat motherhood* as a source of competence and significance. Unfortunately, they soon learn the realities of raising children on their own without the emotional and financial support of a husband . . . The impact [of *early marriage and pregnancies*] on their

future lives proves *devastating* . . . for many girls, physical, sexual, and emotional *victimization* is the first step along the path leading to the *juvenile justice system*. A high proportion of them enter as runaways, seeking to escape *abusive homes*.[27]

By essentializing Latinas and minority girls as victims or future delinquents, Salomone paves the way for her defense of the cultural intervention of TYWLS—a school founded by a white upper-class woman from outside the community. This argument, as well as both Tisch's and Salomone's obsession with the excessively high pregnancy rates of minority girls, is reminiscent of the reproductive interventionist strategies associated with Operation Bootstrap in the 1960s. The poor in ghetto neighborhoods were seen as in need of supervision due to their "proclivity for immediate gratification and inability to plan for the future." This argument justified interventionist practices that ultimately led to massive sterilizations (35% of all Puerto Rican women of child-bearing age) and the largest percentage of births by c-section in the world.[28]

Salomone goes on to describe TYWLS in relation to its host community—Spanish Harlem, which she describes as a "beleaguered community" with "graffiti lined streets." TWYLS, on the other hand, is described as "an oasis of excellence and hope in a desert of poverty, crime, and despair," "a striking contrast with the surrounding neighborhood . . . a safe haven for these girls," a "ticket out of the sub-culture," "a place that is orderly and secure with a palpable sense of energy and purpose" as opposed to the surrounding neighborhood. Underlying this form of discourse is what Henry Giroux calls "cultural deprivation/deficit theory." "In this ideology of 'need fulfillment,' the category of need represents an *absence* of a particular set of experiences. In most cases, what educators determine as missing are either the culturally specific experiences that school authorities believe students must acquire in order to enrich the quality of their lives, or the fundamental skills they will "need' in order to get jobs once they leave school." Underlying this view of experience is the logic of cultural deprivation theory, which defines education in terms of cultural enrichment, remediation, and basics . . . Specifically, the experience of the student as 'other' is cast as deviant, underprivileged, or 'uncultured.' Consequently not only do students bear the sole responsibility for school failure, but also, there is little room for questioning the ways in which administrators and teachers actually create and sustain the problems they attribute to students."[29] In other words, by using language that focuses on the deficits of the cultural group, the school can justify a culture-blind curriculum that reinforces negative stereotypes about the student's home culture. Conversely the overarching socio-historical context is ignored and the dominant society (represented by the school) is presented as benefactor and savior.

At TYWLS, this attitude is evident in the lack of representations of Latino culture in the school and in the curriculum, the lack of school involvement in the family and community life of the students, and the lack of Latino faculty and staff. The question here is, does this absence of cultural representation in the schools adversely affect Latinas? The answer to this is subjective and would have to take into account differing interpretations of success. Paulo Freire in *Pedagogy of the Oppressed* states:

No pedagogy which is truly liberating can remain distant from the oppressed by treating them as unfortunate and by presenting for their emulation models from among the oppressors. The oppressed must be their own example. Pedagogy which begins with the egoistic interests of the oppressor (an egoism) cloaked in the false generosity of paternalism and makes of the oppressed objects of its humanitarianism, itself maintains and embodies oppression. It is an instrument of dehumanization.[30]

The efforts of all external educational, social, and political programs, no matter, how well-intentioned are problematic and suspect, unless they begin as a collaborative effort with the community in question. Such an effort would strive to identify the actual needs of the residents of that community and not their own preconceived assumptions of those needs.

Diane Pollard of the University of Wisconsin, Milwaukee, conducted a research study at an Afro-centric single-sex after-school program in a middle school in Baltimore that attempted to do just that. Her reflections on this study were published in an AAUW journal, "Separated by sex: A critical look at single-sex education for girls." In Pollard's own words, "The impetus for this program and study was the need for broader attempts to implement *culturally* centered educational models. In this context single-sex classes have focused on both formal and informal socialization for boys and girls." The program was aptly named "Rites of passage." This program offered young African American students of both sexes the opportunity to focus on gender issues in an environment that was culturally supportive, nurturing, and even enhancing. The underlying tenet of African-centered education is that schools serving African American children need to be closely *linked* with the communities of their students, and should *build upon and reinforce* the cultural activities of those communities. This orientation suggests that these schools should not be limited to an academic focus, but should also concern themselves with social and personal development. Furthermore this orientation emphasizes the notion that students are expected to use education not only for individual empowerment but also for the promotion and *empowerment of their communities*. Pollard argues that gender issues within minority communities need to take into account the *historical and cultural aspects* of that community, as gender identity and relations are shaped by cultural heritage, colonization, and imperialistic exploitations. Issues related to gender cannot be separated from issues of class and race. Pollard's study emphasizes the need for education that builds on the strengths that minority students, both male and female, bring with them from their home communities. This issue begs for more research that focuses on the intersections of race/ethnicity, culture, and class as these intersect and play themselves out in a single-sex environment.

The literature I have here compiled represents diverse views on the goals of SSE for Latina girls. Riordan's de-contextualized research on parochial single-sex schools repeatedly conflates issues of economics and race/ethnicity. This proves problematic, as it omits other aspects of the historical/cultural development of gender that are crucial to a complete understanding of the significance of SSE in Latin culture. Stabiner and Salomone both present "cultural deficit models" to justify their advocacy of a specific type of SSE, specifically TYWLS, for Latinas. Lexical selections show the "familiar form of negative other presentations, and positive self-presentation" and constructs Latinas as needy and disadvantaged. Diane

Pollard's study introduces a new and alternative brand of SSE.[31] This SSE has emerged as a result of a need expressed by a marginalized community. As a result, according to Pollard, it respects and builds upon the culture of the students and takes into account the socio-historical factors underlying the social realities of their community. The students are presented as active agents with a stake in their own educational processes.

Conclusion: Some Crucial Questions

The United States has a long historical tradition of coeducation. The father of progressive education, John Dewey, argued for equal coeducation as the ideal for a truly democratic society. He believed that separate could never be equal, and he sincerely aspired to full educational equality for women. Unfortunately, studies and statistics have shown that in the case of gender, coeducation does not guarantee equality. Title IX was flawed in that it offered an educational solution to a problem that is societal and cannot be fully resolved within the schools. Until women achieve full equality in American society, schools will continue to replicate these biases and inequalities within our coeducational classrooms.

Single-sex schools offer an alternative that appeals to many parents. Latinas and African Americans in particular have been shown to benefit from this type of education.[32] With the recent popularity of single-sex schools in the United States, and their immense appeal to minority parents in NYC in particular, it is vital that we understand all the factors behind their success. Understanding the history of single-sex education in the Spanish-speaking Caribbean helps to explain this appeal. However, not all single-sex schools are created equally. Differing school philosophies and ideologies make for vastly different educational experiences. The philosophy/ideology of TYWLS, for example, is for the most part Eurocentric, feminist, and color/culture blind. This may not be what most Latino parents have in mind when they think of a single-sex education for their daughters. I would venture a guess that many of the girls (and families) who choose to come to this school do so because they too have incorporated a "cultural deficit model." They choose TYWLS because what this school promotes, full assimilation to American society, is exactly what they have been convinced they need to succeed. However, I do not believe that this is true for the majority of New York City Latino parents. For girls who are more firmly grounded in their Latina culture, this school can become a ground for contestation and identity conflicts.

Latinos are not unlike other immigrants in several important ways. The close geographical proximity of Latin America, and in the case of Puerto Ricans—dual citizenship, facilitates consistent back and forth travel or circular migration. The migrant population is thus consistently replenished, and it becomes necessary to maintain a dual cultural identity. "Deactivation" of the home culture dissolves support networks and erases valuable cultural capital. "Although assimilation has been rationalized by schools on many grounds, recent research on cultural and linguistic identity has challenged the long-standing wisdom that in order to get ahead on must sacrifice one's identity."[33] The research has shown that the more successful Latinas are those that learn to meld the two cultures into a "homogenous, bounded unitary, whole."[34] In addition, the history of the education of Latinos (as described by Nieto), particularly of Puerto Ricans and Mexicans, in the United States has been one of struggle to maintain a bicultural and bilingual identity as both a "defense against a hostile environment and as a nonnegotiable demand for educational improvement."

And so there are several questions we must ask ourselves at this juncture. Why has the discourse on single-sex education resurfaced at this particular time in history? Who are the actors behind this resurgence? Why have Latinas been targeted? Who actually benefits from the legal changes that have emerged from the incorporation of single-sex education?

In a country where Latinos now represent the largest minority population and yet have consistently maintained the lowest educational achievement and economic levels, this research indicates that the curriculum of TWYLS and similar schools merely prepares a select handful of properly assimilated token Latinas for leadership positions in order to "quell discontent among the masses" (De Tocqueville, 1888). In other words, as now and the American civil liberties union (ACLU) have insinuated, TYWLS serves as a distraction to the injustices and educational inequities that confront the majority of Latino children of both genders on a daily basis and in fact, as the numbers show, benefit only a very small minority (recent statistics for TYWLS show a decrease in the graduation rate from 97% in 2002 to 85.7% in 2004, Scholastic Aptitude Test (SAT) scores in both the verbal and math were lower on average than those in city schools and only 35% of 2004 graduates went on to four-year colleges as opposed to slightly over 50% of city school graduates).[35]

In spite of this, the No Child Left Behind Act included a bipartisan amendment sponsored by Senators Kay Bailey Hutchison (R-Texas) and Hillary Clinton (D-New York), which called for single-sex schools and programs as one of twenty-seven "innovative Assistance Programs." In the spring of 2002, the Department of Education announced its intention to loosen Title IX guidelines to allow for single-sex education."[36] The result has been the opening of many more single-sex schools and programs across the country. Though I am an advocate of single-sex education, I do not believe this new brand of American feminist, culture-blind single-sex education can work for the general Latina population. However, with the recent popularity of single-sex schools in the United States, and their immense appeal to minority parents in NYC in particular, it is vital that we understand all the factors behind their success. If single-sex education has proved an effective method for countering the dropout rates of minority girls, then it is crucial that more research be done in this area, but in so doing we must be careful not to abandon our advocacy of culturally sensitive/relevant, student-centered, community-based education, which has likewise been proven successful in these same areas for the greater portion of our Latino students, of both genders.

NOTES

1   R. Diaz, *The Resurgence of the Amazon of Matinino: Women in Traditional and Contemporary Taino Society*, CUNY Graduate School dissertation, 1996.

2   Jimenez de Wagenheim Olga. *Puerto Rico: An Interpretive History from Pre-Columbian Times to 1900* (Princeton, New Jersey: Markus Weiner Publishers, 1998).

3   A.Y. Vargas, *La Mujer en Puerto Rico: Ensayos de Investigacion* (Rio Piedras, Puerto Rico: Ediciones Huracan, 1987).

4   The World Bank Group. Gender Stats Database of Gender Statistics, Thematic Data—Education in Cuba.

5   The World Bank Group. Gender Stats Database of Gender Statistics, Thematic Data—Education in the Dominican Republic.

6   Ibid.

7   H. I. Safa, *The Myth of the Male Breadwinner: Women and Industrialization in the Caribbean* (Boulder: Westview Press, 1995).

8   Mintz, 1974, Martinez-Alier, 1989.

9   Vargas, 1987, Sued Badillo, 1975, Ravitch 2000.

10   R.C. Salomone, *Same, Different, Equal: Rethinking Single-sex Schooling* (New Haven and London: Yale University Press, 2003).

11   *New York City Public Schools Division of Assessment and Accountability* 2001–2002 Annual School Report.

12   National Organization for Women, Comments on the Department of Education's Notice of Intent to regulate on single-sex Education, May 8, 2002.

13   Bailey 1992, Sadker 1994, Hagg 2000, Lee and Bryk 1996, Tidball 1990.

14   Suarez-Orozco 1999, Valenzuela 1999, Espin 1999, and Hurtado 2002, Weiler 2000, Rolon 2000, Ginorio and Huston 2001.

15   A. Ginorio, *The AAUW Report: Si se Puede! Yes we Can, Latinas in School* (Wellesley, MA: Center for Research on Women, Wellesley College, 2000).

16   Ginorio, 2000.

17   O. Espin, *Women Crossing Boundaries* (New York and London: Routledge, 1999).

18   A. Valenzuela, *Subtractive Schooling: US Mexican Youth and the Politics of Caring* (State University of New York Press: New York, 1999).

19   J. D. Weiler, *Codes and Contradictions: Race, Gender Identity and Schooling* (Albany: SUNY Press, May 2000).

20   Ginorio, 2000, Weiler, 2000.

21   C. Suarez-Orozco and M. Marcelo, *Children of Immigration* (Cambridge, MA: Harvard University Press, 1999, 2001).

22   *The Latino Workforce*, a Statistical Brief from The National Council of La Raza, August 2003.

23   S. Nieto, *Puerto Rican Students in U.S. Schools* (Mahwah, NJ: Lawrence Erlbaum Associates, Publishers, 2000).

24   V. E. Lee, and A. S Bryk, "Effects of Single-sex Secondary Schools on Student Achievement and Attitudes" *Journal of Educational Psychology*, 78(5) October (1996): 381–395.

25   C. Riordan, *Girls and Boys in School: Together or Separate?* (New York: Teacher's College Press, 1997).

26   E. Tidball, D. Smith, C.Tidball, L. Wolf-Wendell, *Taking Women Seriously: Lessons and Legacies for Educating the Majority* (Phoenix: Oryx, 1999).

27 Salomone, 2003.

28 M. M. Lopez, "No body is an island: Reproduction and modernization in Puerto Rico," in Ellen Shohat, ed. *Talking Visions* (Cambridge: The MIT Press, 1998).

29 Giroux, Henry A. *Pedagogy and the Politics of Hope: Theory Culture, and Schooling* (Boulder: Westview Press, 1997).

30 P. Freire, *Pedagogy of the Oppressed* (New York: The Seabury Press, 1970).

31 Teun, Van Dijk. *Multidisciplinary CDA: A Plea for Diversity*(London: Sage Publications, 2001).

32 Riordan1990, Salomone 2003.

33 Nieto, 2000.

34 R. Brubacker, and F. Cooper, "Beyond identity," *Theory and Society, 29(1),* (2000): 1–47.

35 *New York City Public Schools Division of Assessment and Accountability 2003–2004* Annual School Report.

36 K. Stabiner, *All Girls: Single-Sex Education and Why It Matters* (New York: Berkley Publishing Group, 2002).

3. How Multicultural Curriculum Development Often Misses the Mark

PEPI LEISTYNA

You will never make colonialism blush for shame by spreading out little known cultural treasures under its eyes.

Frantz Fanon[1]

Before they were forced into chasing the standards of No Child Left Behind, and leave in the wake any programs that are not dedicated to raising test scores, increasingly educators and public school systems were turning to the plethora of research, literature, and practices in multiculturalism to help ensure cross-cultural understanding (among students, faculty, and staff), academic success, and overall school/community harmony.

To combat the violence, racism, cultural strife, and exclusionary practices that plague its schools and community, an effort was made by the *Changeton* school district to create a system-wide multicultural educational program. A volunteer group, referring to itself as the *Multicultural Central Steering Committee* (the "CSC" for short), had been established to shape and direct what it hoped would provide a foundation for working toward what it described as "the affirmation of diversity through educational equity and social justice."

At the time of my research the city's estimated population was racially broken down as follows: there were 74,449 Whites, 12,028 Blacks, 1589 Asians/Pacific Islanders, 5860 Latino/as, 269 Native Americans, and 4453 designated "Others." In addition, there were over 13,000 people living in poverty, and the annual crimes committed in the city totaled 6895, with 1156 violent acts.

When the research began, there were fifteen elementary schools, four middle schools, and one high school in the city. There was a total school enrollment of 14,015 students. Demographically, the schools were 13.6% Latino/a, 29.7% African American, 3.0% Asian-American, and 53.2% White. One in every fourteen students in Changeton had limited English proficiency.

Adding to the system's status of probation with the state because of its failure to effectively desegregate the schools, Changeton had high dropout rates, especially among racially subordinated and low-income youth(s): 9.9% (or 296 students). The high school lost nearly a tenth of its population that year (and the dropout rate for ninth-graders was estimated as 12–14%). The retention rate (those held back) in Changeton was high, 11.5%.

The academic standings throughout Changeton's school system were also bleak. The percentage of high school seniors performing at grade-level goals in math was 25 and in science, 27. Of the 64% of the students who took the Scholastic Aptitude Tests (SATs) that year, the average score was 801—as compared with the state average of 903. In addition, 13.5% of the students throughout the school system, overwhelmingly poor and racially subordinated boys and linguistic minorities, were in Special Education. The development of the CSC was a response to such statistics.

The CSC, which was made up of a diversity of teachers, guidance counselors, principals, specialists, and administrators, had been officially sanctioned by the Superintendent of Schools to direct this system-wide effort. The committee members were given the responsibility to extract from their own individual experiences, as well as from the bounty of research and literature on cultural diversity, ideas that they thought would help their city's schools.

Through a seven-year qualitative study, I documented and critiqued developments in the CSC's work, including professional development, community outreach, and diversifying the faculty and staff. The specific area that I want to address for this chapter is the CSC's effort to revamp the curricula in their schools. It is important to note that while the level of criticism throughout this chapter is extensive, the goal of such research analysis is by no means intended to dismiss the crucial work being done by the CSC. On the contrary, in deconstructing their work, the task at hand is to theoretically approach the complex social conditions that gave rise to the committee in the first place. Such analysis is thus undertaken with the utmost optimism; however, hope for the future requires awareness of the grim realities of so many students in this country and the reconcilable limitations of mainstream efforts to bring about equity and social justice in schools in the United States. The suggestions for the future of multicultural education made throughout this analysis are intended to extend the possibilities of the efforts in Changeton so as to radically democratize public schooling.

The Disarticulation of Theory from Practice

A major obstacle of critical transformative education in the United States is that theory is often devalued among educators, and consequently disconnected from the actual practice of teaching. This divorce of theory from practice is reflected in a great many mainstream multicultural educational models that inspire a search for methods and materials with little exploration of the conceptual framework that informs, or the sociohistorical and cultural realities that give rise to, such practices. Indeed, one of the major dichotomies that initially surfaced in the CSC's work concerned personal awareness versus prioritizing practical materials. Some members commented on the importance of developing "our own self-consciousness before we go into the classroom," and others wanted more "how tos."

Figuring either that theory was irrelevant, or that their focus on affirming diversity—on sensitizing teachers to differences and making classroom curricula more inclusive of all backgrounds so as to resolve intergroup antagonisms, and consequently help all students to achieve academically—was enough, the CSC main goal was to provide classroom materials to local educators. As one member insisted, "People want curricula, check out the research" (referring to the original needs assessment). Other such comments included:

"What teachers hear doesn't beat when they see a room full of materials."

"We need more how to nuts and bolts rather than theory!"

"I walked away with very little for my staff."

"We need curricular strategies for those people who are on the fence."

"I don't just want talk . . . When all is said and done, more is said than done . . . I want concrete tools that can be taken back!"

One committee member stated, "After the central needs of schools are identified, then it's our job to scramble around and find out what's available." The problem here is that *needs*, and not political awareness, are the impetus for searching out appropriate materials. The critical question is, how can you know what you are lacking, or even understand the specific problems within a particular context, without deep theoretical analysis—without exploring the *whys* of *what* is happening? Active theorizing is crucial for the administration, teachers, students, and the community at large to make sense of the educational process, the world that shapes such a social dynamic and their interactions therein. Without a sense of praxis—the on-going process of reflection and action/theory and practice—the CSC risked turning teachers into efficient multicultural technicians/distributors rather than creative and critically engaged public intellectuals attempting to understand and confront the predicaments that they face on a daily basis.

A Depoliticized Approach to the Curriculum

Knowledge guides the ways in which people understand and interact with the world. Because knowledge is always a product of representation, it is important for educators to understand how ideologies (i.e., values and beliefs) are produced, disseminated, legitimated, consumed, and reproduced or resisted by the larger society. It is also crucial within a critical multicultural model of education to excavate whose values, understandings, and agendas are at the core of public schooling. Far too often, multicultural educators do not question the basic structures and goals of society and schooling, and how they are deeply implicated in shaping identity, situating difference, and reinforcing forms of understanding and control.

The CSC talked about working toward a "bias-free" classroom curriculum and to "review curricula to see that it is not culturally biased. . . ." However, instead of balancing out the curriculum so that it is not one-sided, educators should be encouraged to understand, name, and eradicate the ways in which mainstream curricula so often systematically (rather than arbitrarily) turn a blind eye to the realities of so many people. Rather than simply adding elements of diversity to existing classroom content, the committee should encourage an examination of the traditional curriculum's distortions, its hidden motivations, and its role as a sorting machine for labor within the logic of capital.

The CSC basically understood that groups were being excluded, but such systematic silencing was simply being treated as an omission that could easily be remedied by adding new materials to the old. Arguing for inclusion, at the exclusion of any analysis of society's unequal power relationships and long history of institutional and socially sanctioned oppressive practices, one committee member's comment reflects the group's direction:

> The white kids would respect the others if they knew more about them, and at the same time, the others would feel part of the exclusive fraternity that invented and discovered.

This vision of cultural harmony can invite simple social and educational reforms, but such a comment is actually implicated in the process of creating "Otherness." By attempting to get the "culturally different" to fit in (to feel part of the exclusive fraternity), the committee member seems to accept Whites (a complex category that went unexplored) as the norm, and apparently looks to them for approval.

Instead, the CSC should follow the lead of the African American youth worker from a local community-based organization, who when asked by a White parent, "Why should such a heavy emphasis be placed on Black History?" immediately responded:

> You can't keep permeating a fraud. Current history textbooks depict Blacks only as slaves and ignore their accomplishments, such as founding colleges and making medical breakthroughs. Children of all ages are left with the impression that Blacks were slaves, from slaves we went on to welfare, and we have never made a contribution. The books have to change. My generation grew up learning to suck up to racism and was erred by telling its children that racism was a thing of the past.

What makes this position critical, rather than merely supplemental, is its understanding of systematic silencing and historical engineering that distort the ways in which so many groups are represented. The CSC solicited extensive lists of multicultural activities taking place in the Changeton schools, and as these lists pointed out, there were indeed lessons on Latino/as and African and Native Americans. Relegating such discussions to food, dance, costumes, and uncritical celebrations of Thanksgiving are not sufficient for understanding, let alone changing the historical present.

As opposed to realizing a bias-free curriculum, it would be more productive to have students and teachers interrogate modernist notions of *universality, neutrality,* and *objectivity* in education. In this way, Changeton educators could confront the Math and Science Departments (fields of study that are traditionally seen as neutral and universal), which made no effort to infuse multiculturalism in their work. In addition, with a more critical understanding of the social construction of knowledge and identity, the CSC could contest the Physical Education Department's refusal to change their approach to gym class—activities are coeducational with no significance attached to color, race, sex, or national origin. They could dialog with students about the dangers of popular representations of Black athletes, the essentialized predispositions of Black rhythm and dance, the sexist treatment of women in sports, the racial and gender make-up of cheerleading, how social class limits certain people/groups from participating in a number of sports, the lack of images of wheelchair sports, or the sexualized stereotypes that most female athletes and gym teachers are Lesbian, and the idea that only Gays become male dancers or ice skaters.

Moving beyond Exoticizing and Romanticizing Cultural Realities

The multicultural lists gathered by the CSC were loaded with lessons and events that recognized and celebrated cultures from abroad. There were curricular activities centered on such superficial aspects as Leprechaun traps, Japanese Doll Day, flag displays, and Chinese New Year. It seemed that a great many of those who participated in adding to these lists were reducing culture to national origin. This assumption not only reduces the multiplicity of cultural realities within a nation to one portrait—disregarding intra-national differences across gender, language, social class, religion, sexuality, race, etc. It also separates groups of people with geopolitical borders, extracting culture out of international and transnational relational developments.

What these nation-focused approaches also speak to is the trend in discussions of multiculturalism to focus predominantly on "immigrant experiences." The focus on immigrants should not obfuscate the reality that many of the people who face extreme obstacles in public schools in this country have been here for generations—African- and Native-Americans, Native-Hawaiians, Chicano/as, Puerto Ricans, women, Gays and Lesbians, the poor, the disabled, and so forth. These are not histories of immigration. They are the products of such engineered forces as enslavement, conquest, and systematic exclusion. Many of these voices rupture the simplistic notion of pluralism and the liberal demands to satisfy the needs of the so-called newcomers. Many of the youth in Changeton have their cultural roots in the housing projects around town and have never been to the countries of their ancestors. If well-intentioned teachers want to create culturally responsive models that link home life to schooling, they are compelled to engage in the actual conditions within which people live—and not solely in some romanticized version of culture elsewhere.

This is not to say that affirming aspects of international cultures is not a step in the right direction. But it is by no means enough. For example, handing out sugarcane and discussing its production (as one school in Changeton did to celebrate Haitian culture) without an historical analysis of colonization, capitalism, and slavery, will not give learners a sense of the complexities of culture, and in this case, the bittersweet realities of the cane itself.

If educators are to address immigration, and they should, it is important to problematize their understanding of this phenomenon. Teachers need to develop historical clarity as to why people come to this country. In this way, they can better understand the relative insignificance of nice things that are often superficially used to define culture, and delve into the traumatic realities of what many students have experienced—war, starvation, displacement, and so on, and how these experiences are often a product of US foreign policy. One committee member's emphasis on the "Afro-diaspora" in the curriculum—"We [Blacks] all came along the same pipeline where this is now our national heritage . . ."—could bring these issues to the surface for students. However, this suggestion would need to avoid essentializing history and identity, and examine how immigrants from countries such as Cuba, the Dominican Republic, Jamaica, and Cape Verde do not necessarily have the same sense of history or point of identification as African Americans. It would also need to confront the reality that, within the stigma around both experiences that circulates in the ideological air that we breathe in the United States, these groups often experience intergroup antagonisms: on the one hand, immigrant groups often do not want to be associated with African Americans, and on the other, African Americans do not want to be camped with the negative representations of immigrants. One committee member acknowledged this very problem:

> Take one Afro-American kid walking down the street and he sees other people of color speaking in different languages. He doesn't identify with them. He sees the color from a distance, but as he comes closer he doesn't really identify with them. As a matter of fact, he may or she may say, "Ahh, it's them." . . . It's no different from when you walk in a corridor in school and you see those divisions.

Unlike the Superintendent's call, at the original all-faculty in-service, for the need to "emphasize the darker side of history in the classroom: Indians, stereotypes, and slavery;" and to make ourselves more aware of issues such as "race superiority and prejudice," the overwhelming majority of activities on the established lists of multicultural lessons and events consisted of superficial add-ons to the existing curriculum (with no engagement with the ideological make-up of the traditional body of knowledge), and scant looks at history and culture, with no real analysis of the effects of capital, neoliberalism, social-class structures, racism, sexism, homophobia, and other oppressive social formations, logics, and practices.

Some CSC members and the Superintendent of Schools did mention the importance of not treating superficially such events as Martin Luther King Jr. Day. Nonetheless, there was little effort by the committee to recognize and insist upon utilizing the very political nature of these historical figures and events to generate discussions among learners and teachers about oppression in society as well as in schools. Educators should also avoid limiting the dialog to central personalities and cultural icons, at the exclusion of everyday folk, including those in Changeton, that have been making a positive difference in people's lives.

One potentially critical activity listed in the Changeton survey data was the "World Food Day Awareness Project." The Home Economics teacher responsible for the course described it as "students through problem solving were made aware of racism and prejudice and its effects on world hunger." In a very different tone, this lesson was described by the local paper:

> More students were expected to attend the class today, when World Food Day is observed with an international teleconference from Washington D.C. and other forums to educate the public about hunger and starvation . . . Students gathered in the computer lab to learn about the challenges facing citizens of farflung lands trying to survive drought and poverty so they can put food on their family's table.

To understand relational histories, such a lesson should address how neoliberalism, US foreign policy, and corporate exploitation contribute greatly to the very poverty that countries around the planet experience. As about 400 transnational corporations control two-thirds of the earth's fixed assets and 70% of the world trade, and organizations like the World Bank, the International Monetary Fund, and the World Trade Organization are shaping the New World order and forging global misery, students in a course on world hunger should be encouraged to explore these issues and power politics. In addition, such lessons need to examine the United States' racialized policies when working with different countries around the world. If this world food awareness exercise is to be effective, it should also examine the extreme poverty, hunger, and homelessness in the United States or in Changeton for that matter rather than just assume that what is in fact sanctioned misery and not random acts of mother nature only happens in "farflung lands." It should also take a hard look at environmental issues and pollution, the corrupt powers of agribusiness, the fast food industry, biotechnology, and genetic engineering.

Some may argue that the reason that the majority of multicultural activities the Changeton schools offered were about food, and fun is that they were being served up to children: the idea being that elementary school children are too young to be exposed to hard and painful issues such as violence, racism, and poverty. However, the reality is that many youth already know what it is like to hear about a kid shooting a classmate. As one of the teens that I interviewed testified, "Man, the playground we call the dead ground . . . ." Many children have experienced what it is like to be ignored because they do not speak English fluently, to not be invited to birthday parties and sleepovers because of the color of their skin or their religion, to witness domestic violence, to be evicted from their home, to be hungry, or to lose a family member or friend to illness, murder, drinking and driving, suicide, or a drug overdose. Many have an experiential sense of being sexually molested, bullied, rolling the halls alone in a wheelchair, being called a freak because they do not fit in, being considered ugly or overweight, walking grounds littered with trash, or seeing violence and sex on TV—including in cartoons. In addition, great numbers of children have been stigmatized by being in lower academic tracks or in Special Education, Bilingual Education, and Free Lunch Programs.

The sad reality is that kids at a very early age are racialized, sexualized, gendered, and positioned and marked by the structures of social class. Here are just a few of the names that

I have overheard young people use in the hallways and classrooms and on the playgrounds of Changeton: spic, nigger, Jew boy, towel head, camel jockey, chink, cracker, white trash, fag, dyke, butt fucker, pussy, slut, bitch, gimp, fat shit, and project rat.

The CSC was right to insist that they get to students in their early years—"This is where it begins!" However, in order to effectively achieve critical consciousness among the very young, that is, the ability to read into the values and beliefs that inform the knowledge that they are exposed to and wield, educators need to move away from the idea that children exist in an abstract age of innocence, and instead apprentice them, with age-appropriate strategies, into analyzing social relations and texts that they are readily exposed to, such as movies and cartoons. Being well-informed and instilling civic responsibility at an early age would be a crucial step in the direction of preparing students for democratic participation in a complex world.

Problematizing Eurocentrism

In search of a bias-free curriculum, the CSC had some concerns about Eurocentrism. However, the few times that Eurocentrism was addressed, it was not engaged in a way that named the asymmetries of power within which groups are portrayed and often devalued. Instead, in a relativistic manner, the term functioned as a measuring cup to quantify curriculum use in terms of how often a certain worldview is or is not mentioned. One committee member stated, "I don't think that we are conscious of the European overdose in schools, to a population that gets the feeling that they've contributed nothing. . . ."

Another member attempted to target the knowledge–power relationship that informs Eurocentrism when she talked of a "world or global approach to education." She made reference to the "Western legionaries" who "want to separate the two . . . ," and alluded to the ways in which certain bodies of knowledge are legitimized, usually at the expense of others. What her point also revealed is that it is in fact the "Western legionaries"—the E.D. Hirsch Jrs., Arthur Schlesingers, Lynne Cheneys, William Bennetts, Chester Finns, and Diane Ravitchs that support standardization and canonization of knowledge—who are actually advocating a form of separatism (which they readily accuse multiculturalists of doing) as categories like "Western," and canons by their very nature, exclude.

A major problem with using "Western" when identifying a particular view of the world is that African Americans' and other racially subordinated groups' struggles and forms of resistance are also part of Western history. One in-service facilitator expressed to the committee, "Four hundred years of slavery has had an impact on the consciousness of Whites and people of color . . ." and he insisted that people, especially educators, "need to understand how we are related historically." It is this relational history and its concomitant cultural manifestations that need to be engaged. Otherwise, the use of "Western" creates a reductionistic binarism that obfuscates the complex interrelationships that shape a politics of identity and difference. For example, by insisting that teaching a "Eurocentric curriculum when such a large percent, [age] of the population is not Euro is ridiculous—it is not important to them!," one committee member abstracted the traditional body of knowledge reinforced throughout society from the realities of oppressed students. In fact, it is this very body of knowledge that in part shapes and works to ensure the reproduction of dominant culture, which in turn produces oppression here in the United States and globally.

The reverse of this logic—that non-Euro students will not be interested in the existing curriculum—is that because Whites may be able to identify with certain traditions, that they are necessarily good for them. Consequently, White students are often not encouraged to recognize the fact that they are also racialized, gendered, sexualized, historical, and thus ideologically driven—and that they are so often dehumanized in the process.

Eurocentrism's links to White supremacy also went virtually unaddressed by the committee. During meetings and in-services, CSC members were given ample opportunity to confront the ideological construction of whiteness embedded in Eurocentrism and its effects on classroom content, and to work to be able to eradicate its oppressive nature. As one high school teacher interjected:

> It's time to get to the classroom, to show that everything is not centered around white people . . .

Nonetheless, the conversation would consistently be rerouted into a debate over inclusion.

The idea is not to simply throw things out because they are of European origin. Instead, all bodies of knowledge need to be engaged and critically appropriated from. What is key is that teachers/learners make connections between the sociopolitical realities that shape their lives and interests, and the body of knowledge that is in part implicated in the formation and maintenance of those realities.

There are ample opportunities in all classrooms to engage in critical dialog around relational histories and cultural production. For example, the Changeton High School Jazz Ensemble has won five gold medals in international competition, and has been highly touted by the local press. As an interdisciplinary approach to multiculturalism, this particular course should explore the history of social struggles and creative resistance to racism, unemployment, poverty, and hunger that come with the kinds of economic oppression and political disenfranchisement that have and continue to inspire the music in the first place. In this way, the class could explore the links among Blues, Jazz, and Rap/Hip Hop culture and connect such musical forms not only to their roots, but also to the realities of contemporary popular culture in this country. Such an approach to education would require a critical understanding of popular culture and its formative role in shaping subjectivity and identity.

The Absence of Popular Culture in Curriculum Considerations

The formative images embedded in media and popular culture play a central role in shaping identities and social relations. Unfortunately, the CSC, as do most mainstream multicultural educators, failed to take seriously the pedagogical implications of popular culture in a way that would compel them to insist that analysis of such issues and materials be a significant part of classroom practice. Disregarding the impact of popular culture is a major oversight in that kids in general get more from these pedagogical images and sounds than they do from formal schooling—initial ideas of the world that enter the classroom. Some of the interviewed youth(s), who had been kicked out of school mentioned the formative dangers of popular culture. For example, one Latino stated:

> This town didn't use to be like this, it wasn't until the movies and shit. I mean I remember after the movie Colors that this dividing of the city began. Now the east side fights the west . . . it's endless.

The youth(s) also alluded to pop culture's junk mentality, and its commodifying powers within capitalist social relations:

> Olavo: You couldn't walk with Nikes. If you have Nikes on, they'd take them off your feet.

When asked, "What do you do with the money that you make on the streets?" Dion responded, "Sneakers yo! You want sneakers, you want some gear, you know what I'm sayin." Olavo added, "Buy cars, buy clothes . . ."

One of the in-service facilitators, in the company of the CSC, made the most extensive analysis of representational politics:

> We have inherited a mindset that color is a cultural and intellectual deficiency. The TV shows this, the stereotypical roles Blacks play as secondary to Whites. Blacks have also internalized a great deal of this—it's even in our folklore. In schools, the curriculum doesn't take this into account—look at the Dick and Jane texts. This creates in the minds a sense of inferiority and inadequacy.

The educator explained that, bombarded with negative images of themselves, "students of color" internalize such misrepresentations and stigma. What he did not speak of is the need to have young people develop critical media skills (critical literacy), so as to be able to analyze the values, beliefs, and agenda buried in the images that they are constantly subjected to, and to realize that these are not really reflective of what their lives are or should be measured by.

Critical forms of multicultural education require that educators create classrooms within which students analyze representations in popular culture and the ways in which such discursive practices come to life and shape people's sense of reality. With a more cultural studies approach to the curriculum, students develop the ability to recognize and confront their own cultural assumptions that have developed as a result of the vicarious teachings of the media. It is only then that one can begin to see how people are turned into atoms of consumption, how prestige gets inscribed on the Nike symbol, and how people buy into such false notions of status and prestige.

Critical multicultural education is meant to facilitate deep interactions between teachers and students in a way that focuses on ideological analyses and political actions capable of eradicating oppressive practices and institutions both in schools and society. In dialog, students are encouraged to be theorists and to theorize about the world around and within them. The idea is not to simply turn people into uncritical sponges of theory, but rather, the goal is to nurture them into being active theorizers. In this sense, theory works through students and not simply on them. For critical educators influenced by the wisdom of Paulo Freire, the concept of *dialog* is not simply about having a conversation with students. He states:

> The teacher who seeks to dialogue has to be very reflective, constantly refining his or her view of the world. Educators can't merely repeat information. For a real dialogue to take place, the teacher also needs to engage the students in epistemological uneasiness in a way that inspires them to revisit the knowledge that they already possess in order to get a better understanding of, expand upon, or rewrite, it.[2]

This type of engagement moves beyond just "affirming diversity" and takes everyone's culture and identity as a point of analysis, critique, and transformation. In other words, through such investigations, people can begin to see how it becomes possible to reposition themselves in the world. This type of classroom interaction would require fundamental pedagogical changes in mainstream education.

The Absence of Pedagogy in Curricular Considerations

Educators who are trapped within traditional ways of teaching, in which the teacher is at the front of the room dispatching what is deemed official knowledge to what are perceived as passive tabulae rasae, work to reconfirm dominant views of identity, meaning, authority, and interaction, whether they are aware of it or not. This type of restrictive interaction often creates a pedagogical battlefield on which participants fight over not only whose values and portraits of the past will be voiced in the educational process, but also how they will be included. The battle could manifest in the form of student silence, resistance to course materials, boredom, acts of deviance, clowning around, skipping class/school, etc.

It is thus surprising that pedagogy was not a central issue in the seven years of work conducted by the CSC. Instead, the group emphasized getting materials and establishing "baseline inventories." As such, they never really engaged the importance of not only what is taught (curriculum), but also how it is taught (pedagogy). When it came to methods and strategies that teachers could use to democratize the classroom, there were very few recommendations and concerns. The only comment that supported the need for critical literacy was never discussed—"Provide workshops on participatory learning and critical, emancipatory, liberatory educational methods and strategies. . . ." Even sparse suggestions around such things as cooperative learning went unexplored.

If and when the CSC eventually takes up the issue of pedagogy, it should avoid falling into the uncritical appropriation of any approach, strategy, or method that claims to be multicultural. It appeared as if any mention of multicultural education on the solicited lists of activities was accepted at face value by the committee. For example, the high school claimed to have a "new curriculum emphasizing a multicultural perspective on literature." However, from this ambiguous statement, it is unclear what a "multicultural perspective" implied. As it turns out, "authors of color" were being included in the syllabus, but there was no mention as to how they were included or engaged.

It is important to note that the CSC, as its work progressed, was beginning to understand that approaches to multicultural education are not recipes that can be mechanically followed. One committee member alluded to this when he explained to the CSC that in his school, teachers had developed the multicultural transformation of their building all on their own, and that there was "no one way to do it, no road map." Likewise, methods and content can only be generated when teachers create the necessary pedagogical spaces in which they have access to and can have an understanding of their students' realities and needs. As the intern for the CSC stated:

> We need to draw out of people, not just put information in them . . . we need to draw out of everyone—teachers and students, by identifying their location . . . who they are.

Others added, "Teachers need to be learners;" "Ask the Students, let them teach us." With the goal of drawing out of the students, critical forms of multicultural education rely on dialog and creating the self-empowering conditions within which all participants in the learning process—students, teachers, parents/care-givers, and the community—come to voice and play active roles. A real danger for teachers, even well-intentioned ones who do a great deal of research (which is important), is objectifying their students—not allowing them to present themselves. Rather, they use empirical representations and existing theory to situate the person/cultural group in the classroom.

Reinventing Changeton

It is important to acknowledge and support the CSC for working extremely hard—educators volunteering their valuable free time—as it diligently surveyed, assembled, and distributed lists of the needs of Changeton teachers, and the types of activities that local schools were enacting to "affirm diversity." The CSC also scrambled to gather together community resources, and they struggled to develop a home for such materials, one that the group hoped would be updated on a regular basis, and available to everyone. It is especially important that the committee wanted a more system-wide, interdisciplinary, and interdepartmental diversification of the curriculum. However, while these extensive efforts bore some fruit, unfortunately the group's over-eagerness to turn toward practical materials at the expense of theorizing the problems they faced, a generally depoliticized approach to knowledge and classroom content, and a disregard for engaging popular culture and pedagogy, stifled the possibility for substantive curricular and pedagogical growth in Changeton public schools. This, in part (as there are other systemic forces at play that work against the best interests of critical education and social transformation), was implicated in the fact that the appalling statistics mentioned at the beginning of this chapter remained, as did the antagonistic intercultural social relations in the schools.

However, rather than simply dismiss the multicultural efforts in Changeton, or simply reject any such practice that gets in the way of teaching to the standardized test, educators can critically appropriate from this lesson and work to realize democratic education. The analysis and suggestions herein are offered as a step in the direction of making "colonialism blush for shame."

NOTES

1 F. Fanon, *The Wretched of the Earth* (London, Penguin, 1961), 179–80.

2 P. Freire and P. Leistyna, *Presence of Mind in the Process of Learning and Knowing.* In P. Leistyna, *Presence of Mind: Education and the Politics of Deception.* (Boulder, CO: Westview, 1999), 48.

4. Urban Youth and Biographical Projects

Notes on Educational and Employment Transitions

RICHARD D. LAKES

In apprehensive and uncertain times such as these, one needs a transitional plan to ensure job-related success and mobility. Processes of individualization present young people with reconsiderations about educational preparation in the transition to work.[1] Late modernization has heightened self-reliance and independence accompanying personal assessment of risk aversion which gives rise to carefully choosing one's life course and reflexively constructing one's biographical project.[2]

Decoupled from traditional social structures, young people become agents of their own making; planning and organizing for one's livelihood means engaging in personal decisions about schooling, transportation, career ambitions, fashion and dress, etc. Yet individuals function in a state of dependence upon institutional structures operating within a market economy. Because the idea of career is built upon risk—or as Beck noted, the individual's "susceptibility to crises"—young people's options are regulated by conditions of uncertainty and instability.[3] That is, individuals are directed into formal schooling (and must learn the hidden curriculum of success) as a way to gain a livelihood and to repel cultural marginality. "Denied access to either [a job or an education]," Beck advised, one "faces social and material oblivion . . . . Those rejected by the vocational training system fall into the social abyss."[4]

This chapter offers an examination of the ways urban youth make meaning of their educational and employment futures, and how critical education might be positioned to help avert uncertainties in life and to repel cultural marginality.[5] In the next section, I will describe the new post-industrial realities for urban youth through the term *social exclusion*—used by sociologists primarily in Europe to frame discourses around the plight of unemployed young people denied access to further education and jobs.

Social Exclusion

The concept of social exclusion was originally developed in French policy circles in 1974, to characterize individuals and groups of people without social insurance; and faced with declining revenues France was unable to reach these individuals through universal welfare benefits—rupturing the social contract between citizen and the state that was once a major feature of Western European life.[6] Over time the meaning of the term has changed to encompass a much broader condition in the United Kingdom and continental Europe (all of the advanced industrialized countries of the West in general) of the unemployed who fall through the cracks of the social safety net. Impacted by globalization and technology, a decline in labor-intensive manufacturing, and a rise in neo-liberal economic reforms, the socially excluded could be described as "a reserve army of labour, continually changing places with those in low-status employment".[7] Denied access to the labor market often for the first time, a young person has little income to pay for health care and housing; lacking further education the recent immigrant maintains a language barrier that segregates one into residential neighborhoods in the city without access to job retraining. In the United States, we sometimes use the term "ghettoization," "marginalization," and "the underclass" to denote those individuals living in poverty.[8] Theorists of social exclusion recognize that young people face future threats to their well-being, including long-term unemployment, family disintegration, homelessness as well as an inability to make the transition from full-time schooling into the full-time, paid workplace.[9] Contingent labor with part-time hours and few if any benefits are features of low-skilled labor in the new economy. The structural conditions of advanced capitalism necessitate resource allocations that undermine the longstanding social contract between labor and capital.

Some young people on the margins of the new economy are aware of the challenges they face in terms of social mobility and economic advancement. Ball, Maguire, and Macrae interviewed post-16 youths in the Northwark area of London, England, and found that working-class white males without qualifications, sacked from one retail job after another, still clung to traditional values, even though they were just "'making out,' hanging on to aspirations and possibilities" in the new economy.[10] For instance, one boy named Rees, who left compulsory schooling with low grades on his exit examinations (four D–G grades on the

General Certification of Secondary Education) and whose father is a part-time plumber, typified a naive optimism when asked about his future plans:[11]

> I have got to start making goals for myself. I can't say anything for sure but I reckon I will be all right. I just want the same as everybody else, a job, a car, a house or a flat even, a girlfriend. That's about it. But I have to get a job first. That's my goal because you ain't going to get the rest if you ain't got a job.

How much longer will these young people buy into a success ethic, even though they are unfavorably positioned in the labor market?

Nowadays urban youth seek ways to alleviate risks at the individual level. For example, the differentiation of skill requirements in the new economy leads to varying educational plans for work. School-to-work transitions are prolonged or elongated for adolescents who desire training and job preparation. "Subjectively young people are forced to reflexively negotiate a complex set of routes into the labour market," Furlong and Cartmel argued, "and in doing so, develop a sense that they alone are responsible for their labour market outcomes."[12] Yet others just give up looking for work altogether.

Among mostly homeless and unemployed London youth ages 17–25, for example, Blackman (1997) found that in a study of survival narratives, economic improvement had fearful consequences.[13] In other words, once the risks of personal advancement did not resolve themselves, one could fall harder into sub-standard existence. One twenty-year-old named Dave said:[14]

> If I could leave the world of the homeless, I'd do it today. Say if I leave, what happens if I don't make it again? I will end up having to move on. But if I stay homeless I have my friends, contacts, people I know. This is my world why should I throw it away?

Social networks operate among excluded youth and provide a strong source of support for hard times.[15] Feminist girls using Web sites and zines have encouraged their peers to take the opportunity of unemployment in order to pursue creative endeavors and self-interests "on their own terms"—a disruptive notion that "shift[s] the image of young women without work as losers . . . [and] questions the meaning of work and programs to get youth into work."[16] Still, the promise of steady work is a tension that appears in the lives of those hoping for an opportunity to succeed.

The idea that "one can achieve anything if they are committed enough," is a psychic challenge to young people faced with the realities of low-skilled employment—too many qualified applicants for a few jobs.[17] Serge and Rob, unemployed Australians from the poor West side of Melbourne declared:[18]

SERGE: You've gotta know someone to get a job these days.

ROB: I went for a job yesterday. There were about 200 people lined up. It was at a biscuit company in Abbotsford. There were six jobs. I'd lost concentration by the time I got there . . . I got interviewed but they reckon they'll call me [generally understood to mean that you haven't got the job].

The point here is that outsiders are expected to act in their own self-interest, such as appropriating a personality that fits into the entrepreneurial demands of post-industrial settings. while eschewing the social network of their peers and the experiences of community norms as marginalized beings. What passes for employment readiness in some quarters, particularly for the socially excluded or unemployed, is a type of training in aesthetics that dwells on impression management, a make-over that focuses more on presentational or corporal aspects of packaging oneself for potential employers.

Beck clarified that the life course for young people is no longer carefully scripted from birth and socially prescribed by class or family.[19] Due to societal changes under globalization, clearly defined age-linked transitions from school-to-work have eroded; the cultural context in planning one's biographical path requires new improvisational strategies for avoiding risk. "The individual must therefore learn, on pain of permanent disadvantage," Beck observed, "to conceive of himself or herself as the center of action, as the planning office with respect to his/her own biography, abilities, orientations, relationships, and so on."[20]

Du Bois-Reymond agreed with Beck that the life course for young people has changed under late modernism; no longer are youths just adopting a cadenced adolescent-to-adult pattern of training and career preparation.[21] Now faced with so-called choice biographies, young people base decision-making upon uncertainty and risk management—that is, distinguished by reversibility and synchronicity in the life course. Some may choose unemployment without feelings of negativity and anguish, rationalizing that a temporary condition of joblessness is featured in an unknown future.[22] Still others adhere to traditional biographies characterized by habitual and sequential movements through age-identified status passages.

In a nine-year longitudinal study of Dutch youth, Du Bois-Reymond asked a number of questions to students and parents detailing perceptions of uncertainties and planning for educational and occupational futures in the risk society.[23] With the most recent round of qualitative interviews, the researcher found five major core concepts or themes that indicated the complexities of pathways for young adults with choice biographies.[24] They are:

Gaining time—variety of options: This concept allows individuals to forestall finalizing one's plans by entering training programs without a clear picture of the job market.

A *profession, in connection with developing one's own personality*: This concept confirms that post-adolescents value, and prioritize social contacts and communications—"having fun"—over wages and financial gain.

A *professional future, being flexible*: This concept recognizes that young people keep their options open to the realities that at times they will drift in and out of the labor market. There is always a fallback plan if things do not work out as once anticipated.

Partnership, family, and job: Delayed marriage and childbirth plus suspension of active sexual life are some of the features of this concept.

Growing up later or never: Becoming an adult signifies a routine work life, a monotonous schedule, and a host of responsibilities—aspects of maturity that are rejected out of hand as too confining and rigid.

Young people face tensions between opportunity structures and social exclusion in life course biographies at this moment in time.

Haywood and Mac an Ghaill underscored the impact of globalization upon shrinking labor markets and noted changes in the way young males (boys-at-risk) viewed occupational expectations and social roles as breadwinners.[25] The growing alienation of working-class males, these two British scholars indicated,[26] is now part of a generation whose transition into adulthood as workers, citizens, and consumers is in the process of being reconstituted as a result of high rates of unemployment, the de-regulation of youth labor markets, and punitive legislative changes that have led to the withdrawal of financial state support for young people.

In particular, they referred to the abolition of wage protection for young people under age 21, the removal of restrictions on adolescent working hours and conditions, and the withdrawal of social security benefits for teens. By the mid-1990s, post-recession declines in national job training programs in the United Kingdom accompanied the rise of post-compulsory schooling where young people "learn not to labour"—institutions where the working classes prolonged education to avoid unemployment.[27]

Because there are many inconsistencies in the notion of risk aversion, scholars such as Furlong and Cartmel claimed "an epistemological fallacy" in late modernity sustained the widening gap between objective and subjective conditions.[28] "People's life chances remain highly structured," the authors clarified, "at the same time as they increasingly seek solutions on an individual, rather than a collective basis."[29] For example, both genders might manage insecurity and doubt in subjective ways that account for decision-making practices in transitions to adulthood. Some researchers realized young girls and females attained "biographical consciousness and reflexivity" sooner than boys.[30] While school-aged females internalized the late modern norm of a full work life (even if it is relegated to service-based employment), they too were beset with uncertainty because of conflicting realities and myths about balancing the demands of a family and a career. "Even if they are in a favourable position," Du Bois-Reymond concluded, young people still "take into account the ways in which things may change to their disadvantage, especially in the field of (un)employment."[31]

In the next section, I will detail how critical education operates in communities of urban young people making sense of their biographical histories. These projects are based upon what Pierson termed a "social action framework"—aimed at reversing exclusion—ones that give voice to the participants, "exploring what common experiences they share and what stories they have to tell."[32] "The social action approach bears strong resemblance to the process of neighborhood capacity building," he continued; "The objective is for young people to acquire the confidence, standing and recognition to achieve a variety of ends that are transferable across time."[33]

Critical Education

The real challenge for urban educators is to assist young people in developing optimism in the face of hopelessness. Traditional training schemes and further education simply are unable to provide much psychic motivation and emotional self-confidence, and certainly do not utilize the rich context of lived experiences in shaping pedagogical activities that offer empowerment. Even now, authoritarian, neo-liberal public policy prescriptions for transforming alienated youth into disciplined and docile conformists remain instantiated because the notion of the marginalized as having deficits is a key feature of programmatic efforts. Called for are novel approaches among service providers and community agencies devoted to enhancing school-to-work transitions that recognize the new realities of employability. Colley summarized the three-pronged thrust of policy initiatives along these lines: (a) accept the fact that youth-at-risk will be working on the periphery of the new economy; (b) help young people reinvent their own identities so that they can overturn negative outlooks and viewpoints and; (c) facilitate their pathways into employability through guidance, careers education, and mentoring—emphasis upon the so-called soft skills that lead to job satisfaction.[34]

I have written elsewhere about the usefulness of engaging urban students in critical education tied to green neighborhood renewal and community development.[35] Furthermore, I have suggested that community service organizations might lead youths to new workplace values modeled by employed adults in places where justice and equity are encouraged and nurtured.[36] The formation of moral vision devoted to designing, planning, and executing projects for social change in peer-led learning communities gives voice to teens devoted to critical literacy. Critical educators believe that youth must appropriate a set of humanizing values devoted to social, cultural, and political reform instead of marketplace dictates glorifying corporate greed and the business rhetoric of success.[37] Through examples of living democratically, as citizen-activists, teachers might redirect their view toward communities and neighborhoods that are greening America.[38]

Formal education for school-aged youth modeled along the lines of the Rindge School in the United States might become an important platform for launching city youths into the community for purposes of studying, planning, and then implementing a variety of small-scale business enterprise and employment activities.[39] Other scholars concurred that at the school, in the 1990s, urban teens had the knowledge based upon which they could problematize ways to reclaim their own neighborhoods. Wirth recognized authentic sociotechnical pedagogy at Rindge, and honored its "rich tradition of respect for education that is technical and liberalizing."[40] Gregson argued that Rindge embodied truly cooperative learning through a critical approach.[41] Rosenstock contended that students gained insight into "the unmet needs and underutilized resources" that drove community economic development.[42] Apple and Beane touted its emancipatory potential: "Through the lens of community development, students arrive at a very different and more positive vision of what it means to be a vocational student."[43]

Critical education works best when kids and young adults engage in participatory decision-making and practical democratic actions. Non-profit organizations are suited to attracting students voluntarily, willingly, and non-coercively in activities, particularly when focused upon urban education and community development.[44] Delgado argued that capacity-building approaches to youth development for marginalized populations is a way to combat what Mclaughlin and Heath labeled "social death;"[45] in other words, reverse the process in which young people's "lives are devoid of meaningful employment and social mobility and . . . low self-confidence and belief in themselves."[46] He highlighted a number of neighborhood beautification programs in the United States such as murals, gardens, playgrounds, and sculptures that improve the quality of city life, and remarked that the locations in which to practice youth development are limitless as "new frontier settings."[47]

Grassroots approaches to youth transitions appear more promising when adults recognize young people have agency and act upon it within groups of like-minded citizens. Sustainable or capacity-building development in urban areas is best orchestrated when these groups welcome technical advisers and other outsiders to participate and collaborate in creating or renewing organizational infrastructures. At sites of production dedicated to cultural struggles for social justice, youth workers offer young people a viable way to solve real-life problems in critical practices which "embody a pedagogical project aimed at enabling ways of thinking and structures of feeling that open and sustain actions that express an ethically informed expansion of human possibility."[48] The pedagogical project becomes a vehicle for transformative learning: students are engaged in understandings that challenge comfortable taken-for-granted assumptions about self and society. Youth workers facilitate the learning process by helping the socially excluded to reframe ethical and moral commitments through "questions, analyses, visions, and practical options that people can pursue in their attempts to participate in the determination of various aspects of their lives."[49]

The visual and performing arts offer one such possibility for disenfranchised young people to explore their biographical histories and lived experiences. Teens and young adults are given spaces to express their world in ways that showcase peer productions. The arts for inner-city youths are democratizing influences reaching outward to new communities of individuals engaged in the creative process and to new venues for attracting audiences interested in these forms of cultural expressions. Kids react positively when their works are legitimized in public spaces as mural designs on street corner buildings, as sculpture in transportation centers, or as theatrical performances in park district buildings. Furthermore, the arts offer anti-elitist messages derived from the positionality of youth on the margins of society. Their creative displays of ancestral origins, identity politics, and subcultural alliances describe both literal and figurative meanings of street life. In addition, the arts may provide a variety of complex psychosocial meanings depicting the anomie and despair in the city, where life histories can be confirmed and legitimized as well as planned and reformed.[50]

For example, unemployed young people living in Lisbon (Portugal), Liverpool (England), and Mannheim (Germany) were provided an opportunity to explore through the theater arts what Alheit termed "biographicity"—defined as the self-reflexive process that offers agency and self-confidence in redesigning one's life course.[51] The evaluation team of European Union (EU) researchers who studied the three youth development projects recognized that education and training programs must allow "young people to make sense of their youth biographies."[52] Traditional job-related skills acquired in training and employment programs only offered false promises of prospects in the labor market. The alternative thinking in transitions training, they argued, shifts the curriculum away from teacher-centeredness toward critical education in which young people have an investment and say in learning about their own life course. Presentation spaces shape everyday realities and assist peers in uncovering and assessing strengths and weaknesses. The researchers explained at length:[53]

> Individual perceptions and interpretations have to be expressed in the public sphere, either in the context of a group or in front of an audience. This exchange between the internal "self" and external feedback potentially leads to the very core of biographicity: it provides a context in which individual life histories can be legitimized. In this setting and in this social network young people are able to relate individual experiences and orientations to the local opportunity structure as regards, education, training and employment. In short young people can play out their own biographies in a creative context in which those biographies are accepted and nourished.

Interestingly, improvisational theater for biographical analysis was implemented in these projects, specifically among the Turkish and Italian migrant youth in Mannheim.

The Boal technique of empowerment in part was favored in the drama workshops because of heightened self-confidence and communication skills development, and as a motivational source for peers to name their oppressions.[54] Created by Augusto Boal in the 1970s as the forum theater, and coterminous with the pedagogical work of Paulo Freire (both radical educators were devoted to critical inquiry and social action among the rural poor in native Brazil), the theater actors identified a protagonist and an antagonist along with the audience members who were facilitated by an intermediary. Together they engaged in problem-posing activities and collective storytelling—a laboratory for heightened self-expression and group consciousness-raising. Contemporary workshops fashioned along the lines of Boal have been put into a wide variety of practices: in social work and therapeutic settings among marginalized populations, within schools tackling the theme of bullying, at universities for leadership development classes, and among political activists in general.[55]

In the Mannheim project, for instance, the theater group met twice weekly for three hours per session and incorporated generative themes developed from among the peers' daily lives. But first the young people were initiated into drama via an initial "animation" phase of four weeks requiring basic breathing exercises, relaxation, and movement techniques; followed by an "improvisation" phase of six to eight weeks that entailed voice and mime exercises; and, finally, the "production" phase where a collage of scenes are prepared and acted out for public screening.[56] Theatrical vignettes were developed from the lived realities of street life for these non-native-born youth faced with few prospects for full-time employment in Germany. One such scene involved a role play between a local employment officer at the

Berufsberatung (vocational guidance and career counseling center)—described as "a moody bureaucrat who only cares about how to keep his office furniture clean and safe from the young people who enter to seek advice"—as he attempted to counsel an angry and disgruntled young man who became more discouraged over time at the power imbalances and communicative battles there.[57] Other scenarios included themes such as forced parental expectations, and the actor's "relationship with their friends, jobs, girlfriends, drugs, and attitudes toward violence."[58]

As a final point, the participants in the Boal method did not learn performance techniques as an occupational goal in order to pursue an acting career in and of itself. After all, these students were resistant to formal learning—a feature of their biographical histories that was never denied or silenced. Instead, the projects affirmed informal learning processes and cultural expressions among at-risk youths, and "provided a forum in which young people were given a relaxed atmosphere in which they could discuss the pros and cons of their particular training 'biographies.'"[59] Additionally, the youths were not schooled in self-reflection skills and therapeutic approaches; yet the theater group facilitated self-examination without dictating normative, moral behaviors by adult youth workers like the drama coach.

Conclusion

I have argued in this chapter that biographical projects assisted urban youth in understanding transitional passages in their life course. Situated as border workers, critical educators offered marginalized groups the ways to understand self-reflexivity in the context of alternative planning under the new economy. Young people's transitions are no longer evenly scripted and more often constructed as do-it-yourself projects with fragmented training, periodic employment, and episodes of unemployment.[60] Structural inequalities of class, gender, and race impact transitions for marginalized populations of city youths and young adults—time and age differentials such as length of schooling, entry into full-time work, periods of unemployment and the like, are pathways that privileged children can negotiate with relative advantage due to desirable school-based experiences and educational credentials.

The popular perception of under- and unemployed youths is one of apprehension and fear; heightened social exclusions fuel talks of control over this rising public menace. Too often the popular press and television media portray young adults in dysfunctional roles as criminals, thugs, and delinquents. Way suggested kids are viewed as a "feared and seemingly ineradicable stereotype, the urban teen: pregnant, drug-addicted, violent, fatherless, welfare dependent, poor, black, and uneducated."[61] Kelly illuminated that Australian youth training policy was conceptualized as a containment process for the inhabitants of wild zones.[62] What he meant is that contemporary populations of youth labeled at-risk are increasingly viewed by neo-liberal governments as ungovernable and jeopardizing the future polity because they reject the good life by constructing pathological biographies (with negligent parenting) outside of those considered responsible or accountable. The neo-liberal turn ushers forth more regulation and social control of youth. Neo-liberal governments obfuscate equity issues and negate social justice agendas which talk about self-reliance and self-help; a posture that instantiates choice models, at the same time ignoring the reality of social structures—tiered, gendered, and raced labor markets, lack of domestic job creation and off-shore flight of industries, and limited access to skills training and further education, among others.

On the other hand, I have witnessed urban youth engaged in health positive social justice activities; dance ensembles where choreographic presentations are featured as a kind of critical pedagogy of lived realities in the city, and a youth-driven newspaper that uses dialog to build a community of peers. It takes courage to shed inhibitions as critical viewpoints are upheld and honored. These are projects where Freire's dictum to practice what he termed "co-intentional education" results in a model of leadership development amplifying critical consciousness.[63]

Finally, a critical education research agenda—one that honors the meaning-making cultural expressions and agency-identity processes of youth—is useful for gaining deeper understandings of young people's subjectivities in the new economy. O'Donnell and Sharpe studied social constructions of masculinity in the UK for instance, and excavated a complex array of boys' emotions to both real and projected changes in their work patterns.[64] McDowell's longitudinal study of English working-class males is informed by theories of risk aversion as well: her charting of "the feelings and beliefs" of those in school-to-work transitions offered empirical evidence to the arguments surfacing over individualization in late modernity.[65] All of this is to suggest that future research on urban youth and young adults socially excluded by race, class, and gender advances what Apple named "an agenda of interrupting dominance"; one that exposes conservative state policy-making in the reforms of curriculum and schools, colonizing discourses in the production of knowledge, and resistance to hegemonic command through progressive social movements.[66]

NOTES

1   C. Haywood and M. Mac an Ghaill, "'What about the boys?' Regendered local labour markets and the recomposition of working class masculinities," *British Journal of Education and Work, 9(1)* (1996): 19–30; M. Mac an Ghaill, "'What about the Boys?' Schooling, class and crisis masculinity," *The Sociological Review* (2001): 381–397.

2   A. Giddens, *Modernity and Self-Identity: Self and Society in the Late Modern Age* (Stanford, CA: Stanford University Press, 1991).

3   U. Beck, *Risk Society: Towards a New Modernity* (London: Sage, 1992), p. 133.

4   Ibid., p. 133.

5   S. J. Ball, M. Maguire and S. Macrae, *Choice, Pathways and Transitions Post-16: New Youth, New Economies in the Global City* (London: RoutledgeFalmer, 2000); S. Miles, A. Pohl, B. Stauber, A. Walther, R Manuel, B. Banha and M. Gomes, *Communities of Youth: Cultural Practice and Informal Learning* (London: Ashgate, 2002).

6   C. Gore, "Introduction: markets, citizenship and social exclusion," in G. Rodgers, C. Gore, and J.B.

Figueiredo, eds. *Social Exclusion: Rhetoric, Reality, Responses* (Geneva, Switzerland: International Labour Organization, 1995), pp. 1–42.

7   T. Burchardt, J. Le Grand, and D. Piachaud, "Introduction," in J. Hills, J. Le Grand, and D. Piachaud, eds. *Understanding Social Exclusion* pp. 1–12 (Oxford, England: Oxford University Press, 2002), p. 2.

8   Ibid., p. 2.

9   D. Byrne, *Social Exclusion* (Birmingham, England: Open University Press, 1999); Hills, Le Grand and Piachaud, "Understanding Social Exclusion," R. MacDonald, ed. *Youth, the "Underclass," and Social Exclusion* (London: Routledge, 1997); J. Pierson, *Tackling Social Exclusion* (London: Routledge, 2002).

10   Ball, Maguire and Macrae, *Choice, Pathways and Transitions Post-16*, p. 145.

11   Ibid., pp. 133–134.

12   A. Furlong and F. Cartmel, *Young People and Social Change: Individualization and Risk in Late Modernity* (Buckingham, England: Open University Press, 1997), p. 39.

13   S. J. Blackman, "'Destructing a Giro': a critical and ethnographic study of the youth 'Underclass'" in R. MacDonald, ed. *Youth, the "Underclass," and Social Exclusion*, pp. 113–129.

14   Ibid., p. 116.

15   M. Heikkinen, "Social networks of the marginal young: a study of young people's social exclusion in finland," *Journal of Youth Studies*, *3(4)* (2000): 389–406.

16   A. Harris, *Future Girl: Young Women in the Twenty-First Century* (New York: Routledge, 2004), p. 169.

17   K. McDonald, *Struggles for Subjectivity: Identity, Action and Youth Experience* (Cambridge, England: Cambridge University Press, 1999), p. 41.

18   Ibid., p. 41.

19   Beck, *Risk Society*.

20   Ibid., p. 135.

21   M. Du Bois-Reymond, "'I don't want to commit myself yet': young people's life concepts," *Journal of Youth Studies*, *1(1)* (1998): 63–79.

22   A. Furlong and F. Cartmel, "Unemployment, integration and marginalisation: a comparative perspective on 18–24-year-olds in Finland, Sweden, Scotland and Spain," in T. Hammer, ed. *Youth Unemployment and Social Exclusion in Europe: A Comparative Study* pp. 29–43 (Bristol, England: The Policy Press, 2003), p. 38.

23   Du Bois-Reymond, 'I Don't Want to Commit Myself Yet.'

24   Ibid., pp. 69–76.

25   Haywood and Mac an Ghaill, 'What about the Boys?'

26   Ibid., p. 23.

27   Ibid., p. 24.

28   Furlong and Cartmel, *Young People and Social Change*, p. 4.

29   Ibid., p. 4.

30   Miles et al., *Communities of Youth*, p. 19.

31   Du Bois-Reymond, '*I Don't Want to Commit Myself Yet*,' p. 76.

32   Pierson, *Tackling Social Exclusion*, pp. 107–108.

33   Ibid., pp. 107–108.

34   H. Colley, "Engagement mentoring for 'disaffected' youth: a new model of mentoring for social inclusion," *British Educational Research Journal*, 29 (4) (2003): 521–542 (quoted at pp. 526–527).

35   R. D. Lakes, *Youth Development and Critical Education: The Promise of Democratic Action* (Albany: State University of New York Press, 1996).

36   R. D. Lakes, "Community Service and Workplace Values: Toward Critical Pedagogy," *Journal of Vocational Education Research*, 23(4) (1998): 311–323.

37   M. L. Rehm, "Vocation as Meaning Making Narrative: Implications for Vocational Education," *Journal of Vocational Education Research*, 24(3) (1999): 145–159.

38   D. Orr, *Ecological Literacy: Education and the Transition to a Postmodern World* (Albany: State University of New York Press, 1992); G.A. Smith, and D. R. Williams, D.R. *Ecological Education in Action: On Weaving Education, Culture, and the Environment* (Albany: State University of New York Press, 1999).

39   M. W. Apple and J.A. Beane, J.A. *Democratic Schools* (Alexandria, VA: Association for Supervision and Curriculum Development, 1995).

40   A. G. Wirth, *Education and Work in the Year 2000: Choices We Face* (San Francisco: Jossey-Bass, 1992), p. 173.

41   J. A. Gregson, "From critical theory to critical practice: transformative vocational classrooms," in R. D. Lakes, ed. *Critical Education for Work: Multidisciplinary Approaches* (Norwood, NJ: Ablex, 1994), pp. 161–180.

42   L. Rosenstock, "The walls come down: The overdue reunification of vocational and academic education," *Phi Delta Kappan*, 72(6) (1991): 434–436 (quoted at p. 436).

43   Apple and Beane, *Democratic Schools*, p. 46.

44   Lakes, *Youth Development*.

45   McLaughlin and Heath cited in M. Delgado, *New Frontiers for Youth Development in the Twenty-First Century: Revitalizing and Broadening Youth Development* (New York: Columbia University Press, 2002), p. 139.

46   Ibid., p. 139.

47   Ibid., p. 159.

48   R.I. Simon, *Teaching Against the Grain: Texts for a Pedagogy of Possibility* (New York: Bergin and Garvey, 1992), p. 46.

49   Ibid., p. 47.

50   D. Mattingly, "Place, teenagers and representations: lessons from a community theatre project," *Social and Cultural Geography*, 2(4) (2001): 445–459; A. Taylor, "(Auto)biography and drama: life history work with adult returners to education," *Research in Drama Education*, 5(2) (2000): 249–261.

51   Alheit cited in Miles et al., *Communities of Youth*, p. 24.

52   Ibid., p. 3.

53   Ibid., pp. 24–25.

54   A. Boal, *Theatre of the Oppressed* (London: Pluto, 1979).

55   S. Houston, T. Magill, M. McCollum and T. Spratt, "Developing creative solutions to the problems of children and their families: communicative reason and the use of forum theatre," *Child and Family Social Work*, 6, (2001): 285–293; K. Monks, P. Barker, and A.N. Mhanacháin, "Drama as an oppor-

tunity for learning and development," *Journal of Management Development, 20(5)* (2001): 414–423.

56 Miles et al., *Communities of Youth*, p. 46.

57 Ibid., p. 52.

58 Ibid., p. 49.

59 Ibid., p. 127.

60 D. E. Stephen and P. A. Squires, "'Adults don't realize how sheltered they are': a contribution to the debate on youth transitions from some voices on the margins," *Journal of Youth Studies, 6(2)* (2003): 145–164.

61 N. Way, *Everyday Courage: The Lives and Stories of Urban Teenagers* (New York: New York University Press, 1998), p. 1.

62 P. Kelly, "Youth at risk: processes of individualization and responsibilisation in the risk society," *Discourse: Studies in the Cultural Politics of Education, 22(1)* (2001): 23–33; P. Kelly, "Wild and tame zones: regulating the transitions of youth at risk," *Journal of Youth Studies, 2(2)* (1999): 193–211.

63 R. D. Lakes, and B. M. Weiss, "Youth communication in Atlanta," in D.M. Hughes, and S. P. Curnan, eds. *CYD Anthology 2002* (Sudbury, MA: Institute for Just Communities, 2002), pp. 126–131; T. Bowers-Young and R. D. Lakes, "What's love got to do with it? Teen dancers on community service learning," in J. Claus, and C. Ogden, eds. *Service Learning for Youth Empowerment and Social Change* (New York: Peter Lang, 1999), pp. 109–126 Freire quoted at pp. 122–123.

64 M. O'Donnell and S. Sharpe, *Uncertain Masculinities: Youth, Ethnicity and Class in Contemporary Britain* (London: Routledge, 2000).

65 L. McDowell, "Learning to serve? Employment aspirations and attitudes of young working-class men in an era of labour market restructuring," *Gender, Place and Culture, 7(4)* (2000): pp. 389–416 (quoted at p. 391).

66 M. W. Apple, *The State and the Politics of Knowledge* (New York: Routledge, 2003), p. 221.

5. De Facto

Zero Tolerance

An Exploratory Study of Race and Safe School Violations[*]

VICTOR GOODE AND JENNIFER D. GOODE

[African American female, age 11] "Hides out in the school and was not going to class. She continuously does not listen in class and disrupts the learning process of other students." The officer arrested the student and took her to Juvenile Justice Center to be booked on a safe school disturbance.

Introduction

The consequences that follow misconduct in public schools have changed. Increasingly the penalty for misconduct is entry into the juvenile court system. Legislative bodies from Congress to City Councils have passed "safe school" laws whose object is to accomplish this by providing local officials with additional legal ability to prosecute certain violators. A vast

[*] This chapter contains excerpts from The Toledo Safe School Ordinance: An Exploratory Study of Race and Safe School Violations (2002), released by Northeastern University and the Harvard Civil Rights Project.

number of these apparent violators are students of color. A recent study of the American Bar Association (ABA) on the Ohio juvenile justice system, *Justice Cut Short*, notes both the overrepresentation of minority youth and the excessive reliance by schools on the courts. Similarly, researchers have found that safe school laws and similar zero tolerance policies are more likely to be applied to ethnic racial minority and economically disadvantaged students .[1]

While some researchers contend that racial disparities in confinement are a result of differential involvement in crime, other research suggests that differences in the offending rates of white and minority youth cannot explain the minority overrepresentation in arrest, conviction, and incarceration.[2]

A review by Pope and Feyerherm of existing research found that about two-thirds of the studies examined showed that racial and/or ethnic status did influence decision making within the juvenile justice system.[3] Subsequently, a large body of research has accumulated across numerous geographic regions reinforcing these earlier findings.[4] These authors also found that research indicates a large amount of variation across rural, suburban, and urban areas. Feld's notion of "justice by geography" suggests there are marked differences in outcome depending upon the jurisdiction in which the youth is processed.[5] Caucasian urban jurisdictions, for instance, are more likely to receive severe outcomes at various stages of processing than are cases in non-urban areas.[6] Since communities of color are concentrated in urban areas, this effect may work to the disadvantage of youth of color and result in greater overrepresentation.[7]

At the same time, some juvenile public defenders who work in rural and urban Ohio counties have noted the availability of fewer resources for rural juveniles and thus fewer options for rural juvenile court judges when it comes to disposition of the youth who appear before these judges. At some point, extreme disparities between counties, whether based upon measures such as resources available to the courts or severity of outcomes for the defendants, should raise an issue of equal protection under the Ohio Constitution, as has been the case in the public school finance context. Legalities aside, extreme disparities between counties also raise important public policy issues. Extreme intra-county disparities raise similar concerns.

In 2000, the Racial Fairness Implementation Task Force (RFITF) was created to develop an action plan to implement recommendations of the Ohio Commission on Racial Fairness. The Ohio Supreme Court created the Commission to examine racial justice in the state court system. RFITF acknowledged an inadequately understood link between overrepresentation of minority youth upon referral to juvenile court, and enforcement practices and referral patterns.[8] RFITF also endorsed the need for better information about informal sanction processes (e.g., school discipline, unofficial handling of referrals to juvenile court).[9]

This latter point is especially important since it is possible that some students may receive "only" a suspension for particular misconduct, while other students are arrested for (or charged with) safe school ordinance violations for the same conduct. Indeed, it is conceivable that some are charged with both—or even that others are charged with neither. This recommendation by the RFITF, regarding the need for better data, meshes with the declaration of the ABA that no national data system exists to track the number of school-related delinquency petitions filed against students, or the number of crime reports filed on school-based conduct. The absence of such comprehensive information system makes it difficult to gauge the breadth of this problem in Ohio and elsewhere.[10]

This chapter explores the Toledo Safe School Ordinance, hereafter referred to as TSSO.[11] Since TSSO has no provisions providing for progressive discipline, the ordinance and its enforcement constitute a de facto zero tolerance policy and practice. Hence, the ordinance functions as a direct pipeline into the juvenile justice system. Using police report data on incidents of safe school violations in Toledo, Ohio we examine the racial and ethnic contours of the safe school violations, and the kinds of conduct that precipitate such charges. This chapter concludes with public policy recommendations.

Historical Context

Dear Members:

We, the members of the Burroughs School P.T.A. wish to express to you our views on the proposed 'Safe Schools Law.'

Conditions have gotten so bad in some of the Toledo schools, that parents of the decent law-abiding children, both black and white, are fearful of allowing their children to travel to and from school alone. Some of these parents may be seen accompanying their children to and from each school session in order to keep them from being attacked in some way by persons who have no respect for the laws, or the rights of others.

When incidents occur, such as have been occurring in some of our high schools, it seems to mushroom until it encompasses nearly every school and neighborhood. We urge you, our representatives, to do something about this situation and do it quickly. Please pass the 'Safe Schools Law,' and see that it is enforced to the fullest extent.

Respectfully submitted
Burroughs School P.T.A12

In order to provide context to the enforcement of TSSO, we begin with a brief discussion of the history of the ordinance. The City passed TSSO in the wake of Toledo's 1967 race riot. Street crime was also a hot issue during this period, and the local National Association for the Advancement of Colored People (NAACP) had accused the mayor of *racializing* crime via pre-Willie Horton-type demagoguery. Other proponents were frustrated with the way the juvenile court was handling youth crime. Parent–Teacher Associations at two schools in predominantly white neighborhoods explicitly used the issue of race to show that this was everyone's problem and that the proposed remedy was everyone's solution. The legislative record, however, does not show that any African American organizations were part of the legislative process. Even when one of the Bill's proponents went to the well-respected black principal of the only African American high school to discuss the problem, city council notes suggest that he was shocked to learn that the principal did not share his view of a problem with "off-campus hoodlums." The principal was not alone. Although they eventually came around, neither the superintendent nor the only school board member to take an active interest in the issue saw the "crisis" that the proponents had manufactured to support their agenda. Toledo, in short, was part of a nationwide white conservative reaction to crime, riots, courts' handling of crime, including juvenile crime, and an increasingly urbanized black underclass. The TSSO was a fruit of that frustration.

Purpose of the Study

The purpose of this study is to assess the racial and ethnic contours of individuals charged with safe school violations, as well as the nature of those violations (e.g., threat, disturbance, or assault). As such, our research question is "Against Whom Is the Safe School Ordinance Used?" What constitutes a threat, disturbance, or assault is defined by school and/or police officials and reported as such on the incident report.

Data and Methods

The research sample is a subset ($n=4824$) of all reported incidences of safe school violations, victims and suspects, within the Toledo Public School District (including Washington Local) between January 2000 and December 2002.

The police data (report dataset) included an assigned unique identification number to identify each specific incident. This dataset had information that included the reporting officers' name, the beat and areas of patrol, and the zip code area of incident. The incidence data (person dataset) also included the same identification number for each incident. The person dataset also included other information such as location of violation, race, gender, and age of suspect. Using the unique identification number, the two files (person data and report data) were matched to the particular suspect. Because our study specifically focused on the racial contours of the safe school violations, only those cases with valid information on race were included in the study.

The person and report data sets were received in Excel format and converted into Statistical Package for Social Sciences System (SPSS). We further assess the research question by utilizing data compiled by Great Schools to determine enrollment, race/ethnicity percentages, and percentage of students participating in the federal free or reduced price lunch program.[13] Student enrollment information was cross-examined with the Ohio Department of Education data for accuracy. The study also makes use of population statistics for the Greater Toledo Area derived from the US 2000 Census.

Results

Descriptive statistics of the sample derived from the police data are found in Table 6.1. More than half of the suspects were black (65.6%) compared to 33.8% white, and 0.6% "other".[14] With regard to gender, male cases were the largest category of suspects (66.3%), with female incidents comprising 33.7% of the sample. The modal age category is 13–14 (39.1%), followed by subjects between the ages of 15–16 (25.5%); ages 10–12 (25.3%), and ages 17–19 (10.1%).

Approximately over half (51.3%) of the type of safe school violation committed by suspects in all incident reports were assaults. Disturbances and threats accounted for 29.4% and 19.3% of the reported safe school violations, respectively. With regard to location, 63.4% of safe school violations were reported to have occurred within the school setting, while 36.6% occurred outside of the school.

Geographically, the highest percentage of safe school violations occurred in the Downtown (central) area (29.9%), followed by East Toledo (15.4%), Northwest Toledo (15.3%), South Toledo (12.7%), University Neighborhood (10.5%), Southwest Toledo (9.4%), and North Toledo (6.6%). A frequency distribution on the percentage of offenses committed in each year (January 2000 through December 2002) revealed that approximately 36% of all types of safe school violations occurred in 2000, 40% in 2001, and 24% in 2002.

Bivariate analyses were performed to assess the relationship between the variables of interest. Figure 6.1 shows that for each year examined, black students received more safe school violations than their white counterparts, irrespective of offense type (i.e., disturbance, threat, and assault). More specifically, among males, black males were more likely to receive a disturbance charge than white males (67.1% versus 32.7%); black males were more likely to receive a threat charge than white males (58.7% versus 40.8%); and black males were more likely to receive an assault charge than white males (64.4% versus 34.9%). For girls, black females were more likely to receive a disturbance charge than white females (72.6% versus 27.1%), black females were more likely to receive a threat charge than white females (64.7% versus 35.0%), and black girls were more than twice as likely to receive an assault charge as white females (68.7% versus 30.8%).

In regards to age, we found that both black (37.9%) and white (40.7%) students between the ages of 13–14 made up the largest category of suspects across all violation types compared to their other respective age categories. Consistent with the vast amount of literature on crime and delinquency, males were more likely than females to commit all types of safe school violations regardless of racial category. Overall, males accounted for 69.2%

Table 5.1 Demographic Characteristics of the Sample

VARIABLES	N	%
Age		
10—12	1221	25.3
13—14	1884	39.1
15—16	1230	25.5
17—19	489	10.1
Gender[*]		
Male	3190	66.3
Female	1621	33.7
Race[*]		
Black	3150	65.6
White	1620	33.8
Other	29	0.6
Safe School Violation		
Assault	2475	51.3
Disturbance	1416	29.4
Threats	933	19.3
Violation Location[*]		
School	2910	63.4
Outside School	1682	36.6
Geographic Location[*]		
Northwest Toledo	732	15.3
North Toledo	317	6.6
Downtown	1428	29.9
East Toledo	735	15.4
Southwest Toledo	450	9.4
University Neighborhood	501	10.5
South Toledo	607	12.7

[*]   *These variables have missing observations: Gender [13]; Race [25]; Violation Location [232]; and Geographic Location [55], therefore percentages in these categories are valid ones. Collectively, other race/ethnicity (i.e., Asian and Indian) of suspects comprised 1% of the sample. As such, they are not included in the analyses. Latinos and Latinas were not identified in the police dataset. There were a few suspects over the age of 19 that were not included in this analysis. This was a small number of individuals who could possibly be parents, relatives, or "over-aged hoodlums."*

of safe school disturbances, while females account for 30.8%. Males also committed more threats than females (65% and 35%, respectively), and more assaults (65.2% and 34.8%, respectively) than females. Moreover, black males were almost twice as likely as black females to be charged with a safe school violation (64.6% and 35.4%, respectively) and white males were twice as likely as white females to be charged (69.4% and 30.6%, respectively).

In regards to violation location (i.e., in school/outside of school), we found that safe school violations were more likely to occur within the school as opposed to outside of the school. Among blacks, 63.8% of all safe school violations were committed in school, and 36.2% outside of school. Similarly, among whites, 62.7% of all safe school violations were committed in school, and 37.3% outside of school. In terms of type of safe school violation, overall, 78.5% of disturbances occur in school, with 21.5% occurring outside of school. Threats were almost three times as likely to occur in school (72.5%) as opposed to outside of school (27.4%), while more assaults occurred inside of school (52.4%), than outside of school (47.6%).

Relative to the geographic location, 38.6% of black suspects were from Downtown area schools, with 15.1% from the University Area, 12.3% from South Toledo, 10.4% from Southwest Toledo, 8.9% from Northwest Toledo, 8.2% from East Toledo, and 6.4% from North Toledo. Moreover, for blacks, in every category of violation, Downtown area schools had the largest percentage (45.9% disturbances, 38.5% threats, and 38.6% assaults). For whites, 29.4% of the suspects were from East Toledo, 27.9% from Northwest Toledo, 13.5% from South Toledo, 13% from Downtown, 7.5% from Southwest Toledo, and 7.1% from North Toledo. Additionally, for whites, the largest percentage of disturbance charges took place in East Toledo; the largest percentage of threat charges occurred in East Toledo (28.7%), though Northwest Toledo was close (28.1%); and the largest percentage of assault charges took place in Northwest Toledo (30.5%).

Discussion

Based on our sample, we do find some evidence of overrepresentation of black students in school discipline. This finding is consistent with extant literature on the overrepresentation of students of color in school discipline and in the juvenile justice system. In our sample, blacks accounted for approximately 66% of all safe school charges. Yet, blacks were approximately 40% of the student population during the same time in the school districts we examined. Additionally, in an earlier study, we reported on Lucas County Ohio juvenile court data showing that for each year between 1997 and 2001, black juveniles had the highest number of safe school ordinance court filings. Still, because our sample is a selective sample, it is not clear that blacks are overrepresented in the total number of safe school violations received between 2000 and 2002 in the Toledo and Washington Local Public School Districts. Specifically, we do not know if the overrepresentation of blacks in our study is the result of more thorough information provided in the police reports on black student suspects versus white student suspects. Moreover, future research is needed to examine the extent to which black students may be either more closely scrutinized or held to a higher standard in their decorum compared to their white counterparts.

We found that the highest percentage of safe school violations occurred in the downtown/central city area. This is consistent with theories that suggest crime in the schools reflect the patterns of disruptive behavior that exist in the surrounding neighborhood, though our analysis did not examine such patterns outside the TSSO context. It may also be consistent with theories that suggest that what is "crime" or "deviance" is socially constructed and determined by relationships of power.

The two-to-one ratio of male to female violators of the safe school ordinance is consistent with a vast amount of research in the juvenile justice and criminal justice fields regarding sex differentials from arrest to incarceration. What is surprising, however, is that in our sample, black females and white males were charged with almost the same number of safe school violations. Specifically, over the three-year period black females received 1114 safe school violations, while white males received 1121. This suggests that race is more of a predictor of safe school violations than gender, at least in our sample.

For each of the three categories of safe school violations, blacks had the highest frequency of violations. However, the gap between blacks and whites was largest in the categories of assaults and disturbances. Also, for each of the three years, blacks had approximately twice as many violations as whites. These results parallel actual juvenile court filings. For example, for each year between 1997 and 2001, black juveniles had the highest number of safe school ordinance filings. Also, for 2000–2001, the ratio of safe school ordinance filings against black juveniles compared to the safe school ordinance filings against white juveniles has been two-to-one, with twice as many cases filed against blacks.

Safe school ordinance charges increased for blacks and whites from 2000 to 2001. However, the increase was greater for blacks. Although in 2002 the total number of safe school charges decreased for both groups, blacks consistently received more safe school violations than whites during the three-year period covered in this study.

Limitations

Data derived from police records have their limitations. One point of concern is the systematic errors police departments make in recording crime data. Systematic errors include the fact that some crimes are unreported (especially threats) and therefore go unaccounted. Also, using police data to assess safe school violations may be biased due to racial and ethnic discrimination at the report and/or arrest stage. Procedural errors include the data entry errors and definitions of the violation. Because our sample is a selective sample of all reported safe school violations with valid information on race, the issue of selection bias is apparent. As earlier implied, there is ambiguity in what constitutes a threat, disturbance or assault although there is less ambiguity in the latter.

Relative to coding in the incident reports, officials did not code for *Latino*. Thus, our black and white data presumably mask the TSSO charges against *Latino* students. We assume their particular experience is camouflaged, rather than that they do not face safe school charges, for three reasons. First, we know from the Toledo City Schools suspension data that *Latino* students are suspended at greater rates than whites and others (non-black), though we also know that suspensions do not always produce TSSO charges. Second, we know from the Juvenile Court data that some *Latino* students were charged with TSSO violations. Third, our review of some hard copies of the police reports revealed that some *Latinos* were indeed charged.

Conclusion

While recognizing the potential benefits of safe school initiatives, the concern here was with how safe school violations can be yet another way in which minority, disadvantaged youth are disproportionately sent through the juvenile justice system. One of the most interesting findings was the triviality and ambiguity of many of the safe school violations. However, this is not surprising given the ambiguous wording of the TSSO itself. We began this chapter with an illustration of a student who received a safe school violation for the type of misconduct that was formerly handled internally by the schools. The following are illustrative of some other instances of triviality and ambiguity taken directly from the written police report:

> '[African American, male, age 12] was sent to the office for being unruly in the lunchroom. He was also very unruly yesterday when his table wasn't called first to get into the lunch line. Today when his lunch table wasn't called he became upset and got up and went to the lunch line when his table wasn't called. When he was advised to go back and wait until his table was called, he became very upset and yelled at the assistant principal that he was going to egg her car for not letting his table go first at lunch. He was charged with a safe school threat.'
>
> [African American, female, age 15] and [African American, female, age 15] were involved in a dispute over hearsay remarks, causing a disturbance in the hallway. Both students were taken to the Dean's office and issued ten day suspensions for violating the safe school policy. The students were then taken to the Child Study Institute without incident. Each was charged with a safe school disturbance.

There is also an important link between school safety and No Child Left Behind that should be considered. As a result of the latter, students in Ohio should be allowed to transfer from schools deemed "violent" for a certain period of time. Consequently, at least in theory, certain schools' approach to discipline may come back to haunt them because parents are increasingly voting with their feet. The state's experiment with charter schools has opened the door for some of that already. It is possible that we saw such a significant drop in Safe School Ordinance charges in 2002 because school officials were aware of these implications of No Child Left Behind and communicated their concerns to the police.

As earlier noted, there is a concern that schools use the safe school ordinance as a "dumping ground" for many matters that should be handled in the classroom or in the principal's office. As such, we are left with the question, "Where do we go from here?" In the following recommendations, we suggest areas that local officials and the community should carefully examine as a basis for policy development and potential reform. Despite the challenges, not the least of which are the interactive or supplemental systems of "school discipline" and "juvenile justice punishment," this issue deserves our attention amidst the numerous competing concerns of public education.

Recommendations

We have several recommendations, outlined below.

Given the national scope of overrepresentation, and given the federal funding by the US Department of Justice of municipal police departments and by the US Department of Education of school districts, it may be helpful for a national coalition of stakeholders to begin having conversations with these funding agencies. The discussions should focus on developing and enforcing guidelines for addressing student discipline and juvenile justice referrals consistent with statutory principles of equity for juveniles of color and non-discrimination for students of color. Uniform data collection and reporting protocols also merit discussion.

Whether or not lobbying the Department of Justice and the Department of Education for better enforcement makes sense [stakeholders might also lobby the President for an Executive Order instructing the federal agencies to issue and enforce guidelines, possibly joint guidelines], at the state levels we might encourage the governors to establish commissions to study the problem of equity and school discipline, including the issue of excessive referrals of students by schools to juvenile court. Alternatively, there may be legislative committees or state auditors that are willing and able to conduct the appropriate analyses.

The dual school-juvenile system of discipline/punishment should be examined collectively by the schools, the City, including the Police Department, the juvenile justice system and the community. As part of this project, at least the Toledo City Schools should re-examine its approach to student discipline. The district should adopt a collaborative evaluation process that includes, along with educators and other school staff representatives, parents and organizations based in communities of color.

Part of the above process should include a careful analysis of the more subjective and/or vague categories of Safe School Ordinance charges (i.e., "disturbance" and "threat"). This analysis should also determine to what extent incidents of disturbance or threat are trivial.

In addition, a study should be done in Toledo City Schools to determine the nature of the relationship, if any, between student suspensions and Safe School Ordinance charges. That is, to what extent do suspensions serve as an early warning system or predicate to Safe School Ordinance charges? To what extent are students charged with a SSO breach *and* suspended for the same, single incident? Do social differentials predict which students who commit the same acts are charged with SSO violations only, and who are suspended only?

Since incidents of Safe School Ordinance violations declined in 2002, further research should be conducted to determine what was different and why (e.g., referrals from schools, police response to those referrals, student conduct).

The Juvenile Justice and Delinquency Prevention Act, 42 U.S.C. Section 5633, requires the State to provide assurance that youth in the juvenile justice system are treated equitably on the basis of gender, race, family income, and disability. The ABA study, with its findings of overuse of the court by schools and minority overrepresentation, implicitly reinforces the importance of the State of Ohio taking the initiative to examine how implementation of the Toledo Safe School Ordinance raises equity issues for students of color.[14] An examination of these issues could be a part of the State of Ohio's broader approach to addressing Disproportionate Minority Confinement (DMC) under the JJDPA.

NOTES

1   R. J. Skiba, R. S. M, A. C. Nardo and R. Peterson, The Color of Discipline: Sources of Racial and Gender Disproportionality in School Punishment, *Indiana Education Policy Center, Policy Research Report #SRS1*, 2001; M. Fine and K. Smith, "Zero tolerance: reflection on a failed policy that won't die," in W. Ayers, B. Dorhn, and R. Ayers, eds. *Zero Tolerance* (New York: The New York Press, 2001); R. Verdugo, "Race-ethnicity, social class, and zero tolerance policies," *Education and Urban Society, 35(1)* (2002), 50–75.

2   Office of Juvenile Justice Delinquency Program, *Juvenile Offenders and Victims: A National Report* 91–92 (August 1995).

3   Ibid.; C. Pope and W. Feyerherm, "Minority status and juvenile justice processing," *Criminal Justice Abstracts, 22(2)*(1990): 327–336 (Part I); *22(3)*, 527–542 (Part II).

4   OJJDP, *infra*, at p. 92.

5   Ibid.

6   Ibid.

7   Ibid.

8   Racial Fairness Implementation Task Force, *Action Plan*, at 38, 75—Appendix II (September 2002)(adopting recommendations of 1993 study on race and juvenile justice in Ohio by Giordano and Cernkovich).

9   Ibid.

10   *See* American Bar Association, *Justice Cut Short*, Chapter 3 at p. 49 (March 2003)[hereinafter ABA].

11   Toledo City Ordinance 537.16:*Assault upon a teacher; disrupting school activity. (a) No person shall assault, strike, threaten or menace a teacher, instructor, professor, person in charge of a class of students or any employee of any school, college or university, while in the performance of his duties, or disrupt, disturb or interfere with the teaching of any class of students, or disrupt, disturb or interfere with any activity conducted in a school, college, or university building, or upon the campus or grounds thereof, or in any public place, or improperly and unlawfully assault, strike, threaten, menace, follow, pursue or lay hands upon a student or other person in a school, college or university building, or upon the grounds or campus thereof, or upon the way to or from*

any school, college or university sponsored activity. (b) Whoever violates this section is guilty of a misdemeanor of the first degree.

12   Letter from Burroughs School P.T.A. to Toledo City Council (12–26–68)(regarding passage of Safe School Law); *see* Letter from Marshall School Mothers Club P.T.A. to Members of City Council (11–27–68)(regarding passage of Safe School Law).

13   Great Schools is a non-profit organization that profiles all public elementary, middle and high schools in the United States. All information is gathered from the National Center for Education Statistics (NCES) and the US Department of Education.

14   For further information on the State's DMC obligation and approach to fulfilling that obligation, *see* The Children's Law Center, Inc., *A Practitioner's Guide to Juvenile Detention in Ohio* at II-7 to II-13 (April 2004).

APPENDIX A

Safe school violation was coded [1] disturbance, [2] threat, and [3] assault. Race was coded [1] black, [2] white, and [3] other race. Gender was coded [1] male, and [2] female. Age was recoded into four categories such that [1] 10 to 12 years of age; [2] 13 to 14 years of age; [3] 15 to 16 years of age; [4] 17 to 19 years of age. Location of violation was coded [1] school, and [2] outside school. The geographic location was derived using a Toledo Police Department unit identification system city map (by beats). Beat area falls under the defined areas: 100–199 Northwest Toledo; 200–299 North Toledo; 300–399 Downtown; 400–499 East Toledo; 500–599 Southwest Toledo; 600–699 University Neighborhood; and 700–799 South Toledo.

6. Who You Think I Am Is Not Necessarily Who I Think I Am

The Multiple Positionalities of Urban Student Identities

REBECCA A. GOLDSTEIN

Introduction

"There are a lot of stereotypes out there right now. And when you fit a stereotype, you are really not given a chance for people to find out who you are just because they look at your skin color. And a lot of opportunities, you do not get to have because people look at your skin color" (Gina, age 14).

When I first met Gina, she was a ninth-grade student attending a large comprehensive high school in a mid-sized city in the northeastern United States.[1] Like many of her peers, Gina struggled with different aspects of who she was, not just because she had recently entered a new school, but because she was also acutely aware of how others—peers, adults, and the wider community—viewed her and made decisions about who she was. Gina was trying to figure it out for herself, to become somebody who she wanted to be, in spite of what was going on around her and who others expected her to be. However, she was frustrated because she encountered many assumptions about who she was because of her race, gender, and the community from which she came. People assumed who she was before they got to know her and expected somebody very different from the intelligent, thoughtful, goal-oriented young woman she was.

Too often when people conduct research on adolescent identity, they view high schools as logical places in which to collect their data. On the surface it makes sense to conduct research in such a manner, because one is then able to work with a population of young people who are more or less held captive by societal norms and expectations about who they are and how they behave, and what role public schooling ought to play in creating active American citizens out of them.[2] But there is also a corresponding danger, particularly for students of color and other marginalized groups, because of who ultimately benefits from such research.[3] What happens when researchers use the high school as a mere repository of adolescent bodies from which to collect data without exploring the complex set of meanings that students construct about and for themselves and others within the physical confines of school? And, perhaps more importantly, what do researchers overlook when they expect to see a certain set of behaviors or meanings associated with adolescent identity development and only look for those constructs? What happens when one strips data of the subjective positions—the lived experiences of race, class, gender, sexuality, language, and culture—that students and others and use it to define who young people are? The most important question of all: What happens to students like Gina?

Such questions are particularly important for those who work with urban students and communities. Regardless of whether we (e.g., those who work with urban students) are from those communities or not, learning to listen to urban students, and expanding our own understandings of how they come to understand who they are in (and in spite of) the world requires us to acknowledge the complexity of how people come to understand themselves. This chapter will illustrate how one might read adolescent development and identity formation differently to explore how urban students might construct identities for themselves. How we do so involves moving away from the modern concept of universalism, to a critical understanding of culture and identities in which we recognize positionality in such a way that understanding adolescence involves a much closer examination of how urban young people become the people they are. Positionality refers to people's many subjectivities in action, and concerns how people engage in the lived experiences/subjective positions of race, class, gender, sexuality, physical ability, etc. Doing so enables us to move beyond seeing urban student identity development as being deviant or oppositional, to seeing it as strategic and empowering in light of the political and power struggles in which young people engage.

Universalist Theories and Identity Construction

When many people think about adolescence, they envision a time of turbulent emotions, physical and emotional changes, and a stage that young people must simply get through in order to become healthy, normal adults. Theories that posit that young people must move through various stages successfully on their way to becoming individuated adults are referred to as stage theories, and have become among the most common and powerful ways that many people understand how adolescent development occurs.[4] Nakkula's discussion of Erickson's theory of psychosocial development is particularly useful here. Erickson's theory of psychosocial development posits that people's identities are formed as a result of experiencing and successfully reconciling crisis (or not). Further, as Nakkula points out, Erickson views development as a process that occurs across the life span, from birth to adulthood, so that quite literally "adolescence provides that best last chance to rework some of the prior crises, and thus reset the course for positive subsequent development"[5]

Erickson's contribution to psychology and education represents a theoretical model that holds universalism as a fundamental lens through which one ought to view the world. Universalism implies that what is good for one person is good for everyone, and what holds true for one individual or a group holds true for everyone else. In addition, what people come to know and understand about others and themselves is independent of place and time. As a result of this modernist belief in universalism, people have conducted research on identity development looking to confirm that young people do, in fact, pass through various uniform stages to become normal, healthy adults. Once they draw and apply their conclusions to all groups, researchers then conduct additional research to examine those who do not fall into the normal ranges of development, and pose ways to remediate, that is fix, those who fail to develop normally.[6]

Of particular concern regarding the universalist approach to adolescent identity development is the notion that people can apply what they have learned from one group of young people to all other young people because adolescent identity formation is viewed to be culturally and politically, and value neutral. Identity research in the first half of the twentieth century was conducted on populations of middle-class boys of European descent, and even though other groups did not share the same cultural and social (racial, socio-economic, and gender-based) experiences, researchers believed their findings and theoretical views could and should be applied to all groups. The result? Individuals or groups who did not fit the models evolving from this research were labeled deviant, abnormal, and in need of remediation, whether through education or psychological intervention. In other words, because the universalist approach to identity formation excludes things like race, class, gender, sexuality, and culture (because it views those differences as inconsequential), people who do not fit the norm, (e.g., white, middle-class, heterosexual, Western European male) may fail to develop healthy identities from this perspective.

As a result, places like school have evolved to ensure that students develop "normally."[7] But, how do we define "normal"? Those who work in schools have been historically expected to prepare students to become active members of society. Coincidentally, students are not only expected to acquire attributes to maintain the status quo in society, but also to ensure that universalist theories of development and identity construction remain the defining concepts used to construct who is normal or deviant. For urban adolescents who do not fit the middle class, male of European descent profile mentioned above, constructing one's identity can be problematic. In many cases, urban adolescents are expected to assimilate the values, behaviors, and norms that the dominant society espouses.[8] These values, behaviors, and norms reflect the interests of a predominantly white, middle-class, hetero-sexual masculine society. Simultaneously, these norms construct who people ought to and ought not to be, as well as what their place in society will be.

If we return to Gina, the young woman to whom I referred at the beginning, the dominant culture and society expected her to fit a stereotype: to be poor, ignorant, a high school dropout, pregnant, and a drain on society—all because she was a fourteen-year-old black girl from the inner city. However, the sum of who Gina was and what she was becoming was much more than a stereotype. Not only was she aware of that, but she was also aware of how complex it all was.

> [Stereotypes make] them (black students) feel like there is nothing better to do. If they (whites and people outside of the city) are saying that about us, we might as well live up to that stereotype, which is like the most stupidest thing to think. You should never prove somebody right when you know they are wrong. If you just prove them right, then that just means you have no self-esteem for yourself or for anyone else. Because it's bad enough that the media is, what's the word . . . is exaggerating the facts, and then you gotta come and live up to them. That makes it even more ridiculous, and makes yourself look bad.

What options does a universal theory of adolescent development and identity present urban youths like Gina? Gina's statement captures the conflicts that students of color from urban communities struggle with on a daily basis when they are boxed into or box themselves into a universalist perspective. They have the either/or choice of assimilating into the dominant group in terms of behavior and norms (though they will never "look like" those of the dominant group), or they can resist and develop an oppositional culture.[9] Through such resistance, students may construct identities that are self-affirming; however, these same identities may further marginalize them from the mainstream. And, depending on which avenue they choose, urban adolescents may be seen as not quite a member of the dominant group or sell-outs within their home communities.

Breaking Away from the Stereotypes: Critical Identities in Action

The interplay between stereotypes and the beliefs and actions of urban students is an example of how urban students come to support and perpetuate the struggle between dominant class ideas, and struggle with those ideas on the part of those who are not part of the dominant class. This is because the common sense ideas and beliefs, or ideologies, that groups have about themselves and others are believed to be natural and simply a function of the ways things are.[10] And, because they are common sense, many people accept an ideological position as a natural truth because they do not consciously think about it or where it comes from. Gina recognized that students "living up to that stereotype" was an example of such buy-in and lack of awareness of an ideology, even though it ultimately hurt the student. However, according to Gina, living up to such an expectation was also a matter of poor self-esteem or having no self-respect, which, on a certain level, is also an ideological belief. In Gina's mind, if students only felt better about themselves, things would be OK. Thus, Gina felt that students themselves were in part responsible for the perpetuation of such stereo-types as well as the unequal treatment minorities received. So, even as she recognized how larger social forces shaped her experiences and how people viewed students like her, Gina still relied on many of those common sense beliefs that defined who she and her peers were and ought to be.

Another ninth-grade student, Jen, provided a provocative example of how complicated it can be when stereotypes play out in the lives of urban youth. Jen played in a local youth basketball league during the high school off-season. To be a member, each woman had to "try-out," and was accepted based upon her ability to play. Once on the team, players were expected to maintain a strong academic record, or face removal. Playing on the team also meant a great deal of travel during the summer months and exposure to college scouts. Jen was the only member from the city on her team. In contrast, most of her teammates were from the outlying suburbs. When asked about her experiences on the traveling youth team, she related:

> So they ask me where I am from and I tell them "Urban." And they're like, "Oh you from Urban? You can't be playing on this team; you don't have the grades." And when I tell them I get good grades, and that I'm not a bad student they don't believe me . . . they think that because I'm black, all I can do is play ball. But that's not true. I'm smart. I get the grades. But they think that all I can do is play ball.

Jen's ability to play basketball was never questioned. She made the youth league team so she must be a competent, if not outstanding, player. And, this must be especially true because of the stereotypes about black athletes. Her academic abilities were in doubt, also because of the stereotypes of black athletes. Even after she told them that she was eligible to play on the team, they still doubted her, hinted that the league made an exception (e.g., she needed the "enriching experience") and allowed her to play even though she might not have been a good enough student. Regardless of their real academic and athletic ability, students like Jen were automatically constructed as deviant or deficient when it came to what others thought about them.

There were other ways in which Gina and Jen experienced stereotypes that affected their school experiences. Both women noted that in addition to being under suspicion when they played tournaments outside the city, their peers in school paid attention to their every move. Even as they were a source of pride for the school (the women's basketball team had a win-ning season), people were suspicious of their abilities *because they were girls*. Even though they were talented athletes, there was something decidedly not-girl-like about their abili-ties. You could not be good at sports and still be feminine.

> JEN: It's really frustrating because we are good, like better than we have been in a long time. And so, suddenly there's this rumor going around that we (the girls' team) are gay.
>
> RG: (REBECCA GOLDSTEIN) 'Why do you think people are spreading this rumor?

JEN: I think the boys (team) be spreading it because they angry at us. They don't want us getting all the recognition here, so they are telling people we are gay.

Again, no one questioned their athletic ability; they attacked the women's sexuality, because real girls should not be able to play basketball better than the boys. Kimmel notes that this is one way that homophobia works to create fear in students. For male students, using homophobic language strips them of their masculinity, thus negating a large part of who they are.[11] For girls, such language functions essentially the same way. If a girl is good at sports, and is therefore not feminine, she cannot be a woman in the true sense of the word, no matter how she might try to navigate being an athlete and being feminine.[12] Like homophobia functions for boys, it did so for girls, creating for girls a fear of being called too masculine. The girls on the team could not be both good athletes and "good" girls (e.g., sexually appealing and thus, socially acceptable among their peers). Only the boys could be the athletic stars. The girls were supposed to watch and cheer on the boys, not infringe on a world normally relegated to male athletes.[13]

The rumors and stereotypes about the girls' basketball team had disastrous consequences for one of their teammates. Both Jen and Gina related that one young woman was sent to live with a relative when her mother heard about the rumor. It did not matter whether it was true or not. The rumor took on a life of its own:

Gina: The girls on the basketball team have a reputation. They act a certain way. You know people say things like, "Look at her, she's on the basketball team, she dresses in baggy jeans, she acts that way." So she must be a certain way. She fits a stereotype.

RG: What stereotype is that?

Gina: Well, she must be bi- or gay.

RG: Why?

Gina: If you play basketball, and you dress in baggy clothes, and you're good on the court, they think, "Oh you dress like a boy, you act like a boy, you must be a dyke." Now, I wear the baggy jeans and shirts because they are comfortable. I know there are a lot of girls in this school that wear the tight jeans, the high heels, the shirt, and they're that way (a lesbian). But because they don't dress like a boy, nothing is said.

Gina once again referred to the notion of a stereotype, a category of meaning that functioned to produce her as someone she was not. Because some girls on the basketball team wore baggy clothes and were strong athletes, they did not "act" like girls (however it was that girls "were supposed to act"). Rather, because they were athletes, and dressed like boys, they must want to be a boy, or they must be gay (even if they were not).

Gina's above point is critical. Some of the girls on the team wore "fashion" that was symbolic within the peer community of what lesbians supposedly wore. That, combined with the fact that the women on the team were strong players, confirmed the stereotypes for others, true or not. However, Gina noted that there were a number of girls who dressed in tight jeans, high heels, and tight shirts, girls who dressed "like girls," and were gay, just as there were girls who dressed in baggy clothes who were not. However, they seemed to fall below the radar in many cases, or because they were not as high-profile as their athlete peers, they escaped the most vocal ridicule:

> RG: Are there a lot of girls who are like that (e.g., lesbians) here?
>
> Gina: There are some. But only the ones who dress like a boy are called 'dyke' and given a hard time.
>
> RG: What about the stereotype of the team? Is that true?
>
> Gina: Yeah, there are some, but there are lots who aren't.
>
> RG: So you think that the way the girls dress has a lot to do with the way they are treated.
>
> Gina: Yeah, if they dress like a boy, they are called out. But if they dress all feminine and like a girl nobody says anything to them.
>
> RG: Because they fit the image of being a girl.
>
> Gina: Yeah, so nobody really knows that they are into that.

Clearly, the relationship between fashion, sexuality, and athletics was not lost on the young women I interviewed. Whether they dressed like a "boy" in baggy clothes, or like a "girl" in tight jeans or a skirt, students like Jen and Gina noted that how girls dressed ended up representing gender roles and sexuality. Reflecting upon these two young women's comments, I am struck by how clearly they articulated the fact that students who "fit the image" (e.g., feminine, heterosexual woman) became that image and were able to "pass for straight." On the other hand, it did not matter whether a female student was gay or not, because if she was an athlete or dressed the part (in baggy clothes "like a lesbian"), her peers determined her identity based upon the stereotypes and ideologies regarding gender and sexuality. The girls who dressed like girls were not nearly as suspect and may have been safer from other students' harassment. How young people use the activities, symbols like clothing, music, technology, and positionality to define themselves come together not simply as a series of layers that create uniform and permanent identities. Rather, they are woven together with threads of contradictory meaning, power relationships, and ambivalence that ultimately shape the identity trajectories of urban adolescents' lives.

Reading Urban Adolescence Critically

If one were to continue an analysis of the above narrative from a universalist perspective, one might fail to consider the strategic and political aspects of identity formation that make up an important part of this conversation. Critical psychological perspectives enable those who work with young people to think about how students come to be the people they are in much more complex ways. At its most basic level, critical psychological theory acknowledges the influence of culture, power, and ideology, and challenges the universalist perspective, the Western European belief that time, progress, and scientific study are neutral. Further, critical perspectives focus on the notion that just as our understandings of adolescence are constructed in relation to culture, power, and the subjectivities of race, class, gender, and sexuality, so too is the individual adolescent. In this sense, how "adolescence" and "the adolescent" are constructed involves unequal power relations that enable some to define both the healthy and the unhealthy adolescent. Finally, critical psychology requires us to rethink what we think we know about identity construction for *all* students.

What people might begin to see is that students use their own definitions of difference—in this case gender and sexuality—as a means to "other" or marginalize students and to reproduce various terrorizing and oppressive power relations within the school, even as they challenged others. On one level, one might "read" Gina's comments as homophobic because she defended her right to wear comfortable clothing and not "be that way." Clearly, Gina did not want other students to challenge her sexuality, nor did she want them to think she was gay. When asked about her feeling regarding sexuality, Gina noted, "To me it's a personal thing," which in and of itself ignores larger social and political aspects of sexuality. In her mind, what one did in private was done in private; it had no impact beyond the bedroom. However, she made no connection to larger political struggles that were defined by how young people viewed "what goes on in the bedroom." At the same time, Gina showed a great deal of critical insight into how athletics and fashion relate to gendered and sexual discourses. She connected gender and sexuality to the symbolic and cultural economy, that is, who and what urban students and athletes are and what power they have, and how it became part of students' physical bodies at Urban High. In effect, students' bodies were the cultural medium through which students enacted and performed their identities, and not only on how they appropriated that physical and symbolic space. Fashion became an important symbol that students used to define who they were, in terms of being "urban," having or pretending to have money, and perhaps most importantly, identified females students' availability to and objectification of the male gaze. If a female student was a strong athlete, she might not be available to validate male students' masculinity and power, and fashion became a large part of students trying to figure out who they were supposed to be. For some it maintained the status quo relationship; for others like Gina, it served as a means to reject certain norms.

If one employs a critical psychological perspective to explore how students like Gina navigate positionalities like sexuality, it is necessary to look at how Gina maintained as well as challenged the association of fashion and sexuality in order to protect herself. While she noted that clothing did not connote sexuality, Gina made evident her own discomfort with sexuality through language. She was "not that way" (e.g., a lesbian, a "dyke") and did not want people to think she was. She noted that it was "fine for other people" to be gay, lesbian, or bisexual, but that it was not who or what she was. Thus, she uncritically brushed sexuality aside, implicating herself in, while simultaneously protecting herself from, the heterosexist language and practices of her peers. While it was not OK to label students because of the clothing they wore, or to associate being gay or straight with certain clothes, Gina was clearly ambivalent about sexuality. For Gina, being outspoken about choice of clothing was particularly important because it also served as a means for self-preservation. After all, not only was she an outstanding athlete, she preferred to wear baggy clothing. Female students were expected to be "heterosexual girls" and dress the part, yet these same young women also wanted to be able to dress and act the way they wanted to, including play sports and be academically successful. They thus struggled to balance who they wanted to be with who others expected them to be in regard to their dress, athletics, and their sexuality. In some cases they downplayed their athletic abilities, in others perhaps they chose to dress in more stereotypically feminine ways than they might have otherwise.

In contrast to universalist perspectives regarding adolescent development, a critical psychological perspective requires those of us who work with young people to consider that students struggle with who they are becoming in ways that are non-linear relative to the discourses of progress that we might expect to see. Jen and Gina's voices clearly indicate that the processes of identity construction in which they are engaged involved multiple issues: not just race or class or gender, but all of the above *as well as* sexuality. How all of this played out for these young women depended on who had power in the school and who did not.

Learning to Teach from the Margins

So how is it that those of us working with urban adolescents or working with teachers of urban adolescents might come to a better understanding of the important issues related to identity construction? First, we must critically examine what we believe to be true about urban young people. In that regard, we must really look at our assumptions, what Gina and Jen called "the stereotypes," that people sometimes use to define urban adolescents. However, it is not enough to simply look at them; we must ask ourselves where these beliefs, good or bad, come from and how they might shape the teaching and learning that goes on in classrooms. Looking inward is a definite starting point, but alone it is insufficient in terms of understanding how urban young people come to be who they are.[14]

Second, it is important for us to move away from what we may have believed or been taught about adolescent development in our educational programs. We can no longer assume that one size fits all. Adolescent identity construction is a function of many experiences, both personal and cultural, in which young people create meanings about themselves and the world in which they live. Further, as Jen and Gina's comments above illustrate, who they are becoming is also very political in nature. For Jen, her experiences as a student and an athlete were shaped by race, and what others believed about her because of the discourses of race. In addition, because Jen was from an urban community, that too carried particular connotations that outsiders used to determine who she was, what her abilities were, and what if any future she had. For Gina, athletics, sexuality, and gender shaped who she was becoming in political ways particularly in ways related to the power she had both in school and out. Taking a critical psychological perspective acknowledges "how psychology locks us into descriptions of who we are, descriptions which reiterate and reinforce patterns and relations of social power".[15] Thus, those who work with youths can begin to see how others' expectations of students of color shape their experiences in and out of school in ways that can be destructive to their well-being.

While culturally, adolescence in United States schools is supposed to be a period in which students find themselves, how they do so occurs in such diverse contexts that those who work with young people cannot assume that their experiences will be similar. Nor can they assume that these experiences will affect all young people in the same manner. It is crucial for those of us who work with students from urban communities to rethink how we interpret what they say about themselves as well as how they behave in and out of school. Instead of asking, "What's the matter with kids today?," people should be asking, "What is right about kids today?" That Jen and Gina chose to be critical of the ways in which they were viewed, both by people outside their home communities and their peers from within, should be viewed as a positive rather than a negative. Both Jen and Gina began to see through the transparent power relations related to their lived experiences as African American adolescent women from the inner city, and challenged what was assumed about them and who they ought to be. From this perspective, a critical psychological reading enables us to understand that their resistance was by no means self-defeating; it was an expression of strategic agency that enabled students like Jen and Gina to find strength in who they were becoming, challenge the oppressive status quo, and come to a deeper understanding of who they were according to them, not others.

NOTES

1   A pseudonym. All names, except the author's are pseudonyms to protect the privacy of individuals.

2   Norms are relations that describe who people are, ought to be and how they should behave. They further define what all people should be like, regardless of race, class, gender, sexuality, and ableness, and exclude those who do not fit the Western European middle-class model.

3   S. SooHoo, "Crossing cultural borders into the inner city," in The Social Justice Consortium with S. SoHoo, ed. Essays on Urban Education: Critical Consciousness, Collaboration and the Self (Cresskill, Hampton Press), pp. 163–180.

4   N. Lesko, Act Your Age! A Cultural Construction of Adolescence (New York: Routledge/Falmer, 2001).

5   M. Nakkula, "Identity and possibility: adolescent development and the possibility of schools," in M. Sadowski, ed. Adolescents at School: Perspectives on Youth, Identity, and Education pp. 7–18 (Cambridge: Harvard Education Press, 2003), p. 11.

6   D. Hook, "Critical psychology: the basic co-ordinates," in D. Hook, ed. Critical psychology (Lansdowne: University of Cape Town Press, 2004), pp. 10–23.

7   K. B. deMarrais and M. D. LeCompte, The way Schools Work: A Sociological Analysis of Education 3rd ed. (New York: Longman, 1999).

8   B. Tatum, *Why are All the Black Kids Sitting Together in the Cafeteria? and other Conversations About Race* (New York: Basic Books, 1997).

9   R.P. Solomon, *Black Resistance in High School: Forging a Separatist Culture* (Albany, New York: State University of New York Press, 1992).

10   K.B. deMarrais and M.D. LeCompte, *The Way Schools Work: A Sociological Analysis of Education 3rd ed.* (New York: Longman, 1999).

11   M.S. Kimmel, "'I am not insane; I am angry': adolescent masculinity, homophobia, and violence," in M. Dadowski, ed. *Adolescents at School: Perspectives on Youth, Identity, and Education* (Cambridge: Harvard University Press, 2003), pp. 69–78.

12   S. K. Carney, "Body work on ice: the ironies of femininity and sport," in L. Weis and M. Fine, eds. *Construction Sites: Excavating Race, Class, and Gender Among Urban Youth* (New York: Teachers College Press, 2000), pp. 121–139.

13   N. Lesko, *Act Your Age! A Cultural Construction of Adolescence* (New York: Routledge/Falmer, 2001).

14   K.M. Zeichner and D.P. Liston, *Reflective Teaching: An Introduction* (Mahwah, NJ: Lawrence Erlbaum, 1996).

15   D. Hook, "Critical psychology: the basic co-ordinates," in D. Hook, ed. *Critical psychology* pp. 10–23 (Lansdowne: University of Cape Town Press, 2004), p. 19.

7. Making a Way

Out of No Way

Black Male Students at City High School[1]

GARRETT ALBERT DUNCAN AND RYONNEL JACKSON

Introduction

The Schooled Lives of Black Male Students in Post-Civil Rights America

Established in 1972 in a mid-sized metropolitan setting in the mid-west United States, City High School (CHS)[2] has a national reputation as a racially integrated public school that emphasizes a rigorous curriculum and that produces first-rate students. In addition to its curriculum, CHS is also known for its "caring" ethic, which was instituted by the school's founding principal and is codified in the school's mission statement. Anyone who visits CHS will conclude that its reputation for being a caring, high-achieving school is indeed merited. However, not unlike other fragmented communities that at first glance appear to be internally coherent,[3] CHS has demographic fractures that marble a school that, observed from a distance, appears to be a paragon of academic excellence and educational equity. Black male students, for instance, have not fared as well as their peers at CHS. For example, although the school is racially balanced, females outnumber males by a ratio of 2:1 as a direct result of the dearth of black male students. The absence of these students was realized most poignantly in 1998, a term that the school ranked first on the state's high-stakes examination. The school year concluded with only one black male student, from an initial cohort of 15, walking with his graduating class at commencement time.

Conventional wisdom in society suggests that the exclusion and marginalization of black males from schools such as CHS is a normal, albeit problematic, aspect of the education of this population of students. Studies in the United States and the United Kingdom seem to provide support for this pervasive belief.[4]). Most studies describe how adolescent black males and/or their families contribute to the problem of underachievement, while others also point out the roles of schools in creating these outcomes.

For example, in her study of a predominately black urban high school, Fordham (1996) posits that black families, especially mothers, largely contribute to the problem of under-achievement and maladjustment of black male students by encouraging them to embrace a "two-fold contradictory formula" in their approach to academic and social decision-making. In other words, parents encourage their sons "to concurrently accept subordination and the attendant humiliation (for survival in the larger society), and preserve gender domination (for survival in the black community)" (p. 148). What this means is that black parents urge their sons to downplay the significance of racism in their lives even as they encourage them to adopt patriarchal attitudes and behaviors "to be both non-dominating and successful in a racialized patriarchy" (p. 149). Fordham notes that the formula, however, is complicated by the contradictory status of what it means to be both black and male in North American society. She concludes that black males largely reject their subservient place in the gender hierarchy of schools and appropriate alternative forms of black masculinity that "further stigmatize them, reproducing the patriarchy and their consignment to secondary domination" (p. 165). This is not really a short comment though, perhaps in other words? In other words, Fordham surmises that black families contribute to the educational woes of black male students by providing them with untenable strategies for negotiating hostile academic climates, and that black males further contribute to their problems by appropriating attitudes and behaviors that exacerbate their marginalization and exclusion in schools.

Other ethnographic studies describe how race and gender converge on and through black male students in schools to shape their social and academic experiences, and often to their disadvantage. For example, Ferguson describes the daily interactions between black pre-adolescent male students, their peers and teachers, that illustrate "a disturbing tautology [where] transgressive behavior is that which constitutes [black] masculinity.[5]. Consequently, African American males in the very act of identification, of signifying masculinity, are likely to be breaking the rules" (p. 170). Similarly, in a study of a boys' comprehensive school in Britain, Sewell argues that teachers and peers impose sexualized perceptions on black boys and that black boys appropriate "normative notions of masculinity that act as an oppressive and repressive agent on their schooling."[6]. Sewell explains that schools do not exist in a vacuum though, and that influences from the wider society, including forms of popular culture such as music, also influence how black boys are perceived and perceive themselves.

Likewise, Mac an Ghaill examines the production of heterosexual masculinities in his study of an English secondary school. [7] He posits that black male students, their peers, and teachers construct these compulsory identities within complex sets of power relations that have particular references to class, race, and ethnicity.

Black Male Students: Strange or Estranged?

One may conclude from the overviewed studies that, for black male students, school success comes at a great personal loss, both real and imagined. In short, the literature frames the issue of their schooling in terms of a dilemma where black male students are damned if they do and damned if they do not achieve academically. Unsurprisingly, the typical orientation of psychological, sociological, and anthropological research on black male students is toward explaining the motivational, affective, or cognitive bases of their actions, or on explicating the cultural resources that they bring to bear in making academic and social decisions in school. In addition, researchers devote considerable attention to identifying interventions and strategies to rehabilitate and to incorporate black males more fully into schools; most pedagogical, policy and programmatic responses to the problems of these young men are similarly focused. However, as we describe in the sections that follow, responses to the purported crisis of black males, even when they are guided by the best intentions, do little to enhance their experiences in schools and, in some instances, reinforce their marginalization.[8] We posit that the intransigent nature of the problems black male students encounter in schools is indicative of populations that are socially constructed as fundamentally different from those who are deemed normal in society. Such constructions result in conditions for these populations in which they become estranged from the rest of society.

In previous publications,[9] we argued that the values that typically inform inquiries into the lives of estranged groups, such as black male students, derive from curiosity and control.[10] The aim of such inquiries is to understand better these groups and to determine effective ways to integrate them into institutions, or to devise compensatory programs to support them in attaining some measure of success within these social structures. However, as we noted, critics of "problem-solving approaches" argue that this orientation leaves institutions unexamined for their complicity in reproducing a racist social order [, [11] and reinforces notions that members of oppressed groups are strange [12] In other words, marginalized populations possess values and attitudes that require explication and clarification because they are fundamentally different from those of the rest of society.

It is in this way that society tacitly constructs black males as a strange population and contributes to the widespread perception that their plight in schools is unremarkable: the dominant frame, or storyline, suggests that black males are too different from other students, and oppositionally so. Moreover, it comes as no surprise that they have difficulty in schools, especially in those with high-powered academic programs and codes of conduct that rely on student consent and compliance for their enforcement. Thus, despite the intentions of the researchers who employ it, the problem-solving orientation in research on black male students tends to gloss over the conditions of their estrangement and reinforces the perception of their strangeness, which only contributes to their further marginalization in school and society.

Beyond Love at City High[13]

As we suggest above and describe in previous writings , [14] even well-intentioned "interventions" for black male students function in some ways to reinforce the dominant storyline about their academic engagement and to marginalize them even as they seek to ameliorate their conditions. For example, after one of the initial visits by the first author to CHS in the spring of 1999 to talk with members of the mentoring program that the school's administration created for black male students, one of the younger adult mentors, a 25-year-old black male, shared the following observations:

> Some of the more recent speakers have come speaking to our students as if they have the solutions to ALL of their problems (including [a prominent black educator that had recently conducted an all-day professional development workshop at CHS]), and after the presentation, their problems would be solved. . . . These younger brothers don't need a speech or series of speeches, they need positive and conscious Black men like ourselves to be honest with them, guide them, and truly listen to them. (4/29/99)

The views of this mentor are not unlike Nel Noddings's observation that "our claim to care must not be based on a one-time, virtuous decision but rather on continuing evidence that caring relations are maintained."[15] To address their concerns: "they need the continuing attention of adults who will listen, invite, guide, and support them."[16]

Data from this study indicate that black male students encounter at CHS a school climate that, for them, is characterized by a form of indifference, or estrangement, that contributes to their marginalization and oppression. This point is best illustrated in the contradictory effect of a mentoring program that was established to stave the attrition rate of the black male student population. For instance, during an all-school assembly on the first day of the 2000–2001 school year, the first author scanned the audience for the faces and expressions of black male students during an announcement regarding the mentor program. During the announcement he experienced that "peculiar sensation," described by W. E. B. DuBois, that is brought on by "a world that looks on in amused contempt and pity."[17] For the most part, the young men he observed either looked down or straight ahead, in ways to suggest that they were shutting out the announcement. Their behavior was cause for me to wonder what the program meant to them. In terms of what the program signified for some of their peers is best captured in the following account by a research assistant, composed from field notes and observational data, that portrays an exchange between students in a hallway during a passing period that indicates disdain for the perceived dependency of black males on others at the school:

> When the bell rings to indicate the end of class I notice this white girl, standing next to an African American female student, shouting "hello" to many other students. Her social interactions interest me, so I ease over to listen in on her conversations. At this point, she is leaning over the balcony, shouting to a friend in the cafeteria.
>
> "Hey, are you joining the black male mentor program?" she calls down to an African American male.
>
> "Naw, I don't need that," he answers. There is no hint that he is either startled or offended by her question.
>
> "Well, I'm starting a female Caucasian group," she screams back. She laughs and seems to be unconcerned that she may have offended either of her friends. Neither of the students responds to her last comment and the three take up separate conversations with other students. (02/16/01)

With respect to those for whom the intervention was intended to benefit, all the young men we interviewed stated that they found the mentoring sessions to be helpful. However, the boy's response in the previous exchange and, more generally, the low and inconsistent attendance of black male students at meetings suggested that the program represented something more complicated in their lives at school. Indeed, during sessions, mentors sometimes conveyed contradictory messages to the mentees: they encouraged them to do well academically but also blamed the young men for the stereotypical attitudes that their teachers had of them. For example, on one such occasion during the spring of 2000, Jack, the second author, conducted a group interview at CHS with members of the mentoring group. However, older adult mentors who were present interjected themselves into the conversation. On the one hand, they counseled and encouraged the young men, yet, on the other hand, they peppered their advice with comments that apologized for uncaring teachers and that blamed the young men for their conditions at CHS.

At the same time, the video record of the session captured the young men strategically rolling and closing their eyes as well as glancing at the clock on the wall. We use the term "strategically" because these actions were often embedded in others, such as reaching for a buffalo wing, sipping soda from a cup, stretching, and shifting one's weight in the chair. The mentors, who regularly chastised the students for what they deemed to be disrespectful or inappropriate behavior, never remarked upon and appeared to not notice what the young men were doing, further supporting our view that the young men were engaged in clandestine activities. The boys also appeared to be communicating with one another, not only through eye contact but also through auditory cues, such as synchronized coughs and throat-clearings. A full transcript and analysis of this session is provided elsewhere [18]

The Cultural Resourcefulness of Adolescent Black Males; or, How Aquil Flipped the Script and Lived to Tell About It

Piqued by what we observed in the video footage, we organized a session to conduct stimulated recall interviews with some of the mentees who were present at the mentoring session. This interview session involved reviewing the video tape of the mentoring session. In addition, it was video taped with Aquil and Roger, two students from the mentoring session, at the university. During the university session, Aquil repeated the concerns that his peers raised in the earlier session, namely that adults at the school treat black males unfairly. Specifically, he complained that teachers and other adults at CHS who have marked him as having an "attitude problem" constantly picked on him. Aquil, however, recast "attitude" as an adult problem, as opposed to a black male problem. "Definitely," he contended, "they have an attitude toward us. People like . . . people like have an attitude problem toward us." Aquil also set the record straight about what teachers perceive to be his attitude problem: "She would say, 'that boy has a . . . Aquil has a smart mouth,' I don't got a smart mouth, I just 'respond'—I respond to questions! She asked me a question and I was like, 'huh? What happened? Like, you going to sue me? I ain't got no money. . . .'"

Mark Tappan and Lyn Mikel Brown suggest that the key to understanding the complexity of moral situations is found not only in the relationship between the cognitive and affective dimension, but also in the conative dimension of how individuals construct their experiences.[19] The conative dimension focuses on what people do and, along these lines, of particular relevance to this paper, are aspects of the stories that Roger and Aquil told during the recall interview that provide insight into strategies they employ when they feel authority figures are disrespecting them and when it appears that they have no way out of the situation—where they are outnumbered and outgunned. In the following story told during the recall session, Aquil describes how he got out of a situation at CHS when he felt that he was being unfairly targeted for reprimand by the school's security guard. In doing so, he illustrated how the use of a strategy similar to those that he and his peers also appeared to have employed during the previous mentoring session helped him to survive a testy situation. Aquil recounted the story as follows:

> Well, wait a minute, I was running through the hallway, right? He was chasing me, yeah, he was chasing me because I said something to him. I think I told him that his pants were too [ ] or something. And I ran past this, what was that, uh Mephistopheles, right? [group laughter] straight up, right? And I run past her, right? She looks and I'm like, "whatever." Then I kept on running and then I came back, she said, "Come here. Now, if you would have ran into me, I would have Sued you for assault." And I was like, "huh?" She said, "yeah, I could have just Sued you for assault." "Aw, sue me what?" "You were running in the hallway. If you had bumped into me, I would have Sued you." I was like, "whatever, can I go?. . . ." She was like, "No I want to talk to you." "No," I was like, "I got to go to class . . ." She was like, "I want to talk to you right now . . ." "No, I'm going to be tardy bye." That was all I did. I haven't said nothing to her since. I ain't said nothing else to her at all since then. I would have took her on Judge Judy and sued for some pennies, now. Straight up. But Judge Judy would do that type of stuff, too.

Aquil retold this episode in response to Jack's follow-up inquiry exploring students' complaints about double standards at the school. It was obvious to Aquil that the security guard was subjecting him to a double standard; however, as indicated elsewhere, he was also aware at the time that she perceived him as having an "attitude" problem—recall that "Aquil has a smart mouth." But passive acquiescence is not an option for this young man, as suggested in his words above. At the same time though, Aquil could not directly call the security guard on her unfair treatment of him for, having been in this situation a number of times, Aquil knew that the airing of his legitimate concern would only get him into more trouble. Hence, he is confronted with a dilemma: "Do I do right and suffer, or do I do wrong and get ahead?"[20] .

In his version of events, Aquil reconstructed his story with a variety of indirect languages. Marcyliena Morgan argues that the use of indirection, as demonstrated by Aquil, "has to do with the development of a speech economy in which 'ways of speaking' inherited directly from Africa have been reshaped by the historical experience of Afro-Americans in America."[21] According to Morgan, the African American counterlanguage of the sort that Aquil employed is an expansion of indirect speech in the U.S. that signals "both the social reality of antisociety as well as solidarity among African descendants."[22] The initial use of this counterlanguage is evident in Aquil's reference to the security officer: "And I ran past this, what was that, uh Mephistopheles, right? [group laughter] straight up, right?" The laughter of the group may be interpreted any number of ways. On the one hand, just the use of the term Mephistopheles in the context of this conversation is cause for laughter. However, the laughter in the room, especially as it came from Roger, was more of the sort that said, "I cannot believe that you just went there!," to which Aquil replies, "straight up," or "I sure did!" His use of Mephistopheles illustrates one way that Aquil appropriates a tool borrowed from school for his own end and is also consistent with Bakhtin's view of language. For Bakhtin:

> 'Any word exists for the speaker in three aspects: as a neutral word of a language, belonging to nobody; as an other's word, which belongs to another person and is filled with echoes of the other's utterance; and, finally, as my word, for since I am dealing with it in a particular situation, with a particular speech plan, it is already imbued with my expression. . . . '
>
> These words of others carry with them their own expression, their own evaluative tone, which we assimilate, rework, and re-accentuate.[23]

Clearly, Aquil assimilated, re-worked, and re-accentuated a word that carried with it its own expression and evaluative tone. Mephistopheles, for instance, represents the personification of evil forces, or the devil in Goethe's *Faust*, a book that is required reading for sophomores at CHS. The video footage and transcript suggest that Aquil, cognizant of the fact that his voice and image were being recorded, was rather purposeful in selecting a specific term that would convey his sentiments in a way that elicited laughter and that lent itself to deniability. Clearly the reaction of Roger and Jack indicated that they heard Aquil call the white security guard a *devil*. Although we are inclined to agree with Robin D. G. Kelley who would likely argue that the main purpose of Aquil's choice of words was to get a laugh from his peers, we also posit that his choice has an historic dimension, described by Morgan, that clearly links his narrative across time and space with others throughout the African Diaspora in North America.[24] His use of counterlanguage here employs the style of Martin Luther King Jr., who used snake metaphors to convey essentially the same sentiments as Aquil. This specific use of counterlanguage is in contrast to its use by, say, Malcolm X or Frederick Douglass who explicitly referred to white people as devils in their public speeches and writings.

In addition to Mephistopheles, Aquil also appropriated another official tool of the school. However, this particular use occurred within the actual context of his interaction with the security guard. Here, in the tradition of Nat Turner, Aquil appropriated the use of a tool that school personnel often used against him for his own ends. Specifically, Aquil employed the school's tardy policy to flip the script, so to speak, on the security guard. Although the tardy policy is rarely enforced on this open campus where students come and go as they please and enter and leave class without permission, authority figures selectively enforce it against black males in the same way that the rule against running in the hallway was selectively enforced in this incident. Moreover, Aquil places the security officer in an awkward position by suggesting that she, whose main job it is to enforce school rules, is contributing to the delinquency of a minor.

Conclusion

The aforementioned example is typical of the linguistic and interpersonal resourcefulness that we found among black male students as they sought to "make a way out of no way" at a school where they were always outnumbered and always outgunned. Overall, the experiences of the young men in the broader project evince evidence of unjust conditions at school; they also illustrate the strategies these students employ to negotiate their academic and social lives within these institutions. To what extent may their experiences inform educational practice and policy? The data tell us something about the nature of schooling and even about ourselves as teachers and researchers, that runs counter to conventional wisdom about public education. For instance, if it is true that knowledge is to be found in the relationship between the knower and the known,[25] the analysis in this study may offer alternatives to the pervasive notion that the post-Civil Rights era plight of black males in public schools is simply an expression of anti-intellectualism, academic disengagement, or oppositional identities. Indeed, such an analysis of schooling may also point to more endemic problems related to oppression and domination that place all students at risk and may provide insights on how to reform schools in more fundamental ways.

Along these lines, we posit that the domination and oppression that black male students encounter at CHS are organizational features of schools in general. Problems of domination and oppression are about relationships and, thus, are moral in nature. If this is the case, and we believe that it is, liberation should be the primary term for conceptualizing remedies to the problems that students and the schools they attend encounter. A notion of liberation in this sense fosters cultural democracy,[26] or the nurturing of group differences. As Iris Marion Young suggests, group differentiation, or what we commonly call diversity, "is both an inevitable and desirable aspect of modern social processes. This alternative view of social justice then, requires not the melting away of differences, but institutions that promote reproduction of and respect for group differences without oppression."[27]

Optimistically, we found that a significant minority of students and adults at CHS forged relationships that support the academic success of students without respect to race, ethnicity, gender, or class. Our on-going research suggests that teachers and administrators that support black male students at the school share affiliations with social movements or a commitment to egalitarian ideologies. Further, some of the students at the school also demonstrated their willingness to mobilize around the concerns of black male students to promote change at CHS .[28] These findings suggest to us the possibilities of bringing about the conditions of social justice grounded in the affirmation of, and respect for, group differences. Such conditions will not only foster the academic achievement of black male students but that of their peers as well.

NOTES

1   Earlier versions of this chapter were presented at the 24th Annual Ethnography in Education Research Forum, Center for Urban Ethnography, University of Pennsylvania, PA, USA, March, 2003, and at a forum sponsored by the International Writer Center, Washington University in St. Louis, St. Louis, MO, USA, March 20, 2003. We would like to thank Cleo Brooks for her research assistance and the IES/AERA Grants Program for a 2002–2004 research grant awarded to the first author, and the generous support of the Washington University Graduate School of Arts & Sciences for funding various stages of this project.

2   All names of institutions and persons used in this section are pseudonyms.

3   M. Fine and L. Weis, "Writing the "wrongs" of fieldwork: Confronting our own research/writing dilemmas in urban ethnographies," in *The Unknown City: The Lives of Poor and Working-Class Young Adults* (Boston: Beacon Press, 1998), pp. 264–288; see also C. West, "Black leadership and the pitfalls of racial reasoning," in T. Morrison ed. *Race-ing Justice, En-Gendering Power: Essays on Anita Hill, Clarence Thomas, and the Construction of Social Reality* (New York: Pantheon Books, 1992), pp. 390–401.

4   See, e.g., M. Blair, *Why Pick on Me? School Exclusion and Black Youth* Stoke on the Trent (UK: Trentham Books, 2001); M. C. Brown and J. E. Davis, eds., *Black Sons to Mothers: Compliments, Critiques, and Challenges for Cultural Workers* (New York: Peter Lang, 2000); L. Davis, ed., *Working with African American Males: A Guide to Practice* (Thousand Oaks, CA: Sage Publications, 1999); J. Davis, "Black boys at school: Negotiating masculinities and race," in R. Majors, ed. *Educating Our Black Children: New Directions and Radical Approaches* (London and New York: Routledge/Falmer, 2001), pp. 169–182; G. Dei, J. Mazzuca, E. McIsaac, and J. Zine, *Reconstructing "drop-out": A Critical Ethnography of the Dynamics of Black Students' Disengagement from School* (Toronto: University of Toronto Press, 1997); G. Duncan, Racism as a developmental mediator, *The Educational Forum, 57(4)* (1993): 360–370; G. Duncan, "Educating adolescent black males: Connecting self-esteem to human dignity," in L. Davis, ed. *Working with African American Males: A Guide to Practice* (Thousand Oaks, CA: Sage Publications, 1999), pp. 173–186; G. Duncan, "Beyond love: A critical race ethnography of the schooling of adolescent black males," *Equity and Excellence in Education, 35(2)* (2002a): 131–143; A. Ferguson, *Bad Boys: Public Schools in the Making of Black Masculinity* (Ann Arbor: The University of Michigan Press, 2000); B. Harry and M. Anderson, "The disproportionate placement of African American males in special education programs: A critique of the process," *Journal of Negro Education, 63(4)* (1994): 602–619; R. Hopkins, *Educating Black Males: Critical Lessons in Schooling, Community, and Power* (New York: State University of New York Press, 1997); M. Mac an Ghaill, *The Making of Men: Masculinities, Sexualities and Schooling* (Buckingham: Open University Press, 1994); K. Meier, J. Stewart and R. England, *Race, Class, and Education: The Politics of Second-Generation Discrimination* (Madison, WI:

The University of Wisconsin Press, 1990); P. Noguera, "Preventing and producing violence: A critical analysis of responses to school violence," *Harvard Educational Review, 65(2)* (1995): 189–212; V. Polite and J.E. Davis, eds., *African American Males in School and Society: Practices and Policies for Effective Education* (New York: Teachers College Press, 1999); T. Sewell, *Black Masculinities and Schooling: How Black Boys Survive Modern Schooling* (Stoke on the Trent, UK: Trentham Books, 1997).

A. Ferguson, *Bad Boys: Public Schools in the Making of Black Masculinity* (Ann Arbor: The University of Michigan Press, 2000).

T. Sewell, *Black Masculinities and Schooling: How Black Boys Survive Modern Schooling* (Stoke on the Trent UK: Trentham Books, 1997).

M. Mac an Ghaill, *The Making of Men: Masculinities, Sexualities and Schooling* (Buckingham: Open University Press, 1994).

8   P. Noguera, "Preventing and producing violence: A critical analysis of responses to school violence," *Harvard Educational Review, 65(2)* (1995): 189–212; B. Hamovitch, "More failure for the disadvantaged contradictory African American student reactions to compensatory education and urban schooling," *The Urban Review, 31(1)* (1999): 55–77.

9   G. Duncan, "Beyond love: A critical race ethnography of the schooling of adolescent black males," *Equity and Excellence in Education, 35(2)* (2002): 131–143; G. Duncan and R.Jackson, "The language we cry in: Black language practice at a post-desegregated urban high school," *GSE Perspectives on Urban Education, 3(1)* (2004) (This article may be retrieved from <http://www.urbanedjournal.org/ articles/ article0014.html>

10   J. Laible, "A loving epistemology: What I hold critical in my life, faith, and profession," *Qualitative Studies in Education, 13(6)* (2000): 683–692; P. Parker, *To Know As We Are Known: Education As a Spiritual Journey* (New York: Basic Books, 1993); R. Williams, "The death of white research in the black community," *Journal of Non-White Concerns in Personnel and Guidance* (1974, April): 116–131.

11   Laible, "A loving epistemology: What I hold critical in my life, faith, and profession"; Williams, "The death of white research in the black community"; D. Bell, *Faces at the Bottom of the Well: The Permanence of Racism* (New York: Basic Books, 1992); D. Bell, *Afrolantica Legacies* (Chicago: Third World Press, 1998); R. Delgado, *The Rodrigo Chronicles: Conversations About America and Race* (New York: New York University Press, 1995); K. Crenshaw, N.Gotanda, G. Peller and K. Thomas, (Eds.). *Critical Race Theory: The Key Writings That Formed the Movement* (New York: Routledge, 1995); M. Matsuda, *Where Is Your Body? And Other Essays on Race, Gender, and the Law* (Boston: Beacon Press, 1996); M. Matsuda, C. Lawrence, R. Delgado, and K. Crenshaw, *Words That Wound: Critical Race Theory, Assaultive Speech, and the First Amendment* (Boulder, CO: Westview Press, 1993).

12   Delgado, *The Rodrigo Chronicles: Conversations About America and Race*; P. Tillich, *Love, Power, and Justice: Ontological Analysis and Ethical Applications* (Oxford: Oxford University Press, 1954).

13   Our interpretive framework draws on critical ethnographic and discourse analyses that examine the layers of meanings and multiple viewpoints that are brought to bear on the academic and social experiences of black male students in the study. See, e.g., P. Carspecken, *Critical Ethnography in Educational Research: A Theoretical and Practical Guide* (New York: Routledge, 1996), and L. Chouliaraki and N. Fairclough, *Discourse in Late Modernity: Rethinking Critical Discourse Analysis* (Edinburgh: Edinburgh University Press, 1999). The larger portion of the field research was conducted from the spring of 1999 through the spring of 2003. Data for the study discussed in this paper were obtained from black male students using loosely structured conversations, semi-structured, open-ended question and answer sequences, and stimulated recall interviews; both individual and focus group sessions were conducted. The authors and research assistants collected the interview data reported in this chapter. Additional

data were obtained from interviews with other students, and faculty and staff members. Data related to the culture of the school were collected through systematic participant observations of classrooms and corridors and during assembly sessions and other school-related activities and meetings. Data were recorded in field notes and on digital videotape and audiotape. Data related to demography, standardized testing, attendance, and graduation rates, and documents related to the historical, ideological, and programmatic features of the school augmented the interview and participant observation data in the larger study. Finally, we collected both participant observation and textual (e.g., written assignments) data from an ethics course the first author taught at the school during the 2000–2001 academic year.

14   Duncan, "Beyond love: A critical race ethnography of the schooling of adolescent black males"; . Duncan and Jackson, "The language we cry in: Black language practice at a post-desegregated urban high school."

15   N. Noddings, "Care, justice, and equity," in M. Katz, N. Noddings, and K. Strike, eds. *Justice and Caring: The Search for Common Ground in Education* (New York: Teachers College Press, 1999), p. 14.

16   Noddings, "Care, justice, and equity," p. 13.

17   W. E. B. DuBois, *The Souls of Black Folks* (Chicago: A.C. McClurg & Co., 1903).

18   Duncan and Jackson, "The language we cry in: Black language practice at a post-desegregated urban high school";

19   M. Tappan and L. Brown, "Stories told and lessons learned: Toward a narrative approach to moral development and moral education," in C. Witherall, and N. Noddings, eds. *Stories Lives Tell: Narrative and Dialogue in Education* (New York: Teachers College Press, 1991), pp. 171–192.

20   W. Mosley, *Always Outnumbered, Always Outgunned* (New York: Washington Square Press, 1998); W. Mosley, *Workin' on the Chain Gang: Shaking off the Dead Hand of History* (New York: The Ballantine Publishing Group, 2000).

22   M. Morgan, "The Africanness of counterlanguage among Afro-Americans," in S.S. Mufwene, ed. *Africanisms in Afro-American Language Varieties* (Athens and London: The University of Georgia Press, 1993), pp. 423–435.

22   Morgan, p. 427.

23   M. Bakhtin, C. Emerson and M. Holquist, V. McGee, Trans., (Eds.) *Speech Genres and Other Late Essays* (Austin: University of Texas Press, 1986), pp. 88, 89.

24   M. Morgan, "The Africanness of counterlanguage among Afro-Americans," in S.S. Mufwene, ed. *Africanisms in Afro-American Language Varieties* (Athens and London: The University of Georgia Press, 1993), pp. 423–435; R. D. G. Kelley, *Yo' mama's Disfunktional!: Fighting the Culture Wars in Urban America* (Boston: Beacon Press, 1997).

25   P. Parker, *To Know As We are Known: Education As a Spiritual Journey* (New York: Basic Books, 1993); P. Carspecken, *Critical Ethnography in Educational Research: A Theoretical and Practical Guide* (New York: Routledge, 1996).

26   A. Darder, *Reinventing Paulo Freire: A Pedagogy of Love* (Boulder, CO: Westview Press, 2002).; M. Ramírez and A. Castañeda, *Cultural Democracy, Bicognitive Development, and Education* (Orlando, FL: Academic Press, 1974).

27   I. Young, "Five faces of oppression," in T. E. Wartenberg, ed. *Rethinking Power* (Albany: State University of New York Press, 1992), p. 180.

28   G. Duncan, "At the risk of seeming ridiculous": A post-critical approach to researching the schooled lives of adolescent black males, an unpublished manuscript, 2002.

8. Culturally Responsive Pedagogies

African American High School Students' Perspectives

MARGUERITE VANDEN WYNGAARD

With the intrusion of the No Child Left Behind Act on education, educators are focusing their efforts on serving those students who are identified as members of a "sub-group" population. The "sub-group" population includes students who have been historically marginalized such as those students who are second-language learners, children of color, children with limited abilities, and those children from homes of working poor and poor families. In response, educators are demanding workshops about culturally responsive pedagogy as a tool that would help them address the needs of students who are different from themselves. Unfortunately, many workshops result in the identification of a few model "lessons" but rarely move beyond to ensure that the students are empowered to make sense of and challenge the world through their cultural lenses. Students of color, poverty, linguistically diverse, and those with limited abilities continue to be positioned as "other" as defined by the dominant culture. As context and culture are removed, culturally responsive pedagogy then loses its emancipatory and empowering focus as it becomes a set of lessons based on cultural attributes within each sub-group population, creates cultural understanding through conflict resolution and continues to position the sub-group population as "different" as compared to the position of the "normal" dominant culture.

Empowerment is at the core of the Ladson-Billings definition as she has defined cultur-ally responsive teaching as pedagogy that uses student culture in order to maintain it and to transcend the negative effects of the dominant culture. Specifically, culturally responsive teaching is a pedagogy that empowers students intellectually, socially, emotionally, and polit-ically by using cultural referents to impart knowledge, skills, and attitudes.[1] Culturally responsive pedagogy is often subsumed under the multicultural education banner. While this might be a logical position for this methodology, I will argue that culturally responsive ped-agogy that is not linked to a social reconstructivist position and taught through the eman-cipatory pedagogy or critical teaching framework will result in supporting the status quo by maintaining the position of "other" based on but not limited to race, gender, class, ability, and/or sexual orientation.

The first part of this chapter will honor the "voice" of African American high school students, from a Midwest urban district who participated in a study to learn their percep-tions and definitions of culturally responsive pedagogy and its impact on teacher practice, and empowerment. Second, I will situate culturally responsive pedagogy as a reform model and teaching practice within the larger concept of multicultural education. Last, I will address the re-positioning of culturally responsive pedagogy as an emancipatory framework not merely a teaching strategy for and about "others."

African American students' perceptions: 4Rs = Culturally responsive Pedagogy

(Portions of this chapter are in Soto and Swadener (Eds.) (2005) *Power and Voice in Research with Children*)

The African American high school students in this study defined culturally responsive pedagogy as the 4Rs Theory—Relationship, Respect, Responsibility, and Relevancy. They believed that the 4Rs transcended the classroom, not only represented effective teaching practices, but also supported the learning community as a whole and helped students learn to navigate in the world. Students agreed that their definition reflected similar findings in the original premises of the research of Ladson-Billings.[2] At the same time, while all four components were necessary, these African American high school students clearly identified relationships as the key foundational component to their theory.

Relationship

Students in this study identified several ways in which educators could establish a strong rela-tionship with a student. First, students expected the educator, whether the building admin-istrator or teacher, to be personable, caring, trustworthy, and have an interest and understanding of the lives of their African American students. Trust and caring were by far the most difficult terrain to traverse as teachers. For students, trust was demonstrated by the teacher in not revealing any information given by the student to anyone else. Clearly there were circumstances when the "trust" had to be broken. Caring was also a difficult line as LaShika (18, female) described an African American female teacher as someone whose "intentions were good," but she was identified as a "real busy body." Still, students in this study agreed that the relationship needs to be personal, a one-on-one opportunity to reflect and learn with an adult. "Ms. E. who is African American was good; she was a real good teacher. She was like, I mean she can just talk to you. I could have a little conversation about anything" (Nickole, Grade 10). Tyreek spoke of the principal in similar terms when he stated, "Mr. Okey [principal] really cares about the students, you know as people. He took some time just gettin' to know me" (Tyreek, alumnus, age 20).

The second way teachers could establish relationships was in the divulging of personal opinion and other information about significant issues from outside of school. Tony, one of four teachers identified by the students as teaching from the 4Rs perspective, described a personal experience that he shared with students:

> And so I lost her [his mother] in December of 1995 to cancer—ten-year-long battle—which was devastating to me and I shared a lot of things with the kids. We talked about it through the years, and they've kind of been with me to see me through. Because they're kind of like a reality check. You can talk about anything with the kids. Hi honey [to a student who entered the room]. (Tony, teacher)

Last, teachers established strong relationships by understanding the life experience of the individual students in their classrooms and not being perceived as judgmental of the various situations. Students spoke openly about issues of racism and their desire to not be "lumped together" as a group. While students did not believe that teachers had to live in Yeardley in order to know them, they did believe that teachers had to extend themselves to understand their experience as young African Americans. India stated, "I mean like Tony [social studies teacher], he know what we go through a lot more, and he's a White man" (India, Grade 12).

The personal relationship for these African American high school students was not only linked to the school as community, but also their perceptions of what it meant to be an adult. An adult for them represented independence from being in a subservient position and teachers, who allowed for student voice, utilized multiple methods of assignments and assessment, and were flexible, were perceived by students as treating them as "adults." This created an environment whereby students felt respected; their opinions honored and created a significant difference in the learning environments represented by their middle school and elementary school experience. Racism also impacted relationships as all students spoke of it as "normal kind of things" (India, 18), like being followed in a mall or being routinely being pulled over by police. This assumption of "normalcy" or internalized oppression created the need for students to excel somewhere in relationship with an adult as an adult; as an equal instead of in another subservient role. Teachers who sought a relationship with students adhered to the boundaries and gave the respective student a place for his or her voice, thus establishing a partnership with these students and creating an alliance allowing for more significant learning to take place. This did not mean that the students did not have the choice to participate in non-learning activities. However it did allow for the opportunity and freedom to do so, which is the norm for being an adult.

Respect and Responsibility

The students linked respect and responsibility together since they respected a teacher who was responsible for creating a safe learning environment and acted in a professional manner. Central to respect was the honoring and respecting of student "voice," and responsibility was acting in a professional manner. Combined, the students equated respect and responsibility with professionalism, which included high expectations for learning, and multiple ways in which to learn and demonstrate knowledge. Several key components of respect and responsibility were identified by the students. Teachers they respected created an environment where the student "voice" permeated the classroom instruction and decisions for instruction were based on their needs. "They treated me with more respect. They, they broke things down for me" (Al, Grade 11). Nickole, Grade 10, struggled in some of her classes and also needed teachers to "break it down" so that she could understand. The term "break it down" did not mean "to simplify" or imply a lack of intellect. Rather it was a process by which students could understand components of the idea and through learning activities gain the understanding necessary to rebuild it for complete comprehension. The teachers' understanding of how to meet the needs of the students was a "signal" of respect and responsibility.

> M.: So it was you determining what to study. Is that right?
> Nickole: Um hum.
> M.: Do you like that? How does that make you feel?
> Nickole: I'm in control of my learnin.'
> M.: Do you have that option in other classes?
> Nickole: No, not really.

Not surprisingly, most students in the study placed full responsibility for establishing high expectations within the learning environment on the teacher. Aaron and Al, both juniors, were the only students who specifically stated that the students had some responsibility in this relationship, but also put the burden on teachers to understand the needs and learning styles of each student. "So I think it's just, it's somewhat like a fifty-fifty exchange like," Aaron said, (Grade 11) while Al added "Just sit down, you do your job, I do my job and everything will be straight" (Al, Grade 11).

A third component of respect and responsibility was demonstrated in the teaching practice itself and has a clear overlap with relevancy. The students were looking for teaching practice that had:

(a) High academic expectations.
(b) Was connected with each student's learning needs.
(c) Provided multiple ways for students to learn and demonstrate their knowledge. Respect and responsibility was also demonstrated by the ability of the teacher to.
(d) Make a link between students' prior knowledge.
(e) Clearly articulate a "usefulness" for today and the future.

Relevancy

"They [teachers] need to help it [subject] be good for me today. If I can't use it, why teach it?" (Aaron, Grade 11)

For the African American high school students in this study, relevancy was the ability of the teacher to make a link between prior knowledge, and to understand and utilize each student's life outside of the classroom, and to offer a glimpse into a possible future. Tommy, one of four teachers students identified as teaching from a foundation of relevancy, was observed working on a project in his communication classes. He was dubbing a student-produced film, to illustrate student voice while simultaneously giving students experience in real-world applications of communication technology.

> Okay, this thing that we did that you saw me editing in the class was in a movie. They [students] went through the facets of all they have to go through to put a movie together. For example they have to decide in this scene, what type of music do we wanna use, what's gonna be our dialog. It had to be relevant. Does it pertain to the plot? And so you put them [the students] in the mix. And that's what I mean by the student going into the classroom. And I mean you saw them out there on the screen, you, you didn't see me anywhere. I'm not even in it. (Tommy, communication media teacher)

Al (Grade 11) spoke of Reggie, one of the four teachers identified, and his ability to make instruction relevant for the class. He said, "But yet it may be the hardest class I have, said Al, but it's the funnest, too, because he makes it, he puts a, the lesson to where I can relate to it and some of the students too. But if you can put it to something like I can relate to or something or just break it down, I will learn things" (Al, Grade 11).

Both Nickole (Grade 10) and Tyreek (alumnus) spoke of specific programs and class-time devoted to future planning.

"In one class I be plannin' for the future. Like things we think we would be interested in. Like, um, read about it and do reports on it so we will know exactly what we want to do in the future" (Nickole, Grade 10).

"I was part of the 'Jump-start' program ever since the sixth grade" and they kept tellin' us "you gotta do it in school to get ready for college. This is what you do when you wanna get into college. I think that's what help make me, you know what I'm sayin'?" (Tyreek, alumnus).

The cultural relevancy model created by Ladson-Billings was predicated on three components, which included teacher–student relationships, knowledge as a socially constructed phenomenon, and teacher beliefs about his or her profession and the students in their classrooms. It was suggested in this study that the students supported the tenets of the framework developed by Ladson-Billings. However, without that personal connectedness,[3] and the Relationship component of the "4R's theory" (Relationship, Respect, Responsibility, and Relevancy), respect would be withheld, relevancy questioned and students of color would continue to be relegated to secondary status in society. The African American students at Maya Angelou High School asked for the subject matter to be presented in a manner that acknowledged that they were intelligent, creative in presentation, and constant student involvement in the process (Respect). Second, when their perspectives were requested, and their "voices" heard, students seemed to respond in a positive manner as demonstrated by the teachers who were identified by the students as "bein' real" (Relationship). Third, students also admired teachers for their curriculum choices which centered on or was related to their African American heritage (Relevancy). Fourth, while relevancy was linked often with "learnin' for today," students also had to see a link between what they were learning now and how it could affect them in their careers and life. Last, students admired those teachers immensely for their intellectual demands, their development as "thinkers" and the knowledge and enthusiasm the teachers showed for their subject area and the community (Responsibility).

Multicultural Education: Historical Context

The only question which concerns us here is whether these "educated" persons are actually equipped to face the ordeal before them or whether it, unbeknownst to them, contributes to their own undoing by perpetuating the regime of the oppressor.[4]

The African American high school student's perception about culturally responsive pedagogy makes conscious ways in which oppression works and empowers them to raise questions and take action. The pedagogy that most clearly articulated the study of power, racism and empowerment was begun in the ethnic studies movement of the late nineteenth century and early twentieth century. Schooling was perceived as the way in which to assimilate new citizens and was soundly rejected by the African American population that was here. Led by DuBois and supported in historical scholarship of Williams, they did not separate the indoctrination of racism as part of the consciousness of the former slaves and their families.[5] Education was seen as a vehicle to ensure that slavery would not be forgotten while continuing to move forward as members of the society. Schools were opened throughout the country but with a shortage of teachers to teach, DuBois concurred that if the Negro was to learn, he must teach himself, and the most effective help that could be given him was the establishment of schools to train Negro teachers.[6]

Intergroup education movement followed in the early 1930s and also had an impact on multicultural education as we know it. Its major goal was to help reduce prejudice and create interracial understanding among students from diverse national, religious, and racial groups.[7] While its focus was on intercultural interactions within a common culture, intergroup education did *not* address issues related to institutionalized racism, power, and structural inequality.[8] The return to ethnic studies occurred again by the late 1960s as African Americans, disillusioned with the slowness and ineffectiveness of desegregation demanded university courses focused on the life of African Americans. The questions of control and purpose of education came to a powerful and violent struggle during the mid-1960s as the Civil Rights Movement forced schools to change, albeit, superficially.

The Civil Rights Movement, alive with its particular traditions of liberation, provided the spark; the war in Vietnam gave a lurid illumination to the system's deficiencies: its incipient violence; its injustices; its racism; its indifference to public opinion and demand. The short-lived effort to reform education and provide compensation for damages done by poverty and discrimination could not halt the radical critique of America's schools.[9]

Multicultural Education: Reform and Practice

Banks, like other foundational developers of multicultural education in the United States were all influenced by ethnic studies founders and were working in ethnic studies prior to participating in the formation of multicultural education.[10] While multicultural education has its origins in ethnic studies, multicultural theorizing has many different ideas and various viewpoints. Because theorists work from a variety of disciplines and training and situated viewpoints, multicultural education may be practiced from vastly different foundations depending on the region of the United States or country of the world. The multiple perspectives alluded to have led to a wide variety of meaning as to what multicultural education is. While the definitions are many, they fall within four categories including an (a) idea or philosophy, (b) reform movement, (c) process not product, and (d) instructional program. For the purposes of this chapter, I will only focus on its role as a reform movement and practice, which support the students' ideas about culturally responsive pedagogy as a high-quality teaching practice.

Multicultural education is an idea, an educational reform movement, and a process whose major goal it is to change the structure of educational institutions.[11] This original construct was expanded to include a larger group of people as well as supporting the social reconstructivist position. While all theorists recognized that there were ramifications with classroom instruction, most believed that multicultural education is a process and not a product. As such, it is a way of thinking and behaving within education and influences the entire schooling philosophy, process, and practice.

Taking this one step further, the African American high school students in this study argued that their definition of culturally responsive pedagogy would not have the impact to cause a change in the learning environment or empower them to be change agents without a commitment to help them learn how to challenge, question, and change the status quo. Al (18) attended a forum on racism and put it this way, "they coulda went through an extra step just to give real people who are really in school and really talk about race. I think people more my age or a little older than I am could have done much better because they woulda spoken honestly without worryin' about tryin' to impress everybody else." Students in this study wanted to participate and engage in a learning community that honored their voice and they wanted to learn strategies in making their voices and opinions heard. For this author, the obvious connection is to engage in teaching practice from a foundation in critical social theory and education that is multicultural creating a practice that reflects critical multicultural theory. To be critical, an inquiry must also challenge directly underlying human interests and ideologies. The task of critical theory is to penetrate the world of things to show the underlying relations between persons ... to see the human bottom of non-human things. Critical social theory is criticism of ideology created by dominant society which prevents agents in the society from correctly perceiving their true situation and real interests.[12] The ideology or false consciousness serves society to mask social contradictions,[13] including diverting attention away from real interests. It is the "diversion" that students believed is the practice of today and where they believed their 4Rs theory would be most susceptible and demonstrated in what they would call "fake" teaching. "C'mon Ms. V., you know when they [teachers] really don't care about your opinion, you're just supposed to give them the answers they want. We go to Mr. Tony's class if we want to have a challenging discussion" (India, 18).

Multicultural Education and Culturally Responsive Pedagogy

Supported by the African American students in this study, the teaching and learning practice that best represents the philosophy of critical multiculturalism is culturally responsive pedagogy. This evolution of multicultural education from theory to reform model, to emancipatory and culturally responsive practice allows for a pedagogy that challenges the relationship between "difference" and "other," and creates the opportunity for all members and especially those who have been historically underserved to challenge prevailing assumptions. This offers the students the opportunity to question and gain a critical perspective as too often, it seems the point is to promote the appearance of difference within intellectual discourse, a "cele-bration" that fails to ask who is sponsoring the party and who is extending the invitations.[14] Students in this study were suggesting that we need a rewriting of difference as difference-in-relation followed by attempts to dramatically change the material conditions that allow exploitation to prevail over relations of equality and social justice.[15]

Conclusion

With the imposition of the No Child Left Behind Act on education, educators are responding in a lock-step fashion in requesting help in seeking teaching strategies to help historically underserved students be successful in schools. They are turning toward culturally responsive pedagogy which the African American high school students in this study would argue is an appropriate pedagogical practice. It supports the education of the student from their specific cultural framework while addressing real-world issues in an effort to empower students to wrestle with "big questions" develop strategies with their peers to address them and take action to change the world in which they live. Education in the name of cultural relevancy can also be used to maintain the status quo as it diverts attention from empowerment to become a tool of unrelated activities with little academic expectations or empowerment as a goal. No Child Left Behind has caused the conversation to focus on sub-group populations which is probably a good thing. However, as a consequence this national obsession has translated teaching practice into a learning process to "fix those" kids. Without empowerment at the core of the practice, culturally responsive pedagogy is reduced to another missed opportunity for historically marginalized students and the purpose of schooling to maintain the status quo, and sort people into expected occupations is served again by the national agenda.

NOTES

1   G. Ladson-Billings, *The Dreamkeepers: Successful Teachers of African American Children* (San Francisco: Jossey-Bass, 1994).

2   Ladson-Billings, *The Dreamkeepers*.

3   L. Depit, *Other People's Children: Cultural Conflict in theClassroom* (New York: The New Press, 1995).

4   C. Woodson, *The Mis-education of the Negro*. 6th ed. (Trenton, NJ: Africa World Press, 1990).

5   W. E. B. DuBois, *Black Reconstruction* (New York: Harcourt Brace, 1935); G. Williams, *History of the Negro Race in America from 1619 to 1880: Negroes as Slaves, as Soldiers, and as Citizens 2* (New York: G. P. Putnam's Sons, 1882–1883).

6   DuBois, *Black Reconstruction*.

7   J. A. Banks and C. Banks, *Handbook of Research on Multicultural Education* (New York: Simon and Schuster Macmillan, 1995).

8   Banks and Banks, *Handbook of Research on Multicultural Education*.

9   M. Greene, "In search of a critical pedagogy," *Harvard Educational Review*, 56(4) (1986): pp. 427–441.

10   Banks and Banks, *Handbook of Research on Multicultural Education*.

11   Banks and Banks, *Handbook of Research on Multicultural Education*.

12   R. Geuss, *The Idea of a Critical Theory: Habermas and the Frankfurt School* (New York: Cambridge University Press, 1984).

13   B. Fay, *Critical Social Science* (Ithaca, NY: Cornell University Press, 1987).

14   b. hooks, *Yearning: Race, Gender, and Cultural Politics* (Boston: South End Press, 1990).

15   P. L. McLaren, "White terror and oppositional agency: Towards a critical multiculturalism," in C. Sleeter, and P. McLaren, eds. *Multicultural Education, Critical Pedagogy, and the Politics of Difference* (Albany: SUNY Press, 1995),, pp. 199–217.

9. Spoken Word and Hip Hop

The Power of Urban Art and Culture

PRIYA PARMAR AND BRYONN BAIN

In the most populace of American cities, one can attend a spoken word poetry reading or hip hop concert any night of the week. Hip hop and spoken word poetry embody a postmodern aesthetic in that they reach a wide range of audiences at national and international levels, regardless of race, culture, and ethnicity. In a cultural context, both use powerful language to articulate the experiences and marginality that African American and Latino working-class people experience. Rap music and spoken word give voice to these communities and other groups protesting the oppressive conditions experienced in the neighborhood, workplace, and institutions of learning.

The art of spoken word, a revival of oral poetry movements dating back to ancient times, utilizes the dynamic range of the voice and engages the nuances of vernacular speech. Commonly referred to as simply "spoken word," the naming of the form itself stands in contrast to the "written word" in which the verse of the Western literary canon is traditionally composed and experienced. "Performance poetry" has also been used interchangeably with spoken word poetry. Both terms suggest the meaning of a spoken word poem cannot be realized completely until performed or recited. As one pioneering spoken wordsmith of the renowned Nuyorican Poets Café observes, "A performance poem is a poem written to be performed . . ."

Spoken word poets regularly appear as "opening acts" for major hip hop artists at rap concerts, and their poetry has an increasingly noteworthy presence in theater, film and on television. As a result, there are incresingly more of writing conferences and poetry-oriented programs for urban youth, such as Youth Speaks and the Living Word Project in California, Young Chicago Authors in Illinois, and Urban Word in New York. With the widespread popularity of poetry "slam" competitions, literary poets, historically embraced by publishing houses and academic institutions, now have a far more considerable audience than they once had. Thousands of graduate students are also enrolled in Master of Fine Arts programs across the country seeking to further hone their writing and performance skills.

Hip hop culture is experienced worldwide in a variety of contexts. Briefly, the original elements of hip hop culture are described as follows: (a) graffiti art also referred to as "graf writing" (b) DJing (deejaying), also referred to as "turntabling;" (c) MCing (emceeing) also referred to as "rhyming" or "rapping" and (d) b-boying, a gendered reference to the style of hip hop dance, commonly referred to as "breakin" and "break-dancing," which was also popularized by "b-girls" from its inception.

Mainstream media and postmodern techno-culture have capitalized on hip hop culture as evidenced by the increasing number of advertisements, films, and television programs that use it to attract audiences to buy products. Other obvious examples are the selling of clothing lines, especially athletic clothing and footwear, beverages (both alcoholic and non-alcoholic), and beauty/make-up products. Although all four elements of hip hop culture exist simultaneously, MCs have been the focus of mainstream media attention because rap was more easily packaged, marketed, and profited from as a commercial product than the other three elements.

The high quantity of sales and profit rap music has garnered may account for the flood of images of rap artists used to merchandise various products. According to the Recording Industry Association of America (RIAA), rap's share of the popular music market doubled from the late 1980s to the 1990s. Rap and rhythm "n" blues together accounted for 23% of sales in 1990, up from 16% in 1989. Because the popularity and sales of rap music alone skyrocketed so much in 1998, the RIAA announced that rap was the best-selling musical genre in the United States. Furthermore, what had traditionally been known as "Black music" had crossed the color line. In fact, Nielsen SoundScan, a company that tracks retail sales, found that in 2001 more than 70% of rap consumers were white suburban youth. In 2003, for example, Soundscan found that Rap and R&B songs comprised 70% of the top 40 songs that made the weekly top 100 list in 2003. It should be noted that these sales figures and statistics do not account for the widely popular practice of selling bootleg copies (a lower quality replica of a tape, movie, or CD), thus resulting in a misleading gauge of rap's popularity. In addition, advances in computer technology have allowed easy and often virtually free access to songs downloaded (or file sharing) from the Internet, making it even more difficult to accurately depict the sales or distribution of any musical genre, much less determine the racial, cultural, and/or ethnic makeup of its consumers.

Mainstream media tend to over-publicize, over-glamorize, and over-glorify those rap lyrics that promote sexist, violent ("gangsta" rap), homophobic images, thus, perpetuating false perceptions and stereotypes of African American, Latino, and other marginalized people who represent the music and culture. hip hop poet and slam champion Jerry Quickley explains that while hip hop may be the most revolutionary artistic movement to emerge in the last hundred years, it is riddled with all of the problems and contradictions any global movement with millions of participants can be expected to possess. The problems are not the hip hop stars of the moment, but those he refers to as the "gatekeepers": massively consolidated radio conglomerates, concert promoters, and record executives (CBS, Polygram, Warner, BMG, Capitol-EMI, and MCA who, by 1990, controlled record chain distribution) effectively control what rap music is released, and place the vast majority of their resources behind. Today's commercial hip hop music, according to poet/actor Saul Williams, is mainly concerned with the portrayal of rough street life with little hope of reaching success, or over-representations of material wealth reflected through designer wear and lifestyles with virtually no critical analysis or social commentary. As media conglomerates capitalized on an increasingly white suburban hip hop consumer base, commercial rap records have come to be criticized by hip hop generation poets as no more than " . . . amazing ways to talk about the same ol' shit."

Quickley also maintains that "underground hip hop" represents the overwhelming body of rap music produced globally. Unfortunately, regardless of their work's content, most of these artists never receive nearly the support their talent warrants. The commercialization and over-amplification of a very narrow segment of rap music is a problem that has inspired many hip hop generation poets to seek other forms of creative expression. Although spoken word poetry began to provide a space beyond these tensions more than a decade ago, as the art form has been increasingly popularized and commodified, the circumstances constraining the evolution of rap music threaten to arise within the spoken word arena as well.

Although the following series of essays is not an exhaustive account of the rich aesthetic traditions that comprise hip hop culture or the spoken word movement, we attempt to present an introduction to the historical evolution of both. Our position is that hip hop and spoken word provide legitimate forms of a cultural pedagogy worthy of study and practice within the context of urban education, in both public schools and teacher education programs. Cultural workers must be knowledgeable, well-informed, and respectful of the history of these cultural and artistic forms for their inclusion in the classroom to be effective.

The first part of this series, entitled "Spoken Word: From the Ancient Storyteller to the Urban Scribes," traces the history of the spoken word movement, from its roots in ancient civilizations to the Black Arts Movement of the 1960s and 1970s, continuing into and beyond the postmodern era. The second series entitled, "The Original Elements of Hip Hop Culture: Tags, Beats, Rhymes, and Breaks," explains the evolution of hip hop, describing how the four urban elements from which hip hop emerged have contributed to the development of a broader cultural phenomenon. The second series ends with a brief description of how hip hop has evolved to include other elements such as fashion and entrepreneurship.

Finally, we conclude with "Poetry of the Oppressed: Pedagogy of the Urban Lyricist" which examines hip hop culture and spoken word poetry as postmodern texts. Based on the work of Brazilian educator Paulo Freire, we argue that the implementation of hip hop and spoken word is an empowering, liberating pedagogy for students, educators, and prospective educators in teacher education programs.

The Spoken Word: From Ancient Storytellers to Urban Scribes

The Origins of the Spoken Word

Spoken word poetry is a contemporary art form fusing elements of verse, music, and theater. Though widely popular throughout the United States in the early twenty-first century, its roots can be traced from the protest songs of the Civil Rights Era, to the blues and sermonic traditions of the American South, and as far back as the ancient storytelling tradition of the African "griots." Historical influences notwithstanding, the unprecedented global impact of hip hop culture, and specifically rap music, have helped to usher into existence this renaissance of oral poetry which simultaneously defies, embraces, and expands the boundaries of previous poetic movements.

The current literature suggests this popular revival of poetry has been marginalized by academia in part because of its emphasis on oral performance. Not only has spoken word been relegated to the status of "poor poetry" by some academic critics, it is written off entirely by others as not poetry at all. As a cultural practice inextricably linked to African oral traditions, this tendency is consistent with colonial scholarship which has historically dismissed the oral traditions of pre-colonial African societies as "primitive". Zulu praise-poems, for example, were once labeled "artless and uninformed repetitions of tribal culture" and considered no more than a "crude accompaniment to tribal dancing."

Although such highbrow mandates for what poetry ought to be are not the source of this turn-of-the century movement, their popular rejection has certainly helped it to gather momentum. While a "poetry" section has yet to be included in most record stores in America, you are more likely to come across a compact disc bin with recordings labeled "spoken word." Titles such as the compilation, "Eargasms," or "All That and a Bag of Words," or even "Grand Slam! The Best of the National Poetry Slam," are among those commercial releases categorized under this heading.

Historical Significance of the Spoken Word

Oral poetry is by no means an anomaly in human civilization. On the contrary, it is a recurring aspect of cultures around the world, from the meditative poetry of the Eskimo to the mediaeval European and Chinese ballads. Oral poets have composed and passed through the generations the lengthy praise-poem honoring the nineteenth century Zulu warrior Shaka, with hundreds of lines of verse, as well as the compact imagery of the Somali "miniature" lyric. Orally composed European works such as the Homeric epics, *The Iliad*, and *The Odyssey*, have passed through the generations in written form and become the subject of widespread Western scholarship.

It has been argued that the epic is the most developed form of oral poetry. The epic is a form that has been widely disseminated throughout the world for several millennia. Consistent with other epics passed on from generations past, the legendary epic of Mali, "Sunjata," comprises a long narrative poem emphasizing the heroic. The category runs the gamut from the Congolese Mwindo, the early Irish Tain Bo Cuailgne, lengthy nineteenth and twentieth century epics recorded in the former Soviet Union, and the West Sumatra recordings of Anggun Nan Tungga, whose recitation takes as much as seven nights to complete. Other epics range from the sacred works such as the Indian Mahabharata, and the ancient Sumerian epic of Gilgamesh, to the "Gesar" epic circulated throughout Tibet, Mongolia, and China. For centuries, the essential aspects of the extensive Gesar epic have survived dissemination throughout a vast region reaching parts of China, Tibet, and Mongolia. Even more astounding is the Indian Rgveda, containing 10 books, over 1000 hymns, and approximately 40,000 lines which has been handed down orally since its composition around 1500-100 BC.

Through the ages, the yogis and seers of India have worshipped the "word" god. Yet the Hindus are not alone in placing this centrality on the human utterance. The Judeo-Christian tradition also attaches mystic significance to the sacred word. In the Bible, the first audible expression is considered the earliest and most exalted sign of life: "In the beginning was the word, and the word was God." The Islamic tradition reserves a comparable sanctity within its doctrine of the mystical word. Parallels of this kind can also be found in the traditions of the Zoroastrians, whose religion predates the lives of Buddha, Christ, or Mohammed.

The power of the spoken word holds a sacred position in religious and spiritual traditions the world over. Whether through mantras, prayers, hymns or calls to worship, the link between these varied traditions lies in the understanding that the sound vibrations of a particular utterance possess the power to bring about change. This belief is the ancient seed sprouting forth from the fertile soil of urban America in the spoken word movement today.

Spoken Word Poetry Today

Since the 1990s, the spoken word poetry movement has given rise to the re-surfacing of poetry on the American cultural landscape. Poets now perform and workshop their original work at community centers, colleges and universities, correctional facilities, coffee houses, poetry cafes, and open mike nights in bars and clubs nationwide. The performance of poetry has become so widespread that it is increasingly common for poets to tour the nation sharing their poems with audiences in each state in the union. Every year a different American city hosts a poetry tournament, which brings together teams of performance poets from over fifty US cities and Canada to compete for a national title.

As with other examples of oral poetry, the spoken word must be experienced in context to be fully comprehended. If the performance space or time is changed, or if the same piece is performed by another poet or before a different audience, the identity of the poem is altered. The performance is not peripheral, rather it is an integral part of a "communicative event" requiring both the oral delivery of the poet and the aural reception of the audience. The mood of the audience, the ability and attitude of the performer, the purpose and location of the event, the sound, lighting, and aura of the venue, as well as the sequence of performers are all aspects that may contribute to the meaning of a poem. The verbal text may be recorded and replayed, but audio and visual recordings fall short of capturing the full effect of a live performance poem.

Early Twentieth-Century Influences:
Uptown Blues and Downtown Beats (1920s–1950s)

The Harlem Renaissance and Langston Hughes

As the final shots of World War I were being fired, a cultural explosion began roaring through the streets and salons of New York City's Upper West Side. Between 1917 and 1935, a northern migration spawned a renaissance that transformed Harlem into the epicenter of the African experience in the Americas. Initially referred to as the "The New Negro Movement", The Harlem Renaissance marked an era when black artistic expression was redefined. Poets and writers such as James Weldon Johnson, Claude McKay, Georgia Douglas Johnson, Jean Toomer, Sterling Brown, Anne Spencer, Arna Botemps, Countee Cullen, and Angelina Grimke were among the most influential figures of this era.

While Marcus Mosiah Garvey mobilized millions with the Universal Negro Improvement Association (UNIA), white patrons funded the high-society black writers and artists that Zora Neale Hurston dubbed the Harlem "Niggerati." Seeking to embrace and honor the essence of black folk culture, Langston Hughes chose not to emulate his "New Negro" peers then mastering traditional western literary forms. Along with noted writers such as Jean Toomer and Claude McKay, Hughes experimented courageously. Enduring the chastisement of poets more concerned with gaining acceptance among white patrons of Negro literature, Hughes drew inspiration from the folk *orature* of blues artists such as Gertrude "Ma" Rainey and Bessie Smith in much of his poetry.

In so doing, Hughes laid a rebellious aesthetic foundation that would be emulated by generations of poets to follow. Hughes' profound respect for his own heritage and history, as well as his personal struggles with race, class, and sexuality, foreshadowed much of the terrain to be traversed by poets for the remainder of the century ahead. Indeed, aspects of

Hughes's celebration of folk culture are echoed in the later work of Bob Kaufman, Ted Joans, and the Beat poets.

The Beat Poets

Having grown up during a dismal depression and survived the Second World War, in 1948 Jack Kerouac coined the phrase that would become widely used to describe the post-war sense of malaise experienced by his immediate circle of writers: the beat generation. Notions of spiritual enlightenment, sexual liberation, and what was commonly considered "anti-establishment" values inspired the writings of the Beat poets.

Like Langston Hughes, Kerouac would abandon a life of letters at Columbia University and ultimately become one of the most influential poets of his generation. The quintessential "beatnik," he is lauded as a legend among contemporary poets in part because of another manner in which he followed Hughes's footsteps. By looking to jazz and the blues tradition to inspire his experimental writings, and dismissing the standards established by the academic poetry critics of his day, Kerouac mirrored the improvisation of black American folk music in his spontaneous writings. Like many spoken word poets writing and performing today, Kerouac sought not to see "what the poem was," but to see "what life is," and to demonstrate that beauty in the creation of the poem.

His close friend and fellow poet, Allen Ginsberg, looked to the cadence of popular speech, song, and various aspects of the Biblical tradition for inspiration. Well-known for his avant-garde poetics, politics, and experimentation with illegal drugs, Ginsberg's personal life also paralleled that of Hughes in that both challenged the dominant mores with regard to sexuality. Furthermore, Kerouac and Ginsberg both possessed an extraordinary stage presence that resonates remarkably with the performance-oriented culture of spoken word poetry today. In 1956, a historic Bay-area reading by Ginsberg pointed further in the direction of movements to come by recognizing the need for poets to do more than merely read or recite poetry to an audience. More than any other work of that time, his performance of "Howl" is said to have been a prelude of the performance poetry that would emerge nearly half a century later.

The Beats' image as drug-induced, renegade-roadsters came to symbolize a national counterculture that only began to wane in the late1960s. With Vietnam emerging as the next arena of international conflict, social and political art saw increasing prominence. With the assassination of Rev. Dr. Martin Luther King Jr., shortly after he spoke publicly in opposition to the Vietnam War, the frustrated progress of the Civil Rights advocates would give rise to the more militant demand for Black Power. As it was before, race would once again be an issue of critical concern for the wordsmiths of the day.

Mid-Twentieth Century Influences:
The Black Arts Movement (1965–1975)

The Black Arts Movement was an informal association of black nationalist intellectuals and artists during the mid-1960s to the mid-1970s. Associated with the militant advocacy of armed self-defense, separation from "racist American domination," and pride in and assertion of the goodness and beauty of Blackness, the Black Power and Arts movements brought together participants with a wide range of political and philosophical perspectives, including a spectrum of ideologies reaching from pan-Africanism and ideologies upheld as remnants of pre-colonial societies, to womanism and revolutionary Marxism. The divergent perspectives within the movement were often a source of great debate and controversy, yet consensus was met in the urgent demand for black liberation and self-determination that was heard nationwide.

The notion of "performance art," as an artistic practice referred to as such, was being newly established in the 1960s and 1970s. The predominance of poetry readings during this time was seen as rooted in a "communal tendency" toward the oral tradition. This is in part because of the central place of orality in the traditions enslaved Africans brought to the Americas during the transatlantic slave trade, but was reinforced by laws that made it illegal for slaves to read and write. The continuing impact of this era must be considered here since it is common for the members of the current generation of Black poets to link their artistic work to that of Black Arts pioneers.

Elements of the Movement (Africana and Jazz)

The Role of the Arts

Poetry, drama, and music (especially "free" jazz) were among the most widely enjoyed artistic genres of the era. This was due in part to the facility with which music, theater, and verse could be incorporated into movement events. Protest rallies, marches, speeches, demonstrations, and community organizing meetings were brought to life in innovative ways with the inclusion of the performing arts.

As with the contemporary spoken word movement, it is difficult to pinpoint exactly when the black arts movement began. One possible beginning might be the 1965 founding of the Black Arts Repertory Theater/School (BARTS) in Harlem by Amiri Baraka (Leroi Jones). His Obie Award-winning play, Dutchman, was published in 1964, and by the following year a broader black arts movement had taken hold of the nation. Black musicians were significantly impacted by Black Power politics and Black Arts aesthetics. Anthems recorded by best-selling artists such as James Brown and Curtis Mayfield urged popular music in the direction of black pride, self-love and self-determination with anthems like "Say It Loud (I'm Black and I'm Proud)" and "Keep On Pushing." Among the most visible artists of the movement were jazz musicians like Sun Ra and Archie Shepp.

National Organizations

The Nation of Islam, and specifically its chief spokesman in the 1960s, Malcolm X, introduced many jazz musicians in the 1960s to notions of black consciousness that would later drive the Black Arts Movement. The foundation for the movement was also laid by pioneering organizations like Umbra, a network of black writers that emerged in the Lower East Side of New York City. As artists became involved with organizations like Collective Black Artists in New York, they honed innovative ideas about their traditions and new identities as artists, activists, and intellectuals.

From the ranks of such groups emerged renowned Black Arts activists and intellectuals including Ishmael Reed, David Henderson, and Askia Muhammad Toure. A nationalist politic infused the work of artists in nearly every black community, and on college and university campuses where organizations increasingly engaged the art and culture of the African diaspora. The close of the Black Arts Movement is as much a challenge to locate as its genesis. As the membership of Black Power organizations like the Black Panther Party began to diminish during the mid-1970s, Black Arts groups and activities slipped away as well.

Whenever it came to an end, it was destined to have an impact on art, culture, and politics in America long after it disappeared. Within contemporary hip hop music, for example, strains of the movement's urgency, militancy, and cross-genre aesthetics can be found even today.

Leading Figures of the Movement

Among the leading writers of the Black Arts Movement were playwright Ed Bullins and novelist Toni Morrison, and poets Gil Scott-Heron, Larry Neal and Haki Madhubuti. The work of black editors like Addison Gayle Jr., and scholars such as Harold Cruse, helped to shape the vibrant debates between artists and intellectuals of the day. Musicians like Abbey Lincoln, Max Roach, and Charles Mingus challenged the economic inequalities of the music industry, linked their own experiences with it to larger social issues, and performed explicitly political material.

Amiri Baraka/Leroi Jones

Amiri Baraka is widely regarded as one of the most influential figures of the movement. Baraka's poetry, theater, cultural criticism, and commentary were fiercely radical. He presented the art of the 1960s as an extension of African culture and spirituality, and argued the Black Arts Movement to be the cultural arm of the black liberation struggle. Written off by as anti-white, anti-semitic, sexist, and homophobic by his critics, they could not deny that his work deployed an inspiring vision of unity for black America which proved tremendously significant in defining the widespread public conversation surrounding the "black aesthetic. "

Before founding BARTS, Baraka's work had a critical influence on black nationalist drama throughout the late 1960s. Furthermore, as Salaam observes: Baraka was a highly visible publisher (Yugen and Floating Bear magazines, Totem Press), a celebrated poet (Preface to a Twenty-Volume Suicide Note, 1961, and The Dead Lecturer, 1964), a major music critic (Blues People, 1963), and an Obie Award-winning playwright (Dutchman, 1964). Other than James Baldwin, who at that time had been closely associated with the Civil Rights Movement, Jones was the most respected and most widely published Black writer of his generation.

Nikki Giovanni

A native of Knoxville, Tennessee, Nikki Giovanni is a groundbreaking poet who began writing during the Black Arts Movement and who continues to celebrate black culture and life in her writing today. The poetry books she published in the late 1960s built for her a name as among the most accessible of the young poets voicing the call for black solidarity and revolution.

If Baraka was the most influential male poet, Giovanni's controversial and gendered demand for blacks to, "Learn to kill niggers/Learn to be Black men" led her to emerge as the most influential female writer of the movement. Giovanni was also well-known for dynamic performances of her poetry, and the several albums she recorded of her work set to music, including the best-selling "Truth Is on Its Way" in 1971. In her poetry, as in her essays and speeches, Giovanni continues to celebrate black identity, which she sees as the defining characteristic of African American poets.

Sonia Sanchez

Born Wilsonia Driver in Birmingham, Alabama, Sonia Sanchez moved to Harlem as a young girl. Sanchez has become an influential writer, activist, and educator, focusing on black women's struggle with racism. Sanchez was radicalized first by the Congress for Racial Equality, and then by Malcolm X and the Nation of Islam (NOI). Sanchez parted with the NOI in the early 1970s in protest of the Nation's treatment of women. Much of her poetry from this period, experimental and irreverent in form, content, and presentation, pointed to the problematic nature of the black nationalist project as characterized within Black Arts poetry. Sanchez became known for bravura spoken word performances that sung the cadences of black speech patterns in the United States.

The Last Poets

Despite their name, critics have argued that the Last Poets' innovative and communal lyricism made them the first rap group. In 1968, Abiodun Oyewole, David Nelson, Gylan Kain, and percussionist Nilija formed the original group at a Harlem memorial gathering for

Malcolm X. From their inception, the poetry of the Last Poets represented the militant politics that drove the Black Arts Movement. Their music emphasized both African-inspired
drumming and the spoken word. In the mid-1980s the Last Poets was discovered by a new
audience when young hip hop musicians began sampling and quoting selections of the Last
Poets' songs in their own work.

Late Twentieth Century Influences:
The Poetry of Hip Hop Culture (1970s-present)

Contemporary Poetry Competitions

Hip Hop Battles

Beginning in the late1970s, rap "battles" emerged as the ultimate test of lyrical skill in hip hop
culture. A battle involves at least two lyricists, accompanied by an instrumental track, engaged
in a back-and-forth rhyming competition. Likened to a lyrical boxing match, a victor is customarily determined by audience applause. Increasing with the rising popularity of rap during the 1980s, battle rhymes ultimately came to be recorded, and could either significantly
enhance or severely damage the career of the wordsmith judged to have won or lost.

   Historic rap battles during the early1980s featured clashes involving rap icons such as Kool
Moe Dee and Busy Bee, and the Brooklyn-based rap group UTFO versus. Queens native
Roxanne Shante. One of the most legendary battles of the past three decades featured a feud
between another Queens rapper, MC Shan, and South Bronx-bred KRS-One. KRS-One's classic "The Bridge is Over" was a response record to MC Shan's pioneering release, "The Bridge."

   In the 1990s, Tupac Shakur and the Notorious BIG both topped the charts as fans eagerly
awaited the release of their next battle record. The murders of Tupac and BIG in 1996 and
1997 brought an end to their exchange, and for the next few years high-profile battles on
record came to a hault. More recently, rap stars have revived the tradition by responding
to each other's "diss" records. Most notably, these battles have included clashes between rappers such as Ja-Rule and 50 Cent, Nas and Jay-Z, and the lesser known rapper Ray Benzino,
who only appeared on Billboard's top-selling chart after launching his controversial attack
on multiplatinum rapper Eminem.

From Poetry Bouts to Slam Poetry

In 1981, bartender and poet Al Simmons ran his first "poetry bout" in Chicago. Inspired by
the idea of putting on a lyrical boxing contest, not unlike the rap battles launched years earlier in New York City, Simmons's first bout was a three-fight card featuring a ten-round fight,
billed as the WPA's "Main Event" Poetry Fight. The poets traded poem for poem and verse
for verse. Simmons held two additional bouts later that year in Chicago's Old Town, and

the other at a club in the Wrigley Field area. By the mid-1980s, *The Chicago Tribune* reported of another local poet and performance artist, Marc Smith, who was hosting poetry competitions not entirely unlike Simmons' bouts. Smith dubbed his bard battles "slams" and staged them at the Green Mill Lounge, a landmark jazz bar and former Al Capone Speakeasy, in Chicago's Uptown area.

The poetry slam is a contest in which judges are randomly selected from the audience, and asked to rank each poem performed on a scale of one to ten. While the specifics may vary depending on the particular venue, the initial rules allowed each poet three minutes to perform an original poem. Smith launched the slam in Chicago and encouraged the audience to let each poet know exactly what they thought of their work by reacting to the performance as they saw fit. By establishing an environment in which crowd participation was expected, poetry slams have helped to build a broader audience for the spoken word. The weekly poetry slam in Chicago spread across the nation in the years following its inception, with individual poets and poetry teams from every state in the union ultimately convening for an annual spoken word poetry tournament. More than fifty cities were recently represented in Chicago for the tenth anniversary of the poetry slam. Beyond its rapid spread within the United States, slam championships have been held internationally in England, Germany, Israel, and Sweden.

Smith praises the slam as responsible for bringing together people from diverse backgrounds, moving everyday folks to become passionately involved with art, performance, words and ideas, and having given others a sense of purpose and direction by challenging them to examine themselves. Nonetheless, Smith acknowledges how the slam has also afforded young poets the opportunity to mimic the voice of others they hear on a CD or see on television. He regrets that the wide range of styles, personalities, characters, and subject matter alive in the early years of slam poetry have come to be homogenized into a "rhetorical style" designed to secure winning scores.

Whether it is to the credit of the Chicago-inspired poetry bouts and slams that have swept the nation, or the pioneering New York City rap battles that laid the foundation for the global impact of hip hop culture, spoken word poetry today enjoys a growing worldwide audience in cafes, coffeehouses, concert halls, bars, theaters, and increasingly within the academy. Poetry anthologies seemed to reproduce themselves, literary magazines that would formerly have perished after a year remain in print, independent publishers have gained substantial readership, and there is an abundance of CDs and videos introducing the next generation to new paths to poetry.

The Multimedia Poetry Renaissance

The Impact of the Nuyorican

At the epicenter of the national spoken word explosion is the Nuyorican Poets Café, as well as the various poetry venues its alumni have established over the years: Bar 13, CBGB's

Urbana, and the Bowery Poetry Club. One of the oldest and most influential spoken word cafes in the country, poet and producer Bob Holman brought the poetry slam to the café in the early 1990s. The Nuyorican continues to hold a packed-to-capacity slam each week, in addition to its regular schedule of youth events, theater festivals, and the longest running hip hop open mike night in New York City.

Rap music was propelled into the global spotlight during the first decade of heightened media focus on hip hop culture; 1980s motion pictures like *Wildstyle, Breakin,' Beat Street*, and *Electric Boogaloo*, to name a few, would be followed by the advent of popular television shows such as *Yo MTV Raps* and *The Fresh Prince of Bel Air*. Beginning in the 1990s, a series of theater productions, television shows, and films would similarly bring widespread attention and acclaim to spoken word. While the poetry slam had taken root in Chicago bar rooms and been replicated by thousands around the nation, the multimedia attention that would introduce millions to the art of performance poetry would reflect the aesthetic of artists emerging from New York's innovative underground arts scene, and, most notably, from the Nuyorican.

In 1996, a groundbreaking ensemble musical entitled: *"Bring in Da' Noise, Bring in Da' Funk,"* took Broadway theater by storm. Winning four Tony Awards with the direction of George C. Wolfe, the choreography of Savion Glover, and the poetry of Nuyorican slam champion Reg E. Gaines. In the same year, Emmy-winner Paul Devlin directed a highly regarded feature-length documentary entitled "SlamNation" about the 1996 National Poetry Slam in Portland, Oregon. Devlin approached the event from a sports-journalism perspective, using interviews and live footage of the competition. The performances of record-setting national slam champion and former *Boston Globe* columnist Patricia Smith, newly elected Poetry Slam International president and slam veteran Taylor Mali, and Nuyorican Grand Slam champion Saul Williams, among others, welcomed a new era for poetry in this adrenaline-driven film.

The following year, a Chicago-based poet, performer, author and national slam champion, Regie Gibson, would help catapult the impact of the spoken word movement even further. His life and work were the inspiration for New Line Cinema's 1997 motion picture, "Love Jones," starring Larenz Tate, Nia Long, Bill Bellamy, and Isaiah Washington. In 1998, director Marc Levin's totally improvised, low-budget film, *Slam*, was named Best Feature Film at the Sundance Film Festival with a multicultural cast including the same acclaimed hip hop-inspired poet who had entered the spotlight two years earlier in Devlin's documentary, Saul Williams. Another Nuyorican wordsmith previously featured with Williams in "SlamNation" appeared as a character appropriately named "Poet" on the prison drama "Oz." Using the poetic sensibility poet/actor Mums the Schema had also honed at the Lower East Side cafe, Homicide producer Tom Fontana took viewers inside a fictive experimental correctional facility, and worked to bring a philosophical perspective to incarceration in this HBO series.

In 2001, a film capturing the true story of the turbulent life of Puerto Rican poet, playwright, actor, and Nuyorican founder, Miguel Piñero, was released by Miramax Films.

"Piñero" tells the story of a Latino icon who captivated New York City's elite in the 1970s and 1980s. Piñero was a formerly-incarcerated Tony Award-nominee, a heroin addict whose poetry was a pre-cursor to hip hop, and a writer of hit TV shows whose life was cut short at age forty. The film chronicles his rise from prison to his work in the renowned New York Public Theater and his success on Broadway with his play "Short Eyes."

By December of 2001, HBO aired its first season of Def Poetry Jam. This televised show-case has featured both well-established and up-and-coming poets from across the country, and was accompanied by the release of the 283-page anthology, "Bum Rush the Page: A Def Poetry Jam," edited by acclaimed poet Tony Medina. This weekly 30-minute TV series placed spoken word center-stage in homes throughout the United States and abroad, using the revised format of its predecessor, Def Comedy Jam, also backed by hip hop mogul Russell Simmons and aired on HBO. A staged version of this televised poetry reading soon followed at the Longacre Theater in New York City. Simmons once again enlisted the expertise of Stan Lathan, along with a hip hop DJ, and a dynamic troupe of young, seasoned poets to present Def Poetry Jam on Broadway. Six of the nine poets comprising the cast, from cultural backgrounds as vastly different as acclaimed Palestinian author/activist Suheir Hammad and internationally renowned Chinese-Jamaican performance poet Stacey-Ann Chin, joined the Tony-award winning show after several years of performing at the Nuyorican as well.

Despite the acclaim the show has received, critics argue that the popularization of poetry under the Def Poetry Jam brand threatens the integrity of the art form. Medina makes clear his apprehension with regard to the rush of poets to gain the exposure offered by these televised and staged shows. In the opening pages of Bum Rush the Page, he argues that not all poets who are referred to as "spoken word artists" are genuinely concerned with performing poetry to promote social change; rather they are in the "business" in hopes of gaining approval or status. As a result, serious poets, especially artists of color, are not taken seriously as writers.

The Original Elements of Hip Hop Culture:
Tags, Beats, Rhymes, and Breaks

Hip hop originated in the predominantly African American, economically-depressed South Bronx section of New York City. This borough experienced radical changes in the 1960s because of poor urban planning, which included construction of an expressway through the heart of the Bronx and a huge apartment complex, which later was sold to slumlords because of its high vacancy rates. Thus, the neighborhood deteriorated, leaving many run-down and vacant buildings. When middle class families of Italian, German, Irish, and Jewish descent moved out of the Bronx because of the diminishing quality of life, poor African American and Hispanic families soon replaced them. There was a rise in crime, drug addiction, and unemployment. Eventually, these poor living conditions and economic disparities led young people to engage in graffiti painting, DJing, MCing, and b-boying, which comprise hip hop culture. Many people predicted hip hop would be a passing fad or trend, but this "fad" endured and came to be known as hip hop culture.

Tags or Graffiti Art

Graffiti art (or taggin') is considered to be a form of non-mainstream art. Gang members, in general, use graffiti as a means of expression. Gangs in the 1950s used graffiti for self-promotion, marking territorial boundaries, and as a method of intimidation. Street gangs emerged in the southeast Bronx in 1968 and grew rapidly, reaching their peak in 1973. Steven Hagar in *"Hip hop: The illustrated history of break dancing, rap music, and graffiti"* contends that their behavior stemmed primarily from normal adolescent concerns: the need for peer respect and approval, security and protection, group support and acceptance, and age and sex role identification. Street gangs in the 1950s differed slightly from gangs in the late 1960s. While gangs in the late 1960s had similar characteristics, in 1969 gangs in New York City used graffiti as a means to communicate in code the language, behavior, and meeting places for its members.

In 1968, seven teenagers calling themselves the Savage Seven laid the groundwork for the domination of street gangs in the Bronx for the next five to six years. Within a short time, gangs appeared on every street corner, and names like Black Spades, Savage Skulls, Seven Crowns, Latin Kings, and Young Lords, to name a few, could be seen in graffiti everywhere. Gang activities reached their peak in 1973, and then slowly died out one after the other for several reasons: rival gang members wiped out many gangs; some gangs were too heavily involved in the drug scene; and others grew to be so large that their members did not want to be involved anymore. Times were also changing as people in the 1970s became more interested in frequenting parties and club scenes to dance to the rhythm of the music. In addition, the number of gangs decreased because an increasing number of people and former gang members were becoming interested in the new activities of hip hop culture. The basic idea of hip hop culture is to compete, not with violence, but through one of the four elements of hip hop culture. The driving force behind all these activities was the impetus to break out of anonymity, to be heard and seen, and to spread one's name.

Hagar and S. Jenkins in *"Graffiti: Graphic scenes, spray fiends, and millionaires"* argue that this shift led to the graffiti movement made famous in the early 1970s by a young Greek American teenager named Demetrius, who resided in the Washington Heights area of New York City. Demetrius signed or "tagged" his name TAXI 183 ("TAXI" being Demetrius' nickname and "183" being the street number where he lived) whenever and wherever possible, but mainly on the walls throughout the New York City subway system. This trend soon spread rapidly, as many artists began "tagging" their names not only throughout the subway system but also in New York City neighborhoods and on city buses when they stopped to pick up passengers. Other famous tag names found in the city at that time were PHASE 2, TRACY 168, and LEE 163d.

Graffiti art became so popular by 1975–1976 that youth in the Bronx, Queens, and Brooklyn were spray painting colorful murals, not only with their names, but also with portraits of their deceased loved ones, particularly those who lost their lives to gang-related violence. In addition, imagery from underground comics and television, and even Andy Warhol-style art began to emerge on the sides of subway cars.

Although graffiti art was initially associated with inner-city youth, "artists" from all economic backgrounds began displaying their work. Whether it was created by upper-class white kids from the Upper West Side or by middle-class Black kids, graffiti art had embedded itself in the lives of many New York City youths. This colorful art form gradually evolved into art works with a wide array of images, ranging from block letters to figures, signs, and symbols (stars and flags), to full-size cartoon characters like Mickey Mouse and Popeye, which could be seen virtually everywhere, inside and outside of subway cars, often even obscuring commercial maps and billboard advertisements.

The Metropolitan Transit Authority responded with dogs, barbed-wired fences, paint-removing acid baths, and undercover police squads. As a result of the Transit Authority's attempt to clean up the city, Lee Quinones, a graffiti artist well known for his subway murals, resorted to painting on handball courts. Quinones' court murals intermingled cartoon imagery with a strong moral sensibility (e.g., one mural pleaded for the end to the arms race). Quinones' passion and obvious talent for drawing soon caught the attention of Fred Brathwaite, another local graffiti artist, who later became known as Fab 5 Freddy, the host of *Yo! MTV Raps*. Brathwaite approached Quinones about painting murals for pay. Quinones agreed, so together they formed a graffiti mural painting group known as the Fab 5. The other members were Lee, Doc, and Slave.

At this time, the Fab 5 graffiti artists painted for personal pleasure rather than for monetary reward. Later, however, the Fab 5 placed an advertisement in *The Village Voice*, offering to paint murals at a cost of $5.00 per square foot. In an article in the February 12, 1979, *Village Voice*, after interviewing Brathwaite, Harold Smith implied that it was absurd to try to sell graffiti art works when the city was trying so hard to eradicate graffiti. Brathwaite, however, used his "street knowledge" to respond to Smith's comment, describing graffiti art as the purest form of art that New York City had ever created, and revealing that his Fab 5 was heavily influenced by New Wave artists such as Warhol, Crumb, and Lichtenstein. It was reported that Brathwaite, in fact, knew that graffiti muralists were not influenced by, nor had they even heard of, these New Wave artists, but he responded in this way in an effort to link graffiti art to the hip downtown New York art scene. Nonetheless, the *Village Voice* article caught the attention of Claudio Bruni, an Italian art dealer, who invited the Fab 5 to display five of their canvases at an art show in Rome. All five paintings sold for a thousand dollars each. Soon other influential art dealers in the United States, Europe, and Japan were exhibiting graffiti in major galleries, giving it the kind of recognition and exposure that allowed this art form to reach mainstream audiences.

In the 1970s, the United Graffiti Artists (UGA) and the Nation of Graffiti Artists (NOGA) were formed, aiding in the development of workshops where youngsters could paint and display their graffiti art in gallery shows. However, at the same time that graffiti art appeared to be prospering, it was receiving negative press, with stories and headlines that read, "Subway Graffiti Here Called Epidemic" (*The New York Times*, February 11, 1972); "Defacing New York has Become a Real Art" (*The Toronto Star*, October 20, 1972); and "Question Plan to Use Dogs to Fight Graffiti" (*The New York Daily News*, July 31, 1974) (Jenkins, 1999). Graffiti art had a twofold effect, because it reappeared in the 1980s as the background for music videos by artists such as Blondie (in her video with the song "Rapture"), in documentaries (*Style Wars* by Henry Chalfant), and in books (*Subway Art* by Henry Chalfant), as well as in movies (*Wild Style* and *Beat Street*).

Among the events that popularized graffiti art in the 1970s and 1980s, Hagar contends that one in particular played an instrumental role in connecting graffiti to hip hop culture. An article by Richard Goldstein in *The Village Voice* in December 1980 is credited with making this first connection. Goldstein, who was also the first to write about the positive value of graffiti art in a New York magazine in 1973, claimed that graffiti artists were not antisocial as they were often portrayed. Rather they were bright and intelligent people, who used this form of art to express the conditions in which they lived. In his article, Goldstein went on to link graffiti art and rap music, claiming that both originated from the same cultural conditions. His claim and/or assumption was the first of its kind. It has been argued that Goldstein's assumption was valid because of the success of some prominent graffiti writers, including PHASE 2 and Fab Five Freddy (Brathwaite), who later became a successful rap artist.

Beats or DJing

Kool Herc has been credited with being the first major hip hop DJ, beginning in 1973. Herc was born in 1954 as Clive Campbell in Kingston, Jamaica. He moved to the Bronx in 1967, uniting with his mother who had already migrated there in hopes of achieving a better life for her family. While attending high school in 1970, Campbell was given the nickname "Hercules" because of his impressive physique and aggressive style on the basketball court. Hercules was later shortened to Herc and soon after to Kool Herc, the tag name he used when he took an interest in graffiti writing. In addition to his strong passion for sports and graffiti writing, Herc was fascinated with music.

Herc's fascination with music stemmed from his upbringing in his native Jamaica. As a young boy, he frequently sneaked peeks through fences at yard parties. These parties were known as "dancehall culture" or "blues dances." One definition of "dancehall culture" frequently used today likens it to modern-day reggae. However, dancehall culture was simply a place where dances took place, whether it was in a large hall or in a slum yard in a ghetto of Jamaica. The rising popularity of rhythm "n" blues music introduced by Black American sailors stationed on the island, as well as by Black radio stations in nearby Miami, caused it to be in high demand. Some favorite rhythm "n" blues artists were Fats Domino, Amos Melburn, and Roy Brown.

Dick Hebdige in *"Cut'n'mix: Culture, identity and Caribbean music"* asserts that since local Jamaican bands were unsuccessful at replicating the sounds of American rhythm and blues artists, mobile sound systems with recorded music were created and were the largest, loudest, and most powerful mobile discotheque systems in Jamaica. These systems were comprised of roadies, engineers, and bouncers. In the spotlight of these sound systems were the DJs, who frequently talked over the music they played, a technique known as "toasting," which is considered to be the direct forebear of modern rap. "Toasting" is a rhymed monologue, which tells stories in the first person and which often thrived in prisons, street life, and the army. John Szwed, in *"The real old school"* defined "toasting" as an AfricanAmerican (rather than a Jamaican) poetic form that typically retells the stories of heroes who often spoke against the grain or status quo of society. Furthermore, David Toop in *"The rap attack: African jive to New York hip hop"* described toasts as lengthy rhymes told mostly by men who are usually "violent, scatological, obscene, misogynist," and were "used for decades to while away time in situations of enforced boredom, whether prison, armed service, or street corner life." A DJ would "toast" over the music by screaming short phrases to liven up the crowd and dancers. Examples of simple toasts were "work it, work it" or other popular phrases or slang expressions being used at that time. It was common to hear the DJ acknowledge people who were in attendance at the party as well.

Kool Herc took his knowledge of Jamaican culture, with its mobile sound systems and toasting, to the Bronx with him and began practicing extensively in his parents' apartment. According to S.H. Fernando Jr., in "Back in the day: 1975–1979" in 1973, Herc made his first DJ appearance at his sister's birthday party in a recreation center in the lobby of his apartment building. Soon thereafter, Herc began playing at block parties, parks, and community centers, slowly gaining popularity and a reputation as a skillful and talented DJ. His popularity grew so much that he started playing at then famous clubs like The Twilight Zone and the T-Connection.

What set Herc apart though, from other popular club DJs who played continuous music of the day (then it was disco music), was the revolutionary technique he created to spin the records. Herc never played an entire song, only the section that excited people the most, or the "break." This was the part where the beat was played in its purest form, where just the drums, bass, and rhythm guitars took over. Because the breaks of the songs were only a few seconds long, Herc expanded them by using two turntables with two records. He learned to extend the breaks indefinitely by using an audio mixer and two identical records by which he continuously replaced the desired segment or percussion sections of the day's popular songs. This technique became known as "beats" or "break-beats," which laid the foundation for "MCing." The MC or master of ceremonies is an entertainer on the microphone who amuses the people and makes them dance to his rhymes, which is called "b-boying." (Rhyming and b-boying will be discussed later.) Break-beats have also been credited with giving rise to much hip hop, dance, techno, and jungle or "house" music today.

Another feature that set Kool Herc apart from other DJs at the time was that he used various musical genres to break-beat in addition to disco. He played funk songs such as James

Brown's "Give It Up or Turn It All Loose" and soul and R&B (rhythm and blues) records such as Baby Huey's "Listen to Me" and Jimmy Castor Bunch's "It's Just Begun" to emphasize the loud percussion sounds during the break segment of the songs.

Herc incorporated Jamaican toasting with his DJ style at first by shouting short phrases but soon leaving the "shout outs" and microphone duties to others, due to the concentration he required to mix the beats in new and creative ways to move and entertain the crowd. Hebdige reported that Herc passed the microphone to two of his friends, Coke La Rock and Clark Kent, who subsequently became the first MC team called Kool Herc and the Herculoids. Herc's now-legendary status inspired other underprivileged youth to take an active interest in DJing, opening the doors for others to create new styles and techniques of their own, contributing to the development of hip hop culture today. Two other notable DJs worth mentioning are Afrika Bambaataa, known as Bam, and Joseph Saddler, known as Grandmaster Flash.

Kool Herc left an especially lasting impression on one particular youngster from the Bronx River Projects on the South Side—Afrika Bambaataa (born Kahyan Aasim in 1957) or Bam for short. The name Afrika Bambaataa originated with a famous nineteenth-century Zulu chief and meant "affectionate leader." Bam became known and respected as the "godfather" or the "grandfather" of hip hop culture. He was also the leader of one of the largest and most notorious street gangs in the city called the Black Spades (mentioned earlier).

Bam was an avid record collector and DJ. His interest in Kool Herc's DJ style inspired him to DJ more frequently, thus perfecting the skills that eventually gave him an opportunity to run a sound system at the Bronx River Community Center. Although Bam was the highly respected leader of the Black Spades, he formed The Organization, a community activist program that educated people about the threat of violence and drugs. Bam was so extremely intelligent and articulate when speaking about his visions of uniting Blacks and Hispanics to work toward positive change that in 1974 he actually inspired many gang members to participate in the projects under The Organization.

That same year, Bam reorganized The Organization and renamed it The Zulu Nation, inspired by his studies in African history and, more specifically, about the Zulus who fought with honor and simple weapons against colonialist Britain, in spite of these Africans' feelings of inferiority. Bam and The Zulu Nation comprised of DJs, MCs, break dancers, and graffiti writers, thus continuing to build upon the tradition of hip hop culture.

Bam's success as a DJ and his work with The Zulu Nation continued well into the late 1970s as he formed a relationship with Tom Silverman from Tommy Boy Records. This association led to the formation of the group Afrika Bambaataa and the Jazzy 5, who soon released the song "Jazzy Sensation" from the album *Tommy Boy 2*. In 1982, Bam's hit "Planet Rock" helped Silverman build Tommy Boy Records into a reputable leading record company as well as begin the electro-funk revolution, a sound that was later sampled in the works of popular artists such as the Chemical Brothers and Fatboy Slim. The Zulu Nation is known today as the Universal Zulu Nation, defined as "an international hip hop movement that upholds such principles as knowledge, wisdom, understanding, freedom, justice, equality, peace, unity, love, and respect in their manifesto."

Another important and relevant contributor to hip hop culture was another Bronx DJ with Jamaican roots by the name of Grandmaster Flash, born Joseph Saddler. Grandmaster Flash earned his nickname by his impressive hand-eye coordination when he mixed beats by listening to one record through a set of headphones while the other record continued to play. Although Theodore Livingston, the brother of Flash's partner, Mean Gene, invented the art of the "needle-drop," Flash is often credited with mastering the art, consequently surpassing Herc in skill and popularity. Needle-dropping prolonged short drum breaks by playing two copies of a record simultaneously and moving the needle on one turntable back to the start of the break while the other played (the two records did not need to be identical as was the case with Herc's break-beat style). A technique known as "scratching" was invented around the same time by a DJ named Grand Wizard Theodor. Scratching is very similar to needle dropping in that the DJ slides the record back and forth underneath the needle in order to create rhythmic effects.

Flash incorporated a drum machine known as the "beat box" into his performances, which gained him even more respect and popularity as a DJ. The beat box was a manually operated machine, which produced an electronic beat with which Flash would drum a part in time with the track. This phenomenon led to later rap groups using their mouths, lips, and throats to produce sounds often referred to as the "human beat box."

Rhymes

Rhyming allowed DJs to express their thoughts and feelings in a creative, expressive, and energizing manner, thus spreading a feeling of anticipation and excitement among the audience. Along with Herc, Flash has been credited with introducing and popularizing the art form known as MCing, as part of hip hop culture. As mentioned earlier when defining the DJing element of hip hop culture, MCing occurred when DJs "rapped" or "rhymed" short phrases over their music. Among the wider variety of oratorical precedents cited for MCing besides the Jamaican style of toasting, were the epic histories of the West African griot (the African oral traditionalist or storyteller who recites the history of his/her tribal community), talking blues songs, jailhouse toast (long rhyming poems recounting outlandish deeds and misdeeds), and the dozens (a ritualized word game based on exchanging insults, usually directed toward members of the opponent's family). Other influences on MCing included the hipster-jive announcing styles of 1950s rhythm "n" blues DJs such as Jocko Henderson, the Black Power poetry of Amiri Baraka, Gil Scott-Heron, and the Last Poets, as well as the rapping sections in recordings by Isaac Hayes and George Clinton.

"Rapping," although not called that at the time, was heard in America as far back as the 1850s. The trading of tall tales, the rhyming and trading of insults (the dozens), and creatively producing one's own rhythmic "chest-whacking," "thigh-slapping" sounds originated in West Africa. All of these forms have been known to contribute to hip hop culture and rap music in one way or another. Many of these traditional African tales or toasts celebrated mythical bad men boasting about how "bad" and/or powerful they were. Toasting with style and clever rhymes gave one status and power among one's peers.

While it is acknowledged today that rap music had its roots in a variety of sources, including those mentioned above, Jamaican reggae music contributed just as much to rap's development. Fernando describes the connection and similarities found between both genres of music, claiming that both emerged from oppressive environments that mirrored the attitude and reflected the lifestyle of the ghetto, both are rhythmic forms of music emphasizing the sounds of the bass more than any other chord, and both found their roots in African griots and Jamaican toasting.

As the lyrical art form of toasting or rapping evolved, it offered unlimited challenges for many. The only rules were to create authentic rhymes that synchronized with the beats of the music. This art form was accessible to anyone—rich, poor, or the inexperienced (no lessons were needed). One simply needed to practice and perfect his verbal skills in order to rhyme freely. The content of rap could be about anything, allowing for one's imagination to run freely. The MC strived for originality and to be considered by one's peers as being imaginative, inventive, or in slang, "def" (cool). In 1977, Grandmaster Flash used his DJing skills once again to impact hip hop culture, by popularizing and implementing the use of MCs in his performances. He formed a five-member group of his own known as Grandmaster Flash and the Furious Five (similar to Afrika Bambaataa's Zulu Nation). Members of the Furious Five included Cowboy (Keith Wiggins), Melle Mel (Melvin Glover), Kid Creole (Danny Glover), Scorpio (Eddie Morris), and Rahiem (Guy Williams). Grandmaster Flash and the Furious Five have been credited with pushing MCing to an entirely different level because of their complicated routines such as back-to-back rhyming, in-tandem flows, and choreographed moves. The Furious Five were unique in that although they would break up phrases and all were rhyming, their rap sounded as if only one person was actually doing the rhyming. They were synchronizing in perfect harmony with one another.

By 1978, MCs became even more popular than DJs since they interacted more directly with the crowd, evoking unlimited surges of energy, excitement, and liveliness when dancing to the recorded sounds of music. Other famous MCs following in the Furious Five's footsteps were Grand Wizard Theodore and the Fantastic Five, and the Treacherous Three.

Breaks or B-Boys and B-Girls

The word "b-boy" is derived from "break-boy" ("b-girl" meaning "break-girl"), a term DJ Kool Herc often used when describing the person(s) who stepped out and danced during the instrumental break in the music (break on the breaks). Breaking emphasizes various forms of body movement that create a unique style of dance and expression. Breaking involved dance moves that incorporated many different dance styles, reminiscent of every period from the Lindy hop or the jitterbug era to the African-rooted Brazilian martial art of capoeira. Many also claim that the "b" in "b-boying" originated from the African word "boioing," which meant to "hop" or "jump." All of these styles of dance can be seen in some shape or form in breaking known today as the "old school" style of dancing. The "old school" style included break-ing, locking, and popping, whereas the present-day term "new school" style of dance incor-porates all of the "old school" dance styles, but with more creative and futuristic moves.

DJ Kool Herc started using the term "b-boy" in the ghettoes of New York City in the early 1970s. The term eventually became common urban vernacular when describing true, devoted hip hop males or females ("b-girls") who understood the history of the culture. In the beginning, most b-boys/b-girls tended to be Black, underprivileged youth from the New York City ghettoes. However, b-boying generated so much interest and popularity among Latino youth from the same area that it quickly became associated with them as well. B-boys/b-girls emphasized creating their own style and moves. The more difficult and creative a move was, the more likely one was to be given the prestigious label of being a "b-boy/b-girl." Some popular moves still known and practiced today are the windmill (legs are spread in a v-shape while b-boy spins around from his upper back to his stomach, then returns onto his back, and so forth), the flare (legs spread in v-shape, b-boy supports himself on hands while spinning legs around him), the head spin (spin using the head as the pivot point), the body wave (move where it appears as if an invisible wave is traveling through the body), and the robot (mimicking robots seen on television in the 1970s), to name a few.

As mentioned earlier, real hip hop dancing (b-boying) originated in the streets and served as a substitute for violence (although at times, breaking caused fights to start due to the intense nature of the competitions). Many of the participants (as was the case with graffiti writing, MCing, and DJing) were former gang members who, rather than fighting, competed in breaking competitions to earn respect. Every element of hip hop culture described thus far involved earning respect and gaining recognition through competitions. "Breaking bat-tles" involved "breaking crews" (groups of dancers who practiced and performed together) who were in competition with one another for the reputation of most creative and original moves.

The first known breaking crew was The Nigga Twins, followed by Afrika Bambaataa's Zulu Nation, The Seven Deadly Sinners, Rockwell Association, Starchild La Rock, and the Rock Steady Crew. Breaking battles took place in a variety of places, ranging from the streets to parks, and eventually, to downtown nightclubs. According to Fernando, perhaps the most notable b-boy, who brought breaking to national exposure, was Richie "Crazy Legs" Colon, a member of the Rock Steady Crew. In 1983, representatives from Paramount Pictures approached Crazy Legs after witnessing his dancing skills at a previous show held in the Roxy. He was offered a cameo appearance in the movie *Flashdance*. He was to fill in for Jennifer Beal's character during one of the dance scenes involving a backspin. It was at this point, and to the chagrin of Crazy Legs, that the media coined the term "break-dancing" as an art form. Crazy Legs (cited in Fernando's, *"The new beats: Exploring the music, culture, and atti-tudes of hip hop"*) explained that the b-boys in the parks would dance when the DJ's took a break from their beats. Crazy Legs was adamant in noting that the b-boys were referred to as "break boys" in the streets and not as "break dancers" as mainstream media termed the dancers.

Hollywood capitalized on the new "fad" of breaking as more movies and documentaries attempted to portray hip hop culture the way "they" interpreted it to be. For example, in 1984, Harry Belafonte produced *Beat Street*, a movie portraying the lives of legendary b-boys from the crews Magnificent Force, Rock Steady, and the New York City Breakers. However, the actors in the movie were much older than the real life b-boys, and their feeble attempts to sound as if they had grown up on the streets were ill-received, as they were viewed as being fake and unrealistic. The barrage of media exposure that breaking received at this time (on *David Letterman*, *20/20*, prime time's *Fame*, and in performances for Queen Elizabeth and Prince Charles, to name a few) ironically also killed its popularity by 1984. The 1990s to present-day have, however, seen a revival of the art form, reintroducing breaking to the stage as an integral part of hip hop culture.

Hip Hop Fashion

As mentioned earlier, hip hop culture is continuously growing and expanding as it also includes its own fashion, language, and lifestyle. The baggy style of clothing commonly worn by today's youth may be considered by some as the "new school" style of hip hop, but it should be made clear that this style did not originate from hip hop culture. Such common misperceptions are often perpetuated through the media, as well as by youth today who do not fully understand the history and culture of hip hop.

The style of clothing that b-boys, graffiti writers, DJs, and MCs wore included cheap Addidas and Puma sneakers, tracksuits, and hooded sweatshirts to hide the writers' identity and protect their heads from the wire fences at subway yards. There are other theories that deserve mentioning and that have credibility. One explanation that people living in urban communities offer for the baggy clothing was the poverty in which they lived. Many poor families could not afford to buy clothes for all of their children, so once older siblings outgrew their clothes, they would pass them along as "hand-me-downs" to their younger siblings. Another valid argument is that this "style" actually originated from prisons as the outfits worn by prisoners were often too baggy and/or loosely fitting (no belts were allowed for obvious reasons); thus many prisoners walked around with their pants hanging off their hips. Upon release, these prisoners (often, young minority men) brought this style back to their old neighborhoods, thus creating a style of dress that would continue for many years to come.

Poetry of the Oppressed: Pedagogy of the Urban Lyricist

Rap Music as Postmodern Oral Poetry

In the wake of the heightened social and political consciousness of the 1960s, postmodern perspectives on popular culture began attempting to breathe life back into art by focusing on form rather than authorship. What a text says, as a function of how it says it, came to mean more than what an author was attempting to express. The form became the art. Hip hop lyricists, commonly referred to as "MCs" or "rappers," emerged within this postmodern milieu and reformulated oral poetry by fusing rhymed lyrics with musical tracks recorded and replayed using advanced technologies.

Since its emergence in the South Bronx, rap music has drawn heavily on the lyricism and layered meanings within the black vernacular and sermonic traditions. Failing to acknowledge the significance of these linkages, some critics have attempted to reduce rap to its roots in the "toast" tradition by claiming it had more to do with "talking hype" than with oral expression or poetry. Arguing for a more expansive view, acclaimed poet Tracie Morris in M.D. Jones's "*SOULS: Understanding the New Black Poetry*" observes, hip has been the primary force behind the resurgence of the "spoken word" movement even for those who do not use the techniques.

While rappers may not commonly regard themselves "spoken word artists" because of the particular structure and aesthetics associated with "MCing," the link between these art forms has grown considerably during the last decade. The live energy of both the hip hop concert and the spoken word performance resurrect a sense of spontaneity in poetry. The simultaneously distinct and interconnected nature of these related forms challenges rigid traditional notions of form altogether. The melding of these two art forms in this manner is not only enriching for each art, it also allows audiences new ways to interpret and participate in each art. If hip hop and spoken word poetry have the liberatory potential to create such energetic, inspiring responses and encouraging audience participation that elicit social consciousness, we contend that each art form can easily be integrated into and practiced simultaneously in classroom contexts at all education levels.

Based upon the philosophy of Brazilian philosopher Paulo Freire, hip hop and spoken word poetry are just one example of a cultural literacy that, as a political discourse, all people can assert their right and responsibility not only to read, understand, and transform their own experiences but also to reconstitute their relationships with the wider society by writing, voicing, and performing these experiences.

All four original elements of hip hop culture (graffiti art, DJing, rhyming, and breaking) can be considered postmodern texts that can be deconstructed, critiqued, and analyzed because of their creative, energetic, and expressive nature, as well as their empowering potential to excite crowds whether it be visually, verbally, kinesthetically, or auditorily. For example, graffiti art is a postmodern text because of its constantly changing and creative means of expression. Furthermore, graffiti art expressed the untold story of oppressive social and living conditions; DJing is a postmodern text due to its expressive, creative, and ever-evolving nature as employed by the DJ when playing, mixing, and talking over records played from a turntable; rhyming provides an empowering postmodern text because of the potential liberatory and empowering interpretations the lyrics may evoke; the creativity and unique body movements involved in the art of breaking can be read, analyzed, and deconstructed just as an English teacher has students read traditional written texts. The expressive nature found in all four elements or texts can lead to many different interpretations and inferences supporting the ideologies reflected in critical pedagogy.

Critical pedagogy invites students to look at "what is" to determine "what could be," and to find a way to move from "where we are" to "where we want to be." Analyzing, critiquing, and interpreting hip hop texts and ultimately performing them through the spoken word from a critical perspective allows students to ask and answer such questions. Critical pedagogy also means taking a close, critical look at schooling and society, and employing a historical perspective to determine how we came to be where we are. Critical pedagogues often refer to this kind of critique as historical materialism. Within this context, we are forced to ask questions such as these: How is it that the material conditions we are currently experiencing are the result of the progress of history? What actions can we then take to effect changes? What are the obstacles to change? Why are they there? How can they be overcome? The obstacles to freedom cannot be overcome until one is aware that they exist. This questioning and coming to awareness is what Paulo Freire called *consciencization*.

In order for students to study hip hop texts and perform their spoken word poetry, cultural workers like Freire emphasize that we must first explore the history of hip hop and the spoken word movement by introducing students to the origins and culture of both hip hop and spoken word. Freire believed that freedom begins with the recognition of a system of oppressive relations and with the realization of one's own place in that system. Incorporating hip hop and spoken word as critical pedagogical tools in the classroom enables members of an oppressed group to develop an awareness or critical consciousness of their situation as a beginning point of liberating and emancipatory change. This liberating practice requires reflection and action, as well as interpretation and change. In the classroom, Freire's critical, liberatory pedagogy translates into the deconstruction and interpretation of hip hop texts that transcend to praxis in the form of performance (spoken word) poetry.

The critical, liberatory pedagogy Freire refers to helps students develop the skills necessary to critically examine the social, political, and economic injustices that affect their lives. Empowering students in such a way gives them a "voice" that has previously been silenced, thus legitimizing their power. Critical pedagogy encourages students to think critically, to question conflicting sources of information, and to formulate and understand concepts themselves. According to cultural worker Melissa Fernandez' (leadership trainer, poet, and artist) testimonial, "hip hop, poetry, and spoken word are tools in the leadership training experiences I design for children and teens throughout New York City. By reading and understanding the lyrics of other great poets, the power of words, ideas, and visualization in poetry become a tangible, recognizable reality. In writing poetry, students are given the opportunity to explore and identify their own feelings, an important part of personal development and growth. They are also afforded the opportunity to realize the universality of their individual experiences and hopefully recognize that poetry and art are instruments they can use to liberate their greater human self expression."

Critical educators or cultural workers who, as Freire suggests, "talk to learners and with them" and "from listening to learners to being heard by them" is similar to what James Beane in "*Curriculum integration: Designing the core of democratic education*" refers to as "integrative learning" or "unforgettable learning experiences." Beane describes integrative learning as having constructive, reflective experiences that not only broaden and deepen both parties' present understandings of the world but that also enable both students and teachers to learn from one another in such a way that new and subjugated knowledge may be formed, carried forward, and put to use in new situations. By collaborating with each other, both teachers and students feel less of a need to compete, and tend to be more thoughtful and cooperative. Empowering students in this way actually frees the teacher to join their students in facilitating growth rather than constantly having to monitor, direct, and supervise their learning and behavior. A curriculum organized around personal, social, cultural, economic, and political issues builds a sense of community and belonging, as well as brings the notion of democracy back into the classroom.

Educators are cheating both themselves and their students by not working in and with the various mediums that speak loudest to their students. Excluding the various forms of hip hop texts from the curriculum excludes voices from being heard, denying the valid existence of life experiences, languages, and cultural expressions of many students. The refusal to incorporate such a pedagogy supports the belief that the culture that students bring to the schools is not legitimate or valued. The inclusion of the students' views (subjugated knowledge) creates an awareness that all individuals can claim an identity on their own rather than one forced on them. Kincheloe and Steinberg in *Changing multiculturalism* argue that when individuals reach such awareness and are able to create their own identity, they are then able to confront the forces that have previously shaped them, which ultimately moves people to redefine their worldview and way of seeing.

A testimonial by Núrí Chandler-Smith, Ed.M., who has taught hip hop at Northeastern and Harvard Universities asserts, "Hip hop is a conduit for youth expression and a means for transforming the world through its social commentary. Because of this, and the tremendous influence hip hop has on the lives of young people on a global level, it can be used as an incomparable tool for education. Learning is more meaningful when it's not just about gathering knowledge of facts and figures that someone else thinks are important, but when you can see that the world you're learning about is your world. Students learning through hip hop become engaged in the material immediately because they can relate to it, because hip hop is the soundtrack of their existence." As testimonials of educators already integrating hip hop texts and spoken word poetry into their classrooms prove, both art forms are one kind of cultural literacy whose addition to the classroom curriculum renders positive benefits that include the legitimation of student knowledge, student voices, and student agency.

10. Urban Youth Engaging Poetry and Creating Learning Communities

KORINA M. JOCSON

Research shows that cultural relevance in the classroom is key to teaching and learning.[1] To improve the education of urban youth, critical educators not only recognize that students enter the classroom with loads of cultural knowledge, but also identify them as resources in the learning and teaching process.[2] In previous studies, the integration of students' culture(s) in the curriculum has had major implications on how teachers can scaffold students into understanding certain texts, or increase their fundamental interest in reading and writing. For example, it has been noted that students' cultural practices are valuable tools for learning and, in the case of African American students, how signifying and "speakerly" texts can incite fruitful discussions, assist in literary interpretations, as well as convey history, culture, and experience in the classroom.[3]

Increasing cultural and linguistic diversity looms large in many of today's classrooms. As educators, how do we (continue to) take on the challenge of seeking multicultural and anti-oppressive means to improve teaching and learning?[4] Indeed, there are myriad ways of valuing students' cultures and responding to students' needs in urban classrooms. One found to be effective is to devise a curriculum for high school English classes that incorporates the use of rap music and hip hop culture, aligning it with canonical texts such as novels and poetry, to promote academic literacy among urban youth.[5] Another is to mix genres of literature and film to engage students in thematic and structural development related to writing and popular culture.[6] Yet, despite these innovative practices and efforts to bridge school and home cultures, there still seems to be a kind of silencing that misses the expressive voices of youth, that is, the "brave new voices" in poetry.[7]

In recent years, despite cuts on arts education, I have seen youth increasingly participate in out-of-school activities that provide them opportunities to be creative and expressive.[8] Such activities have included poetry writing workshops and teen slam competitions, among others. Certainly, poetry has become one of those critical spaces where urban youth can speak their minds while accessing an artistic, learning community. The (re)emerging cultural phenomena in spoken word poetry as rooted in the African diasporic oral traditions of storytelling has also served as a site for uplifting marginalized voices and building a sense of community.[9] From my decade-long experience as a high school teacher in Los Angeles and researcher in the San Francisco Bay Area, I have come to understand the nature of writing instruction in many classrooms and, for the most part, the lack of opportunities for students to express themselves in more critical and profound ways, not to mention establish a sense of community. One exception is the work behind June Jordan's Poetry for the People program in Northern California.

Poetry for the People, or P4P as it is commonly known, is a UC Berkeley program that is in partnership with several organizations, including a high school, a church, and a prison. It is one in which a group of college student–teacher–poets (STPs) with the guidance of the late professor and poet June Jordan, collaborate with teachers, community members, and other artists to implement two significant objectives: (1) to create a safe medium for artistic and political empowerment, and (2) to democratize the medium of poetry to include "the people," or populations that have been historically denied equal access and representation.[10] Through my teaching and outreach work with P4P, I saw and imagined the potential of poetry in young people's lives. Hence, in my subsequent ethnographic study about urban youth poetry, I sought to investigate a number of high school students and their experiences in the context of P4P, and their poetry-related literacy practices both in and out of school. For the purposes of this chapter, I examine the experience of one male urban high school student named Naier to suggest how poetry can create learning communities, and facilitate the kinds of writing instruction that would further recognize the salience of urban youth culture in the classroom. In what follows, I represent his voice in selected quotations and include two of his poems. I begin with a brief description of Naier and his literate activities.

Writing Poems and Other Multi-Literate Activities

Nigerian American 16-year-old Naier attended Bellevue High School located in the San Francisco East Bay Area. He grew up with 10 other siblings in disparate cities and, at the time of the study, resided in a two-bedroom backhouse with his mother, stepfather, and seven-year-old brother Isa. Their home-centered between the 580 MacArthur and 880 Nimitz Freeways, was a place where, according to Naier, for "quiet time in this busy neighborhood." He carved his own space by "drowning" in literate activities such as listening to music, reading magazines, watching television, and writing poetry.

Naier started writing poems in the eighth grade when, in the process of repeating a previously "flunked" English class, his summer school teacher approached him and positively commented on what he recalled as "the very first piece" he ever wrote. Though that "(that poem) was really not that good," Naier recognized this experience as a critical moment that eventually led to his passion for poetry writing. Since then, he wrote "wherever and whenever, on the bus, BART [Bay Area Rapid Transit], waiting in line for something," in restaurants, in class, at home, or just "out and about everywhere." For Naier, these omnipresent literate episodes became a way of being that consisted of "reading his daily" (surroundings, that is) and jotting down words that "hit" him unexpectedly.[11] Not only did they reflect in writing what went through his mind between social encounters, but these episodes also shaped how he processed his realities and, consequently, how such realities shaped the way he responded to them. Furthermore, they were important in defining what was meaningful, in developing a particular kind of practice that was socioculturally embedded with, as well as situated in, his beliefs.[12]

In examining his poetry, I discovered Naier's ideological stance "about the world" as well as the political statements he made related to American society in concert with his personal values. Ironically, these statements were shaped *and* being shaped by the very thing that he wrote about. Like a critical ethnographer making observations, he recorded what he saw in relation to how he felt through his own/visceral reactions about power structures and social inequities.[13] He did so in the following poem, inspired by a "racial profiling" experience:

Hung On Past Ideas

Rage consumes me
as the noose of past generations
is tightened around my neck
Am I the southern Negro here to prance around
with a grin from ear to ear
like Amos & Andy
Yessa, ssorryssa, can I get that fo yasa
feeling like a boy
avoiding the whip of his father
Or am I the Negro with the caliber at my waist
protecting my 20-inch chain and my ounce of dope
because they mean more to me
than my 5-year-old son on welfare with my baby momma

Or am I just the Negro who knows to stay in place
pushing the envelope is impossible
Or if I ever get over
it's because I play football or act
I get thrown off the edge
10 years later my obituary says
Hung On Past Ideas

In his elaboration of why and how he wrote poetry, particularly the one above, Naier noted that he was often adamant about "not missing out on a thought, phrase, verse, line, stanza, rhyme, or just anything that comes to mind." He found any and every available writing tool—from his personal notebook to scratch paper, napkins, and/or old receipts—so that he could "capture the moment." In the classroom, such practices as in Naier's case can become relevant points of departure for writing instruction. The question is, what else should teachers know about their students' everyday experiences to innovate their practice and invigorate their curriculum? Here is one possibility and a closer look at Naier's life.

Like many of his high school peers, Naier was in school from 8:45 A.M. to 3:30 P.M. and enjoyed hanging out with friends in between. He stayed late after school to do homework to improve his overall 3.0 grade point average.[14] Whenever he arrived home around dinnertime exhausted from his day's activities, he either watched TV, read magazines, talked on the phone, played with his brother, or escaped the world through his headphones. He listened to various types of music from contemporary jazz to neo-soul, R&B, and Rap, and followed artists such as Najee, Jill Scott, Alicia Keys, Case, Ginuwine, Beanie Sigel, and Talib Kweli.[15] In addition, Naier also watched music videos on BET or MTV, and sometimes engaged himself with the History or Discovery channels. While he kept up to date with "who's who" or "what's hot" by reading *Ebony, The Source,* and *Jet* magazines, he also maintained what he termed "cultural awareness" by reading African American texts such as the *Assassination of the Black Male Image* that his parents made available at home, or *Bearing the Cross* that his English teacher provided in the classroom. Considering his eclectic interests, it was evident that Naier's literacy practices were embedded and situated in his sociocultural environment, through interactions with music, magazines, books, etc. In short, he was shaped *and* being shaped by this outside world because popular media and their variegated cultural forms and icons, which have a degree of influence on one's literacy and can transfer into school literacy.[16] Thus, from the perspective of teaching and learning, it is important that such forms be considered and integrated in classroom curriculum and instruction. Asking students to bring physical samples of their interests could mark the beginning of insightful discussions, activities, and projects that make relevant subject matter content to their lives.

In many of his poems, Naier extracted from his everyday experiences as a young African American and remained conscious about identifying with those of others. He sought motivation from within himself and reached out to what he called the "likes of cultural renaissance makers" of his time. Upon blending various aspects of his environment in his poetry, Naier befittingly expanded the notion of literacy from being sociocultural, to that of being discursive at the same time. He did not only find himself situated within certain social and cultural spaces that he entered, exited, and navigated, but also used the discourses associated with them. One such example is a discourse community he participated in on a voluntary basis called Poetry for the People Too (P4P2), a name coined by members themselves. P4P2 was first initiated in 2001 when two sophomore high school students were invited to speak and discuss their poetry as well as writing processes at a conference sponsored by the National Council of Teachers of English held on the UC Berkeley campus. The duo gradually grew as six other students joined the group in later classroom talks held at several locations in the San Francisco Bay Area, including a city college and elementary school. Naier was one of P4P2's original members. For high school teachers, it is important to understand how and why he created and participated in this community.

Creating a Learning Community Youth Call Their Own

P4P2, a high school STP group, convened on certain occasions to present written poetry to different audiences. At the time of my study, it consisted of eight Bellevue high school students, all of whom were involved with the university–high school partnership aspect of the P4P program. P4P2 derived from P4P, a unique poetry program that, as described earlier, utilizes UC Berkeley college STPs to serve and work with high school students in their respective English classes. With their newly acquired and mediated knowledge about poetry, these eight members of P4P2 continued to follow P4P's writing guidelines and, in turn, took on the role of STPs themselves. Similar to the notion of an apprenticeship (i.e., master–student relationship), they were novices (beginner poets) who looked to college STPs (intermediate/advanced poets) as experts in and for their own construction of poetry—a situated learning activity that they as well as many of their peers experienced inside their English classes. For P4P2 members, however, what transpired as a result of this situated learning experience is a practice that began to extend *beyond* the classroom. Poetry writing as a learned activity gradually became an integral part of these students' lives, where "legitimate peripheral participation," that is, a generative social practice occurring over time, took place.[17] In other words, as the students' interest in poetry changed, so did the nature of their participation. Unlike the more consistent and structured schedule of P4P, P4P2 members met spontaneously by way of occasional "invitation-only" presentations in high school and college settings, and/or by swift exchanges during lunch or after school. Fellow English teachers and other Humanities or Social Science instructors interested in incorporating poetry and poetry writing in their own classes often were the ones who provided opportunities for such presentations.

P4P2 members as a whole, including Naier, wrote poems at their leisure. One stark difference between P4P and P4P2 writing activities was that students did not base what they wrote about on assigned prompts; rather, they chose their own topics or themes. Much like in P4P, however, students constructed poetic texts that reflected "truths" about their lived experiences and illustrated negotiations with their social worlds, which I found were often critical and ideological in nature. Everyday social realities were, according to Naier, "so forceful" and "so real" that making meaning was significant in the process of shaping how they saw themselves as urban youth and how such identities were shaped by external influences. Unfortunately, such realities were often not given priority in their social environments, particularly in school and inside classrooms. Hence, it is important for teachers to take the knowledge they have of students' experiences and utilize them critically to delve into issues that not only make them relevant, but also connect with them in ways that build more meaningful relationships. For Naier, "extreme emotions" like anger, joy, and love caused him to pick up his special blue ballpoint pen and poetry notebook, and started to write what naturally came to him. *Wastes Away*, a poem from January of 2000 when he was in the tenth grade, about his slain older brother, illustrates this type of negotiation and reality. Naier revealed that he began to write this poem exactly two days before his brother's death, a prophetic yet painful reality he was still living through and coming to accept everyday:

Wastes Away

1   As he twists & turns through life
     His soul spins from divine to unkind
     Will he forever be punished
     For past sins of his lifetime
5   As he dies I see the whites of his eyes
     Burn red from greed
     He feels the need to lie, cheat and steal
     All to make that bill he thinks
     He needs so badly
10 But doesn't he see that while he's a G
     His gun is destroying equality for you and me?
     Doesn't he realize that he's erased the tracks
     Made by the broken backs
     Of his ancestors
15 But as he proceeds his family bleeds
     The pain which he causes
     And as time pauses
     He falls into a cycle of ill-begotten dreams
     That shatter like glass
20 That last for a lifetime
     He says he cherishes his life
     But cold enough to take another

Demand his family to love each other
But slap around his baby's mother
25 He's running for cover
As the cold, hard wind of reality hits his face
And the sun rises up, shines away
The last strand of darkness
He hides from the light
30 Afraid that his mask will decay
And dare I say
He wastes away

In the case of Naier and others, P4P2 as a discourse community provided youth some space to mediate their everyday realities through poetry. The production of poetic texts became one means of reifying the social meanings they made out of experiences from home, school, the streets, and places in between. In addition to social meanings, this community also engaged its members in the more rudimentary writing process that many teachers (continue to) emphasize in their writing instruction. According to Naier, the "raw, untouched, and unrevised" draft in his notebook turned into another draft by incorporating constructive comments from P4P2 peers. After subsequent workshops, he would then draft other versions on loose-leaf pages before "typing a decent one up." Understanding the complexity of the writing process, Naier stated that "a poem is never perfect" and recognized the importance of having poems workshopped or revised at least once, a stage of co-construction that allowed him to gain more confidence about his writing. Generally for him a poem could be cut short to be more precise in length and meaning or lengthened if/when it became necessary to expand on a point or "play up a metaphor" to build imagery, which to say are all choices in his discretion. Sometimes, he would change certain words for diction, others for rhythm and rhyme. Understanding the significance of language use, he noted that with P4P2, he was able to co-construct his poems with "stronger and more descriptive words" to make his writing more purposeful.

Through this process, Naier also exposed himself to a secondary "acquired" discourse (i.e., literary devices and language in poetry writing) that allowed him to participate more fluidly in constructing realities occurring in his primary "learned" discourse (i.e., everyday language use).[18] As his participation changed over time from periphery to center, he was both acquiring *and* learning at the same time. However, most interesting in all of Naier's writing was that he used this same arguable notion of a secondary discourse to critique happenstances within others' secondary discourses. For example, in *Hung on Past Ideas*, he challenged "blaxploitation Amos & Andy-type characters" (see lines 5–8), yet tied his critique to semantics adopted by descendants of African slaves as imaginatively illustrated in "Yessa, ssorryssa, can I get that fo yasa." Also and more broadly speaking, as seen in *Wastes Away*, he depicted his "brother's dim world through [his] own" understandings of American society, indicative in his question, "Doesn't he see that while he's a G/his gun is destroying equality for you and me?" (see lines 10–11).

Conclusion

For youth like Naier, literate practices, such as poetry writing, were shaped by multiple negotiations in his social practice. In P4P2 Naier created and sustained a discourse community set against a backdrop of larger communities of practice. The several talks of which he was a part demonstrated to others (i.e., the audience) the possibilities of poetry and related practices they could employ in their lives. What he learned in his own participation in P4P2 allowed him to actively exercise this access not only to influence others, but also to expand other present day communities of practice. His membership in P4P2 engaged him to further produce "meaning," mold "identity," sustain "practice," and define "community."[19] As I have illustrated here, P4P2 as a discourse *and* learning community, asserted these four key elements that, in turn, manifested in Naier's own poetry writing *and* actions as an STP in other classroom settings. For teachers who seek ways to improve student participation and social dynamics in the classroom, it is important to consider creating smaller communities of practice, in the form of teams or groups, that could potentially activate students' membership and learning processes.

Despite his high level of confidence and abilities as a student, Naier still felt disengaged "whenever and for whatever reason" in his own classes. So, instead of total disengagement, he would write poems to get him through the hour. He would jot down what came to him, smile at its potential, and simply keep it in his notebook. Perhaps rather than waiting to be read and shared at the next P4P2 presentation, these "hidden" poems consisting of "hidden" realities should be provided space *inside* classrooms, particularly in English/Language Arts classes. Perhaps then, a mere literacy episode such as a writing of a haiku on the bus or a "dope line" sparked by a rap song on a piece of scratch paper can serve as an impetus to innovate writing instruction, as well as a reason to expand more communities of practice that engage students in thinking about how their realities are relevant to teaching and learning. Ever since the eighth grade, Naier sought to grow and develop a more sophisticated way of expressing his "extreme emotions" through poetry. P4P2 as a discourse and learning community provided the critical space for this kind of expression that he had hoped soon his current classes would make available.

NOTES

1   G. Ladson-Billings, *The Dreamkeepers: Successful Teachers of African American Children* (San Francisco: Jossey-Bass, 1994); L. Delpit, *Other People's Children: Cultural Conflict in the Classroom* (New York: The New York Press, 1995); K. Gutiérrez, Baquedano-López and M. Turner, "Putting language back into Language Arts: When the radical middle meets the third space," *Language Arts* 74(5) (1997): 368–378.

2   L. Moll, "Mediating knowledge between homes and classrooms" in D. Keller-Cohen, ed. *Literacy: Interdisciplinary Conversations* (Cresskill, NJ: Hampton, 1994), pp. 385–401; C. Sleeter and C. Grant, "Mapping terrains of power: Student cultural knowledge versus classroom knowledge" in C. Sleeter, ed. *Empowerment through Multicultural Education* (Albany: SUNY, 1991), pp. 49–67; C. Lee, *Signifying as a Scaffold for Literary Interpretations: The Pedagogical Implications of an African American Discourse Genre* (Urbana, IL: NCTE, 1993); J. Mahiri and S. Sablo, "Writing for their lives: The non-school literacy

of California's urban African American youth," *Journal of Negro Education, 65(2)* (1996): 164–180; E. Morrell and J. Duncan-Andrade, "Promoting academic literacy with urban youth through engaging Hip Hop culture," *English Journal, 91(6)* (2002): 88–92.

S. Nieto, *Language, Culture, and Teaching: Critical Perspectives for a New Century* (Mahwah, NJ: Lawrence Erlbaum, 2002).

3   Lee, *Signifying As a Scaffold for Literary Interpretations.*

4   Nieto, *Language, Culture, and Teaching.*

5   E. Morrell and Duncan-Andrade, "Promoting academic literacy with urban youth through engaging Hip Hop culture."

6   D. Allender, "Popular culture in the classroom," *English Journal, 93(3)* (2004): 12–14. See also E. Morrell, *Linking Literacy and Popular Culture: Finding Connections for Lifelong Learning* (Norwood, MA: Christopher-Gordon, 2004).

7   J. Weiss and S. Herndon, *Brave New Voices: The Youth Speaks Guide to Teaching Spoken Word Poetry* (Portsmouth, NH: Heinemann, 2001). For a discussion on silencing, see M. Fine, *Framing dropouts: Notes on the politics of an Urban Public High School* (Albany: SUNY, 1991).

8   E. Soep, *"The Art of Critique: Learning from Youth Making Media,"* talk presented at the Graduate School of Education's Language and Literacy, Society and Culture colloquium series (University of California, Berkeley, CA, 2003); G. Hull and M. Katz, "Learning to tell a digital story: New literate spaces for crafting self," paper presented at the meeting of the *American Anthropological Association* (New Orleans, LA, 2002); S. Heath and Smith, *Art show: Youth and community development* [Documentary] (New York: Partners for Livable Communities, 1999); S. Meacham, "Reader writer freedom fighter:" Tupac Shakur and the struggle between liberatory literacy and 'thug life' in Hip Hop music," talk presented at the *meeting of the American Educational Research Association* (Chicago, IL, 2003).

9   M. Fisher, "From the coffee house to the school house: The promise and potential of spoken world poetry in school contexts," *English Education 37(2)* (2005): 115–131. To clarify the term, "spoken word" is a type of poetry that centers on the oral form, or performance, of a written poem. Here I focus on poetry as a written form. For more on the history and present-day manifestations of the spoken word movement, see M. Algarin and B. Holman, *Aloud: Voices from the Nuyorican Poets Café* (New York: Henry Holt, 1994); Z. Anglesey, *Listen Up! Spoken Word Poetry* (New York: Ballantine, 1999); G. Glazner, *Poetry Slam: The Competitive Art of Performance Poetry* (San Francisco: Manic D, 2000).

10 L. Muller and the Poetry for the People Blueprint Collective, *June Jordan's Poetry for the People: A Revolutionary Blueprint* (New York: Routledge, 1995). Also see J. Jordan, *On call: Political essays* (Boston: South End. 1985).

11 S. Heath, "What no bedtime story means: Narrative skills at home and at school," *Language in Society 11(2)* (1982): 49–76; These literate episodes derive from what Heath calls "*literacy events,*" that is, any set of human interactions mediated by print/writing. Also see Gee (1996) for a discussion on literacy and Discourse, see J. Gee, *Social Linguistics and Literacies: Ideology in Discourses* (Bristol, PA: Taylor and Francis, 1996).

12 B. Street, *Literacy in Theory and Practice* (Cambridge: CUP, 1984).

13 Mahiri and Sablo, "Writing for their lives."

14 At the writing of these notes, Naier no longer had the time to do homework after school. He either went directly to work at a BioTech company or attended organizational group meetings held by Youth Together or the Black Student Union. He did his work when he got home.

15 At the writing of these notes, Naier listened more to artists such as Nas, Cee-Lo, 50 Cent, and Goapele than those previously named.

16   A. Dyson, *Writing Superheroes: Contemporary Childhood, Popular Culture, and Classroom Literacy* (New York: Teachers College, 1997).

17   J. Lave and E. Wenger, *Situated Learning: Legitimate Peripheral Participation* (Cambridge: CUP, 1991).

18   See Gee, *Social linguistics*. See also Delpit, *Other people's children*. This shift from one discourse to another implies that acquisition (not just learning) can also take place in one's primary discourse. Delpit argues that the separation between primary and secondary discourse, and/or other levels of discourse for that matter, is not as plainly rigid as Gee's theory explains it.

19   E. Wenger, *Communities of Practice: Learning, Meaning, and Identity* (Cambridge: CUP, 1998).

11. Urban African American Female Students and Educational Resiliency

VENUS EVANS-WINTERS

As raced, classed, and gendered subjects, urban African American female students are multiply affected by racist, sexist, and classist research paradigms and their resulting educational policies. Needless to say how these racist and sexist frameworks have affected research on or about Black girls and women, as researchers and the researched. In the lives of African American girls and women, racism, sexism, and classism are three interdependent control systems. Simultaneously and interdependently, White racism has suppressed urban Black girls within racialized identities; patriarchy has subordinated them and deemed them powerless; concurrently their lower-income and working-class status has forced them to the periphery of society. Their raced, classed, and gendered bodies have made them both invisible and hyper-surveillanced in educational policy and within the urban school system.

Because African American females experience the intersection of race, class, and gender simultaneously, they become easy targets in the subordination and legitimation process in Western society.[1] As articulated by Patricia Hill Collins,[2] "Portraying African American women as stereotypical mammies, matriarchs, welfare recipients, and hot mommas, helps justify US Black women's oppression".[3] Collins further states that these socially constructed images are designed to make racism, sexism, and poverty, and other injustices appear to be a normal part of life.[4] Politicians, the media, social service personnel, religious groups, and researchers tend to focus on teenage pregnancy and high school dropout rates among urban African American adolescent girls. The generalized depressing statistics about poor minority girls erases the role of discriminatory practices in education and other social structures.[5] Very rarely do we hear discussions about the majority of Black girls from urban and inner-city communities that graduate high school and college. There is a need for more urban education research and pedagogical reform efforts that look at how urban girls are resilient despite their risks and vulnerabilities.

Resiliency Research

Resiliency studies ask questions pertaining to the motivation and persistence of students. Research on resilience is more likely to ask the following question: What resources do students identified as "high-risk" have in place to support educational achievement? Resiliency is the ability to recover from or adjust to problems, adversities, and stress in life.[6] For women and African Americans, academic achievement has been associated with social and economic mobility. However, very little research has focused on factors that enhance positive educational development among African American females. Instead, the majority of research on Black female students focuses on social problems, such as school dropouts, drug and alcohol use, welfare dependency, and teenage pregnancy.[7] The discussion below focuses on educational resiliency in the lives of a group of African American female students living in a midsize urban city in the Midwest.

Researching processes of resiliency

The results reported below are based on a three-year ethnography that followed five students from their eighth grade school year to their junior year in high school.[8] Data was gathered in the form of field observations in family homes, neighborhoods, and schools, as well as open-ended interviews. The original purpose of the study was to look at how the interaction of racism, classism, and sexism impacted the school experiences of urban African American female adolescents. However, after implementing the study, the theme of resiliency dominated over the theme of subjugation in the lives of the selected students. I learned from the most educationally resilient students that support from the family, community, and school simultaneously buffered adversity and fostered school resiliency. Three of the five students were found to be educationally resilient, as measured by school persistence.

All the students in the study lived in low-income and working class neighborhoods. They also attended the more high-risk middle schools and local high school, which were identified as such by their high student dropout rate, high mobility rate, and the number of low-income students who attended the school. I found that resilient students in the study did not dichotomize or order the significance of their stressors. Most of the stressors that the students experienced occur at the intersection of their race, class, and gender. Consequently, these stressors have affected the young women's educational experiences. In the discussion following, I attempt to extract out the stressors and support systems that the resilient students experiences as urban girls.

Context-specific stressors

Four of the five students experienced some kind of medical problem that impeded on the schooling process. For example, one student, Nicole, reported that she was hospitalized for pneumonia, and as a result required home schooling for the first three years of her education. She also reported that she was diagnosed as having Attention Deficit Hyperactivity Disorder, prior to entering middle school. To cope with her medical problems, Nicole and her mother were required to integrate their resources from the Department of Children and Family Services (DCFS) and the school, which included at-home tutoring provided by the school and paid for by DCFS. In Nicole's case, the family, community, and school came together to help her achieve academically.

Likewise, another student, Zora, reported that teachers thought she had a learning disability, because she had refused to talk at school for a period of time. Obviously, it is not known if a student's environment, income status, or biology caused any of their health conditions. However, from other research it is known that there exists a relationship between poverty, health problems, and student deficits at school.[9] Zora eventually thrived, despite the circumstances that may have caused her speech delays. Two of the students who were found not to be educationally resilient, but resilient nonetheless, left school due to early pregnancies.

Other stressors that the students in the study reported encountering were racism and classism in the larger community, police or government intervention in family affairs, violence and drug trafficking in their neighborhoods, hostile school environments, etc. All the students described how negative media perceptions of their school have affected students' interactions with teachers and staff. As Zora explained about her high school, "It's like every year, they get a new rule, and it gets stricter and stricter." Using the pregnant body as a point of reference, Pillow explains how the female body is a "site of paradoxical social attention and avoidance."[10,11] Like the pregnant body, the bodies of African American female adolescents have always been sites monitored, avoided, and scrutinized by those holding power. Whether the power holders are caregivers, slave masters, legal/political bodies, or school officials, the Black female adolescent body has been the targeted culprit.[12] Zora is conscious of her and her female peers' targeted bodies.

Many of these factors had not only affected the Black girls' individual (micro-level) school experiences, but it had managed to affect them on a broader (macro) level. For example, the students in the study were affected by teacher shortages and were less likely to have an African American female as a teacher. Yet, they were more likely to be educated by bitter

White teachers, who found themselves with low pay, few resources, and teaching in an environment that was "culturally" different from their own. I can only presume that these were the "prejudiced" teachers the students described in their life stories. As for resilience, the most resilient students located resources that countered prejudicial behavior. For instance, Nicole located an African American teacher at school, who she felt understood her emotional needs growing up as an urban girl. The third resilient student, Yssis, who had more trouble finding solace in the school building, located a mentor through a community organization. Zora, on the other hand, found solace in her own acquired skills, by interacting with and mentoring students who were considered outsiders by their peers.

Another example of gender and cultural-specific stress that is linked to their context, is that the young women in the study also found themselves being surveillanced by policies that dictated what they learned, how they dressed, and how they behaved. For example, all the girls in the study complained of school policies that appeared to allude to the sexual messages in their styles of dress (i.e., girls were not permitted to wear sleeveless blouses or tank tops). Most of the girls alleged the policies served to try to prevent sexual molestation or rape by controlling young women's behaviors. These policies are racist and sexist in thinking. First of all, the policies are targeting the potential victim's behavior. Second, the policies assume there is going to be a victim. As we hear from the girls, many of the policies at their schools were put into place because the larger community views them as uncivilized heathens, who need to be contained. Even more, it is assuming that the Black girls in the school building are jezebels, who tempt the potential rapist (or some may conclude the girls' victim).

Fortunately, the most resilient students in the study were conscious of how the images held by members of the larger community and society affected the rules and discipline policies of their local school buildings. What is even further interesting is that the most resilient students attempted to guard against "tainting" their own images. They strived to maintain the "good girl/good student" image by avoiding sexual relationships with boys and participating in the labeling of "those girls" who fit the "loose girl/bad girl/bad student" stereotype. These gender-specific resilient strategies have worked to the advantage of the resilient students.

In sum, all the gender and cultural-specific stress, derived from their families, communities, and schools, only caused more stress between the students themselves. Therefore, it was even difficult for students to turn to their peer group for support. Only one of the three students, Zora, expressed a somewhat high attachment to other students attending her high school. None of the students reported spending time with peers located in their immediate neighborhoods. In the case of the resilient young women, community organizations and extracurricular activities at school at least provided a supportive environment for the opportunity to foster peer relationships. All the girls had participated in community and school student groups.

I argue that the stressors that the young women experienced throughout their educational career are related to their race, class and gender, and where they live and attend school.

I also argue that these gender and cultural-specific stressors required the most resilient students to draw on gender and cultural-specific resiliency fostering supports.

Resilience and African American female students

After reading the stories of the most resilient students, we are able to begin to answer the following questions: Who are the students who are more likely to stay in school? What factors contribute to students staying in school? When were the profiled African American female students at their most resilient? What are the historical, economic, and political conditions that affect their schooling process? And, how do the most resilient African American female students cope with, resist, or buffer adversity?

I found that the most resilient students were those young women who received support from their family, community, and schools simultaneously. Because the young women's stressors could not be dichotomized, neither could their support systems. For example, in the conversation below, Nicole's words demonstrate how outside forces affect the schooling process.

> N: It was kind of hard when I was in kindergarten, because my mom, we got taken from her, and all that kind of stuff. So, it was kind of hard for us. For me, because I was the baby in kindergarten. It was hard. We would like go to the courthouse almost everyday. They come pick us up from school and stuff.

It appears that those families and students, who were more adept at blurring the boundaries between family, community, and school, were the most resilient, for their stressors were very rarely easily divisible; thus, their resources were not stratified either. The more a student was able to utilize resources at home and in the community, the more likely she was to stay psychologically (measured by school involvement in extracurricular activities) and physically (measured by school attendance) attached to the school building.

Community support

Community resources that assisted in educational development usually included after-school programs like tutoring, mentoring, or group-related activities. In most cases, community participation usually depended on its relevance to school. Participation in religious services was the exception. Most students attended church, because they had family members who attended the church, they felt it was the "right thing to do," or simply to worship. However, church appeared to be very important to all three resilient students. Educational resilience many times was also reinforced at the community level, by programs that offered the young women temporary job opportunities during the summer or after school. Even in the community work programs, the most resilient students still took preferred job assignments that focused on education or learning in some capacity (i.e., tutoring younger students or providing childcare).

Besides, most of the resilient students associated out-of-school interns or work programs as learning opportunities. For example, Nicole tutored children, because she thought that it gave her the chance to see what it would be like to be a teacher who cared. Another example includes Yssis' decision to continue working at her summer job with children, because it offered a college scholarship incentive to long-term employees.

It is important to restate that in some cases lines were blurred between stressors and resources. For example, Zora and Nicole both received intervention services through DCFS, which may be categorized as potential stressors or distractions to a student's education and development. Postmodern tenets remind us that we must avoid binarial thinking that would force us to order stressors and buffers, because the two may actually be working bi-directionally. For example, I found that all the resilient students were very concerned with their grades. The students' over concern with grades may actually produce more stress and strain in her life, while also encouraging her to work harder as a student. Looking at stressors, support systems, and individual agency simultaneously, reminds us that resiliency-fostering factors are dynamic in nature.

In this particular study, the resilient students and their families utilized community resources as a mediating entity as they negotiated a space of their own in the realm of education. The resilient student understood that community resources assisted in their educational development by providing networking opportunities (i.e., community mentors), and needed resources such as paid work, community mentors, tutoring services, or a safe space beyond their schools and homes. Yssis sums up the role of community organizations in the lives of resilient Black girls. When I asked Yssis how her community could help her with school, she responded:

> Well, they do got a lot of programs and stuff around, but all the commotion around the neighborhood . . . I think that we should move somewhere, like away from this drama. People fighting everyday, arguing, saying stuff that kids don't need to hear . . . But, it's a lot of programs around the neighborhood that'll help you with your school and stuff. If you need to just talk, somebody always there to talk to you.

School support

Like with community resources, the most resilient students were keen at taking advantage of resources available to them at the school itself. For instance, all three of the resilient students in this study at some point sought tutoring in at least one subject. Moreover, the resilient students were also more likely to participate in extracurricular school activities that supported their long-term goals. Because all the young women had planned on completing high school and going on to college, all three participated in Junior Recruitment Officer Training Corp (JROTC), with the goal of receiving a college scholarship. Resiliency studies show that students who are involved in school activities are more likely to be academic achievers and to complete school on time; thus, these students early on had increased their chances of completing high school.[13]

Furthermore, the resilient students appreciated stern but understanding teachers. Also, all the resilient students voiced the need for Black female teachers. I do not believe that the girls necessarily felt an African American female teacher could teach them more or any better than a White teacher. My hypothesis is that the students associated African American female teachers as being stern and empathetic to their needs and the adversities they faced in life (qualities similar to their mothers). As pointed out by Lisa Delpit,[14] some African American teachers bring a teaching style to the classroom that is congruent with the parenting styles that some African American children are accustomed to at home. It too was assumed by the students that African American teachers had the potential of mixing caring and sternness to provide an ideal learning environment. Moreover, the students welcomed those teachers, regardless of race, who were fair.

In contrast to other ethnographies, this study also found that even the resilient young women were in opposition to unjust school policies and discipline procedures. Oppositional behavior was displayed in "talking back" to teachers and other school staff, refusing to carry out a punishment, or simply choosing to ignore a school rule or policy. Different from other studies on resistors, the resilient young women continued to attend school and soon enough decided to conform to what it took to graduate from high school. Their conformity was marked by their advocacy for more school programs and extracurricular activities that made education fun, like it was prior to high school.

Even though all the resilient students generally had a negative attitude about their schools' environment (staff and other students), most had positive feelings about at least one adult in their school. A positive feeling toward an adult in the school was usually a result of one-on-one contact, such as after school tutoring. For example, Nicole, an honor roll student, stated, "those teachers don't understand us ghetto children." When I asked her to explain her comment further she explained, "We need some Black teachers. The teachers are prejudice. Get us some books." Interestingly, this same resilient student named her White resource teacher as the one person who has helped the most at school with her schoolwork. As a side note, Nicole also mentioned the emotional support that she received from an African American female in her school, who was not a teacher. Therefore, research on gender and cultural-specific resilience programs might emphasize that the race of a teacher is less important than the caring nature of the teacher and the ability of the teacher to understand the cultural experiences of the students.

These findings on teachers' caring attitudes toward students are consistent with Valenzuela's work with Mexican and Mexican American students' perceptions of schoolteachers.[15] As Valenzuela found in her research:[16]

> The individual histories that teachers and students bring to classroom encounters necessarily influence the chances for successful relationship building. Still, in most cases, there is likely to be some room to maneuver that is, if the situation is approached literally "with care."[17]

Because caring relationships with teachers were not very frequent, the family members of the students also contributed to support school persistence. Although all the students' families had experienced crisis of their own at some point in their child's educational career, they were able to meet the educational needs of their child. Most of their crisis situations were related to their social and economic positions in the city in which they lived. For example, Yssis family had survived a divorce and the incarceration of her father; Nicole's biological mother had lost custody of her children; and Zora experienced the death of her biological mother in the middle of her freshman year of high school. Ironically, none of the students lived with both their (biological) mother and father during the time of the study. Yet, all of the resilient students named a family member as their main source of support. More specifically, the young women named their female caregiver as the one person who has helped them "get this far" in school.

Familial support

In my view, family support was the most dynamic in nature amongst the resilient qualities of students. Family support defied almost everything I have ever learned in sociological theory about educational resilience. For instance, most hypotheses state that those students who come from two parent (heterosexual) families are going to be more competent in society. However, I learned that the most resilient or competent students were those students who felt love in their family. Although Yssis and Nicole admitted having missed building a relationship with their fathers, none of the resilient students felt that living in a single-parent household (or not with their biological parents) negatively affected their education. All three of the resilient young women felt that their parents cared about their educational accomplishments and wanted them to do well in school. More importantly, all the students reported that a family member helped them directly with some aspect of their schooling, like completing a homework assignment or providing assistance with studying for an examination. In the dialog below, Yssis, as a junior, discusses her mother's role in her educational development:

> V: Tell me who has helped you get this far in school?
> Y: Mainly, my mom, because she really like pushed me to get good grades and stuff. Like if I ever brought home like a "D" or something, she'll be like, "Well, you just gotta work more in this subject" or whatever. Then, I'll probably get an "A" in it the next week. She helps me a lot too.

Aside from emotional support (i.e., girls reported that mother is "there for me when I need her"), or financial support (i.e., providing housing or clothing), family support also included monitoring school participation (i.e., intervening with discipline problems at school or even punishing a student for not doing well in school). Nevertheless, very high attachment to a female caregiver was very significant in the resiliency process. For example, the forms of support listed above were more likely to come from a primary female caregiver, such as a mother, grandmother, or aunt. The study found that relationships between maternal caregivers and students fostered resilience, when students experienced a "muse" relationship with their mothers.

Muse relationships are relationships that are more natural in nature, as opposed to mentoring relationships, where an adult guide is usually assigned to a student. With muse relationships, students are able to choose their own role model, who usually is someone from a similar background or community as their own.[18] Furthermore, muse relationships, like the one's that appeared to have been more worthwhile and effective for the resilient students, teach girls life lessons by sharing from one's own experience. This study found that female caregivers, who were reportedly more open and honest with their daughters about their life experiences, produced stronger mother–daughter relationships. Even more, it was also found that regardless of other available mentors or role models, resilient students always named their female caregiver as the main source of support.

Individual Agency

Although support from the family, community, and school is significant in fostering educational resilience, students' individual intentions and motivations also play a significant role in school persistence. For instance, all the resilient students in the study looked forward to completing high school, and eventually going on to college and having a long-term career. In fact, the most resilient students had already developed a plan for their life course. For example, in the eighth grade, Zora's goals were to go to high school, get into the nursing academy, and get involved in school activities, graduate from high school, and go to college. Of course, not all of the girls' goals worked out as planned, but it is still important to mention that the most resilient students had some type of plan in place. Maybe their articulated goals actually served as a buffer to school failure.

Grades also appear to be very important to the most resilient students. The most resilient students seemed to be always conscious of their grade evaluations, and usually strived to do better in school or in a particular class. I found grade evaluations to be a stressor for all the resilient young women, instead of serving as a reward or positive reinforcement. Regardless of the level of real or perceived stress, the resilient students asked for help or sought out useful resources in their family, community, or schools. Despite their ability to seek out social and academic resources in the community, the most resilient students were also those who had low attachment to their community neighborhoods. Yssis, for instance, simply chose not to associate herself with any of her peers at school or in the neighborhood. Nicole and Zora's parents simply forbade them to hang out in their neighborhoods. Definitely, the most resilient students were not "social butterflies" in their immediate neighborhoods, by choice or by force. Notwithstanding their low attachment to their immediate neighborhoods, the most resilient students and their families were more likely to have a low mobility rate. Nicole and Zora have lived in the same neighborhood and homes from kindergarten through high school, and Yssis from approximately fourth grade through high school. Therefore, low mobility was also a supporting factor in the students' resiliency.

Another significant finding to point out about the character of the most resilient students is that these young women were also very attuned to and vociferous about intimate relationships with boys, sex, and the possible negative consequences of an early unplanned pregnancy. The resilient young women rationalized from the experiences of others around them (i.e., peers, neighbors, or family members) that sexual activity was a potential threat to their educational and career goals. In other words, intimate relationships with boys and pregnancy were viewed as a threat to their long-term goals, and were behaviors that they were almost always conscious of and articulated often in their educational stories.

Also, it is important to mention that resilience is a process. The most educationally resilient students did not necessarily display the qualities listed above all at once or all the time. Just like any other skill, building relationships with adults, asking for help, and participation in extracurricular activities, require skills that we are more adept or comfortable with at a particular time. For instance, some students in the study had to work on improving their school attendance, or others ended their participation in a school organization. Yssis, for example, had decided that she no longer felt comfortable participating in after-school activities offered at a local community organization. Similarly, Zora's relationship with a boyfriend interfered with her attendance record, and Nicole found that her plans for joining the cheerleading team had to be altered. What is more important about the resilient students is that they showed resilience over time. The most resilient students had the motivation and resources to access the available support systems that were necessary to bounce back from adversity.

Implications for Urban Education Reform

Not only does structural inequality shape the specific stressors in urban girls' lives, but it also shapes the systems of support that Black girls depend on to cope. Unfortunately, current literature on resiliency does not acknowledge the interaction of race, class, and gender, or the influence of individual agency and social structures on African American female students' educational development. A new and more inclusive cultural and gender-specific look at school resilience has the potential of having a transcending effect on school reform. For example, this new focus in resilience research can assist reformers in producing more cultural and gender-specific resiliency programs. Also, this new perspective may bring cultural and gender-specific issues (i.e., concerns that Black feminists have traditionally addressed) to education policy and pedagogy discourse altogether. Resilience research has the potential of assisting policymakers in identifying the impact of race, class, and gender oppression on educational experience and outcome. Many researchers in urban education have studied the impact of race and class discrimination on urban education,[19] but very few have studied gender oppression in urban education. Even more important is the fact that little or no research has focused on the ways in which women of color cope with and overcome many forms of gender, race, and class oppression, and maintain resilience in the face of adversity.

Rigsby reminds us that resilience is contextually bound in time and place and culture.[20] African American female students' educational experiences are impacted by their race, class, and gender status. Their educational experiences are also influenced by where and how they live. Multiple identities and multiple oppressions require that minority females draw on unique cultural and gender-specific systems of support. From past research with African American females, their families, and their communities, we are able to recognize resilience-fostering factors.[21] We also realize the need for a more inclusive definition of resilience and a need to reconstruct resilience. Finally, gender-and culture-specific resilience research has the potential to help facilitate progress in urban education reform initiatives. Resilient African American female students struggle against race, class, and gender oppression. For instance, African American female students are more likely to attend schools in urban neighborhoods with high poverty, unemployment, and high crime rates than their white counterparts,[22] and to live in a world that privilege White over Black, male over female, and wealth over poverty. In spite of social and institutional racism and sexism, the majority of African American females have been able to achieve academically. More resilient adolescents may obtain support from the family, community, and/or school, that serve as protective factors against academic failure.

NOTES

1   L. F. Miron, *The Social Construction of Urban Schooling: Situating the Crisis* (Cresskill, NJ: Hampton Press, Inc., 1997).

2   P.H. Collins, *Black Feminist Thought: Knowledge, Consciousness, and the Politics of Empowerment* 2nd ed. (New York: Routledge, 2000).

3   Ibid., p. 69.

4   Ibid.

5   B.J.R. Leadbeater and N. Way, *Urban Girls: Resisting Stereotyping, Creating Identities* (New York: New York University Press, 1996).

6   J.B. Ashford, C.W. LeCroy and K.L. Lortie, *Human Behavior in the Social Environment: A Multidimensional Perspective* (Pacific Grove, CA: Brooks/Cole, 1997).

7   Ibid.

8   V.E. Evans-Winters, *Reconstructing Resilience: Including African American Female Students in Educational Resilience Research*. Unpublished Dissertation. (Urbana-Champaign: University of Illinois at Urbana-Champaign, 2003).

9   I.A. Canino and J. Spurlock, *Culturally Diverse Children and Adolescents: Assessment, Diagnosis, and Treatment* (New York: The Guilford Press, 1994).

10   W.S. Pillow, "Exposed methodology: The body as a deconstructive practice," in E.A. St. Pierre, and W.S. Pillow, eds. *Working the Ruins: Feminist Poststructural Theory and Methods in Education* (New York: Routledge Press, 2000), pp. 199–222.

11   Ibid., p. 201.

12   A.Y. Davis, *Women, Race, and Class* (New York: Random House, 1981); D. Roberts, *Killing the Black Body: Race, Reproduction, and the Meaning of Liberty* (New York: Random House, Inc., 1997).

13   M.C. Wang and E.W. Gordon, *Educational Resilience in Inner-City America* (Mahwah, NJ: Lawrence Erlbaum, 1994).

14   L. Delpit, *Other People's Children: Cultural Conflict in the Classroom* (New York: The New Press, 1995).

15   A. Valenzuela, *Subtractive Schooling: U.S. Mexican Youth and the Politics of Caring* (New York: University of New York Press, 1999).

16   Ibid.

17   Ibid., p. 73.

18   A. M. Sullivan, "From mentor to muse: Recasting the role of women in relationships with urban adolescent girls," in B.J.R. Leadbeater and N. Way, eds. *Urban Girls: Resisting Stereotypes, Creating Identities* (New York: New York University Press, 1996), pp. 226–254.

19   J. Anyon, *Ghetto Schooling: A Political Economy of Urban Educational Reform* (New York: Teachers College Press 1997); C.M. Payne, *Getting What We Ask For: The Ambiguity of Success and Failure in Urban Education* (Connecticut: Greenwood Press, 1994); R. Taylor, "Risk and resilience: Contextual influences on the development of African American adolescents," in M.C. Wang, and E.W. Gordon, eds. *Educational Resilience in Inner-City America: Challenges and Prospects* (Mahwah, NJ: Lawrence Erlbaum, 1994), pp. 119–130.

20   L.C. Rigsby, "The Americanization of resilience: Deconstructing research practice," in M.C. Wang, and E.W. Gordon, eds. *Educational Resilience in Inner-City America: Challenges and Prospects* (Mahwah, NJ: Lawrence Erlbaum, 1994), pp. 85–96.

21   C.A. Bagley and J. Carroll, "Healing forces in African American families," in H.I. McCubbin, ed. *Resilience in African American Families* (Thousand Oaks, CA: SAGE, 1996); A. M. Cauce, Y. Hiraga, D. Graves, N. Gonzales, K. Ryan-Finn and K. Grove, "African American mothers and their adolescent daughters: Closeness, conflict, and control," in B.J.R. Leadbeater, and N. Way, eds. *Urban Girls: Resisting Stereotypes, Creating Identities* (New York: New York University Press, 1996), pp. 100–116; M.L. Clark and D. Scott-Jones, "The school experiences of black girls: The interaction of gender, race, and economic status," *Phi Delta Kappan, 67* (1986): 520–526; A. Henry, "Invisible and womanish: Black girls negotiating their lives in an african-centered school in the USA," *Race, Ethnicity, and Education, 1(2)* (1998): 151–170; J.A. Ladner, "Introduction to tomorrow's tomorrow: The black woman," in S. Harding, ed. *Feminism and Methodology* (Bloomington: Indiana University Press, 1987).

22   J. Anyon, *Ghetto Schooling: A Political Economy of Urban Educational Reform* (New York: Teachers College Press, 1997); M. Fine, *Framing Dropouts: Notes on the Politics of an Urban Public High School* (NY: SUNY Press, 1991); W.J. Wilson, *When Work Disappears: The World of the New Urban Poor* (New York: Random House, 1996).

12. "I Still Fear I'm Gonna Slip"

A Case Study of African American and Latino Males in an Urban College Preparation Program

NOEL S. ANDERSON

Introduction

To create greater educational equity and to increase opportunity in the United States, millions of federal, state, and private dollars have been allocated to college-preparation (or early intervention) programs at the secondary level. These programs are designed to increase high school graduation rates, enhance college access, and ultimately close the college enrollment and degree gaps among under-served groups.[1] Advocates of these programs suggest that they provide a vital safety net for thousands of poor African American and Latino students who are inadequately supported in their school environments.[2] However, as many as two-thirds of low-income and minority students enrolled in these programs drop out of them.[3] For example, in a recent evaluation of Upward Bound, a thirty-six-year old federally funded early intervention initiative, almost 40% of the students enrolled dropped out of the program before completing the first year.[4]

This article is based on a case study that was conducted at one Upward Bound program in a large urban center in the Northeastern United States that is grappling with high attrition of African American and Latino males. Interviews were conducted with program administrators, faculty, and African American and Latino male students over a year until no new information emerged, as well as participant observations and document analysis.

The purpose of the study was to examine the assumptions about equity underpinning the design of a college preparation program serving young men of color and to understand how this approach to increasing educational opportunity plays out in the lived experience of young men served. Further, the assumptions of interpretive interactionism as discussed by Norman Denzin provided a useful methodological framework for the purposes of this study. Through interpretive interactionism, we make the world of lived experience directly accessible to the reader, capturing the voices, emotions, and actions of those studied as they strive to succeed in an educational program that is designed to serve them.[5] The goal is to perhaps shed light on some of the challenges and potential interventions educators and policymakers can have in increasing the graduation and college going rates of African American and Latino young men.

Case Study

Eastern University campus is like a fortress, with ornate iron gates at all entry points. The urban campus is wedged between a largely black and Latino working class neighborhood and a growing population of white professionals most are largely affiliated with the university. With this racial and ethnic mix, the neighborhood is visibly multicultural. Black and Latino teenagers regularly play among white toddlers in nearby parks, and trendy coffee shops are just blocks from working class Latino "bodegas."

It was this glaring disparity in resources between the university and surrounding neighborhood that led progressive white students at Eastern to found the College Access Initiative (CAI) program in 1965, becoming one of the first Upward Bound programs in the country. Their goal was to strengthen the relationship between the university and neighborhood residents, to open the gates of the university to the community.

"Students really do take ownership of this place. This campus is like their second home," Craig, the Executive Director of CAI, states. A tall, middle-aged African American man, Craig is a striking presence. His deep resonating voice reveals a slight southern drawl. His family roots are in the deep South. He migrated north over twenty years ago to attend college. He has a formal manner and a wry sense of humor, often slipping in a joke when you least expect it. He is also a constant presence in program workshops. "I try to know as many kids as possible" he states, "that is more for me than for them. I want them to see me as a support."

In his desire to "give back," Craig is integrally involved in the day-to-day operations of the program, including student recruitment and selection, and curriculum and workshop development. Craig is very concerned about serving the students in his program. CAI supports a maximum of 150 students each year, so it is a relatively small program. The majority of participants in CAI identify themselves as African American/Caribbean Black (38%),

Latino/Hispanic (27%), multi-ethnic (19%), and Other (16%), which includes those of Asian background and a variety of other backgrounds.[6] Most attend comprehensive public high schools in the city and apply to the program. Craig views the small program size and diversity of neighborhood kids as an indication of the effectiveness of the program in fostering university school linkages. He states, "as long as CAI stays consistent with our vision we will continue to keep the university doors open." In fact, much of CAI's outreach is to schools in the area, not only promoting the program but the larger university.

"Our academic program is no joke:"
Preparing students for the rigor of college life

As part of the CAI mission to open the university doors, the program emphasizes a "college preparation curriculum" through year round after school programming. CAI students participate in an intensive summer program, which Craig calls "the summer grind," and they attend academic classes on Saturday throughout the school year. The goal of the intensive academic program is to help prepare students of color for college. Craig states:

> Kids need to know that college is a real commitment," Craig states emphatically. That's why our program is no joke. Our CAI curriculum compliments what students are getting in their schools. They find out what classes they should take. Wherever they need help, they get it here.

Craig stresses that the goal of the Saturday program is to compliment and provide academic support for what students are learning in school. As a result, the academic classes at CAI tend to mirror the classes students take at their respective public high schools. Since students attend schools all over Central city, much of the curriculum at CAI is shaped by the numerous academic standards and standardized tests designed and promoted by the city school board. For instance, the tenth grade history curriculum at CAI is driven by the Central City history examination. The course objectives, lessons, and assessment reflect the test. In fact, students take sections of the examinations for practice drills and pre-assessment, and teachers constantly refer to the examination during class lectures.

"Motivation can overcome poverty:"
Rugged individualism and academic achievement

"Students must be motivated to do well in this program," Craig says, discussing the rigorous nature of the CAI program. Although exposure to campus life should inspire kids, Craig believes that motivation is the driving force needed to succeed in CAI. To Craig, motivation is especially important for poor children, not only for achieving at CAI but to succeed in life. Craig has little interest in discussing the ways in which poverty may limit many students' abilities to succeed in school. When discussing how poverty affects kids' performance in schools, he quips:

We saddle people with that stuff. Whatever your circumstances are you view it as normal. I grew up in Texas; the town was half white and half black. I thought the whole world was like that. It was because that was my world. Your reality is your reality. Someone had to tell you that something is limiting you. When my mom was growing up they were all in the Depression but they didn't have a sense I can't do anything because I was poor because everyone was like that. So you keep those things on people. So if you buy into it, I am in poverty so I can't learn, no. We are taught that.

Craig's belief that people have to be told that poverty is limiting them is greatly informed by his own experience growing up. He asserts that breaking the cycle of poverty is an individual act of will. To Craig, motivation is an individual concern. This stance is inextricably rooted in the rugged individualism promoted in the United States. Historic arguments for the "freedom of man" and "individualism" are articulated in the Declaration of Independence, as well as in the US Constitution. Supporting Craig's perspective, scholars today have argued that rugged individualism advantages students in achievement. In fact, scholars have argued that students who are not socialized into an ethic of rugged individualism may experience greater difficulty in school. Suarez-Orozco and Suarez-Orozco, for example, refer to literature that blames the underachievement of Latino students on a failure of the culture to embrace individualism.[7]

Craig believes that CAI must counter cultural values that undermine student achievement. Because he sees motivation as central to succeeding in school as well as in life, it permeates the CAI program. "Formal state-sanctioned barriers to individual mobility are removed, any continuing inequality must result from the personal failure of individuals".[8] From this perspective, the notion that students are "under-motivated" is solely a personal matter and a personal problem. To Craig, dropping out of the program is clearly evidence of a lack of motivation.

Students need to focus on the future

Similarly, Craig believes that in order for students to be successful in CAI and life, to stay motivated they need to focus on future goals and remain disciplined to achieve. He maintains that it is logical for students to separate their neighborhood from their academic aspirations and career goals. In fact, he views this division as "natural" and conducive to success. He reflects on his own experience:

Students will always separate their neighborhood from school. It is natural. I mean, I have my personal life and then I have my professional life at CAI. I mean its normal to have them separate.

Craig's notion that students "naturally" separate their neighborhood and academic worlds is rooted in a prevailing belief that in order for students from poor and working class inner city communities to excel academically or obtain success (e.g., an education or higher social class status), there must be some psychological and social distancing from harsh present day realities. In other words, most inner city communities are rife with deprivation and deficits (i.e., poverty, the absence of social capital, inadequate health care and education, crime and drugs) that a child's neighborhood, peer group or family arrangement can be potential obstacles.[9] Ogbu argues, for instance, that a great many black students from poor and working class communities are conditioned to believe that academic success is an attempt to "act white." Consequently, significant numbers of black students are intentionally underachieving for fear of alienating themselves from friends and/or community.[10] To Craig, a CAI student should be disciplined to maintain a vision for the future in the midst of present day pressures. Yet, given the high dropout rates among young men in CAI, one wonders what value students place on the program? How do the young men served in CAI experience the program?

Craig: "Motivation can overcome poverty"

Angelo: "I struggle to stay focused"

Angelo is a soft-spoken kid, with a brown complexion and small twists in his hair. He is 16 years old and lives in Lawrence Heights, a largely poor Dominican neighborhood. His stylish dress makes him stand out among his peers. Angelo aspires to go to a college to study computers. He believes that "computers are everywhere and the future." A self-proclaimed "B student," Angelo recently joined CAI in the fall. He learned about the program through a presentation by a CAI staff member at his public high school and left the meeting believing that CAI would "help me get into the college I want." Angelo attends CAI pretty regularly, commuting over an hour by subway to get to the program.

Angelo's future goal to attend college is challenged by the daily obstacles in his life. Angelo's mother is a single parent and has been a constant, strong presence in his life. He has no relationship with his father since his parents broke up, and he struggles to establish a close bond with his brothers, Roy, age 25 and Jose, age 31. Both brothers have dealt with chronic unemployment and encounters with the law.

Angelo shares a bedroom with Roy and watches Roy waste hours in bed, because he is unemployed. "My brother who lives in the house he just likes sleeping," Angelo says, a tinge of frustration in his voice. "He sleeps a lot. He is probably sleeping right now. He just doesn't do anything. He just lays around." On the surface Angelo presents a nonchalant attitude to his brother's idleness. Yet when describing the challenges his other brother, Jose, is facing, Angelo is reflective about how it impacts his life. He describes the events that led up to his brother, Jose's, arrest for burglary and assault:

> [Jose] was caught breaking into an apartment. When a security guard came up to them, apparently he hit him with a pipe or something like that and knocked the man out. He had to get mad stitches. My brother and his boys thought the apartment was empty but it wasn't. The people were just away for a while but they got caught like a few hours later. The police came by looking for him. But he was uptown at one of his boy's house. It was like three of them who tried to get in and they got caught.

Angelo's brother's unlawful behavior is indicative of his fairly troublesome teenage years. Angelo reflects on his brother's life:

> My brother always got caught doing stupid stuff, like trying to rob people and stuff like that. He was doing stuff when he was a teenager. My mom had a hard time with him. He usually got caught, do like probation and spend like only a few months in jail. This is the first time he like had to go for a long time. He got 5 years.

Angelo confesses that much of his ambition to go to college is fueled by the fear that he will end up like his brothers, unemployed or in the criminal justice system. To Angelo, college is simply a better alternative to incarceration. He states:

> I mean I never got in trouble, but I could have. I used to hang out with some people who could have gotten into stuff like that. My friends back in the day used to steal stuff, candy and stuff from stores. One time my friend got caught trying to steal from a Korean store. But the guy told us to get out. Nothing serious. But it was scary . . . But I caught myself. When my brother got caught, I was like, man, I don't want to be in prison like fighting for a bunk or something. I don't want to be calling my mother and asking her for stuff or having people visiting me with prison clothes. That's not the life I want. I just realized that I would end up in jail like my brother or dead.

Angelo flirted with crime, engaging in mischievous behavior with friends, but, "caught himself" after his brother was incarcerated. Although he was never a victim of violence or engaged in a life of crime, Angelo still has a fear that he will "slip" into adverse situations because they are pervasive in his family and larger community.

Nussbaum argues that concerns with bodily integrity pervade the lives of individuals living in poverty. Bodily integrity is an innate concern with one's safety from assault and one's ability to move freely without fear of violence, in various forms.[11] This concern is further exacerbated by negative media images which portray inner-city young men of color as either victims or perpetrators of violence and other social deviant behavior.[12] Hence, for young men like Angelo growing up in under-resourced communities, there is a pervasive fear of bodily assault as well as deep-seated fear of failure that shapes actions and motivation.

To Angelo, watching his brother succumb to "the streets" impacted his ability to stay focused on the future goal of college. At points in the year, the stress of his brother's incarceration coupled with the demands of school led him to ponder dropping out of the CAI program. He states:

> The court case and stuff was a lot. I didn't want to go to the jail and see him. My mom and brother did that. It was a tough time. On top of that sometimes I get too much homework between school and CAI, it is a lot. Sometimes I forget to do my homework for my Saturday classes so I get behind. At times I didn't want to come. During the summer program, I was so stressed out. I struggled to stay focused. It was so much work and concentrating on classes. I wanted to drop out at points.

For Angelo, the additional academic work of CAI coupled with "feeling stressed out" because of his brother's incarceration led him to ponder dropping out of the program. In this story we see that when Angelo's brother was put behind bars for five years, his faith in and motivation to continue in the program wavered.

Craig argues that young men of color must stay motivated in spite of the obstacles they face. They must keep their eye on their goal to get an education and let nothing get in their way. However, in this story, we see that Angelo struggles to stay motivated and achieve academically. He looks around his community and at his brother, and his faith in what is possible is severely shaken. He begins to wonder, why am I doing this? What is my future, anyway? In essence, Angelo's daily struggles greatly impact his outlook on the future and his capabilities to succeed. He needs help thinking through the fears of failure that haunt him.

However, CAI does not provide this kind of support, so he keeps his fears to himself, fears that sometimes make dropping out of CAI seem like a rational choice.

Craig's assumption that students must be motivated to continue in the program underplays the myriad of problems that quell young men's desires as well as their freedoms to achieve. Clearly motivated to succeed, Angelo experiences difficult personal and academic challenges that affect his work participation at CAI. Yet, CAI is not geared toward addressing the life difficulties young men of color face each day. Therefore, Angelo is constantly coping with present day challenges and struggling not to lose sight of the future.

Craig: "Students must focus on the future"

Miguel: "It felt like I was sinking"

Miguel wants to be a computer engineer. An outgoing, tall tenth grader who struggles to juggle family and academic responsibilities, Miguel has an earnest bearing and engaging smile. Miguel joined CAI a year ago to help fulfill his dream of being the first person in his large Dominican family from Lawrence Hill to attend college. He attends a comprehensive high school in Central that is known for gang activity. Yet Miguel struggles to ignore the negative influences in school and stay committed to his academic goals. He states:

> I am a good student. I get nothing but Bs and B-pluses on my exams. I like Spanish, history and gym. History is good because it helps you to understand things. It is fun. I like watching the history channel cuz it is interesting. I knock history out.

Like Angelo, Miguel works hard to juggle the responsibilities of school, CAI, and family. Miguel recently encountered major family challenges that sidetracked him from CAI and his goals. At one point the pressure was overwhelming that he even dropped out of CAI. He recalls:

> My mom was like real sick and stuff. She had like tumors or something in her uterus. So she had to like get it taken out so she was in for a while and like then was home cuz she couldn't work. She was going to the doctor a lot so I was picking my brother up from school cuz my dad had to work. It was a lot. But like coming here to CAI and then like doing homework, taking care of my brother, it was a lot. I was tired all the time. I was like slipping in my work. I went from like a B in one class to like a D in like only a few weeks. I was missing tutoring a lot. It was too much. I wanted to come but didn't have the time. So I was like I should just stop this year and come back like next summer and start over or something.

Miguel found himself looking after his younger brother and doing more of the household chores while trying to maintain his demanding academic schedule. He had very little support, even from his father during this time. His dad works long hours as a grounds keeper and needed to support the family financially. Miguel's only support came when his aunt came from the Dominican Republic some months later to help out. Overwhelmed by the events in his family and seeing very few avenues for support, Miguel struggled to cope with the situation on his own, but eventually he decided that he had to drop out of CAI. He did not even let his parents know that he had dropped out:

> My pops would ask me if I was going to CAI and I would say yeah, even though I wasn't going. I eventually had to talk to JT [an advisor at CAI] about it cuz I was missing class. He just told me to

make up as much work as I can and come like again in the spring. It was just too much . . . I was just like sinking or something, it was like quicksand. It was like quicksand all the time. Sinking. You know how quicksand is, like takes you under and stuff.

Miguel's feeling of "sinking . . . like quicksand" highlights the overwhelming pressure he feels to balance his increasing responsibilities. It is not uncommon for children from poor and working class communities to assume responsibility for taking care of younger siblings. Many young adults, in fact, must defer future plans and take on employment to support their families.[13] Miguel saw dropping out of CAI as the only viable way to manage his overwhelming responsibilities. For Miguel, CAI was not a place where he could talk about the pressures he was feeling. Instead, the program was one more burden that he could not bear during this difficult time. YMC might have been such a place, but Miguel did not see the program as a place where he could talk about his concerns. When he finally did talk to his counselor at CAI, it was only after he had made the decision to drop out, and the counselor offered no alternative to dropping out of CAI for a period of time, leaving Miguel alone to face his problems.

In this story, we see that Miguel's future plans became secondary to his family's needs. Sen states that the poor are particularly vulnerable to unanticipated problems like ill health and because of systemic deprivations.[14] In Miguel's story, we see how these deprivations limit one's legitimate choices. Miguel's obligation to help his family compels to renegotiate his future to put his education on a back burner.

Craig: "CAI replicates what schools are doing"
Shawn: "I am a good student trapped"

Shawn is a bespectacled young man, with a rich dark brown complexion. Charming and easy going, Shawn is known to crack jokes or share humorous stories with friends. He lives in the Harbor Hill section of Central City, a predominately poor and working class African American community, with his mother, Dorothy. Shawn is always well dressed, preferring white Oxford shirts and dress shoes to the popular athletic jerseys and fashionable, expensive sneakers worn by his peers. He wants to become the next "Johnny Cochran." He chose the flamboyant attorney who became internationally recognized during O.J. Simpson's murder trial as a model for his career aspirations because he is "smooth, has money and can work the law." Like many African American kids from poor or working class backgrounds, Shawn views being a lawyer as a stable avenue to financial security. However, when describing the ability of his high school to help prepare him for college and his professional goals, Shawn sees glaring weaknesses. He states:

I go to Central High School. My experience there has been alright. The school is your typical large high school. You know, about 2000 kids. It used to be one of the best in the city, but now it is getting a reputation for not doing so good . . . a lot of students are failing the standardized exams, so there are questions about the school and the academics.

Shawn describes his urban high school as a school in decline. He views the low passing rates of students on standardized tests as an indicator of its failure. A survey of over 1000 New

York City high school students reveals that two-thirds believe the schools they have attended have either stayed the same or worsened over the last five years.[15] Since the publishing of *A Nation at Risk* the majority of public schools, nationally, are utilizing some form of standardized measure for student performance.[16] The results of these measures have been used to shed light on teacher competency and school effectiveness.[17] The biggest impact of these high stakes measures is in under-resourced urban schools where tests have increasingly been used as benchmarks for a school's survival.

In light of these developments, very little research has been done on how students perceive themselves, academically, or how they view their school in a high-stakes environment.[18] Shawn feels the pressure of tests in his school. In fact he views himself as a "good student trapped" in a failing school:

> I classify myself as a good student trapped in an alright school. I am a good student cuz academically I am strong and I get mad support from home. But I do well cuz I have other things going for me. I just focus on getting through the classes and passing the exams. I do what I got to do, you know. Go to class, take my notes and bust the exams out. I just do what I have to do and pass the tests.

To Shawn, simply listening to the teacher, taking notes, doing homework and passing tests are characteristics of being a good student. Freire argues that the traditional task of [the teacher] is to 'fill' the students with the contents of his narration".[19] Freire describes this broadly as the "banking concept of education, in which the scope of action allowed to the students extends only as far as receiving, filling, and storing deposits".[20] Shawn's notion of what makes a good student is influenced by the narrative character of his teaching and learning experience. In a high-stakes, examination-intensive environment, students' test scores become the primary evidence of academic achievement. Often curriculum and pedagogical practices are altered to meet test objectives leading others to argue that these practices are resulting in little more than "killing through drilling," or "too much schooling and too little education".[21]

Shawn heard about CAI a year ago during a presentation in his high school English class. The majority of the recruitment of students for the CAI program is done by staff members going into comprehensive high schools in Central City and using charismatic pleas to encourage students to attend. Many of Shawn's classmates took applications that day, but only he and two girls actually signed up.

At CAI, Shawn attends math and English classes on Saturday and participates in the Young Men's Collective workshop on Friday afternoons. Shawn's Saturday classes are an intensive hour and a half each and begin in the morning and conclude in the early afternoon. Shawn sees his classes as being "cool." He attends regularly and is an active participant during class discussions. When comparing the quality of CAI classes to ones at school he reflects:

The classes [in CAI] are a lot smaller. You don't feel crowded. The classes are more college focused as opposed to school. You work on harder material and you are tested like every 5 weeks. So you have to be on top of the material. The classes are on Saturday, which is cool during the fall, but spring it gets harder to come cuz it is getting warm and stuff. Other than that the classes are set up like college so you get an idea of what to expect.

To Shawn, CAI classes are "cool" because they are taught on a college campus and are modeled after college courses. His class sizes are smaller and they are taught by college students. The overall environment simulates college life. However, Shawn struggles to draw distinctions between instructional approaches at CAI and at his high school. He states:

> Teachers in CAI kind of teach the same way as in my school. Just at CAI they ask you more questions on the reading, you know you have to be up on the work or they put you on the spot in the class. But teachers just kind of expect you to do the readings, assignments and participate.

During one of Shawn's Saturday math classes, the teacher spends a great deal of time lecturing and reviewing city-wide sample examination problems. She is a young Asian college student, zealously writing on the chalkboard, illustrating steps to solve quadratic equations. Students diligently take notes, raising their hands occasionally to ask for clarification. Much of the hour is spent taking notes and doing sample problems. Shawn reflects:

> That's how most of the classes are. You listen to her talk, watch her do the problems then you ask for help if you need it . . . it's o.k. I just do what I need to do. Much of that stuff I get in school anyway. So I don't really think about it.

Shawn's impression of his teachers in the CAI program generally mirrors that of his school day instructors. The real difference between his CAI and high school classes is related to the setting, class size and quantity of assignments. In fact, the smaller class sizes seem to provide a greater level of intensity to his academic work. The low student–teacher ratio, which provides for greater demands of students' participation, is evident in teachers "putting you on the spot in class." Although Shawn views the academic assignments at CAI as harder than at his high school, "harder" is a response to an increase in the quantity of assignments. As for the actual content of the assignments, Shawn states, "much of that stuff I get in school anyway . . . Its just more work to do and you come in and do it."

In essence, Shawn's academic experience at CAI is consistent with Craig's goals and intended outcomes. Craig asserts that the CAI academic program is "no joke" and that he wants to replicate what "schools are doing." Craig believes that CAI should be an extension of public schools and that academic assignments should be geared toward the high stakes tests. In math, for instance, the curriculum focuses more intensely on aspects of the city-wide examination, having students do sample problems and ask for help from the teacher. Consequently, since Shawn is familiar with this form of instruction in school, he responds to the math class in the same pragmatic fashion evident in the school day, by being a "good student." He "listens to her" and "does what he needs to do," which is taking notes and doing the sample problems.

Freire argues that in traditional forms of teaching and learning "verbalistic lessons, reading requirements, the methods for evaluating 'knowledge,' the distance between the teacher and the taught, the criteria for promotion: everything in this ready-to-wear approach serves to obviate thinking".[22] He states that, consequently, "classrooms die as intellectual centers when they become delivery systems for lifeless bodies of knowledge".[23] Shawn's inability to draw meaningful distinctions in his teaching and learning experience at his high school and in CAI classes illustrates the effective way Craig has successfully aligned the program with the curricula and instructional approaches prevalent in public schools in Central City.

However, Craig's assumption that simply replicating the school day will lead to academic success and, ultimately, college access plays out quite differently in Shawn's life. In fact, since joining CAI, the dimensions of his work and life have increased, causing Shawn to once question his ability to persist in the program. He states:

> Last year, I thought about dropping out. Stuff was hectic here after the summer program. I was at Central doing a lot. I felt like just coming home after school and relaxing. I did not want to go in and do more work. It was a lot.

Shawn's feeling of being overwhelmed by the quantity of work at school and CAI created frustration and anxiety. In this circumstance, juggling all the work became too hard for Shawn. In fact, Shawn also states that none of the CAI administrators were aware that he was contemplating dropping out.

Discussion and Concluding Remarks

By examining the assumptions of the program as well as how these assumptions play out in the lives of three academically oriented students at CAI, we achieve greater insight into why young men of color may be opting out of these programs in large numbers.

CAI is grounded in the belief that academic achievement is vital to increasing the educational opportunity and life chances of young men of color. Therefore, the program is geared toward increasing students' level of achievement by providing additional course work and skill development in key academic subjects. For Shawn, Angelo, and Miguel, we see that this increasing demand for academic performance without adequate support for learning how to cope with and address the life problems and pressures they were facing, proved problematic. The young men's narratives illustrate the need for an expanded notion of achievement, one that includes the ability to navigate social and academic worlds.

The vulnerabilities to violence or family challenges that these young men experience often make a college dream a too distant and seemingly unattainable goal amidst the more immediate and pressing problems of street and family life. Although Craig insists that students must maintain a clear vision of and focus on their future goals, and distance themselves from negative influences of the streets, we see that these young men are grappling with serious life pressures that directly influence their motivation and their freedoms to achieve. All three boys are struggling to believe in CAI's prevailing message that dedication and focus on future goals of college and material comfort will ultimately overcome their present conditions. However, on a daily basis, these boys are confronting family and community problems that make the academic demands of CAI overly burdensome and their educational goals precarious.

The stories these boys tell support Nussbaum's argument for treating children as whole *human beings*, rather than as *students*. She argues that human beings need support for human concerns. Clearly, this is the case for Shawn, Angelo, and Miguel. In their stories, we see how fears of failure stemming from physical and emotional integrity often undermine their abilities to stay focused, believe in their future, and stay in school. Yet, CAI and schools more broadly tend to ignore issues of bodily and emotional integrity entirely.

The findings of this study raise serious questions about the efficacy of the overtly academic turn that has taken place in our schools as well as in support programs like Upward Bound. In the end, we see how this focus on academic achievement, and the failure to address issues of bodily and emotional integrity, simply increases the pressures these boys feel, and makes dropping out of the program seem like a rational choice.

NOTES

1   L. Perna and W.S. Swail, "Early intervention programs: How effective are they at increasing access to college?" Paper presented at the *Association for the Study of Higher Education*, Miami, Florida, 1998.

2   L. Perna and W.S. Swail, "Pre-college outreach programs: A national perspective", Paper presented at the *Center for Higher Education Policy*, University of Southern California, 2002.

3   R. Nozaki and B. Shireman, "The effectiveness of college preparation programs," *Chronicle of Philanthropy*, 57 2001.

4   Moore, *A 1990s View of Upward Bound: Programs Offered, Students Served and Operational Issues* (Washington, D.C.: Mathematica Research, Inc., 1997).

5   Denzin, *Interpretive Interactionism* (Newbury Park, CA: Sage Publications, 1989).

6   Philliber Research Associates, *The Upward Bound Program* (New York: Double Discovery Center 1999–2000).

7   M.M. Suarez-Orozco and C.E. Suarez-Orozco. "The cultural patterning of achievement motivation: A comparison of Mexican, Mexican immigrant, Mexican American and Non-Latino White American students," in W.A. Cornelius ed. *California's Immigrant Children: Theory, Research and Implications for Educational Policy* (San Diego, CA: Center for U.S.- Mexican Studies at the University of California-San Diego, 1995).

8   L. Guinier and G. Torres, *The Miners' Canary: Enlisting Race, Resisting Power and Transforming Democracy* (Cambridge, MA: Harvard University Press, 2002).

9   J. Coleman, *Foundations of Social Theory* (Cambridge, MA: Harvard University Press, 1990).

10 J. Ogbu, *Next Generation: An Ethnography of Education in an Urban Neighborhood* (Philadelphia, PA: Elsner Science and Technology, 1994).

11 M. Nussbaum, *Women and Human Development: The Capabilities Approach* (Cambridge, England: Cambridge University Press, 2000).

12 Poussaint and A. Alexander, *Lay My Burden Down: Unraveling Suicide and the Mental Health Crisis Among African Americans* (Boston, MA: Beacon Press, 2000).

13 M.T. Moore, *A 1990s View of Upward Bound: Programs Offered, Students Served and Operational Issues* (Washington, D.C.: Mathematica Research, Inc., 1997), p. 24.

14 Sen, *Inequality Reexamined* (Cambridge, MA: Sage Publications, 1992).

15 Citizens Committee for New York, *New York City High School Students Review Their Schools Performance* (New York: Citizens Committee for New York, 2001).

16 D. Meier, *Will Standards Save Public Education?: A New Democracy Forum* (New York: Beacon Press, 2000).

17 H. Kantor, "Equal opportunity and the federal role in education," *Rethinking Schools II,(2)* (1997).

18 Citizens Committee for New York, *New York City High School Students Review Their Schools Performance* (New York: Citizens Committee for New York, 2001), p. 10.

19 P. Freire, *Pedagogy of the Oppressed* (New York: Continuum Publishing, 1995).

20 Ibid., p. 52.

21 T. Asher and C. Flaxman. "Students of color and school success," *Demography, 42* (1987): 462–503.

22 P. Freire, *Pedagogy of the Oppressed* (New York: Continuum Publishing, 1995), p. 56.

23 Ibid., p. 58.

13. Appreciating the Landscape that Urban Youth of Color Must Navigate to Become Effective Social Actors in Our Civil Society

kecia hayes

"Each generation out of relative obscurity must discover their mission, fulfill it or betray it."

Frantz Fanon, *The Wretched of the Earth*

Our contemporary social discourses, policies, and practices that structure the lives of urban youth of color substantively ignore their understandings of who they are as social actors; and instead, privilege racialized and classed stereotypes of them that radiate from the mediated social imagination of our hegemonic society. "The increasingly familiar script suggests a correlation between urban public space and rampant drug use, daily assaults, welfare fraud, teenage mothers, and young black men caught in the ritual behavior of thug life, prison, and moral irresponsibility."[1] Research by Dorman and Schiraldi demonstrates that 76% of the public depend on the media to formulate their opinions about youth crime; and that African American youth are more likely to be shown as perpetrators of criminal activity in the media.[2] As noted by Marable, "You become a social actor in the real world not on the basis of any objective criteria, but by the stereotypes imposed on you externally by others."[3] The depictions of city kids of color that engulf the public domain position them as social actors who are destructive and problematic rather than as social actors with a sociopolitically valued mission informed by the ways in which they make sense of their lived experiences.

The relative obscurity out of which urban youth of color "must discover their mission, fulfill it or betray it" is, in part, socially constructed by complex societal forces that converge upon them. Most often, we uncritically read their participation in civil society as a failure or betrayal of themselves, and their communities. However, perhaps the real problem is that we ignore the extent to which our socially constructed milieu either fails to nurture their efforts to define and fulfill the mission; or empowers their ability to betray the mission. The civic engagement potential of urban youth of color, our most vulnerable youth, needs to be fundamentally appreciated and nurtured. This discussion seeks to elevate attention to the civic engagement of urban youth of color within our social discourses through an initial examination of the social dynamics that impact their work to define, articulate, and fulfill a mission in society. With such an understanding, we can better empower and support them as effective agents of social change.

There are several considerations relevant to this inquiry. First, urban youth culture, like other subcultures, emerges from the social, historical, political, and cultural contexts in which the members live; and represents the performance of a struggle against social forces that hegemonically structure their lives. Consequently, an understanding of these larger social contexts is essential. Second, we must examine not only the usage of conventional modalities of civic participation but also non-conventional methods as sites where urban youth of color are attempting to articulate and fulfill a mission. Third, the ability of urban youth of color to effectively mobilize the full range of their agency as social actors is significantly impacted by the ways in which our social institutions and the society interact with them.

The social contexts from which urban youth subculture surfaces is best discussed through a theoretical lens offered by the Center for Contemporary Cultural Studies at Birmingham University, which sought to "locate them [youth subcultures] in relation to three broader cultural structures, the working class or the 'parent culture,' the 'dominant' culture, and mass culture."[4] Clarke, Hall, Jefferson, and Roberts conceptualize the notion of *double articulation* as the instance where youth subcultures are not viewed as existing in isolation from larger cultural contexts but as positioned within a dialectical relationship with other cultural formations.[5] Within this paradigm, the subculture of urban youth of color is effectively situated as a type of interlocutor with other cultural formations. They are engaged in negotiation, resistance, and struggle with the dominant culture, the subordinated parent culture, and mass culture. Efforts to understand the work of urban youth culture devoid of any examination of these three broader cultural structures are fundamentally problematic, so we will consider the role of each cultural formation in the dialectical relationship with the subculture of urban youth of color.

The context of the dominant culture, at least during the high-growth economic period of the 1990s, is best described as a " . . . relentless defunding and dismantling of public and private support for the young by the richest generations of middle-aged and elders in American history . . . divesture of the coming generation is reflected in, and justified by, political and special interests who engage in blaming every social ill, from crime and violence and poverty and drug abuse to personal immorality, upon our most victimized adolescents."[6] A specific example of the dominant culture's assault on America's urban youth of color is the hypercriminalization of their behaviors, the hyperpolicing of their spaces, and the simultaneous creation of educational inequities. This multifaceted assault is especially pernicious because it has been institutionalized within youth-dominated spaces, including schools.

Kitwana explains how criminal justice spending and legislation during the 1990s specifically targeted inner city youth. Reagan's 1980s "War on Drugs" efforts, which privileged punishment over rehabilitation, and endorsed criminal sentencing disparities for crack cocaine—more prevalent in urban communities —than for powder cocaine —more widespread in white suburban communities, was an offensive prelude to the more destructive 1990s. First, there was Bush's Violence Initiative that funded research focused on identifying the behavioral and biological markers for predicting violence in inner-city children. Second, there was the Violent Crime Control and Law Enforcement Act of the Clinton presidency. The Act not only increased funding for prison construction but also sanctioned the use of the death penalty for federal crimes generally linked to urban youth of color; established the "three strikes" penalty for violent felonies and drug crimes; and endorsed the adult prosecution of thirteen- and fourteen-year olds.[7] State and local officials as well as policymakers followed federal trends with similar laws, policies, and practices. These social policies and practices effectively structured and embedded within our society the stigmatization of urban youth of color. The social posture toward urban youth of color during this period can be understood through the comments of John J. DiIulio Jr., who characterized them as morally bankrupt superpredators who threatened American civil society.

The twenty-first century, ushered in by the rhetoric of No Child Left Behind, is not faring any better in terms of the dominant culture's considerations of urban youth of color as evidenced by the social policies and practices that target them. For instance, urban youth of color are being devastated within our urban schools on several levels. Zero tolerance discipline policies and practices have facilitated the co-optation of the educational space of school by the criminal justice system and as such have assisted in the hyperpolicing and hypercriminalization of urban youth. As early as 1989, New York instituted zero tolerance discipline policies that mandated expulsion for drugs, fighting, and gang-related activities.[9] By 1993, the offense threshold of zero tolerance discipline policies was lowered to include behaviors such as smoking and school disruption. Of Paul Robeson High School in Chicago, Dohrn notes that 158 students were arrested for behaviors such as pager possession, disorderly conduct, and mob action with no indications as to whether the actions were violent or simply large gatherings of students.[10] In terms of the hyperpolicing of urban youth of color, John Devine describes how students at a New York City high school are initiated into a culture of constant surveillance and police power with the routine use of metal detectors, X-ray machines, and other forms of "security" technology. He also notes how the introduction of a criminal justice lexicon into the school further aligns the educational culture with the police culture.

In terms of the educational inequities, the Children's Defense Fund (CDF) reports that children of color are far more likely to attend overcrowded schools with larger class sizes; have teachers with less academic attainment than students in high-income, low-minority schools; and are less likely to be placed in gifted and talented classes with advanced college track curricula. They also note that youth of color are far more likely to be born into poverty and without health insurance; and have more chances of going to prison, attempting suicide, never graduating from high school or college than obtaining a PhD, or becoming a lawyer, minister, teacher, or doctor. These outcomes are not surprising considering that 33% of Black youth and 28% of Latino youth are living in poverty, compared to a national rate of 17%, according to the National Center for Children in Poverty at Columbia University's Mailman School of Public Health. They also note that 51% of the children living in poverty reside in urban areas, which is the highest when compared to suburban and rural areas. Children living in poverty routinely lack access to basic services like appropriate educational opportunities.[11]

The convergence of these negative forces is powerfully illustrated through the nation's fiscal activity during 2003 through 2005. George W. Bush and the US Department of Education presented New York City students, primarily youth of color, with approximately $2.6 billion less than promised for various educational initiatives to improve student performance in high-poverty school districts.[12] This shortfall coincided with a $6.25 million windfall from the US Department of Justice to the New York City Department of Education's Operation Impact Schools program, which outfits the City's schools with the presence of police officers. Despite the rhetoric of No Child Left Behind, urban youth of color are being significantly left behind by the social policies and practices of the dominant culture that controls the systems of education as well as the other child and social welfare systems. Within the dialectic between the dominant culture and the urban youth of color subculture, the implicit message is that society is less socially committed to the youth's education and empowerment than they are to the criminalization and impoverishment of young people. William Bennett, former US Secretary of Education for Ronald Reagan and Drug Czar for George Bush, said, "if you wanted to reduce crime . . . if that were your sole purpose, you could abort every black baby in this country, and your crime rate would go down."[13] Based upon our current social treatment of urban youth of color, Bennett's comments might come to typify the tewenty-first century posture toward them as DiIulio's comments depicted our twentieth century attitudes. In our social discourses, we have primarily and inextricably linked urban youth of color to criminality.

The oppressive and disempowering milieu created by the dominant culture reflects only one component of the social dialectic within which urban youth of color must define, articulate, and fulfill their mission; mass culture is yet another. Although the Birmingham researchers specifically name mass culture as one of the three board cultural structures, there is, at least within the framework of this discussion, an overlap between the social policies and practices, and the manipulation or construction of mass culture because both are significantly governed by the dominant culture. With respect to the role of mass culture, it is most important to examine the representations and images of urban youth of color, as earlier mentioned. While the overrepresentation of urban youth of color as criminal perpetrators and their simultaneous underrepresentation as victims is fundamentally problematic, it is significantly exacerbated by the fact that they are not often portrayed as achievers, such as in education. It is the synergistic combination of what is and is not available in terms of mediated images that forms the basis of the problematic representations of urban youth of color in the public domain; and consequently facilitates society's ability to hegemonically position them within mass culture.

Furthermore, despite their contributions to the development of artifacts within mass culture, urban youth of color remain subordinated within it. More often than not, they are not the owners of the media systems that structure the mass culture, and therefore do not exercise any substantial control over the production and dissemination of the cultural artifacts, including how they ultimately are represented within such products. For instance, the commodification and commercialization of the cultural products of urban youth of color privilege particular discourses of the subculture over others. Blair appropriately emphasizes the idea that commercialization threatens the cultural form by "preventing its genuine forms the freedom to fully develop. The expression of Black people is transformed when it is repackaged without any evidence remaining of the Black historical experience."[14]

The cultural product, which begins as a means for the subculture to express its dissatisfaction with the social milieu in which it exists, is transformed into a commodity produced, disseminated, and controlled by the ideological proclivities of the dominant culture. "During this process, subcultural meanings are changed by mass producers (such as advertisers) into more marketable, less radical meanings."[15] This notion is further supported by Tricia Rose who documents how record companies, through their A&R departments, mold artists to fit the best selling genres so that as gangster rap gained market share, artists were steered to include that type of musical form in their overall repertoire. However, there is an irony in the dialectical relationship between mass culture and the culture of urban youth of color that results from the youth's position as producer and consumer of the artifacts of the mass culture, an aspect that will be addressed later. Mass culture works to reinforce the dominant culture's posture toward urban youth of color by promulgating and legitimizing their problematic representations within the public domain. The third component of the dialectical relationship is the subordinated parent culture. There is a disconnect between the promises of their parents' generation and the lived experiences of urban youth of color, especially around issues of social mobility, political empowerment, and leadership. "As the first generation to come of age in post-segregation America, one would think that we, unlike previous generations, would have enjoyed a lifetime of social, economic, and political equality. Nothing could be further from the truth."[16] While it is universally understood that today's urban youth of color are the beneficiaries of the gains of the Civil Rights struggle, their lived experiences remain significantly afflicted by obstacles to equitable social mobility as well as full participation in civil society. Despite the efforts of their parents to achieve social uplift for the community, they are still oppressed by the dominant culture, albeit in different ways.

Urban youth of color are cynical about the issues that comprise the social agenda, the definition of those issues, and the competency of the leadership of their parents' generation to now achieve meaningful social change. "Although the ideas at the core of the Civil Rights era are still relevant to today's political landscape (equality, inclusion, and the like), the manner in which they are now being articulated does not translate meaningfully into the ways these issues are manifest among the younger generation."[17] With the continued escalation of social, economic, political and cultural marginalization of urban communities of color, as evidenced by the research of organizations such as the Children's Defense Fund and the National Urban League,[18] many Black youth no longer believe that a sociopolitical agenda consisting of federal government intervention and social integration as typically embraced by traditional AfricanAmerican organizations and leadership is appropriate in the contemporary context. From their perspective, the traditional sociopolitical agenda and social change methods are bound together as elements of the current landscape of poverty, poor health care, inadequate education, and disproportionate representation in the criminal justice system that has a stranglehold on urban youth of color.

Bynoe makes the point that not only are urban youth of color disillusioned with their parents' sociopolitical agenda but are also scornful of the generation's ability to overlook the indiscretions of leaders like Rev. Jesse Jackson's "baby mama drama," Marion Barry's crack use, and embezzlement by Rev. Henry Lyons, while simultaneously castigating the hip hop generation for their behavior.[19] The hip hop generation, which prides itself on "calling people out" for their transgressions, expresses no sympathy for the Civil Rights leadership that has closed its ranks to them because they refuse to sublimate to the leadership's directives. Urban youth of color substantively have been abandoned by the leadership, which has muted their voice in the social movement's discourse and which is no longer physically present in their communities and lives. In terms of the devaluing of the hip hop generation's voice in the sociopolitical discourse, Kitwana details the NAACP's lack of support for the Million Youth March as an example. Of the leadership's absence from the lives of urban youth of color, Broder notes, "the pursuit of both financial and political success may be drawing black leaders away from a primary concern with the mass of blacks still suffering severe effects of discrimination."[20] As the leadership achieved sufficient economic and cultural capital to secure modest social mobility into America's racialized middle class, they have fled the communities of urban youth of color.

And so, our expectation is that urban youth of color should successfully discover and fulfill their mission within civil society while caught in a social nexus significantly shaped by the oppressive conditions imposed by the economic and political hegemony of the dominant culture; by the dissemination of disparaging and subjugated images of them within mass culture; and by the failure of their parents' generation to strategically evolve their sociopolitical movement to reflect the voice of urban youth of color as well as provide them with viable leadership. The weight of this social context fosters alienation and mitigates against the ability of urban youth of color to develop the necessary sociopolitical efficacy to become effective agents of social change. "Developmental psychologists have reported that, in comparison to middle-class white youth, youth from low-income families and youth of color tend to feel more 'alienated' from their communities and generally have a lower sense of 'political efficacy' . . . Youth living in urban contexts are more likely to encounter obstacles depriving them of knowledge about their communities or access to opportunities to participate."[20]

Urban youth of color are unconvinced that their participation in our sociopolitical system will yield any meaningful gains for them especially considering how such engagement by their parents' generation did not produce sustained achievement of social gains to guarantee the full promise of the Civil Rights Movement for the community. While urban youth of color have not embraced the conventions of our political system to speak their own truth to power, as evidenced by their absence from the ballot, they have not necessarily been silent or inactive.[21] For this discussion, it is essential that we explore the role of urban youth of color in the dialectical relationship. An examination of their cultural products provides a glimpse of the issues that they have identified and defined for a contemporary sociopolitical agenda or mission. Hip hop reflects the complex, contradictory, and multifaceted ways in which urban youth of color are doing the work to discover and fulfill a mission within the social context that we have created for them. "Hip hop is a reaction to institutionalized White racism, American classism, the material, spiritual, and psychological failures of the Civil Rights Movement, the United States government's abandonment of its war on poverty, the horrendous lack of vision and incompetence of 'traditional' Black leadership. . . ."[22] In this way, hip hop can be understood as a vehicle for urban youth of color to negotiate, resist, and struggle against the disenchantment and alienation caused by the dominant culture, mass culture, and the subordinated parent culture.

To be clear, this is not to suggest that the entirety of the music has been radical or progressive in a sociopolitical sense but only that there are artists such as Afrika Bambaataa, dead prez, Common, Black Star, Public Enemy, KRS-One, Mos Def, Salt N' Pepa, Disposable Heroes of Hiphoprisy, Queen Latifah, and Kanye West who, as Gramscian organic counter-hegemonic intellectuals, are defining the issues of their generation. By incorporating political discourses and black history education into their music, they have created a viable context to teach, politicize, and mobilize the youth underclass. As noted by Decker, there is a hip hop nationalist community that has created the basis for a more critical and conscious struggle.[23] He further notes that "While hip hop nationalists are not politicians, they are involved in the production of cultural politics —its creation, its circulation and its interpretation —which is tied to the everyday struggles of working-class blacks and the urban poor."[24] It is through the cultural politics of the nationalistic forms of hip hop that we can begin to understand how urban youth of color are navigating the oppressive social landscape to conceptualize a mission specifically informed by their lived experiences.

According to Kitwana, "Although this agenda has yet to be articulated holistically, it centers around seven main issues: education, employment and workers rights, reparations, economic infrastructure in urban communities, youth poverty and disease, anti-youth legislation, and foreign policy."[25] Considering that education was a touchstone issue for their parents, that schools are the social institution specifically designed to nurture the development of youth, and that we are in the wake of the No Child Left Behind Act, which promises to improve the schools serving America's most socially vulnerable children, Kitwana's delineation of education as an issue is particularly striking. For the majority of their parents, the issue of education primarily was defined in terms of the physical racial segregation of schools and remedy was achieved through litigation that culminated in *Brown vs the Board of Education*. However, the youth, who overwhelmingly attend racially and economically segregated schools, are focused on the extent to which they are not prepared to effectively compete within the contemporary high-tech, global economy, to obtain employment that provides a living wage, and victimized by the dissemination of knowledges that elevate the dominant culture and subjugates their culture.

One powerful example of the youth's sociopolitical discourse on education is "*they schools*" by Dead Prez.[26] The artists initially acknowledge that the same people who control the prison system also control the school system. What follows is a phenomenological critique of school based upon their experiences, with particular focus on the fact that the types of knowledge promulgated within the classrooms reflect that of the dominant culture as opposed to their subjugated types of knowledge; the hyperpolicing of the educational space as a means of surveillance and control; as well as their alienated and disengaged reactions to the entire process. In the second verse, the critique of the ways in which the school violates the minds and bodies of urban youth of color evolves into an articulation of what education means to youth. They are fundamentally concerned with the establishment of educational systems that are culturally relevant and empowering, rather than finding remedy through integration. The artists are explicit in their valuation of education and they imagine it as tool for the empowerment and social uplift of the community. Education is not to simply prepare them to obtain a job but to equip them to effectively exercise their agency to achieve positive change in the social, political, and economic contexts of their lives and their communities. This represents just one illustration of the ways in which sociopolitically conscious hip hop artists are identifying and defining the issues that urban youth of color perceive as relevant to their lives. There are many other important examples across the range of issues delineated by Kitwana.

So if urban youth of color are identifying and defining issues that can help to construct a mission, then why is not that work realized through a social movement to fulfill the mission. In a broad sense, the cultural systems with which urban youth of color must interact have significantly retarded the development of their self-efficacy to conceive of themselves as effective agents of sociopolitical change, and to mobilize their efforts to progress from identifying issues to constructing a movement to address the issues. Self-efficacy "refers to people's assessments of their effectiveness, competence, and causal agency."[27] An individual needs to experience " . . . the quality of the individual-environment interaction, primarily with regard to the opportunities it provides form engaging in efficacious action (e.g., a stimulating, challenging, responsive environment, and the freedom to engage it)."[28] Not only do urban youth of color lack access to appropriate opportunities to engage in efficacious action, but they also lack what they would perceive as credible examples of sociopolitically active possible selves. "An individual is free to create any variety of possible selves, yet the pool of possible selves derives from the categories made salient by the individual's particular sociocultural and historical context, and from the models, images, and symbols provided by the media and by the individual's immediate social experiences."[29] It is difficult to emulate what is not readily there. Several societal forces specifically can be implicated as obstacles to the ability of urban youth of color to develop the necessary self-efficacy and to imagine themselves as competent sociopolitical change agents within our civil society.

One structural obstacle is the educational system. Too often, schools educate poor urban youth of color to develop an instrumental literacy through a pedagogical approach of banking competency-based skills, which prevents them from being able to "read the world" critically and to understand the reasons and linkages behind particular social realities that powerfully affect their lives.[30] The hyperstandardization of the pedagogy of our public schools has forced teachers to forego a focus on developing students' critical thinking skills in order to "teach to the test" that not only determines whether a student will be promoted but also whether the teacher will be assessed as professionally competent. A New York City public high school teacher laments how the time constraints of the test-driven curriculum prevented her from engaging her students in a discussion about their responses to a term paper assignment on the issue of AIDS in Uganda, a global issue that has significant racial, economic, and health implications within the sociopolitical sphere.[31]

To nurture their critical awareness of social issues, schools serving urban youth of color must embrace a critical literacy pedagogy, which " . . . invites teachers and students to *prob-lematize* all subjects of study, that is, to understand existing knowledge as a historical product deeply invested with the values of those who developed such knowledge. A critically literate person does not stay at the empirical level of memorizing data, or at the impressionistic level of opinion, or at the level of dominant myths in society, but goes beneath the surface to understand the origin, structure, and consequences of any body of knowledge, technical process, or object under study."[32] Infusing critical literacy into their academic program would provide urban youth of color with opportunities to engage in efficacious action. Schooling would be connected to their lived experiences in meaningful ways. Students would be equipped to not only challenge or justify the social, political, and economic arrangements of their communities and our society; but also to competently think about ways to effectively leverage their agency as individuals and as a collective within the sociopolitical context of our society. In this way, schools, as the primary social institution engaging youth, could strategically disrupt the impact of the debilitating messages that urban youth of color receive, and that hinder them from effectively moving from issue identification to definition, education, and mobilization for a mass movement within their culture. Education would be truly about developing citizens and not just workers.

Another component of the structural obstacles is the gap between the Black leadership and today's youth. Their disconnect from the poorer black masses is not only physical but also social and ideological; and results, in part, from the leadership's integration into or co-optation by the political mainstream of our civil society. The leadership's co-optation mitigates against their legitimacy as effective social change agents, especially in the minds of urban youth of color. The leadership is seen as far more efficacious in achieving their individual social mobility as opposed to sustained sociopolitical change to continue to uplift the race. It is not unlike W.E.B. DuBois's dilemma with the *Talented Tenth*, when he noted that "This deradicalization process, according to DuBois occurs when more privileged African Americans (re)align themselves to function as a middle class interested in individual group gain rather than race leadership for mass development. Asserting that the New Tenth must remain connected to the mass, he highlights a new leadership in conflict with an assimilated or assimilating African American elite."[33]

The critical problems with the disconnect, in terms of its impact on the ability of urban youth of color to define and fulfill a mission, is that it prevents the necessary transfer of knowledge and training from one generation of leaders to the next generation, fails to exploit the political potential of a united intergenerational coalition, and inhibits a seamless transition within an ongoing social struggle. The failure of the leadership to effectively remain connected to urban youth of color as a means to understand the ways in which they make meaning of the issues, and to mentor them into leadership roles only intensifies the obscurity from which the youth must discover and fulfill their mission. Furthermore, the leadership, prominently positioned within a highly mediated social space, becomes an example of mainstream co-optation or "sell-outs" for the youth. As they look for a pool of possible selves to begin to conceive of themselves as effective agents of social change, they are saddled with Black leaders who are seen to have betrayed their own mission by allowing themselves to be co-opted. Not only do urban youth of color lack a particular competence that comes with appropriate training and transfers of knowledge, but they also have a dearth of leadership models from which to model a possible self as social change agent. This situation only fuels their disengagement from the process.

The lack of visible support by the Black leadership for urban youth of color who are attempting to assert a sociopolitical stance is evident in the recent situation involving Kanye West. In reaction to George Bush's mishandling of the Katrina Hurricane disaster in the Gulf coast area of the southern United States, West commented "George Bush doesn't care about black people." As he came under attack by Laura Bush, who preferred to devalue West's perspective rather than attempt to understand how his lived experiences informed his point of view, West was endorsed by Jay-Z, Sean "Diddy" Combs, Nelly, and a few other artists.[34] The public silence of the Black leadership was deafening and ignored West's critical read of the situation through a racialized lens that is not inappropriate when discussing the social realities of America's hegemonic society. In his commentary, West created an opportunity for us to engage urban youth of color in a critical dialog about fundamental issues of the struggle for racial and economic justice in America, and such opportunities should be embraced and nurtured by the Black leadership. This type of failure by the leadership was also demonstrated on the 30th anniversary commemoration of Martin Luther King Jr.'s "I Have A Dream" speech at the Washington Monument in 1963. When the youth leaders began to address the crowd, the established black leaders began moving off toward the Lincoln Memorial as if to say that the commentary of their young charges was irrelevant.[35] The Black leadership needs to be wholly present so that they can learn how their youth are conceptualizing the issues that impact their lives and consequently develop strategies, in collaboration with the youth, to leverage their more established political power to exact the necessary change.

Another obstacle is the ways in which urban youth of color participate in mass or popular culture. The masses of urban youth of color uncritically consume the commodified cultural products that flood the markets and public domain. In his discussion of popular culture, George Lipsitz makes the point that "culture comes to us as a commodity," and we often do not question its origins or the intentions of the artists behind the commodified cultural artifact. However, there is a need to question the authenticity of the artifact, or more specifically whether the artists, in the production and performance of the cultural artifact, are keeping it real or complying with the dictates of the marketing department of their music label. With this type of interaction, it is nearly impossible to understand what is "keeping it real." Although hip hop artists situate themselves within the communities for whom they articulate resistance to the hegemonic oppression, it must be understood that the performative element that is evident in the commodity is not necessarily an accurate or empowering representation of the lived experiences, but rather of the compromise between the reality and the marketability of that reality. Inherent in the commodification of the subcultural forms in mass culture are decontextualization and compartmentalization of the elements so that they can be repackaged into a marketable cultural product that is disseminated to the public via mass media outlets. Unfortunately, the result is that an industry can insidiously interrupt and destabilize the potential of the public transcripts created by the more nationalistic musical expressions of urban youth of color. As the industry and popular culture elevate the musical forms that position urban youth of color within hyperessentialized thug and gangsta identity formations; while simultaneously not elevating the nationalistic expressions, the potential for their politicization begins to wane and fails to be realized.

Additionally, far too many urban youth of color have made conscious decisions to privilege acquisition of the *bling*, even if it means disparaging members of their culture as exemplified by the misogyny, overtaking any type of a sociopolitical stance, whether it is in their music or within the public domain of civil society; and have failed to take a proactive role in the development of their own critical awareness. "In a world where so many youth believe that 'getting paid' and living ostentatiously was the goal of the black freedom movement, there is little space to even *discuss* building a radical democratic public culture. Too many young people really believe that this is the best that we can do."[36] Despite their raging against the Black leadership for "selling out" and their consequent impotence to bring about meaningful change in the contemporary social context, many urban youth of color are engaging in the same behaviors that allow for their co-optation by an entertainment industry that capitalizes on their lack of critical awareness and social agency. For this, urban youth of color must be taken to task because it is part of the structural link that prevents them from creating a wholly defined mission and effectively fulfilling it. The market of commercial hip hop and rap, especially the genre known as gansta rap, is replete with examples of which the artist, 50 Cent, is one.

He "is muscular, talks about sex and his "Magic Stick," black on black crime, and so forth. The whole image is mostly physical, almost animal like. Nothing mental or spiritual is relayed or embraced. Consider the mainstream embrace of 50 Cent's image and its ties to the traditional American racist depiction of the strong athletic and ultra-sexual black male."[37] In an effort to *get rich or die tryin'*, Curtis Jackson has privileged acquisition of the *bling* and in the process, has allowed himself to be used to promulgate a disempowering script for urban youth of color. While they may be mesmerized with Jackson's socioeconomic assent, what they fail to recognize is that that wealth will not be accompanied with the necessary cultural capital to alleviate, even at an individual level, the oppressive social conditions in which all urban youth of color are living. Just as they are vigilant about "calling out" others, urban youth of color need to critically problematize the behaviors of their peers who reinforce their hegemonic position within civil society. They cannot allow themselves to become divided and, consequently, more impotent by their active participation in the reinforcement of the negative discourses and images of them privileged by the mass culture.

To be fair, the call to hold themselves accountable for their gains and loses is not only being issued outside of the culture but inside of it as well. "Many complain about the cash money, hoes and cars, yet stubbornly and cowardly they do not blame themselves or us as a whole, the listeners and cultural partakers. We need to stop using our music as a scapegoat for our problems . . . Do not blame her when part of the problem is within us, the listeners. Y'all talk a big one but ain't doing shit. It's crazy but know this: sitting on the sidelines or playing the rules does not obtain revolution. Revolution is won through collaboration, intelligence and discipline."[38] Again, urban youth of color cannot escape accountability by claiming a status of passive participant. They create the music, allow for its commodification, actively engage in its consumption, and fail to problematize the commercialized misrepresentations. Just as they seek the necessary education and skills to produce the music, they can similarly educate and mobilize themselves around the sociopolitical issues of which some of them speak in the music. Greg Tate aptly wonders how the political potential inherent in the insights of the subculture can be harnessed for social change rather than continuously elevated into a hyperessentialized substitution for it. Without evolving into a social movement through the leveraging of their social, political, and economic power to dismantle the oppression imposed by the dominant culture, they will "degenerate into simply another way for capitalists to sell back to people a picture of the life that has been stolen from them."[39]

The tragedy that we perceive in our urban youth of color lies not in who they are but in the limitations we place on them as they attempt to emerge as effective social actors within civil society. We need to embrace their phenomenological sense of the world around them and their lived experiences; seek to understand how they make meaning of the sociopolitical issues that they are identifying as agenda items for a contemporary social movement; collaboratively work with them so that they are supported in the development of their own sociopolitical mechanisms to achieve social change; leverage collective political support for their efforts by substantively incorporating their mission and issues into the broader sociopolitical agenda of the community; provide platforms so they can educate the entire polity about the issues of their mission; and build safe and educative forums in which to establish coalitions within and across the racial, economic, and generational divides. Formal and informal structures need to be created and commandeered to inculcate the masses of urban youth of color, from those who are court-involved to those who are in the ivy towers, with critical awareness, leadership skills, and an understanding of the sociohistorical context of the struggle in which they now find themselves.

NOTES

1   H.A. Giroux, *The Abandoned Generation* (New York: Palgrave MacMillan, 2003), p. 129.

2   L. Dorfman and V. Schiraldi, *Off Balance: Youth, Race, and Crime in the News. Building Blocks for Youth—Executive Summary*. Retrieved March, 2005, from http://www.buildingblocksforyouth/media.

3   M. Marable, *The Great Wells of Democracy: The Meaning of Race In American Life* (New York: BasicCivitas Books, 2002), p. 3.

4   K. Gelder and S. Thornton, *The Subcultures Reader* (New York: Routledge, 1997), p. 83.

5   Ibid., p. 101.

6   M. A. Males, *The Scapegoat Generation* (Monroe, ME: Common Courage Press, 1996), p. 5.

7   B. Kitwana, *The Hip Hop Generation: Young Blacks and the Crisis in African American Culture* (New York: BasicCivitas Books, 2002).

8   R. Skiba, "Education policy Briefs—Zero tolerance: The assumptions and the facts, *Center for Evaluation and Education Policy, 2(1)*(2001):1–8.

9   B. Dohrn, in W. Ayers, B. Dohrn, and R. Ayers, eds. *Zero Tolerance: Resisting the Drive for Punishment in Our Schools* (New York: The New Press, 2001), p. 95.

10   J. Devine, *Maximum Security: The Culture of Violence in Inner-City Schools* (Chicago: University of Chicago Press, 1996), pp. 26–27.

11   Children's Defense Fund. (2004). *The State of America's Children 2004*, pp. 87–107.

12   *GOP Convention Primer: Education—No Child Left Behind Underfunded by Bush* Retrieved March, 2005, from http://www.house.gov/weiner/report26.htm.

13   Retrieved October 2005, from Media Matters for America. http://mediamatters.org/items/200509280006.

14   M. Blair,. Elizabeth. in M. Forman, and M. A. Neal, eds. *That's the Joint! The Hip Hop Studies Reader* (New York: Routledge, 2004), p. 497.

15   Ibid., p. 501.

16   B. Kitwana, *The Hip Hop Generation: Young Blacks and The Crisis in African American Culture* (New York: BasicCivitas Books, 2002), p. 26.

17   Ibid., p. 83.

18   See Children's Defense Fund. (2004). *The State of America's Children 2004;* and National Urban League. *The State of Black America, 2005.*

19   Y. Bynoe, *Stand and Deliver: Political Activism, Leadership, and Hip Hop Culture* (New York: Soft Skull Press, 2004).

20   D.S. Broder, In Blake, Jr., Reynard N. "Beyond the Bling: A Look at Hip Hop, African American Leadership & The Black Church: Implications to African American Youth Development," *Journal of Urban Youth Culture* (2003, February). Retrieved September 2005, from http://www.juyc.org/ current/0302/blake.html.

21   B. Kirshner, K. Strobel, and M. Fernandez, (2003). "Critical Civic Engagement Among Urban Youth," *Urban Education Journal* 2(1), (2003, Spring). Retrieved October 2005, from http://www.urbanedjournal.org/articles/article0010.html.

22   K. Powell, "The Hip Hop Generation" in Nuruddin, Y., and Wallis, V. eds. Hip Hop, Race, and Cultural Politics. *Socialism and Democracy, 18(2),* (2004, July–December).

23   J.L. Decker, "The State of Rap: Time and Place in Hip Hop Nationalism" in A. Ross and T. Rose, eds. *Microphone Fiends: Youth Music and Youth Culture* (New York: Routledge, 1994).

24   Ibid., p. 101.

25   B. Kitwana, *The Hip Hop Generation: Young Blacks and the Crisis in African American Culture* (New York: BasicCivitas Books, 2002), p. 178.

26   P. Dead, *They Schools Lets Get Free* (Loud Records, 2000).

27   V. Gecas, "The social psychology of self-efficacy," *Annual Review Sociology, 15*(1989): 291–316, p. 292

28   Ibid., p. 300.

29   H. Markus, and P. Nurius, "Possible selves," *American Psychologist, 41(9)* (1996): 954–969, p. 954.

30   D. Macedo, *Literacies of Power* (Boulder: Westview Press, 1994).

31   D. Meier and G. Wood, eds., *Many Children Left Behind: How the No Child Left Behind Act is Damaging Our Children and Our Schools* (Boston: Beacon Press,2004).

32   I. Shor, *Empowering Education: Critical Teaching for Social Change* (Chicago: University of Chicago Press, 1992), p. 24.

33   J. James, *Transcending the Talented Tenth: Black Leaders and American Intellectuals* (New York: Routledge, 1991), p. 24.

34   J. James. *Laura Bush Says Kanye West's Comments were Disgusting.* Retrieved October 2005, from http://news.yahoo.com/s/launch/20050912/en_launch/23875612;_ylt=AuNwxkqoQgTfcx MyPq5mBGmVEhkF;_ylu=X30DMTBiMW04NW9mBHNlYwMlJVRPUCUl.

35   Blake, Jr., N. Reynard, 2003 "Beyond the bling: A look at Hip Hop, African American leadership and the black church: Implications to African American youth development," *Journal of Urban Youth Culture* (February), Retrieved September 2005, from http://www.juyc.org/current/0302/blake.html.

36   R.D.G. Kelly, quoted by Y. Bynoe, *Stand and Deliver: Political Activism, Leadership, and Hip Hop Culture* (New York: Soft Skull Press, 2004), p. 21.

37   BrooklyniteOne. *Why 50 Cent Sells Records: Commercialization of the Hip Hop Persona.* Retrieved October 2005, from http://www.nobodysmiling.com/hiphop/editorial/81615.php.

38   Dre. The State of Hip Hop, What's Happening to Her?2004. Retrieved October 2005, from
      http://www.nobodysmiling.com/hiphop/editorial/75587.php.

39   Greg Tate quoted by G. Lipsitz, in A. Ross, and T. Rose, eds. *Microphone Fiends: Youth Music and Youth
      Culture* (New York: Routledge,1994).

IV.

TEACHING
CITY KIDS

14. Race, Urban Schools, and Educational Reform

The Context, Utility, Pros, and Cons of the Magnet Example

HANDEL KASHOPE WRIGHT AND SIDONIA ALENUMA

Introduction: (Beyond) Stereotypes of Urban Schools

Magnet schools are well established and by now quite familiar public yet alternative schools in urban areas. They are high achieving, multicultural, multiracial public yet alternative schools of choice with a specialized curriculum focus (e.g., the creative and performing arts, engineering, languages, and computer science) and/or particularly innovative pedagogical approaches and have the principal dual focus of improving educational quality and increasing racial integration. But how have magnet schools come about and how have they come to be an integral part of urban education? In this chapter, we discuss magnet programs as a relatively recent educational reform initiative that have been developed and implemented primarily to address a thorny and recurrent problem in urban education, namely racial and economic (re)segregation of schools and consequent educational inequity.

We concentrate on contextualizing magnet programs in terms of a rich history of American educational reform, traditions of alternative schools and efforts at desegregating schools and creating educational equity for students irrespective of race, ethnicity, location, and socio-economic status. Thus, while our discussion is in a sense about educational improvement, we are dealing not merely with a standards based, supposedly "apolitical" conception of educational improvement but with a decidedly progressive conception, one inextricably linked with the historical struggle for diversity, equity and social justice in and through education.

The designation "urban school" ostensibly refers quite simply to schools located in urban areas. However, urban schools have become, in both the professional and popular social discourse, the repository of a large number of intersecting (and often quite problematic and unfair) connotations. "Urban" has become a euphemism for schools with exclusively or predominantly poor student of color populations (especially Black and Latino) and connote schools that are characterized by underfunding, racial and economic segregation, inefficient administration, poor infrastructure, demoralized teaching faculty, poor equipment, resources and facilities, overcrowded classes, outmoded and largely ineffective pedagogical approaches, student on student and student on teacher violence, chronic classroom management problems, dilapidated and/or dangerous neighborhoods, uninvolved and uncaring parents, etc. In other words, the stereotyping of the worst characteristics of various urban environments and various ethno-racial groups and the poor as well as the worst characteristics of bad education have been blended in the stereotype of urban schools in general.

Given this negative and stereotypical conception of urban schools, it is hardly surprising that, while the entire educational system has been subject to reform throughout much of America's history, urban schools and urban education are considered a perennial and obvious candidate for reform and improvement. Poor functioning urban schools are considered the norm and are either ignored or characterized as typical. Successful and smooth functioning urban schools are considered something of an anomaly and are studied for their surprising success, with everything from "best practices" of individual teachers to evidence of unique elements of administrative efficiency and innovative strategies for parental involvement.

Hollywood depictions reflect the popular social stereotype of the urban school as a gang infested war zone and the American obsession with the power of the individual as heroic change agent. In the futuristic *Class of 1999* the school system employs robot teachers to take on the gangs and in *187* a teacher actually kills gang members and ends up being killed himself. In Hollywood depictions it is the lone and exceptionally talented, determined, resourceful and caring teacher in *Stand and Deliver*, *Sister Act 2* and *Dangerous Minds* or principal in *Boys Town*, *Lean on Me* and *The Principal* who individually pulls the class or entire school up from failure, violence and desperation into academic success and self-worth. Hollywood depictions also reflect (and help create) the popular presentist lens through which urban schools are conceptualized. They focus on a school already "gone bad" with virtually no historical context of the how the problems developed and what measures (beyond the heroic action of the individual teacher or principal) could be taken to address the problems facing an urban school.

While acknowledging that urban schools, like much of the educational system in general can benefit from educational reform and improvement, we want to move in this essay beyond popular culture (mis)conceptions to explore the pros and cons of magnet programs as a specific contemporary educational reform initiative (and indeed movement) for improving urban schools. In contrast with presentist, individual agency focused popular and professional depictions, we concentrate on providing a historical context of the magnet school model and consider magnet programs as a broad educational initiative that involves contributions from everyone from policymakers, school administrators, and teachers to students, parents, and local communities.

The History of Race, Racism, and Educational Reform

The United States has a long history of educational reform initiatives, policy and movements. Although it was preceded by a variety of private, public, and charter school organizations, the common school movement of the 1830s and 1840s represented a milestone in that it conceptualized schooling as serving distinct social and political goals .[1,2] In terms of our focus on sociocultural difference and justice issues, the common school movement was particularly significant since its primary purpose was the initiation of educational equity and diversity with the goal of promoting sociocultural diversity and harmony, and building political community. One author points out, it was argued that if children from a variety of religious, social-class, and ethnic backgrounds were educated in common, there would be a decline in hostility and friction among social groups. In addition, if children educated in common were taught a common social and political ideology, a decrease in political conflict and social problems would result.[3]

Thus, the common school marked an explicit link between government educational policy and efforts to address economic, social, and political problems in American society. Racism is one of the most persistent and pernicious of those problems, both in American society and in schools. Education and educational reform initiatives have been pressed into service to both address racism in the schools and through education to address societal racism. For Blacks, for example, the road to educational equity has been long and difficult, marked by measures that have both enabled and undermined progress. During the era of slavery, Blacks were not only denied an education, they were actually severely punished if they were discovered learning to read and write. Although the Emancipation Proclamation of 1863, and the Thirteenth and Fourteenth Amendments of the United States Constitution brought new rights for Blacks, these were undermined by laws enacted in Southern states and the practice of averse racism or tendency for the races to be granted separate environments and services. Averse racism in the form of segregation was legally endorsed via the emergence of the inherently flawed doctrine of supposedly "separate but equal" environments for blacks and whites.[4]

Segregation took hold not only in privately owned transportation, hotels, and restaurants but also in local and national government run public transportation, departments of the US government and even the gallery of the US Senate.[5] Not surprisingly, there was also segregation in public education. Segregation in education was legally sanctioned and endorsed by the US Supreme Court decision in the *Berea College v Kentucky* in1908 which upheld the right of states to prohibit integration of the races in educational institutions. Although segregated education became the norm in the United States and lasted from the late 1800s till the 1950s, it was not an uncontested norm. It was considered by Blacks to be the primary form of racism in education and therefore became a rallying cause for the formation of organizations such as the Niagara Movement and the National Association for the Advancement of Colored People and the activism of Black intellectual leaders such as W.E.B. DuBois.

Brown v The Board of Education: The End of Segregation?

In the 1950s, five cases were brought before the Supreme Court, each with a different set of circumstances and differences in nuance but all of which challenged segregation in education with the same basic argument that segregation violated the Fourteenth Amendment of the Constitution, the notion of "equal protection under the law." Voluminous and damning testimony from a wide variety of experts including educators, psychologists, and social scientists spoke to the effects of segregation on Black students and on race relations were presented. For example, Kenneth Clark, a social scientist, presented the following forceful and persuasive argument as part of his testimony:

> Segregation is prejudice concretized in the society, and in my work with Negro youth and in my interviewing them, I find this is the way they interpret it: Segregation is a mist, like a wall, which society erects, of stone and steel—psychological stone and steel—constantly telling them that they are inferior and constantly telling them that they cannot escape prejudice. Prejudice is something inside people. Segregation is the objective expression of what these people have inside.[6]

Clark's testimony revealed, in part, the link between what we would now call individual, institutional, and societal forms of racism. Hugh Speer, a professor of education who testified in the second case, *Brown v Board of Education of Topeka*, pointed out that through segregation Black students were denied interaction with Whites, and that this constituted a significant deterrence to social cohesion since American society and culture were predominantly white. In the same case, Horace English, a psychologist, pointed out that because segregated schools were lower achieving generally ending segregation would increase the achievement levels of black students.[7] In general, the experts in the five cases pointed to the effects, especially inferior education, relatively poor performance, the deep psychological wounding, and sense of helplessness that segregated education as a pervasive, legally sanctioned, institutionalized and taken for granted form of racism had on Black students in particular and secondarily on whites and society in general.

The myriad of expert witnesses in the five cases helped make the argument that while not a panacea, ending segregation would be a precondition to developing and promoting more positive self-image among Black students and raising their academic performance as well as fostering tolerance and positive relations between Blacks and Whites in schools and consequently in society. In the end, the *Brown Decision*, handed down by the Supreme Court in 1954, found for the plaintiffs and by the late 1960s had been extended nationwide, made applicable wherever it could be proved that segregation was the result of intentional actions of school boards and administrations. Integration became the new order of the day and the Brown decision brought about what many thought would be the end of segregated education in the United States.

However, while there was acceptance of the call to desegregate schools in some quarters, there was also white resistance to desegregation resistance for a variety of reasons from a general fear of change to balking at the inconvenience of specific strategy of busing, from fear of cultural clash and physical violence to outright white racism. Averse racism joined the search for larger homes, more land, safer environment, smaller numbers in communities, etc., as an additional factor in the movement of the white middle-class from urban areas to the suburbs and later to the margins of the suburbs of American cities. Whatever the impetus has been for various individual white middle-class families, the phenomenon of "white flight" from the inner cities and indeed from the cities in general has had the effect of re-segregating America's schools to a considerable extent. As one author points out, involuntary school integration became a primary cause of white flight from the affected school districts and this consequently led to increased overall segregation by contributing to the concentration of black and poor populations, especially in urban communities.[8]

Magnet Schools, Alternative Schools, and Educational Reform

Although magnet schools are perhaps best understood as part of the tradition of educational reform in general and in particular the tradition of reform initiatives which have social engineering and social justice goals (such as the common school and desegregation and the resulting integrated schools), they are also clearly part of the tradition of "alternative schools" which have a long history in the United States and other countries' school systems. Alternative schools and school systems are usually established with an alternative social, political, or religious worldview in mind, to put in place a radically alternative curriculum or set of pedagogical approaches and/or to serve a specific sub-set of the population. Historically, the rather oppressive and authoritarian atmosphere of public schools of the late nineteenth and early twentieth centuries, combined with the fact that the public schools did not reflect the religious and political views of a variety of sub-sets of the population seemed to some to demand the establishment of alternative models of education.

Thus, for example, modernist schools established in England around WWI reflected the politics of anarchists. They were based on the idea that public education was authoritarian in its approach and that an alternative and far preferable and more effective education was one in which children were allowed to pursue their own academic interests and learn at their own pace. Based on a similar notion of student-centered approach to curriculum and pedagogy that emphasized student interest (though without having anarchism as its ideological base), the Summerhill model was established in England in the 1920s, and by the 1950s there were both schools and even a Summerhill society in the United States. In terms of religion and alternative schools, as early as the nineteenth century the Catholic school system has served the children of Catholics and initially operated as an alternative to the Protestant-dominated public school system.[9]

It is difficult to pinpoint precisely when "alternative schools" transitioned in the United States into becoming "magnet" schools. What is clear is that what was traditionally a progressive form of educational reform, namely alternative schools, were ironically seized upon by conservatives in the 1970s as a much more palatable alternative to enforced integration and busing. As alternative schools were incorporated into desegregation plans, the term "magnet" emerged as a reference to the function such schools played in the new strategy of voluntary integration.

Dissenters from integration in general and the practice of busing in particular received support from high quarters when Nixon promised to curb involuntary busing and in 1972 even requested from Congress a moratorium on the practice. Nixon argued that the principal purpose of the Brown decision, the elimination of a race-based dual educational system (especially in the South), had been achieved. Furthermore, he argued, busing was inconvenient and disruptive to children and their families and ironically was even fomenting the very problem of racism it was meant to address.[10] Nixon advocated greater balance between the goal of addressing racial inequality in education and other goals such as improving schools, convenience and parental involvement. Racially charged incidents in cities like Boston in the mid-1970s served to endorse the view that involuntary integration was indeed problematic and was contributing to racial tension. The result was that conservatives turned to alternative or magnet schools as a more palatable and mutually beneficent approach to promoting and implementing voluntary integration of education, especially urban schools.

Thus, magnet schools have a very complex socio-political history. An author provides the following cogent summary of the history of magnet schools, pointing to how it has its roots in progressive politics but was appropriated by conservatives and has become embroiled in various issues, including levels of parental involvement in school choice:

> The irony in the conservative support of magnet schools was that the concept of magnet schools was a product of a radical reaction to the school system in the late 1960s and early 1970s. The magnet school movement was therefore a product of conservative reaction to desegregation and the alternative school movement of the 1960s. The term *alternative* to the existing public school system. By the 1970s, the magnet school movement became part of the debate over whether or not parents should be allowed to choose a particular public school or program for their child.[11]

Magnet schools are part of a history of efforts at creating more flexible, nuanced, and student-centered alternative educational models. They are also part of the progressive effort to serve and create educational equity for minority groups such as specific religious groups like Catholics and racial groups such as Blacks. Finally, they have contributed to the creation of multicultural learning environments, allowing blacks and whites in particular and in some cases students of a wide variety of races and cultures to interact and learn together. In all these senses they are firmly part of progressive politics reflected in education. On the other hand, they offered a very attractive alternative to busing and introduced for conservative Whites the possibility of voluntary integration of schools. They also offered the white middle-class a strong incentive of an elite education in the form of smaller classes, innovative pedagogy and most importantly a specialized curriculum in fields in which their children might want to specialize. Finally, specialized curricula offered a functionality and specificity that generally reflect conservative views of the utility of education (which have gained prominence in even more recent conservative "back to basics" and "education for the workplace" movements). In these senses they could be considered part of conservative politics in education. Thus, from leftist origins as alternative schools to the more conservative public education, magnet schools were appropriated by the right as a more palatable approach to desegregation of America's schools.

Characteristics and Socio-Political Utility of Magnet Schools

Some authors provide the following particularly concise and accurate definition of the magnet concept when they assert that it refers to:

> . . . a school, or program within a school, that is characterized by a special curricular theme or method of instruction, plays a role in voluntary desegregation within a district, and provides choice of school to students and parents and access to students beyond a regular attendance zone.[12]

Magnet schools are public schools that are also alternative schools in the sense that they have a unique focus and set of characteristics that make them radically different from regular public schools. As some other authors point out, the following are the distinct aspects of schools with magnet programs: program, faculty, principal, school location, quality of school plant, opportunities provided for parent involvement, voluntary nature of the magnet school, and an opportunity for "another chance" for students perceived as having behavior problems.[13]

Magnet schools have a dual focus: improving educational quality and increasing racial integration. This dual focus is reflected in the principal, interrelated characteristics of magnet schools. One such characteristic is a curriculum that is different, special, and distinctive, one that is clearly specialized and distinctive from the regular curriculum in a non-magnet school. A related characteristic is the wide appeal of magnet schools despite their location in urban areas—because of the high quality of the education provided and the magnet focus, they are attractive to the poor and the middle-class and to all races. Thirdly, magnet schools are by design multiracial and multicultural, open to students of all races on a voluntary basis.[14,15]

One of the primary functions of magnet schools is for the desegregation of schools and their multicultural, multiracial character is a product of that function. In fact, the first magnet schools utilized for the purpose of school desegregation were court sanctioned (though with a cap on the racial distribution of their student populations) and enrollments are cur-rently regulated by school policy to ensure a racially mixed student population.[16] The result has been schools that include students of various cultural, racial, and economic back-grounds. Since this diversity has come together through choice (indeed magnet schools have also been referred to as schools of choice), there is, presumably, greater inter-group toler-ance in magnet schools than there was in schools that were forcibly integrated through the practice of busing.

To achieve the goal of school integration (and resultant de-facto racial economic and cultural diversity school population), magnet schools have to possess broad appeal. An author asserts that magnet schools that prove successful in attracting white students to travel to mixed or predominantly black, often urban neighborhoods have such characteristics as an image of educational excellence, a distinctive principal and faculty with reputation for ped-agogical success and a specialized curriculum. These same characteristics combined with the fact that the magnet school is in fact a neighborhood school are what makes magnet schools attractive to the local mixed raced or black, often poor local community, parents, and students.[17]

In terms of their utility primarily for students and parents and secondarily for the work-force and communities, a bewildering variety of magnet schools have been established which fit the specific academic and professional interests of specific students in various cities. Some authors observe for example that by the 1980s the Houston school system offered alternative schools specializing in engineering, criminal justice, the petrochemical industry, health serv-ices, advanced academic work, and the creative and performing arts. Philadelphia, they point out, offered a similar range of specialized programs in its magnet schools along with programs in foreign affairs. A third example they provide is the Cincinnati school system which offered magnet programs in computer sciences, athletics, advanced academic work, mathematics and science, creative performing arts, and languages. The astonishing variety of magnet pro-grams is reflective not only of a response to students' interests but also a reflection of the respec-tive urban school systems' response of industries, businesses and the general labor market.[18]

Difference and Socio-Economic Justice:
The Pros and Cons of Magnet Schools

The rationale for the establishment of magnet schools is that they are a means of integrat-ing America's schools, providing quality education, and countering the effects of income level on educational quality and opportunity. Although they are often discussed as being inher-ently positive and innovative, there are both pros and cons to magnet programs when one considers their effects and levels of effectiveness.

As a voluntary alternative to the unpopular and involuntary practice of busing, mag-net schools have proved a much more effective strategy of desegregation and the racial, mul-ticultural, and economic integration of America's schools. It is clear that White and middle-class families and students have benefited from magnet programs in terms of the elite, specialized education provided, the richness of multiracial and multicultural schools and neighborhoods, the preservation of property values, etc. Poor and minority families have also enjoyed many of these benefits.

However, it is also clear that poor and minority families and communities have borne the brunt of the sacrificing that has had to be done to attract white and middle-class students to magnet schools and staunch the flow of whites and the middle-class from urban neighborhoods. One author points out that "poor people in the District . . . want very much to keep the middle-class children, white and black, from fleeing the city's schools".[19] His assertion illustrates that what is commonly referred to as "white flight" is equally "middle-class flight" from urban areas and with the rise in the Black middle-class, the struggle to prevent white flight has become a struggle to prevent a general middle-class flight. The poor in America's cities accept a dual system of magnets for the wealthy and traditional neighborhood urban schools for the poor (with some examples of both located within the same school building) as the price they have to pay to attract and/or keep middle-class students in local schools.[20]

Magnet schools are also a double-edged sword in terms of academic excellence. With their specialized curricula, charismatic principals, effective teachers, innovative pedagogy, etc., it is hardly surprising that magnet schools in general have provided a superior education for their students. Because the students are a mix of middle-class and working-class and various races and cultures, magnet schools provide quality education for all its students, irrespective of racial and socio-economic background. On the other hand, although the initial aim was in part to improve the quality of the education that poor children received, the fact that magnet schools have concentrated on attracting and keeping the middle-class combined with the fact that they tend to select the academically gifted and motivated students from the surrounding poor community means that the vast majority of poor children do not benefit from magnet programs. This discrepancy is particularly glaring in instances where there is a magnet program within an otherwise regular school. Thus, while magnet schools and programs do provide quality education for a select few poor students and students of color, they also leave the vast majority to local regular schools and therefore fail to seriously impact the discrepancy of quality of education received by students based on socio-economic status.

The problem of educational inequity is both ameliorated and exacerbated by magnet schools which both provide quality education for all students irrespective of racial and economic background, and yet contribute to an inherently unfair two-tiered educational system. The following informed observation and critique from a Cincinnati resident who is both the father of a student enrolled in a magnet school and a teacher in a non-magnet school goes to the heart of the matter:

> I guess my biggest gripe is, why should magnets be deemed better if this is a public system? Why should anybody not want to go to the better schools? You are setting up a hierarchy. Somebody is losing out. If the schools aren't all equal, then why aren't they all equal?[21]

Conclusion: Magnet Urban Schools
and Educational and Socio-Cultural Equity

As we have illustrated magnet schools have a rich, complex and at times contradictory history, set of characteristics, uses and effects. They are at once part of the long tradition of schools established as alternatives to public schools and part of the public school system. They are based on leftist politics and yet were championed by conservatives. They were utilized as a more palatable and effective strategy for racial school desegregation, and yet have also contributed to more economic-based segregation of students. They have contributed to raising the quality of education in urban schools yet contributed to the establishment of a two-tier system of urban schools. They have made significant contributions to creating urban schools that have a multiracial, multicultural student population and yet it is often the poor in urban areas who have had to pay the price of such diversity by accepting lower-quality regular schools for the majority of poor and minority students. These characteristics are not simply a direct result of the nature of magnet programs but of the complex interaction of the persistence of sociopolitical problems such as averse racism, poverty and waves of efforts at addressing them in the general society.

In this chapter, we have put forward an explanation of the historical, social, and educational circumstances in which magnet schools were developed and in which they currently operate in an attempt to provide a context for understanding magnet schools that reaches beyond the often superficial, presentist, sensationalist, negative, and stereotypical images of urban schools found in popular culture and even at times in educational discourse. Such depictions tend, on the one hand, to sensationalize urban schools as virtual war zones where virtually no learning takes place and on the other to present simplistic solutions to the problems of urban education such as the ability of the teacher or principal to effect virtually miraculous change through individual heroic dedication and force of personality. As we have illustrated in the chapter, things are and always have been much more complicated for urban schools.

We took up the magnet concept and initiative as our example in order to illustrate that urban schools have a history and their present state of affairs is complex and reflective of historical and socio-cultural as well as educational context. The magnet example also allowed us to point to the fact that change in urban education has been effected not merely and not usually by the heroic efforts of individuals but by law, national and local government policies, the initiatives of educationists, and the efforts of school administrators, teachers, students and communities. Our discussion of magnet programs helps to illustrate that the successes and setbacks of efforts at achieving quality, diversity, equity and tolerance in education and through education in society are a reflection of the progress and setbacks of the society in general in dealing with such problems as averse racism, poverty, and other forms of discrimination and inequality.

NOTES

1   J. Spring, *The American School 1642–1993* 3rd ed. (New York: McGraw-Hill, 1995).

2   W. Urban and J. Wagoner, *American Education: A History* (Boston Burr, IL: McGraw-Hill, 2000).

3   Ibid., p. 63. See note 1.

4   W. G. Stephan and J. R. Feagin, *School Desegregation: Past, Present and Future* (La Cruces: New Mexico State University, 1980).

5   T.F. Gosset, Race: *The History of an Idea in America* (New York: Schocken, 1965).

6   R. Kluger, *Simple Justice* (New York: Knopf, 1976), p. 495.

7   Ibid., see note 4.

8   Ibid., see note 1.

9   Ibid.

10   Ibid.

11   Ibid., p. 354.

12   R. K. Blank, "Educational effects of magnet schools," in William Clune and John Witte, eds. *Choice and Control in American Education* Vol. 2 (London: Falmer Press, 1990), p. 78.

13   E. Royster, C.D. Baltzell, and F.C. Simmons, *Magnet Schools and Desegregation: Study of Emergency School Aid Act Magnet School Program.* Summary Report. Cambridge, MA: ABT Associates. (ERIC Document Reproduction Service No. ED 177 263, 1979).

14   C. Ascher, "Using magnet schools for desegregation: Some suggestions from the research," in N. Estes, D.U. Levine, and D.R. Waldrip, eds. *Magnet Schools: Recent Developments and Perspectives* (Austin, Texas: Morgan Printing and Publishing, 1990), pp. 3–30.

15   C.B. McMillan, *Magnet Schools: An Approach to Voluntary Desegregation* (Bloomington, Indiana: Phi Delta Kappa Educational Foundation, 1980).

16   C. Smrekar, and E. Goldring, *School Choice in Urban America: Magnet Schools and the Pursuit of Equity* (New York and London: Teachers College, Columbia University Press, 1999).

17   C.H. Rossell, "What is attractive about magnet schools?" *Urban Education, 20(1)* (1985): pp. 7–22.

18   K. Borman and J. Spring, *Schools in Central Cities* (White Plains, NY: Longman,1984).

19   J. Kozol, *Savage Inequalities: Children in America's Schools* (New York: Crown Publishing Inc., 1991).

20. Ibid., p.185.

21   Ibid., p. 112. See note 16.

15. Becoming Whole Again through Critical Thought

A Recipe[1]

ROCHELLE BROCK

To the reader:

I believe a requirement of any effective Urban Education program is instilling in students the ability and knowledge to critically deconstruct the world that constructs them. Students in Urban environments are subjected to a myriad of issues that they do not always understand. Although they are aware of the poverty that surrounds them, the knowledge to analyze the reasons of the poverty may not be in their immediate grasp. Without such knowledge they mistakenly believe poverty is only the fault of the individual because they are not aware that in 2005 the Black unemployment was 10.8% compared to 4.8% for White unemployment[2] or that the causes of high unemployment are due in part to outsourcing, systemic racism that attempts to ensure that even if qualified they will not be hired, poor schools that either do not adequately prepare students for the job market or are so problematic that students drop out before graduation. The student is not aware of the governmental policies that create and maintain the condition under which they live/survive.

As a teacher committed to social justice for Black students, I work to make my curriculum such that it forces students to think in new ways. I know the phrase "thinking outside the box" is overused, but it provides the perfect conceptual intent I want my students to visualize. The box is that place that confines the mind and body of the students, subverts their drive toward realizing their full humanity. When students think outside of the box, their thinking is not at the margins but at the center. They succeed in turning the box inside out.

An often-asked question of teachers concerned with critical thinking is how to "do-it" in their class, in their curriculum, in their pedagogy. I so wish I could provide a fail-safe lesson plan to be used in any and every situation. But of course that is impossible if we understand and acccept the changing nature and fluidity of critical thought. Instead, I offer an assignment I have given my students, which provides the space to question and reflect on a specific issue utilizing critical thought/critical cognition as the vehicle to understanding.

When working with my students on issues that are difficult to understand, I ask them to write a dialogical play, complete with stage directions. The play is written in the questioning Socratic method and the characters (preferably only two) represent the confusion the student feels about the subject matter. Writing in dialogue allows the students to talk to themselves, question what they have just written, think in deeper ways about the parts that make up the issues they are writing about. Like a two-year-old, the dialogical play provides them the opportunity to constantly ask 'why'? Besides that, it's fun and allows the students to stretch their creative juices by tackling sensitive issues as another person.

Inform your students that the stage directions should convey in a literal and metaphorical way both the mystification and enlightenment the characters (and by extension the students) experience. The process of conceptualizing and writing the play allows students to question themselves, constantly delving deeper into obscure meanings. As a conclusion for this exercise, you can either have certain students perform their play for the entire class, or depending on class size and time available, all of the plays can be perfor*med in a culminating event for the class. Sell tickets, invite the community, open the knowledge to others. After all, is that not one of the goals of critical thought in education?*

The first stage in the assignment is to share with my students a "play" I wrote about my internal struggle and search for self. Please share my journey into self . . .

Ingredients to make a Black goddess:

- spirit of ancestors,
- a healthy dose of love for students,
- ability to read the world
- a complex vision of urban education,
- patience,
- theoretical understanding of all and everything,
- wholeness of being.

Take your ingredients and stir while listening to your favorite jazz tune—preferably Cassandra Wilson. Allow the sounds of a Black woman to seep into your mixture. When everything is smooth (the mixture, not the jazz) get out your old beater and slip a pumpin,' bumpin' reggae cd in, turn it up as loud as you can and twirl and dance as you beat the shit out of your mixture—Remember, you are paying homage to those who came before so do it with the rhythm of your past adding your unique flavor to the batter—then beat . . . the faster the better.

And call her Oshun, the African goddess of voluptuous beauty, the goddess of love, the goddess of fertility, the female master of strategy. Oshun is the sweet and sour taste of life. Do not forget to add a little Yemaya for water purifies and is a giver of life . . . new life.

A goddess was just what Rochelle needed. Not only a higher power but also one from the historical memories of an African past. Created with music and brought to life with rhythm and soul, a goddess with the strength to move the paradigm beyond the margins. She holds a golden chain in her hands, a chain to tie all of her people together. She offers new ways of thinking, new modes of critical thought, new ways to think about urban education. Oshun is the guide to help us re-remember our past, the subjugated knowledge that has been forgotten and denied.

Together Oshun and Rochelle will write and speak their truth. Oshun brings voice to the silence surrounding Rochelle. Rochelle brings life to the historical memory of Oshun. As one they tell you A Black woman's story . . .

■   ■   ■   ■

Stage Directions: Rochelle is sitting at the kitchen table in her apartment, an ashtray, an old battered typewriter, and a stack of blank typing paper is on the table in front of her. A lone light hangs over the table forcing the kitchen to be seen only in shadows. There are several candles on the table in varying heights. A bowl of grapes sits in the middle of the table with a coffee pot on one side. One large purple coffee mug is placed in front of Rochelle. Surrounding the table in a semi-circle are four 6-foot bookshelves. Scattered on the floor are books stacked haphazardly and in varying heights. The books represent the knowledge of the leaders in the field of Critical Thinking, Radical Education, and Black Women's History. Note: The audience should get the feeling of "intellectual chaos" from the books.

The Players:

OSHUN   the African Goddess of Critical Thinking
ROCHELLE   the teacher of all students

Rochelle: (*Looking out into the audience.*) Where can I find the power to understand the feelings I have? Who will hold me; help me traverse this hostile world I find myself in? I sit here confused, stuck, barren. (*Extending hands toward the typewriter and then pulling them back, roughly.*) I cannot even write a facile sentence in a language not meant for me. It's as if I'm fighting an abstract, stubbornly refusing to engage in these words and thoughts that feel alien. Why? (*Standing and moving to the front of the table Rochelle begins to pace.*) My head hurts, I cannot fill my lungs with enough air to speak a thought, even one that is silent. I need to turn away, take a mind-rest, at least for a moment, from this malaise. But I can't. It is too important to work my way through, process my alienation from abstract thought, explain and articulate so all can understand. I must write and complete this article on critical thinking as a means to help Black women understand and fight their status in a racist sexist society. But the pieces will not come together in any type of cohesive whole. Instead, I sit, staring at an empty piece of paper, drinking coffee, killing myself with cigarettes, questioning my intelligence, my critical thinking skills. Why?

Oshun: (*As soon as Rochelle utters "Why" Oshun walks out of the shadows onto the stage. Soft jazz and sounds of the ocean can be heard in the background, which should remain for the entire play. Walking to the kitchen table, she reaches one hand out toward Rochelle.*) I hear and feel your pain and I have come to help you process that pain. Go inside of yourself, reach deep and find the strength to look and think critically about your life. Change your way of thinking—of seeing the world. Use those analytical skills of transgressive critical thought to help and guide you. Remember that you are a conscious being and therefore possess the cognitive skills to consciously control the trajectory of your world. Never forget that racism and all of its manifestations produce a mind-funk[3] that distorts thought and action. What has enveloped your soul is internalized racism; it's taken away your wholeness. You are defining yourself through it, accepting that because you are Black and a woman; your options, your worth are limited. You are forgetting your own power of thought and mind.

Rochelle: (*Still pacing and walking aimlessly, while at times talking to the audience and other times talking to self. Note: Rochelle remains oblivious to the physical presence of Oshun. Rochelle feels Oshun in her subconscious only.*) I once read about this thing called mind-funk. Mind-funk is the nemesis of Black Womanist critical thought, allowing me to believe all that is negative. Caused by internalized racism, it has encapsulated my thoughts, my entire sense of being until I cannot find the words to articulate the things I know. I have become theoretically challenged, not by outside forces but from the inside. I have allowed the words of others to enter my Being, forgotten that their thoughts do nothing but pull me down. I have been violated. But I must find a way to climb out of and far from this mindfunk. Damn, where is my shelter against the pain? My confusion, anger, and isolation increase as I realize that my critical insight into the constructions of Black womanhood does not insulate me from the daily pain of my otherness. (*Laughing*) But then perhaps if I did not possess a critical understanding, I would be crazy rather than terminally depressed. I don't know.

Oshun: (*slowly and gracefully sits in the chair opposite of Rochelle*) Ahhh yes, you are experiencing racism at its finest my Original World daughter.

Rochelle: (*repeating*) I would be crazy rather than terminally depressed.

Oshun: (*Speaking directly to Rochelle*) You are crying, I am happy. For I want you to never lose your passion. Do not become the rational thinker attempting to scientifically analyze your feelings of incompleteness. Instead, feel deeply and allow those feelings to move you to passionately question your world. Racism works at the decomposition of the cultural integrity of Blackness.[4] Close your eyes, walk with me and visualize. Decomposition, the breaking into parts, affords a visual, emotive sensation to describe the realities of racism. In order to remain whole, you must keep a constant vigil against internalizing racism. Anything short allows the space to exist where mind-funk can thrive. You must understand that mind-funk is more than a catchy phrase; it is a consuming way of reading the world and reading the self. It fosters the doubt, which stops a person from moving beyond their prescribed boundaries, to break out of Western psychological assessments of who we are as black women. You were not careful enough, not cognizant enough. You let your armor rest a minute too long.

Rochelle: (*Walking over to the bookcase, Rochelle speaks while looking at the books. Her back is to the audience.*) Could it be that my soul has been raped? Could it be that my armor has been stolen? Or could it be that I'm tired as hell of constantly having to carry that armor! Whatever the reason it's missing and I have no idea how or where to find it. My position as Black and female hinders the ability I need to think my way out of this oppressive frame of mind I find myself in. I let things inside that I should not have. Western positivistic evaluations of my abilities have found their way into my selfhood. What makes it so difficult is this inner turmoil that is blanketing me is caused by something outside of me. (*Turning toward the audience, but speaking to no one in particular.*) I am alienated not only from society but also from myself. And even though I strive for knowledge of my otherness, despite my understanding of subjugated knowledge and objectification, regardless of my awareness and acceptance of critical thinking and its transgressive cognition, I still allow myself to be silenced. Does it really matter if that silence is internal or external? I still become too tired to make my voice and thoughts heard. Such an insipid thing, racism can seep into every pore until it fills you with hate and bitterness and confusion.

Someone please tell me how racism accomplishes the decomposition of the cultural integrity of Blackness? Why am I allowing myself to be silenced and not using the critical thinking skills I have worked so hard to get? How do I find the strength to develop and become a critical agent of change and transformation for all of those Black women I come into contact with daily, and for myself? How do I re-remember the spiritual strength that aided my ancestors during the years of capture, enslavement, colonization, and exploitation? How do I retrieve my wholeness?

Oshun: (*As angry and confused as Rochelle's words are spoken Oshun speaks in a calming, reflective voice.*) Wholeness is delivered when your spirit is strong. Yes. Re-remembering and reconnecting with that which aided our ancestors is essential to your survival and the strength you need. But you ask how do you survive and I answer that you must open your eyes and your heart to all that surrounds you. You must become conscious of the powerful influences which seek to destroy your understanding of self. You must learn to not only use critical thinking to analyze what is outside of you but more importantly what is inside. (*Reaching for the grapes.*) Dig deep and discover that which gets in your way, hinders you as a Black Woman. (*Rises from her seat and moves to the front of the stage, parallel to Rochelle.*)

Rochelle: (*Moves from the bookcase to center stage.*) What is it that keeps getting in my way? Concepts of me as the other. A non-entity. Different, unheard, unwanted, unrespected, unloved, the only, removed, outside of society.[5] My position as a Black woman in America is as *the other*, which is such a strange term to describe a person. What does being the *other* have to do with how I feel about myself? People explain me, they study me, they write about me and if I am not careful I occasionally allow their definitions to seep into my thoughts. Everywhere I look they try to take me out of myself. There are powerful forces that attempt to construct my identity; place me in within an oppressive cage; force me to become the spectacle in their obsession.

Oshun: The decomposition of the cultural integrity of Blackness is cultivated, in part, through an ideology of the *other*. You are greater than the sum total of your parts. Perhaps it is this knowledge that will allow you to dismiss the attempts at decomposition.

Rochelle: (*still center stage, perfectly still*) When I disrobe, lay down my shield, rest, I am left with no choice but to use my *otherness* to define the boundaries of my existence. As the *other* I am removed, standing at the perimeters of normalcy helping to clarify a criterion I can never meet. Those who stand at the perimeters of normalcy are constantly demeaned by mainstream education and psychology's regime of truth.

Oshun: (*Walks to center stage several feet from Rochelle, looks at and speaks directly to Rochelle. Rochelle continues looking out into the audience, still oblivious of*

Oshun.) My child you always have a choice. Yes, you are the *other* but the *other* must never define you—resist that falsely constructed regime of truth. A liberated mind is the manifestation of critical thought. Deconstruct the significance of the *other*. The paradox of your life is that as the *other* you are both despised and yet needed. Although your status threatens the moral and social order of society you are also essential to its survival—your position at the margins of society helps to clarify those very margins. Black women empower the privileged in dominant culture's norm-referenced tests. Without us at the bottom they can't be the superior ones. Know that African American women, by not belonging, emphasize the significance of belonging.

Look for your shield in the knowledge that you are not what they say. Those writings by other people that you speak of do not or should not necessarily mean control. You are giving those who harm you the power to define. Stop! Make clear to yourself the ways in which ideology works.

Rochelle: (*Should be read stilted as if reading from a book in the beginning. As Rochelle reads, the words should become more natural, like she is internalizing the knowledge of the many attempts to define and dominate Black women. The power in her voice representing the ownership she is now experiencing regarding the concept of critical thought and her being.*) I am a political being. My life is politically inscribed. I must make clear to myself the ways in which ideology works. Ideology, socializes us to believe that the taken for granted assumptions are a natural, inevitable function of life. It calls us into being, but a being that is falsely constructed. Historically, Black women have been controlled with an ideology of domination, through legitimization, categorization, reification, mystification, and acquiescence, that ideology has been used to subjugate, objectify, and dominate Black women in America since enslavement. Remember that ideology functions in such devious ways. It becomes legitimate when systems of domination are represented as being worthy of support. Likewise, systems of domination are denied or obscured, and unequal social relations are hidden—"there's no oppression in psychology's testing industry." In other words, ideological forces ensure that oppressed people are either not aware of their own oppression, or aware but cannot necessarily articulate how it operates. Yes, it is becoming clear. Ideology works vis-a-vis fragmentation which occurs when meaning is fragmented and groups and individuals are placed in opposition to each other and to self. Decomposition. Through reification a transitory state is represented as if it were permanent, natural, or transhistorical. I was becoming that which society said I was. Ideology allows society to believe that the constructed images are valid. And more importantly, it allows the individual/the group to believe that the constructed images are valid. In this ideological configuration I.Q statistics are real. I really don't have the ability to make it in the worlds of commerce, academia, knowledge work, technology, helping professions—the hell I don't. (*Read with the pain and joy of giving birth to a new thought*). These forms of ideology are interwoven and occur simultaneously and ultimately work to interfere with my wholeness of being. Once I know and accept this knowledge I can become an intellectually free person.

Oshun: (*Walking toward where Rochelle stands.*) Once you truly understand and internalize the definitions of ideology you begin to develop the strength and knowledge to fight. Can you now begin to see our recipe for wholeness—connectedness to our ancestors, spiritual strength, power through self-definition, and deconstruction of ideology—that come together when we use critical thinking as a methodology? These are your ingredients, but you must still add others, depending on the spiciness you need. Remember the fluidity of critical thought. Move with it. Allow it to take you where it must. There are times when the moon is right and the ingredients for wholeness are few but at other times the weight of racism will threaten to pull you asunder and you must add the spices of your past. Although difficult to find they will bring about a taste favored by the goddesses.

Rochelle: (*Moving away from center stage and from Oshun, Rochelle resumes her seat in front of the typewriter.*) I will write and think myself away from this. I will prove to me that despite the changing faces of racism, spiritual strength and connectedness with the ancestors will and can guide me to wholeness. I will combine all that I know and feel and bring forth my greater truth. I will do it all with the passion that is central to my being. Yes, that is what I will do.

Oshun: (*For the first time Oshun speaks directly to the audience.*) The mind-funk, the depression and confusion which had been smothering Rochelle for weeks began to open, not completely, just enough so that she could see and breathe her way into thought.

Rochelle: (*Speaking as she puts a fresh piece of paper into the typewriter. Should be spoken while simultaneously typing.*) I can craft words to define thoughts to tell a story that is both personal and political. I can do it all while remaining true to my voice. When I stop and breathe and reflect on my life, I know the only way to survive is to give birth to my wholeness. I must recreate and redefine me. (*As these final words are spoken Oshun walks to where Rochelle sits, Rochelle rises when Oshun reaches her and for the first time they look directly at each other and become one.*) I weave a tapestry for the future with threads of hope and humanity.

NOTES

1 A version of this chapter appears in chapter 2 of R. Brock, *Sista Talk: The Personal and the Pedagogical* (New York: Peter Lang, 2005).

2 R. Clemons, "Even as US economy gets better jobs and wealth gap gets larger on the 'equality index,'" http://www.nul.org/PressReleases/2005/2005PR185.html (retrieved 6/17/2005).

3 G. Yamato, "Something about the subject makes it hard to name," in M. Anderson, and P. Hill-Collins, eds. *Race, Class, and Gender: An Anthology* (New York: Wadsworth, 1995), pp. 71–75.

4 P. C. Murrell, "Digging again the family wells: A Freiran literacy framework as emancipatory pedagogy for African American children," in P. Freire, J.W. Fraser, D. Macedo, T. Mckinnon, and W.T. Stokes, eds. *Mentoring the Mentor: A Critical Dialogue with Paulo Freire* (New York: Peter Lang, 1997), pp. 19–55.

5 For a wonderful emotive description of "the other" see A. Madrid "Missing people and others: Joining together to expand the circles" in M. Anderson and P. Hill-Collins, eds. *Race, class, and gender: An anthology* (New York: Wadsworth, 1995), pp. 10–15.

16. Supporting Academic Achievement in Culturally Diverse and Academically Talented Urban Students

SALLY M. REIS AND THOMAS P. HÉBERT

Talented students from culturally diverse populations have existed in large urban environments for generations; yet, many do not achieve at a level commensurate with their ability. Educators must acquire a better understanding of the educational needs of culturally diverse students as many urban school districts address the educational needs of this population. Academically talented high school students from culturally diverse populations who live in cities and attend large urban high schools often encounter difficulties that impede their continued academic achievement. To better understand the culture of talented students in an urban high school, a group of 35 culturally diverse teenagers in an urban high school who achieved and underachieved during their high school years were studied over three years. This chapter summarizes the results of a study that identified why some academically talented urban students were able to succeed, while others underachieved, and in some cases, dropped out of high school.[1]   The findings offer educators useful suggestions and strategies for addressing students' academic needs and supporting their continued high achievement. In this chapter, a case study of one of the high achieving students is presented, findings related to research on academically talented students in urban settings are summarized, and specific strategies, emanating from this research, are suggested, to help educators promote high levels of academic achievement.

A Case Study of Wallace

Wallace kept the sports commentators busy. In any football game featuring South Central High School, Wallace, who was 6'1" and weighed 270 pounds, was the offensive and defensive tackle who could be depended on to produce in any crucial play. The public address system boomed with his name from kickoff to final whistle. Because of his dependability and talent on the field, the South Central High fans looked upon Wallace as a local hero and the Centerfield area sports commentators had only praise for the young African American athlete. Wallace, however, was a modest young man who knew his talents were combined with much hard work to achieve this athletic success, and he explained his realistic outlook came from his upbringing at home.

You come home feeling really proud. You're a champion! And Mom's reaction was "Okay, champion, it's your turn to do the dishes and don't forget to clean your room! You know, you're no better than anyone else." My parents were proud—tremendously! They congratulate me, but after it's over, it's "Go clean your room!"

Wallace had excelled in varsity football since his freshman year. During the winter months, he ran indoor track which he explained, "was simply the coach's breeding for football season." He won a gold medal for his shotput throw in the State Inter-Scholastic Athletic Conference, breaking statewide records. Several colleges had their scouts attending his high school games and investigating the promising young star. Wallace's mail had also included several letters from colleges inviting Wallace to visit their campus and chat with their coaching staffs. This attention was exciting, yet Wallace described how he dealt with the hype when he said, "I block it out. I go out there and concentrate, knowing what I have to do and I work hard."

Wallace and his younger brother, Derrick, a sophomore at the high school, lived with their parents in a modest apartment building in the south end of his city. His father drove a taxi and his mother was a nurse's aide at a convalescent home in their neighborhood. Neither parent had a college education, but they encouraged this dream in both their sons. Wallace's parents had plans for their boys and they wanted to be sure they "followed the right path." They insisted that athletics was not the only ticket and instilled the value of academics. This may have been a struggle with Wallace in the beginning because his elementary school years were not without problems.

Wallace's teachers were concerned about him all through elementary school. His fourth-grade teacher commented in his school records, "Wallace gets involved with students and doesn't control his behavior!" His fifth-grade teacher noted, "Wallace works hard when positive behavior is present. When he is upset, his work suffers. He needs to control his temper." His sixth-grade teacher noted, "Wallace's attitude socially and academically is inconsistent. He requires much supervision because he is far too interested in his neighbors."

Teachers knew that Wallace had the ability to succeed. Achievement tests reflected this; Wallace scored in the 88th percentile in reading and math and 86th percentile in language arts. In fifth grade, Wallace was recommended for the gifted and talented program, but chose not to join the self-contained G/T class, because he did not want to leave his friends. In seventh grade, teachers continued to recognize the high potential in the young man and recommended him for a two-year enrichment program, which provided high-potential students from inner-city environments with field trips and specialized training with professional architects. Through this exposure to creative individuals, Wallace gained a great deal of confidence and he pointed out that many skills he used in his current coursework had been developed through this program.

The high potential and strong ability were recognized again in high school when Wallace was chosen for the Upward Bound Program. He participated in Upward Bound's six-week summer program at a private college in Centerfield and he continued to benefit from the support systems provided by the program throughout the scholastic year. Wallace was also a newspaper columnist, who contributed articles regularly to the *Centerfield Gazette's* "Student Page," and he won a second place prize with two partners in the city-wide Science Fair competition. Wallace's high school program included a combination of honors and academic classes, and he achieved a B average.

By the time he was a senior, Wallace had earned the respect of his peers, as the entire student body understood that this young man was someone they would be reading about after he left South Central High School. Soft-spoken and articulate, he was elected Student Council President. He initially had aspirations of attending Clemson University, playing football, and eventually becoming a public relations expert. These aspirations changed, however, as Wallace began to consider the impact of athletics on many college athletes. He decided instead to accept a scholarship to a small private liberal arts college with an excellent academic reputation.

Background of the Study

Far too little research has been devoted to academically talented, culturally diverse urban youth like Wallace. Ford and Harris examined the relevant literature on minority gifted children, particularly African American, and discovered that of 4109 published articles on high-ability youth since 1924, less than 2% addressed children of color.[2] These numbers are disheartening because less information means less understanding of the academic achievement needs of culturally diverse students in our urban schools. The federal funding of the Jacob Javits Act that focuses on ways to nurture and develop talent in a broader spectrum of students, resulted in more research about how to meet the needs of talented students. Research conducted prior to the implementation of the Javits Act identified some obstacles to the achievement of academically talented, culturally diverse students including: the use of definitions of giftedness that reflect middle-class majority culture values and perceptions[3]; the use of standardized tests that do not reflect the exceptional abilities of children of color,[4] low socio-economic status causing differences in environmental opportunities that enhance intellectual achievement[5]; and cultural differences in the manifestation of gifted behaviors.[6]

More recently, researchers have attempted to explain school failure and underachievement of academically talented culturally diverse students through an examination of social and psychological factors, family and community factors, as well as educational programmatic factors, and have provided multiple theories or explanations regarding why students do not achieve academically. Ford examined determinants of underachievement in high-ability African American students, suggesting that psychological factors played the greatest role in underachievement.[7] Ogbu's work is considered one explanation of underachievement of academically talented urban youth.[8] Ogbu argued that a critically important difference exists between immigrant minorities, people who have moved to the United States because they seek a better life, and non-immigrant, or "castelike," minorities, people whose status in American society is a result of slavery, conquest or colonization. According to Ogbu, immigrant minorities such as Southeast Asians, Chinese or Filipinos, for example, may face seemingly insurmountable barriers once they arrive, but tend to see those barriers as temporary. However, castelike minorities, such as African Americans, feel excluded from the high-quality education received by whites and this exclusion hampers the academic performance of some African American children.

Factors Promoting Academic Achievement in Academically Talented Students

In this study, high-ability students who were identified as high achievers were compared with students of similar ability who underachieved in school. Thirty-five students participated in this three-year study in a large urban high school. Qualitative methods were used to examine the perceptions of students, teachers, staff, and administrators about the reasons that some academically talented students fail to achieve in school. In this research, the factors identified as promoting academic achievement in talented students are summarized in Table 17.1. They include the development of a belief in self, supportive adults, interaction with a network of high achieving peers, extracurricular activities, challenging classes such as honors classes, personal characteristics such as motivation and resilience, and family support. The achieving, academically talented students identified with the beliefs and values of a "culture of high achievement" in their school, that they had helped to create. Some of the high achieving students experienced periods of underachievement in school; however they were supported in their achievement by a network of high achieving peers who refused to let their friends falter in school. For these students, achievement was like walking up a crowded staircase. If students started to underachieve and tried to turn and walk down the staircase, many other students pushed them back up the staircase. Once, however, the cycle of underachievement began, it was difficult to reverse.

Table 17.1: Factors Promoting Academic Achievement in Talented Students

- Development of a strong belief in self-characterized by aspirations and goals, and confidence in one's ability to succeed
- Supportive adults in school (teachers, counselors, coaches)
- A network of high achieving peers and friends who provided encouragement, friendship, and positive relationships
- Extra-curricular activities, after-school, enrichment programs, summer and special programs that expanded opportunities and helped develop advanced abilities
- Appropriately challenging learning experiences/honors classes that provided multiple opportunities to develop self-regulation and effective work habits
- Personal characteristics (resilience, sensitivity, motivation, multicultural appreciation, inner will)
- Ability to solve urban school and community problems and deal with adversity
- Family support, love, and pride

Students who achieved in school acknowledged the importance of being grouped together in honors and advanced classes with other academically talented students. Successful students received support and encouragement from each other and from supportive adults including teachers, guidance counselors, coaches, and mentors. Students who achieved in school took part in multiple extracurricular activities both after school and during the summer. Most high achieving females we studied chose not to date in order to concentrate their energies on their studies. High achieving students had a strong belief in self and exhibited resilience in any negative family, school, or urban environments. Although parents of students in this study cared deeply about their children, their involvement in their children's high school education was minimal.

Several high achieving participants discussed their experiences in the district's gifted and talented program in elementary school. That program, based on Renzulli's Enrichment Triad Model,[9] focused on providing enrichment to a talented pool of students that enabled them to become exposed to a wide variety of topics, gain skills in creative and critical thinking, and problem-solving, and become involved in advanced projects based on their interests and talents. In addition to elementary teachers, these academic achievers mentioned specific high school teachers, counselors, coaches, mentors from the community, and administrators as having been influential. They discussed the importance of a specific group of adults in their high school such as their honors class teachers, coaches, and one or two administrators.

Students also described relationships with guidance counselors and how some counselors supported them. Because a large student load was assigned to each guidance counselor, counselors consistently discussed their perceptions that they spent the great majority of their time dealing with students with problems. It was common to see police, drug enforcement officials, social workers, angry parents, and community members in the guidance counselors' offices. The majority of guidance counselors' time was spent on this population and when they could find time to work with high achieving students, they described it as enjoyable. For example, one guidance counselor, upon hearing of the acceptance and full scholarship of one of the high achieving students in this study to an Ivy League University, explained: "This is the joy of my work!"

In addition to support from adults, high achieving students established a strong peer network. This network was essential to the achievement of most of the participants in this study and all participants acknowledged its existence in a variety of ways. As students grew older, the peer network became stronger as students interacted with other high achieving peers in various extracurricular activities, including National Honor Society and summer programs at private or independent schools. It was at this point during the high school experience that the greatest gap between students who achieved and underachieved appeared. High achieving students worked in peer groups on projects and community issues, and provided support and encouragement to each other in numerous ways. These young students provided an active network for each other, and intervened when problems arose at home or in school, providing help, peer counseling and the support needed to overcome these problems. Opportunities to participate in extracurricular, after-school, Saturday, and summer program experiences also contributed to high achievement in this group of students. Almost all of the achieving students in this study remained in their high school after school to participate in a wide variety of activities on a daily basis. Many of the participants were involved in more than one sport and all were involved in school clubs and optional activities, such as jazz band, foreign language clubs, service groups, and academic competitions. These extracurricular activities and programs appeared to have a major impact on these young people and were consistently cited as being extremely influential in the development of their ability to excel academically.

The special programs helped to expose participants to a different world outside the urban area in which they lived and went to school. Summer programs at a selective private school for high potential students, for example, provided the exposure to other academically talented students who had a positive attitude about education and firm plans for their futures, including attending competitive colleges and considering graduate school at a young age. These experiences enriched the lives of the participants in this study in numerous ways and helped some of them to decide to attend colleges and universities that were in other geographic areas. One Hispanic young woman, for example, initially had problems with her parents when she attended a three-week summer program that was an hour away from her home. However, after her success in that program, her parents became more supportive of her decision to attend an Ivy League School that was two hours away from her home.

Achieving students involved in this study had appropriately challenging learning experiences in school. Not all classes were interesting or enjoyable and not all produced high-level learning experiences, but in most classes, students were expected to produce high-quality

---

Table 17.2: Reasons for Underachievement of High Ability Students

School Factors
- Inappropriate early curricular experiences
- Absence of opportunities to develop appropriate school work habits
- Negative interactions with teachers
- Absence of challenge in high school
- Questionable counseling experiences

Family Issues
- Family dysfunction
- Strained relations with family members
- Problems with siblings and sibling rivalry
- Inconsistent role models and value systems in the family
- Minimal parental academic monitoring, guidance, and expectations

Community Factors
- Negative school environment
- Hostile urban environment (ethnic prejudice, limited opportunities for constructive entertainment)
- Inappropriate peer group issues

Personal Factors
- Behavior problems and disciplinary issues
- Problems with unstructured time
- Confused or unrealistic aspirations
- Insufficient perseverance and low self-efficacy
- Poor coping strategies and self-regulation

---

work. Students indicated that they did their most advanced work in their honors and advanced placement classes. In other classes, students who achieved at lower levels often made fun of their high achieving peers. This situation was never encountered in honors or advanced placement classes, and the achieving students appreciated the academic challenge they encountered in their honors levels courses.

Factors Influencing Underachievement

The high-ability underachievers in the study seemed to attend a different high school program from the one described by the achieving population and the reasons they believed that they underachieved are summarized in Table 17.2. High school students who underachieved in school believed that their achievement problems began due to a variety of reasons, but all believed the most important reason was their particularly easy elementary school experiences. These young people explained that they had never learned to work, primarily because their elementary and middle-school experiences had been too easy, which directly affected their high school experiences. Their daily elementary curricular experiences were inappropriate for them, and that affected their later experiences. Their classes and academic tasks were "too easy," and the participants discussed how they had "breezed" through elementary school, indicating that schoolwork required no major effort. Schoolwork was so simple that students did not acquire appropriate opportunities to develop important academic skills, sophisticated study skills, or effort. In other words, they never learned how to work hard at learning, and some became so accustomed to learning without effort because the work was so easy that when they had to exert effort, they erroneously thought they were no longer smart.

Schoolwork was so easy for them that these students did not acquire appropriate opportunities to develop important academic skills or sophisticated study skills. Their schoolwork habits, self-discipline, and self-regulation in classrooms and at home were not properly developed. These students often had limited access to challenging learning experiences that foster the skills and discipline required for higher intellectual pursuits later in their academic life. Teachers were considered sources of support for the students' learning in high school and if teachers were not considered to be caring and concerned, underachievement was exacerbated. Participants who underachieved believed that although they met "good" teachers during their secondary school experiences, most of their content area teachers were less caring and supportive than those they had encountered during elementary school. All of the underachievers reported that they also began to underachieve if an unrewarding, unchallenging curriculum provoked boredom. Most participants discussed the obvious mismatch that existed between their curricular strengths and the classes they were enrolled in. Their special talents and strengths were often ignored in such classes.

Inappropriate counseling experiences existed for the underachieving students as evidenced by their strengths being overlooked, their negative curricular experiences, and the problems they faced with their guidance counselors. These counseling experiences often thwarted students' paths to success. The majority of the students who underachieved expressed dissatisfaction with the nature of some of their interactions with their counselors. A series of family issues also negatively affected the lives of the high-ability underachievers. Stressful events, such as the serious illness of a family member or relative, a disabled sibling and/or a change in the family structure negatively influenced their home atmosphere that, in turn, influenced their moods, attitudes, and achievement in school. The stress often resulted in a difficult time for all family members. Incongruent points of view regarding cultural values and age-related (adolescent) issues were also found in the case of some students. Conflicting points of view between students and parents were identified in relation to Puerto Rican traditional cultural values regarding interdependence/independence and "respeto" (respect) toward parental authority. In addition to conflicting relationships, tense relationships with siblings negatively influenced students' disposition to learn. Some participants had a brother or sister who had been an academic "superstar" in school. In order to avoid competing, the participants in this study stopped trying and consciously began to underachieve in school. Participants reported that discord with their siblings arose in relation to issues such as the use of the phone, the volume of the radio, unasked advice, and disappointment about family problems.

Many of the high achieving young people in this study faced difficult problems and for some, life was a daily struggle. Most of the underachieving students faced similar problems, yet they were not able to overcome these problems and succeed in school. Some of the other underachieving students had severe family problems, which seemed to contribute to their underachievement. Most underachieving students recognized their parents' interest in having them succeed in school and to "do better" than their parents. Parents tried to encourage their children to succeed in school and life by using their own life experiences as examples to prevent their children from "making the same mistakes." Yet, parental help was frequently of limited quantity and quality, as one participant explained:

> My parents have always told me to do my work. They are always after me, "Do your work. Did you do your homework?" My mother doesn't know English. Well, she knows English, but she never went past fourth grade education. So I can't ask her for help. And my father, he is always working. I can't ask them for help. I have always had to do my work all by myself.

Parents did not become actively involved in the schoolwork required in high school. These parents expected their children to do their homework by themselves, and as a result, doing homework was left up to students who reported that they spent a good deal of time at home just watching TV, talking on the phone, listening to music, or playing Nintendo.

In addition to numerous family problems, the underachievers faced the same types of community problems as did the achieving students, but somehow while the achievers were able to use their resilience to overcome problems, the students who underachieved were more susceptible to issues caused by community problems. Participants discussed the hostile environment, the influence of the surrounding community, and its influence on their personal life and school performance. The local community was plagued with gang-related conflicts, prejudice, and limited opportunities for entertainment. Consequently, students felt unsafe, bored, and uncomfortable with their social life conditions. The urban area was plagued by increasing gang-related incidents involving fights, drug dealing, and homicides. These gangs ran their own drug cartels, and offered young people from poor neighborhoods an opportunity for making money. Gang membership provided an alternative means for economic advancement. In addition to access to better economic conditions, gang membership involved emotional support. After a trial period, gang members counted on the protection of their fellow members. Although none of the participants in this study admitted to active membership in these gangs, they were all aware of the situation. They believed that the common fights and drug dealing in and out of the school, as well as the killing in their neighborhoods, had a negative impact on them. The latest killing of young gang members incited a sense of despair in these participants, who felt threatened, scared, and unsafe.

Minimal opportunities for constructive entertainment were another community factor that participants perceived as affecting their lives. Participants described their city as a dirty, poor, violent, and boring one that offers nothing for young people. With the exception of school sports or clubs, participants believed that there was little for them to do in their urban environment. However, several of the participants who were underachieving were not allowed to participate in school sports because their academic performance was equivalent to less than a C average. The friends selected by the high-ability underachievers also caused problems for some who were having difficulties fulfilling their academic responsibilities. Most of the males in this group faced peer group issues that appeared to negatively influence their attitudes toward academic achievement.

The high-ability underachievers said they were bored with their curriculum, negatively influenced by their peers and their dismal surroundings, and had few strategies for constructively dealing with these problems. Accordingly, they developed personal problems that negatively affected their achievement in school. Many of the young people in this group, particularly males, faced disciplinary problems for poor behavior in school. An extensive collection of disciplinary reports was found in their permanent record files. Several of the young men were repeatedly seen with their heads down on a desk either sleeping or hiding under a hooded sweatshirt, and some teachers would allow them to remain that way, while others insisted they sit up and participate in class.

Several of the participants indicated that they had problems with unstructured time. Two of the underachieving girls read and watched soap operas and other television programs most of the time they were not in school. Most underachieving students appeared to have aspirations that were either confused or unrealistic. Most did not understand the reality of their academic and personal situations. For example, one of the male athletes who had a dismal record of academic failure and discipline problems, dreamed of attending a New England college "not too far from home" a large enough school where he had a good chance of being recognized by professional recruiters. According to the data gathered in this study, participants had difficulty in persevering in several areas of their lives. For example, one young woman reported giving up several things in life. She explained that usually her "interest for something builds up," but then she just "messes around and gives it up." For her, this attitude emerged most often during emotionally stressful times provoked by arguments with her mother, and when she was feeling depressed. "Giving up" was also evident in some school-related interests as well as personal hobbies such as playing the guitar and the flute. In order to protect 'themselves from negative experiences, students reacted negatively and became defensive toward painful family, school, social, and personal experiences. For instance, one tried to commit suicide because of family conflicts. Another decided to stop doing his schoolwork, and instead, devoted his energies to making friends.

Female Students

Some differences emerged between high achieving and underachieving female students. The high achieving girls in this study did not date or become romantically involved, were extremely supportive of other achieving students (especially other female students), were involved in multiple activities, displayed independence, resilience, and were already dedicated to a career. Clear trends emerged regarding parental expectations, as mothers of high achieving students, in particular, encouraged their daughters to excel in school without being actively involved in their daughters' education. The majority of the mothers of this group had never been in the high school their daughter attended, but their support was clear. Their daughters did their homework, put their academic studies ahead of their social lives, did not date, and often were deeply connected with their families and their churches. They had a positive circle of peers and were supported by these young people to continue to achieve academically. They were independent, believed in themselves and wanted a career that would enable them to use their talents. The underachieving girls dated extensively, watched hours of television, read romance novels, and spent hours communicating with their friends out of school. Rather than becoming alienated and underachieving in school, the female achievers in this study created a community of achievement within their school.

Implications

The findings of this research provide specific implications for urban educators of high-potential youth. The support system created by the achievers suggests the importance of strengthening peer-counseling programs for high-potential students. Mentor programs and forums for inspirational guest speakers from the cultural communities could share their success stories as well as details of any challenges in achieving success in an urban setting. Parents of culturally diverse students might benefit from discussion groups held in private homes or in school on topics that would assist them in supporting their sons' and daughters' academic achievement. These sessions could be led by culturally diverse school counselors and teachers and provide a strong sense of community within the families of high-ability achievers. Urban high school administrators and counselors should do everything possible to strengthen Advanced Placement opportunities and maintain honors courses for high-ability students, as well as extracurricular, athletic and special summer programs associated with businesses, private colleges, and state universities.

Leadership programs and youth forum opportunities should also be offered to high-potential and achieving youth who might also benefit from opportunities to investigate the problems of their urban communities. They can be encouraged to plan, design and creatively produce campaigns to raise the social consciousness of their communities and address issues faced in their urban schools and communities.

Summary

Rather than becoming alienated and underachieving in school, the young people involved in this study created a community that supported high achievement within their school. Some of their teachers, counselors, coaches, and parents were an integral part of this community and all were partially responsible for the eventual academic success achieved by the participants in this study. Despite family problems, and all of the difficulties faced in their urban high school, including gangs, violence and drugs, the achievement ideology remained in tact for the participants of this study. The community of achievement they created both developed and protected this ideology, providing them with a haven in which their accomplishments were both valued and nurtured.

NOTES

1   S. M. Reis, T. P. Hebert, E. I. Diaz, L. R. Maxfield, and M. E. Ratley, *Case Studies of Talented Students Who Achieve and Underachieve in an Urban High School* (Storrs, CT: The National Research Center on the Gifted and Talented, 1995).

2   D. Y. Ford and J. J. Harris, "On discovering the hidden treasures of gifted and talented Black children," *Roeper Review*, 13(11) (1990): 27–32.

3   J. Maker, "Quality education for gifted minority students," *Journal for the Education of the Gifted, 6(3)* (1983): 140–153.

4   Ford and Harris; M. Kitano and D. Kirby, *Gifted Education: A Comprehensive View* (Boston: Little Brown, 1986); . S. Richert, J. J. Alvino and R. C. McDonnel, *National Report on Identification: Assessment and Recommendations for Comprehensive Identification of Gifted and Talented Youth* (Washington, DC: US Department of Education, Educational Information Resource Center, 1982).

5   Maker, "Quality Education"; Kitano and Kirby, *Gifted Education*; B. Clark, *Growing Up Gifted*. 2nd ed. (Columbus, OH: Merrill, 1983); J. Gallagher, *Teaching the Gifted Child*.. 3rd ed. (Boston: Allyn and Bacon, 1985).

6   Ford and Harris; Kitano and Kirby; Clark, *Growing Up*; A.Y. Baldwin, I'm black but look at me, I am also gifted, *Gifted Child Quarterly, 31(4)* (1987): 180–185; G. Davis and S. Rimm, *Educaiton of the Gifted and Talented* (Englewood Cliffs, NJ: Prentice-Hall, 1985).

    D. Y. Ford, "Determinants of underachievement as perceived by gifted, above-average, and average Black students," *Roeper Review, 14(3)* (1992): 130–136.

8   J. U. Ogbu, *The Next Generation: An Ethnography of Education in an Urban Neighborhood* (New York: Academic Press, 1974); J. U. Ogbu, "Research currents: cultural-ecological influences on minority school learning," *Language Arts, 62(8)* (1985): 860–868; J. U. Ogbu, "Variability in minority school performance: a problem in search of an explanation," *Anthropology and Education Quarterly, 18(4)* (1987): 312–334; J. U. Ogbu, "Immigrant and involuntary minorities in comparative perspective," in M. A. Gibson and J. U. Ogbu, eds. *Minority Status and Schooling: A Comparative Study of Immigrant and Involuntary Minorities* (New York: Garland Publishing, 1991), pp. 3–33.

9   J. S. Renzulli, *The Enrichment Triad Model: A Guide for Developing Defensible Programs for the Gifted* (Mansfield Center, CT: Creative Learning Press, 1977); J. S. Renzulli and S. M. Reis, *The Schoolwide Enrichment Model* (Mansfield, CT: Creative Learning Press Inc., 1985); J. S. Renzulli and S. M. Reis, *The Schoolwide Enrichment Model*. 2nd ed. (Mansfield, CT: Creative Learning Press Inc., 1997).

17. Pedagogical Practices within The Prison Industrial Complex

L.A. GABAY

What kind of society do educators want to live in and what kind
of teachers and pedagogy can be informed and legitimated by a
view of authority that takes democracy and citizenship seriously?
—Henry Giroux, *Schooling for Democracy:*
Critical Pedagogy in the Modern Age

In this era of diverse and growing urban schools programs throughout the educational system, this is a narrative that focuses on educating an adjudicated youth clientele. The New York City Department of Education offers many alternative high schools for juvenile detention education. Given my current experience teaching in a high school for incarcerated students in New York City, I have become particularly interested in juvenile detention education. This curiosity with the judicial system and its administrative processes, coupled with my commitment to curriculum, has led me to look at issues of education and curriculum development in the prison industrial structure. The particular dynamics of educating

a court-involved cohort leads to specific issues facing education in prison and these pedagogical challenges include teaching methodology, curriculum design, and program
development.

In their chapter in this book "De facto Zero Tolerance: An Exploratory Study of Race
and Safe School Violations" Goode and Goode delve into the issue of ethnic profiling of
detained students with staggering data and analysis. In addition to the highly disproportionate racial dynamic which informs many of the ideas in this paper, over the years I have seen
scores of children with low economic status, learning disabilities, low impulse control, and
a host of other causations, end up either in detention or alternative probation programs. I
would like to explore ways to assist students who fall into this population and help them go
on to get high school diplomas, General Education Diplomas (GEDs), college degrees and
eventually, secure jobs, as the majority of these youth offenders will be released and re-enter
free society. Teachers need the means to better respond to these students' complex and wide
range of circumstances. If they are not educated in prison, then where? Understanding that
the justice system is highly complex and related to intersecting economic, racial, cultural,
and ideological structures of power, I am not suggesting that we need to reduce the prison
infrastructure to rubble. Surely there is a need for these institutions. Individuals need to be
held accountable for their actions, and there are indeed rules and consequences for breaking laws. The mechanisms by which our society constructs criminality is deeply in place; thus,
through deconstruction I suggest that new spaces need to be created.

The students that I teach have not responded well to traditional learning or living environments and need to become attached rather than detached to teaching programs and methods. I do not provide a working blueprint for how things should be. What is most important
in the system's redesign is that we begin to ask ourselves questions leading to productive discussions about how we think about juvenile detention. What do these "punitive and rehabilitative" structures reveal about who we are as a society? When we begin to ask ourselves
this question, we may discover that social justice should be an active ingredient in pedagogy, practice, and curriculum development. It is my belief that through research and
action, educators can construct a more just, humane and creative incarceration curriculum.
Human arrangements are as complex as human beings themselves and this complexity is
greatly multiplied when we attempt to influence the direction of social justice, take sides
and actively try to end oppression.

As a classroom teacher I recognize daily the need to empower educators and cultivate
the strengths of students. Curricula need to reinforce the power of the individual. Adjudicated
students seem to cry for a curriculum and methodology that revolves around self-actualiza-
tion. Prison curricula should promote understanding of the different views of human beings
living in a global world, and pedagogical actions reflect values by supporting the belief that
we are not more or better, but different. Analyzing society, instilling discipline and adding
to a student's confidence is key in my classroom pedagogy. The goal is to demystify much
of the material and make it both relevant and compelling to the student. Many schools and
curricula neglect non-verbal modes of processing and producing information, and tradition-

ally favor verbal modes of processing and expressing knowledge that traditionally has been based on social efficiency. Standardized tests are designed to reflect a certain prioritization of knowledge. Most inmates either are not familiar with or do not respond well to traditional curricula and practices. I know from both personal and professional experience how stressful these traditional modes are to marginalized or alienated students. The students' experiences should be examined and included in the lived school culture by tapping into the urban locales to cultivate their strengths and cognitive abilities.

I have colleagues who teach at some of the "finest" public city high schools that have students who are outstanding test takers but cannot really write. They know vocabulary and can do the writing exercises, but in terms of writing something real, or something at stake for them, they are unable, or more likely ignorant, about how to undertake such a task. It is important to focus on the many variations of writing that can be reflected in many approaches. Methodology needs to encourage a student's leadership and voice. Interactive experiential learning (meaning, fewer lecture and note-taking methods) engages students to ask provocative questions and inspires critical thinking as students connect to each other and other communities. In other words, students need to learn what they *want* and not what they *ought* to know.

Practicum

I teach writing at a New York City public school that provides educational services and programs to young people who are in the custody of the Department of Juvenile Justice or the Department of Probation. The overall goal of this program is to provide credit-bearing classes to empower students with the necessary tools so that they may re-engage in their education and become productive members of their families, communities, and society at large.

The copious procedural obstacles and circumstance that typically affect teaching includes time constraints. On average, students are placed in this program for twenty-three days. Some students stay months while others can be assigned for just one day. Yearly, approximately 4000 students visit this facility. If they are placed in this school they are expected to attend class and complete homework (or hallwork) assignments.

From the instructor's point of view, therefore, any given lesson—even if part of a larger thematic unit—needs to be self-contained and readily accomplished within the forty-five-minute class period to stimulate both the long-term student *and* be inclusive of the new or short-term learners. My school, which opened in 1998, is both similar to and representative of many school programs in juvenile correctional facilities: It has been continuously redesigned and given new names and instructional direction, and as a result is constantly in a fledgling stage of dealing with this clientele that is in desperate need of classroom structure, consistency, and information. Lack of modern equipment and engaging material within the restrictions of the host prison facility further aggravates this situation, challenging the ingenuity and resourcefulness of even the most motivated teachers in their attempts to provide legitimate top-quality classes to serve the needs of their students.

Personal safety is a priority. Format restrictions manifest themselves into physical limitations that prevent provisions of magazines with staples, spiral bound books because they can be used as instruments of harm, current newspaper publications, and pencils with erasers. Classrooms must also be free of electrical and extension chords, food, glue, pins, string art and maps of local areas. These necessary precautions severely alter the technique, implementation, and actualization of a lesson.

I find that classroom management is crucial in creating a successful learning environment. I even find myself implementing a Giuliani-esque broken windows theory, where you attend to the little problems to avoid the larger challenges. For example, if routines are in place, desks are in rows and free from graffiti, fewer fights and confrontations occur while the students are in my care and custody.

The instructional mandate is to follow the New York City curriculum and New York State standards. The framework is cognizant of the twenty-three-day average stay of our students, and administration has suggested either telescoping or spreading out the concepts and activities over two or three days. Surprisingly, the scripted framework of the standards encouraged me to experiment and personalize strategies to make them my own. With provisions for a certain degree of improvisation and spontaneity, many of my lessons follow a self-developed format: I begin to learn who the students *are*, discover their needs as writers and personal passions as a means of seeking to broaden their learning perimeters. During an early lesson on onomatopoeia, a student suggested that a hip hop group The Roots, use this literary technique that creates words based upon sound and effect. With each lesson more hip hop songwriters were being referenced (i.e., for imagery, Tupac Shakur; for narrative, Notorious B.I.G.; for metaphor and simile, Jay-Z). I started bringing these songs into the classroom and asking students to analyze the lyrics as well as use what others had written as a model for their own writing. With such an approach, soon my stagnant lesson was given new life and intimacy, celebrating creativity, history, diversity, intelligence, and personal power.

Curricula need to be fast-moving and continually developing. For instance, a few weeks later, during the mandated lesson on symbolism in writing, a student referenced popular culture's use of iconic symbols such as Nike's "swoosh" and McDonald's "arches." This transformative lived moment ultimately led to an exploration of trends in media consolidation by understanding basic principles of advertising and describing images and symbolism. The next semester I continued with this analysis when teaching imagery, by examining how self-conceptions of body image are influenced by media and the implications these have upon one's attitudes and behaviors. The methodology is such that lesson plans are rooted in the academic areas but are ultimately designed as departure points for further educational exploration. By condoning my use of such a methodology, my school's administration provided both teacher and students the opportunity for agency while simultaneously offering a curriculum that is focused upon breaking the built-in structural antagonisms, thereby changing the tradition hegemonic dynamic often found in schools, while maintaining the legitimacy of school as a place to learn.

The spirit of inquiry and discovery in updating and making courses more meaningful soon provided me with means to include theater and acting in my writing class. A New York professional actor took on the role as co-teacher by sharing a positive, constructive and effective medium in redirecting lives. Building sets and costumes, rehearsing scenes, journal writing, and producing a public performance utilizes a teaching methodology that reinforces the personal lived and experiential elements. The value in such a learning activity is getting students to reflect upon their rich experiences at the micro, meso, and macro levels. The acting project is pedagogically reflective by nature as the learners look at characters and explore issues of self in relation to society. The use of theater in a classroom is certainly reflective in revealing our own locations in the web of reality. The tools of acting and role-play provide the possibility in revealing these personal aspects. The acting program offered a safe, engaging, and constructive environment for people who are most vulnerable and need alternative and productive methods of self-expression. The curriculum provided the students with a more transformative, egalitarian and just context for learning. In his free-writing journal entry, a student expresses this very sentiment with great insight and deep aplomb:

> When I'm alone I try to finally relax and think about the struggle of my parents and what it means for me. I can't just relax though, I need something to twist up or drink down. Just like Hubble [from *Runaways*]) anger has built up because of the hurt. Performing or sleeping keeps me safe because when I'm bored I do stupid things. It is better for everyone if I just chill when I'm alone, I don't know what else to do. (Jonathan, student, age 16)

Jonathan's piece demonstrates different forms of reflectiveness and empowerment. In my classroom, students have opportunities to play out their situations, emotions, and feelings while hiding behind the safety of a costume and character. This training can provide even more engaging opportunities. Rehearsing a play or executing a scene requires long hours of practice, focus, and perseverance, all of which are components of self-discipline, a trait that many students are desperately lacking.

One of my students, Jasmine, is a fifteen-year-old misanthrope. She is moody, nasty, and hated by the entire staff. The words that come out of her mouth can be just lethal. Given the opportunity to perform in the acting workshop, Jasmine's genius began to define itself in the world of performance. She is an amazing dancer, mimic, and has tremendous emotional range that she is not afraid to display in front of an audience. Now that she is engaged in a culture of knowledge production that suits her needs, Jasmine has thrived. Performing has increased her ability to express anger appropriately, communicate effectively with adults and peers, and to cooperate with others while developing other interpersonal skills. During this program, she has also received fewer court referrals compared with her previous write-ups. Truth be told, I still need endurance and courage to deal with Jasmine's uncertainties, heartbreaks, and occasional successes. I cannot say that I enjoy working with her nor do I really understand her, but I do know that she is more than what I previously knew of her. The craft of acting has allowed her humor, style, creativity, and even poise to emerge and even flourish on occasion. It is my belief that the more Jasmine is involved in creating something, the less likely she will be to turn to acts of violence and destruction which are the very reasons that this fifteen-year-old is part of the juvenile justice system.

There is no way to prepare for or plan for any human interaction. The moment-to-moment interpretation, in which we improvise our response to one another, offers the potential to define our own genius or limitations. This is the value of this curriculum.

Opportunities for Change

In *Pedagogy and the Politics of Hope*, Henry Giroux explores the valuable link between what a student learns in the classroom and the environment they function in outside of school. He writes that "teachers need to understand how experiences produced in the various domains and layers of everyday life give rise to the different, 'voices' students use to give meaning to their own worlds."[1] Giroux's suggestion of incorporating the indigenous knowledges from our own backyards and street corners has been useful in my own practice. Utilizing both theater and hip hop music and culture as tools to promote learning has aided me in developing new levels of insight by their role in creating a sense of community in the classroom. These potent life forces which offer an inclusive epistemological shared space are therefore a welcome and necessary ingredient for the meaningful writing classes I try to teach.

Critical constructivists who want to change education to make it more useful and compelling call for teachers to "come up with systematic ways to study and understand the construction of their students' consciousnesses and their effects on their lives in schools."[2] Through this prism one might ask: How are our students' constructions of the world shaped? How did things get the way they are?

Ernest Hemingway advised young writers to write hard about what hurts. My classroom has evolved into a space where students can speak out on what is bothering them and/or what made them happy, sad, or laugh. Independently, students began writing about their own neighborhoods in a unique style that had attitude, confidence, and a visual dynamic. There was often initial resistance to be asked to be culturally self-reflective. Once students know that they were being listened to, these opportunities brought in different energies and levels to the writing class. It was *their* neighborhood, *their* community dialect, accent, and slang. Its representation accommodated different style and points of view about community. The paradigm shift of consciousness and the ability to criticize both oneself and others in public spaces is what Ladislaus Semali refers to as indigenous literacy or, "the ability to use community knowledge so produced from local history to solve problems endemic to the community."[3] This re-conceptualization of education and validation of indigenous knowledge provides a critical understanding of self, place, people, and their knowledge. By bringing back issues of territory, subjugated knowledges are no longer disqualified as inadequate.

In her article *Indigenous Knowledge as a Component of the School Curriculum*, June M. George discusses indigenous knowledge pertaining to various aspects of daily living. George writes particularly about the Calypsos' music and culture but the words parallel the values of acting and hip hop or other innovative coursework. "Calypso serve well to document history, to highlight and comment on current social and political issues and even to prophesy."[4]

George's is an excellent example of a community that has priorities, participates and offers analysis of its membership and language codes. Street realities are explicit and spirited and need to be revealed. In using hip hop in the classroom, these multilogical voices and epistemologies of subjugated knowledges were given amplification. The oppression was indeed about to change. These voices were shared with the wider society and academic boundaries have begun to change. Repression evolved into emancipation to affirmation to celebration to power.

As part of rehabilitation, students in jail need confirmation, motivation, and belief in themselves and communities where they will one day return. The role of education is to guide, empower, and provide individual journeys for students, not to belittle and stifle them. Correlation is not causation; thus as a society our epistemology must not be positivistic in our approach as ideas cannot be reduced or de-contextualized to controlled variables.

From great problems can emerge even better opportunities. New York City's jail education has some great curricula, but it could and should be more nuanced, more complex and more attentive to individual needs. We have the smarts, technology, and the money. The challenges and opportunities within this context are to provide thousands of incarcerated New York City teenagers with safe, ongoing, and uncensored writing and performance opportunities. Teenagers can and must speak for themselves. The key to building self-confidence, honing critical thinking skills, developing imaginative and honest writing, and avoiding retention is to honor what they say and feel.

I am attempting to further expand justice and democracy into alternative-oriented traditions which give people of color, the destitute, emotionally disturbed, mentally ill, and other marginalized groups that predominate the prison population, a shared and vibrant voice. Prison pedagogy cries for progressive and student-centered teaching that simultaneously provides planned, implemented, and evaluated guidance and support.

As reflective practitioners, we teachers are responsible for finding our voice and persona, listening to the students, our colleagues and observing what is successful and what can be improved. Teachers in prisons particularly need to be firm but fair and learn to give respect to gain respect to others and themselves. Therefore the need to critique the many frameworks within the culture of knowledge production and epistemology should duly be applied in refining, reinvigorating, and reinforcing school programs. I wonder if some of our techniques of making students line up walking down hallways or sitting in assigned rows in the classroom actually educates the students to be leaders or simply to follow? It is a difficult task to simultaneously engage students while ensuring order and safety for all involved.

Paulo Freire's idea of conscientization has in many ways inspired my beliefs that students learn to read and write better when these activities are associated with a critical, conscious, or an interactive domain that combats certain professionalizations and standardizations that distance students from the actual learning.[5] Students need the opportunity to be listened to carefully and develop their ideas with their own forms of interpretation. My current classroom experiences support these ideas. Francisco Varela similarly suggests that cognition cannot be separated from environment and therefore must reflect and respect these ever-changing and spontaneous perspectives.[6]

United States prisons now release more than 600,000 people a year, a figure that is more than the entire population of Boston. The pertinent question is: What does this population plan to do on the outside and how can jails better prepare released inmates for this transition? Forty percent of people released form prison will return within three years. Criminal justice dollars are spent in locking people up and keeping them there. Little is spent on transformation. Currently over thirteen million people have been convicted of felonies and have spent time locked up. That is almost 7% of the United States adult resident population, and a figure larger than the populations of many countries, including Greece or Sweden.[7]

Why?

The critical ontology question of who we are and how we act as a society is essential to understanding knowledge, power, discipline, and control. The roots of our epistemological and ideological assumptions, and the structures of the systems currently in place that are influenced by them need to reject singularity and a snapshot approach toward pedagogy, and must move from the aerial perspective to a close-up. Silences can be seductive and safe. Pedagogical discussions always have some advantages and certain disadvantages. Ideas are always problematic as are approaches to research and pedagogy. As an educator I need to remind myself not to forget to look at big ideas or be fearful of critiquing them. Research on prison education programs needs to look at many of the assertions of this paper patiently, carefully, and vigorously.

It is a fertile time for us to consider questions about what we teach and why we teach it. How do we adhere to the rules yet critique things simultaneously? The ability to ask questions and challenge ideas is essential to any educational pursuit. Education is not just information, it is critical thinking. Censorship is more than just what you can or cannot read. It is evidence of the increasingly militaristic state in schools and the adversarial relationships between adults and youth. How we talk to, act towards, and treat the young people is important. For instance, we now have police officers in schools, and there is good reason for this; but in some ways a police presence makes schools a pipeline to prisons by making students always feel constantly under suspicion and/or as though they were already incarcerated.

What goes on in prisons is a microcosm of society and the issues faced in prisons cannot be divorced from the larger society. Discipline must be examined in regard to how it is used and our society's goals. This too reflects the larger society by raising important questions and illuminating them. If prison is a rehabilitative structure particularly for a youth offender, then education is the most significant, if not most complicated, component of prison life. In my future work, I would like to examine what the cultural boundaries of the prison are and dissect their theoretical frameworks and assumptions. In relation to pedagogical issues, learning in jails needs to include empowerment, access, and equality. The focus should be on the students in the classroom. Lessons should, if necessary, be unconventional as the above-described acting workshop or use of hip hop, and provide opportunities for teachers to employ original methodologies that teach as they entertain. Physical control is a necessary part of incarceration, but I question how necessary it is to regulate the intellectual freedom of inmates. In my mind, if you are a friend of totalitarianism, you are an enemy of democracy, as knowledge is power.

I do not suggest that I have the answers to the big questions in education. I am still on my own path to discovery. However, I believe that everything has its own story and everyone has obstacles to overcome and that these may be our greatest teachers.

NOTES

1   H. Giroux, *Pedagogy and the Politics of Hope: Theory, Culture and Schooling* (Boulder: Westview Press, 1997), p. 110.

2   J. Kincheloe, *Critical Constructivism Primer* (New York: Peter Lang Publishing, 2005), p. 6.

3   L. Semali and J. Kincheloe, eds., *What is Indigenous Knowledge: Voices from the Academy* (New York: Falmer Press, 1999), p. 95.

4   J. M. George, in L. Semali and J. Kincheloe, eds., *What Is Indigenous Knowledge: Voices from the Academy* (New York: Falmer Press, 1999), p. 83.

5   P. Freire, *Pedagogy of the Oppressed* (New York: Continuum Publishing Corporation, 1993).

6   F. Varela, *Ethical Know-How: Action, Wisdom and Cognition* (Stanford, CA: Stanford University Press, 1999).

7   J. Gonnerman, *Life on the Outside: The Prison Odyssey of Elaine Bartlett* (New York: FSG, 2004).

SUGGESTED READINGS

L. Bing, *Do or Die* (New York: Harper Perennial, 1991).

D. Hoch, *Jails, Hospitals and Hip Hop* (New York: Villard, 1998).

J. Lott, *A Teacher's Stories: Reflections on High School Writers* (Portsmouth, NH: Boynton/Cook Publishers, 1994).

18. Multicultural Story

Learning from the Experts in Urban Neighborhoods

ELIZABETH QUINTERO

> *Hmong traditional literature takes two forms: oral stories handed down by the elders to succeeding generations, and the story cloths stitched by the women that contain such things as Hmong history, the daily life of a family, the stitcher's personal autobiography, and traditional stories preserved by being stitched. Hmong children were educated this way, through the oral traditions of their culture. Their language did not have a printed form throughout most of their history, and few Hmong-Americans are literate in the contemporary form of their written language.[1]*

Urban neighborhoods and schools have increasing numbers of people representing ethnic, racial, and religious diversity. In my work with children and teacher-education students and their families, I have found dynamic multidirectional learning occurring through multicultural story, in its many forms. In many of the cultural groups who have recently come to the United States, storytelling and art have been the means to pass along history over many generations. Other groups use cultural artifacts to provide the visual and the concrete learning for young children as stories, proverbs and poetry are passed along.

The experts in our newest refugee and immigrant neighborhoods have much to teach us educators, other students, and other families. Teachers and students can use multicultural stories as a way to enter neighborhoods and begin to learn from other stories of the various groups of people. This use of story, art, history, and culture is a tangible hope for better world understanding. In other words, I believe that currently in the United States, we have a dense population of untapped resources in our urban centers from whom we can all learn.

Experts in Our Midst

Of course, children are different and come to us with many differing experiences. In 2003, a teacher-education student in a graduate program in New York City wrote:

> I came from India when I was four and started kindergarten when I was five.
>
> Neither one of my parents spoke English, so when I started school it was a difficult experience for me. I felt so different from the other children and wanted to quickly learn English so that I can be a part of their world. I would run home after school so that I could finally be in a world that was familiar to me, with language and customs I was an expert of. However, at the same time I was angry with my parents for not knowing and therefore not being able to teach me English. I felt very alone in my experience. When my mother would pick me up after school I would beg her to not speak to me in Hindi. I was embarrassed about who I was.

Luis Moll declares that "funds of knowledge" of all families in our communities must be recognized and built upon. To begin to understand a culture, teachers must study the folk tales, legends, history, and current culture of a group of people. Children need the opportunity to react to multicultural ideas through a variety of activities such as picture books, drawing, journal writing, and storytelling. Literacy events use multicultural stories to strengthen children's understanding of various cultures and people. Historically, much of humankind's most profound reflections have emerged in the form of story. Story is the way people learn with all the complexities of related issues in teaching, as in life, intact. Therefore, the danger of stereotypical oversimplification of issues is lessened.[2]

Problem-Posing with Critical Literacy: Personal Story as Teacher

I believe that by using a problem-posing, critical literacy approach with children's literature, even the complex issues of a world in conflict and confusion can be addressed in an ongoing dialog. Problem-posing teaching using multicultural literature supports students' meaningful learning. This method encourages integrated learning that is both developmentally and culturally meaningful, through interacting with story, reading literature, and participating in related learning activities. The problem-posing method was developed by Paulo Freire and critical pedagogists going back to the Frankfurt School of Critical Theory in the 1920s, initially for use with adult literacy students.[3] The method leads students of any age, experience or ability level to base new learning on personal experience in a way that encourages critical reflection. All activities focus on active participation. This method has not been widely used with younger learners, but lends itself well to practice combining theory with practice using this critical literacy framework for focusing on multicultural children's literature and creating contexts for integrated curriculum at all grade levels. I use this method with the teacher-education students I work with, and they use the problem-posing process with all ages of students.

This problem-posing method encourages students to experience and make conscious the transformations that often occur through the reading of and reflection on literature. I believe this natural outcome is not causal, but that metaphors enriched by reading and other creative activities structure our thinking, our understanding of events, and consequently our behavior.[4]

J. R. R. Tolkien in *From a Letter by J. R. R. Tolkien to Milton Walman, 1951*, connects story with history and art:

> After all, I believe that legends and myths are largely made of "truth," and indeed present aspects of it that can only be received in this mode; and long ago certain truths and modes of this kind were discovered and must always reappear.[5]

I am inspired by these ideas, and I feel they can come alive through multicultural story and problem-posing. For example, many stories, dreams, and critical dialogs can come from studying cultural stories. According to Clandinin and Connelly, stories are the nearest we can get to experience, as we tell of our experiences.[6] They say that the act of our telling our stories seems "inextricably linked with the act of making meaning, an inevitable part of life in a . . . postmodern world" and only becomes problematic " . . . when its influence on thinking and perception goes unnoticed" or is ignored.[7] A Montessori teacher of three- and four-year-olds believes:

> Our cultural history is tied to literature. All aspects of history are incorporated into stories. These stories have been told over time and written down. Stories explore a multitude of perspectives about life and truth. Through these perspectives we gain a greater understanding of being part of a culture.

Where's the "Critical" in the Method?

It is always important to keep an open mind regarding what we are all learning and we must always ask what is really going on here? This is true in terms of policy and politics, and it is true in terms of the multicultural children's literature we use in our classrooms. For example, when a teacher-education student found the storybook, *Knots on a Counting Rope* by Bill Martin Jr. and John Archambault, we were all happy to see the beautiful book and have the opportunity to further our knowledge of American Indian people.[8]

The story is about an American Indian boy and his grandfather. The boy is blind and his grandfather tells him the story of when he was born and how his family discovered that he was blind. The grandfather's story helps the boy to deal with his blindness. The grandfather uses a counting rope and adds a knot to it for each time he tells the story—when the rope is filled the boy will know the story by heart. The grandfather tells the boy that he does this because he will not always be here to tell the boy himself.

In addition, the story seemed to be a way into information sessions with children about issues of ability and disability, potential, and barriers. Then we found an article by a Navaho scholar and learned about inaccuracies in the book. She and her collaborator explain that Ted Rand's illustrations suggest primarily that the story is set in the Navajo nation, but his pictures show a mix of material culture from other different nations as well. For example, traditional Navajo men in the story have a variety of hairstyles of the Atsina, Blackfeet, Mandan, and Piegan nations. Also, Pueblo people are shown at a horse race wearing traditional ceremonial clothing that would be inappropriate for such an occasion.[9] Whereas these inconsistent details may seem insignificant, they are very important in terms of critical literacy and the importance of history, as well as to Native Americans.

So, should the book be totally censored and never be used? I think not. I think it is a good way to engage first-grade students in critical literacy and a starting point for them to learn to be critical researchers.

Back to Tolkien's idea that legend (or story) lives on the brink of history, I stress to students that our study of history must be on-going. What does history mean when studying curriculum and learning? Critical literacy is a process of both reading history (the world) and creating history (what do you believe is important?). No one develops or learns out of the context of family, community, country, or world at the present time, or without a connection to the past—the stories of those who have gone before. My students and I believe that learning develops among particularities, among persons and objects in families and communities. Large sweeps of history take meaning from the small stories.

What Does the Method Look Like?

What does problem-posing using story look like? Often there is a Listening, Dialogue, Action format such as this one used in a teacher-education class:

Listening

- Write about a memory you may have of your parents or a family member helping someone who was in danger. What do you remember about what was going on? As a child, how did you find out about this?
- Write about what you know about life among different nationalities and ethnici-

ties of people in the decade before the Civil War.

- Write about a job you had as a young child that helped to contribute to your family's livelihood. How did you feel about this job and how did other members of your family and community feel about your work?
- Read *The lost village of Central Park* by Hope Lourie Killcoyne.[10]

Dialogue:

- In small groups, first discuss any of your group members' knowledge about life among different groups of people in the 1950s. Now, discuss your examples of a family member's helping someone in a difficult situation and your memories about working as a child.
- Now discuss the story *The lost village of Central Park*. What was old information? What was new information? How did your stories from the discussion above relate to anything in the story?

Action:

- Research both primary source and secondary source documents about Seneca Village. Report your findings to your class.
- Research slave narratives about the Underground Railroad and other ways people gave sanctuary to runaway slaves. Report your findings to your class.
- Research the situation of poor families from Ireland who came to the United States and Canada. Where did many families settle? Why? Who helped them? How did they survive? Report your findings to your class.
- Visit one or more museums and document ways oppressed peoples' histories are documented through art. Report, using a visual medium, to your class.
- Read *Aunt Harriet's Railroad in the Sky* by Faith Ringgold and plan a problem-posing activity to share with second graders.[11]
- Read *The Poisonwood Bible* by Barbara Kingsolver.[12] Kingsolver's character Orleanna in *The Poisonwood Bible* states:

  > I was occupied so entirely by each day, I felt detached from anything so large as a month or a year. History didn't cross my mind. Now it does. Now I know, whatever your burdens, to hold yourself apart from the lot of more powerful men is an illusion (p. 323).

- What does this quotation and this story have to do with learning? Report to your class.
- Read *The Watsons Go to Birmingham—1963* by C.P. Curtis.[13] This story is about a family from Flint, Michigan, who travel to visit a grandmother in Birmingham, Alabama. They find themselves in the middle of some of the most chilling moments in the struggle for civil rights in the 1960s. This is a wonderful novel, full of history, that second graders will love. Plan a way to use it with students and share your plans with your class.

Problem-Posing with Young Children

The method can be used with young children as well. The following are examples of how to use problem-posing as a frame for early childhood and elementary aged learners. It is important to note that the key to problem-posing is choice and relevance to student lives and contexts. The teacher may offer choice in the selection of literature pieces and in activity selections. The students' critical participation comes not only in the ultimate action taken after the readings, but in the sometimes tiny steps of choice built in to the whole activity process. This example is a first-grade classroom based on use of the book *The whispering cloth: A refugee's story*, written by Pegi Dietz Shea, illustrated by Anita Riggio, stitched by Youa Yang.[14]

Example from a First-Grade Class

The following observational case documents a lesson in a first-grade classroom in an urban school in a large Midwestern city. The teacher is a twenty-year veteran teacher with the district, a woman of Irish American descent. The student teacher with her is a Hmong male who is from the community where the school is situated. The students in the class consist of sixteen Hmong children, three African American children, and one child from South America. For this lesson, the teacher used the storybook, *Whispering Cloth*, by Pegi Deitz Shea, illustrated by Anita Riggio and stitched by Youa Yang.

Listening

- The teacher began by gathering the children around her in the classroom center area where she unfolded several quilts. She reminded them of previous discussions and stories they had shared about quilts. Then she showed a weaving from Ireland and explained that it was from the country her family came from. Then, she held up a large, colorful "storycloth" which had been made by one of the school staff's relatives who is Hmong.

Dialogue

The teacher asked,
- "Do you think a quilt could tell a story? Do you think you can hear a story from a cloth?" The children discussed briefly what they thought about the question.

Action

- Then the teacher passed the folded cloth around the circle, so that each student could "listen" to the cloth. Then, she showed the class the book and told them just a little about the book. "It is a story about a Hmong girl and her grandmother who live in a refugee camp in Thailand. Grandmother is teaching Mai how to make storycloths and Mai creates one that tells her story." Then the teacher showed the bilingual glossary in the book with Hmong words and English translations, and explained that she would read the story in English in a few minutes, but that first, the student teacher would read it in Hmong.

Listening

- The story was read in Hmong. The students who did not understand Hmong appeared to be fascinated by the words in spite of not comprehending.

Dialogue

The teacher then asked,
- Can you guess what the story was about, based upon Mr. Z's intonations, the pictures, and so forth?

Action

- Then the teacher read the story in English.
- The student teacher explained to the students that he had written a letter to their families explaining what they were learning about. The letter was written in English, Hmong, and Spanish. In the letter, the teachers asks the parents if their child could either share a storycloth, quilt, or other artifact that tells a family story. When the items were brought to school, extension activities were implemented.
- The class made a class storycloth with a contribution from each student's drawing and writing (native language or English or both) during the following days.
- Another example, which honors history and can be appropriate for students from kindergarten to third grade.

Listening

- Write or draw yourself doing something you love to do. Include details about the context. How did you learn to "do" this activity? How did you become "good" at doing it? Were there other people involved in your learning? If yes, in what ways were they involved?
- Read *Diego* by Jeanette Winter.[15]

Dialogue

- With a partner, discuss the story about Diego Rivera and relate any aspects you can from his story to your own that you wrote previously.
- Diego expressed himself through art. How do you express yourself?

Action

- With your classmates, make a Diego Bulletin Board on which students constantly contribute (mirroring the chalkboard walls in the story). During Writing Workshop write about what you have drawn.
- Do a map activity, "Where am I from? Where's my family from?"
- Investigate art history and history books to inform yourself and your classmates about the historical context in which Diego Rivera lived and worked. Why was his hero Zapata? Why was he a colleague of Trotsky? Why are his murals in various national buildings in Mexico City considered a national treasure? Report to your class and make an action plan about how you could relay this historical information to kindergarteners.
- Read the children's storybook *Frida*.[16] How did she maintain her allegiance to what she believed to be most important? Report to your class and make an action plan about how you could relay this historical information to kindergarten students.
- Choose a figure in history that you admire. Research that person's childhood experience and write a report about her/him and try to answer some of the questions you answered about yourself in the listening section of this section. (Your report could be in the form of a children's book like *Diego*.)
- Read, Ancona, G. (1998). *Barrio (Jose's Neighborhood)*. CA: Harcourt, Brace, & Company. Also available in Spanish: *Historias de mi barrio : el San José de ayer*.[17] This is a book about the Mission District in San Francisco. It contains photographs and text which discuss the traditions, customs, art, food, etc., of what the locals call El Barrio. The book does this by following the goings-on of El Barrio through the life of one boy, Jose, and his elementary school. Read the following problem-posing lesson planned by a student teacher using this story:

Listening

- The teacher and children learn about murals and what they are. The teacher then shows the children photos of murals from around the teacher's neighborhood. Children are given time to discuss the murals and ask questions.

Dialogue

- What can you say about the neighborhood that these photos were taken in?
- What stories do these murals tell?
- If there are murals in your neighborhood, please describe them for us.

Action

- The teacher reads only the first half of *Barrio* with the class. This area of the book addresses murals and other forms of artistic expression (dance, song, etc.).

Listening

- Then children might tell stories—through murals or other types of artistic expression (dance, song, etc.,)—about themselves, their neighborhoods, etc.

Action

- Children would decide to either partner up, get into a group, or work individually to create a mural, song, dance, etc., telling a story that they would like to share with the class.
- That evening the children would go home with a letter explaining the day's art activity and suggest that the family create a mural or other form of artistic expression which tells a story about their family. As the children returned with their family projects, extension activities would be implemented.
- Children would also be encouraged to bring in photos of murals or other forms of artistic expression from their own neighborhoods. Again, this activity would be accompanied by follow-up discussions and extension activities.

A Third-Year Teacher Learns from Families

A teacher in the beginning of a dedicated career, teaching an elementary school that is in a low-income neighborhood in New York City. She explains in her journal:

> The students in my school come from many areas such as Puerto Rico, Dominican Republic, Antigua, Africa, and Mexico—to name a few. Some of my students were born in the Bronx and their parents were born in other countries. Other students were born in other countries and have just arrived in New York. Because of the wonderful diversity among my students, I realized that they were the best place to start if I wanted to learn about another culture than my own.

She has learned about language diversity and about how both parents and students want to use their languages to connect with her.

One major cultural aspect of the people in the neighborhood of my school is the rich language diversity. The two main languages are Spanish and English. There are also a small population of children who speak French and various different African languages . . . I have realized how much the parents of my students want to help me, want to open their homes to me, want to tell me about their lives, and most often and importantly, want to feed me! I have had nothing but friendly, open arms and homes upon showing interest and care in the lives and success of their children. Family means a great deal to my parents—everybody helps everybody shares—children are very well taken care of and looked after.

But this teacher acknowledges that the whole situation is not always perfect. Families put up with a lot of hardship on a day-to-day basis.

This is not the case for every family, however. I want to remain positive when discussing culture and yet not forget the extremely difficult hardships that some families must go through to simply survive and get their children to school every day. The reason why I point this out is because I feel like some teachers at my school think that just because the parents have no money and no education that they don't care about and don't try for their children. I really strongly disagree and this activity (a university class activity) has further proved my feelings of disagreement towards these biased views and opinions. My parents really do care and want to be involved and want to learn and give me whatever they can in their own little special way. I think that I have learned the importance of including parents in their children's education.

She tells her fellow teacher-education peers:

We should not be afraid to include, inform, and prepare the parents for what we expect and want for their children. We should also not be afraid to learn new things and let parents help us to help their children.

And she is learning ways to do this.

There are many resources for teachers—like plays, folktales from other countries, and music—that teachers can use to integrate parents into the curriculum in fun ways. I find myself including parents into parties, but am looking for more exciting and culturally educational ways to do this. Parents can help with costumes and making the setting for the stage. Parents can help practice songs with the students and help to authenticate the cultural learning.

This teacher summarizes:

. . . The best place to learn about the people is by the people!

Conclusion

Many teachers, like many well-known writers and visionaries, talk about the importance of the passing on of stories by parents and grandparents. In a study of effective literacy teachers, family story was identified as a primary influence of teachers' lives and the ways they interacted with their students.[18] One teacher smiled as she reported that her West Indian grandmother passed on teaching through folk tales. She also spoke at length about her mother's influence on her reading, in terms of modeling, interest, and actually providing trips to bookstores and libraries. Another teacher talked about both grandfather and grandmother. He noted that passing on stories in his American Indian community during his youth was done orally. They would gather around a campfire, and the eldest would talk—often it was the grandmother.

Although the world is a vast collage of identities and differences, we can all find a connection through multicultural story integrated within our school curriculum to effectively educate and honor all participants in the future generations.

NOTES

1   Hmong Family Group of Duluth, *Hmong Roots with Paper Dolls and Story Cloths: A Look at the History and Traditions of the Lao Hmong in Minnesota* (Duluth, MN: Chang Vang and Vong Xiong, 2003) p. 20.

2   P. Freire, *Education for Critical Consciousness* (New York: Seabury, 1973).

3   L. Moll, 1994 Funds of knowledge: A look at Luis Moll's research into hidden family resources, *CITYSCHOOLS, 1(1)* 19–21.

4   G. Lakoff and M. Johnson, *Metaphors We Live by* (Chicago: University of Chicago, 2003).

5   J. R. R. Tolkien, From a letter by J.R.R. Tolkien to Milton Waldman, 1951. in C. Tolkien, Ed. *The Silmarillion*, (London: HarperCollins, 1977), p. xvi.

6   D.J. Clandinin and F.M. Connelly, "Teachers' professional knowledge landscapes: Teacher stories—stories of teachers—school stories—stories of schools." *Educational Researcher, 25(3)* (1996): 24–30.

7   L.S. Goldstein, *Teaching with love: A feminist approach to early childhood education* (New York: Peter Lang, 1997).

8   J. Archambault, T. Rand, and B. Martin Jr. (Illustrator), *Knots on a counting rope* (New York: Owlet, 1997).

9   D. Reese and N. Caldwell-Wood, Native Americans in children's literature. in J.H. Violet, Ed. Using multiethnic literature in the K–8 classroom (Norwood, MA: Christopher-Gordon), pp. 155–192.

10   H. L. Killcoyne, *The lost village of Central Park* (New York: Silver Moon Press, 1999).

11   F. Ringgold, *Aunt Harriet's Railroad in the Sky* (New York: Random House, 1992).

12   B. Kingsolver, *The Poisonwood Bible* (New York: Pernnial, 1998).

13   C. P. Curtis, *The Watsons Go to Birmingham*. 1963. (New York: Yearling/Random House, 1997).

14   P. Shea, *Whispering Cloth: A Refugee's Story* (Honesdale, PA: Boyds Mills Press, 1995).

15   J. Winter and J. Winter, *Diego* (New York: Knopf, 1991).

16   J. Winter, K. Frida , J. Ana (Illustrator) *Frida* (New York: Levine, 2002).

17   G. Ancona, *Barrio (Jose's Neighborhood)* (San Diego, CA: Harcourt, Brace, & Company, 1998). Also available in Spanish: *Historias de mi barrio : el San José de ayer* (San Diego, CA: Harcourt, Brace, & Company, 1998).

18   M. K. Rummel and E. P. Quintero, *Teachers' Reading/Teachers' Lives* (Albany, New York: SUNY, 1997).

19. Urban Students as Critical Ethnographers

Critical Textual Production through Community-Based Research

ERNEST MORRELL

Introduction

The ills of contemporary urban education have often been documented with good reason. Educational attainment is a prerequisite for critical citizenship and professional membership in the technical, global, multicultural societies of the new century. Educational anthropologists have played a leading role in documenting the disparities that have plagued urban schools in the United States and have provided glimpses of the possible. In this chapter, I move from discussions of ethnography as a tool to understand urban education toward a concept of critical ethnography as a process of pedagogy and textual production in the service of academic achievement and urban school reform. I draw upon data collected from a multi-year study that looks at the relationship between participation of urban students as ethnographers in a research-oriented community of practice, and academic literacy and school reform. I begin with a basic set of questions concerning the relationship between critical post-structuralist ethnography, academic literacy, social praxis, and the discourse of educational research:

- How can a critical, poststructural ethnography serve as a pedagogic tool in urban contexts? What sorts of cultural and textual production accompany the positioning of urban students as ethnographers of urban schools?
- How can collaborative, community-centered praxis illuminate the processes and potential of critical poststructural ethnography?
- How might critical, poststructural ethnography augment or even change conversations within urban educational research?

I begin this journey by visiting the work of Denzin, and Kincheloe and McLaren to outline a critical poststructuralist approach to ethnographic research.[1,2] I argue in this paper that this form of anthropological research can serve as a tool for understanding urban contexts and as a curriculum for social praxis. I then describe the work of the summer seminar and its approach toward students as researchers for literacy achievement and school reform. The data collection and analysis sections outline my focus on the seminar as an activity system,[3] and on a social theory of literacy that views literacy as a set of social practices observable in events that are mediated by written and digital texts.[4] The analysis follows the seminar students through several types of literacy practices most closely associated with textual production. I focus on note taking, electronic journaling, and the production of critical memoirs, research papers, presentations, and iMovies. I conclude by considering the importance of the process of critical poststructural ethnography and the products of critical research for academic achievement, for educational research and for urban school reform.

Critical Poststructural Ethnography

Denzin addresses a triple crisis of representation, legitimation, and praxis that confronts researchers in the human disciplines. In his work *Interpretive Ethnography: Ethnographic Practices for the Twenty-First Century* he argues:

> Traditional ethnographers have historically assumed that their methods probe and reveal lived experience. They have also assumed that the subject's world is always final, and that talk directly reflects subjective and lived experience. The literal translation of talk thus equals lived experience and its representation. Critical poststructuralism challenges these assumptions. Language and speech do not mirror experience. They create experience, and in the process of creation constantly transform and defer that which is being described. The meaning of a subject's statements are, therefore, always in motion . . . There can never be a final accurate representation of what was meant or said—only different textual representations of different experiences.[5]

Denzin promises that the new language of ethnography, heavily influenced by poststructuralism, will be personal, emotional, biographically specific, and minimalist in its use of theoretical terms. The twenty-first century, he claims, will witness ethnographies that take the shape of: new journalism, narratives, autobiographies, documentaries, and performance texts. Denzin further claims that:

... qualitative research in the (sixth) moment discovers what has always been known: we are our own subjects. How our subjectivity becomes entangled in the lives of others is and has always been our topic.[6]

All of this begs a logical and valid question for educational researchers; that is, if all meaning is constructed through language, what is the purpose of doing ethnography? Denzin and others have referred to such questions as a crisis of legitimation, which stems partly from our desire that texts have authority, that they be judged as valid, and that they be generalizable to a larger context beyond the specific site of research. If, as the poststructuralists claim, neither ethnography nor any research in the human sciences can do this, what can they do?

If there is not a method or status of the researcher that confers authority on a text, poststructuralists argue, then the authority must emerge from the content of the text itself. This frees ethnographers to simply tell their stories. As with other genres of writing, the readers will convey ultimate authority on a text. This provides a space for critical poststructural ethnographers to construct ethnographic narratives fully invested with themselves as emotional and ultimately fallible beings. These ethnographers, social scientists, and storytellers, can eschew claims to impartiality, distance, or objectivity that interfere with the telling of the only narrative they have ownership of: that of their own relationship to the stories they present. Stories that they ideally present will all of their honesty, with all of the facts that they can remember or reclaim, with wit, with creativity, and with passion. They simply tell the stories as best they can and in telling honest and compelling stories, add to collective conversations and play a small role in illuminating the human condition in a time of interfacing and border-crossing where such illuminations are badly needed.[7]

Another tradition of anthropologists and critical theorists looks toward ethnography that works toward social change; ethnographic research that is itself part of a process of transforming the world. Kincheloe and McLaren,[8] for example, define a criticalist as a researcher or theorist who attempts to use her or his work as a form of social or cultural criticism and who accepts certain basic assumptions that all thought is fundamentally mediated by power relations that are socially and historically constituted; that fact can never be isolated from the domain of values or be removed from some form of ideological inscription; that the relationship between concept and object, and between signifier and signified, is never stable or fixed and is often mediated by the social relations of capitalist production and consumption; and that the oppression that characterizes contemporary societies is most forcefully reproduced when subordinates accept their social status as natural, necessary, or inevitable (p. 263). In the process of articulating the politics, purposes, and practices of critical research, they offer the following:

> To engage in critical postmodern research is to take part in a process of critical world-making guided by the shadowed outline of a dream of a world less conditioned by misery, suffering, and the politics of deceit. It is, in short, a pragmatic of hope in an age of cynical reason. (p. 294)

Within this criticalist tradition, Denzin advocates a public, civic, or everyday life ethnography that draws on the legacies of the new journalists, that evidences a desire to connect with people and their concerns, and writes ethnographies that move people to action and:

> . . . answers to a new readership—the biographically situated reader who is a coparticipant in a pub-
> lic project that advocates democratic solutions to personal and public problems. (Charity, 1995, p. 146)

It is from this emergent tradition that I offer this narrative; and it is also within this tradition that the actual work of the seminar is situated. What I offer here is but a small portion of my story as an educator and a researcher who had the privilege of working with a
team of parents, teachers, and students as they designed and carried out studies of the
material conditions of the schools within their communities. The seminar offered the space
and the tools to engage in this kind of work with the hopes of using critical poststructural
ethnography to promote academic literacy, individual and collective agency, and urban educational reform. It is to the seminar that I now turn.

Five Summers of Critical Research: 1999–2003

Beginning in 1999, several colleagues and I began convening a summer seminar at a large
west coast university. The seminar brings together students, teachers, and parents from urban
schools and communities to design and carry out critical research projects on issues of
immediate concern to these schools and communities. The students work in groups of four
or five on research teams that are led by a teacher in the local schools. Throughout the five
weeks of the seminar the students read seminal works in the sociology of education and critical methods of educational research; they work in small groups to develop research questions, read relevant literature, collect data, analyze data and create research reports; and they
present these reports to university faculty, policymakers, and, on occasion to regional and
national conferences of educational researchers and practitioners. Students also write individual papers and contemplate the practical applications of their research to the issues in
their own schools and communities. There are multiple goals of the seminar, but two stand
out as primary. One primary goal is to use the seminar space to help students acquire the language and tools they need to function within the academy, what I have called *academic literacy*.[9] Customarily, the student populations that we have worked with have not been well
represented within colleges and universities throughout the state. We wanted to demonstrate
to the schools and universities that dismissed these students that the students were indeed
capable of college-level work. At the same time, we wanted to use the context of critical,
community-based research to help the students gain the literacy tools they would need in
order to be successful at these universities.

A second goal of the seminar relates to the research itself. My colleagues and I at West
Coast University held the sincere belief that teachers, students, and parents were the most
legitimate collaborators for the kind of community-based praxis-oriented research that we
ourselves were interested in. In other words, the research studies were not merely a context
for literacy learning; the products themselves were important to the struggle for educational

justice within the teacher education program, with the local districts, the greater metropolitan area and even statewide. The student-participants and their work would influence policy and practice across all of these settings. This chapter points toward a third important outcome of the seminar research, an outcome that pertains to questions of method. Throughout the various seminars, I have come to learn a great deal from our research community about the purpose and process of critical ethnography as a pedagogical tool and as a tool for textual production.

The seminar has met at a major university for each of the past five years in the Graduate School of Education and the Law School. The thirty or so student participants attend all-day sessions for five weeks to earn four semester credits for a university course. As a part of the seminar, students are exposed to critical theory, cultural studies, educational sociology, legal history, social theory, and critical qualitative research methodology, as they design and conduct research related to issues of equity and access in urban schools and communities. In this way, the seminar seeks to address these issues of access both in terms of course content and desired outcomes for its students. Over the past five years, the seminar has addressed the following themes: *Language, Youth Culture, and Transformational Resistance in Urban Schools* (1999), *Youth Access and the Democratic National Convention* (2000), an *Educational Bill of Rights* (2001), *Equity and Access in California's Public Schools* (2002), and *Oral Histories of the Educational Experiences in Post-Brown Los Angeles from 1954–2003*(2003). Student participants have presented their research conducted from the seminar to university faculty, local and state politicians, teachers, community members, and parents. Additionally, this research has been presented at regional and national conferences and has been featured by local and national media, including CNN.

Data Collection and Analysis

As an ethnographer attempting to study ethnography, I drew upon many traditional data sources in order to understand pedagogy and production in the research process of the seminar. These data sources include: field notes, digital photographs, digital video footage, interview data, student essays, and student research reports. As an active participant in the research seminar, it was often difficult to take field notes while actually in the field. I would have to wait until evening to record my observational notes. There were, however, exceptions to this rule. For example, when the students themselves were in the field and taking notes, I was also able to take notes, though my gaze was often pointed toward them instead of the conditions they were studying. I was also able to capture video footage of all of the seminar sessions and field days. Additionally, I also had access to the students' collected data, which provides another lens into the activity system of the seminar. I found the digital photographs and digital video captured by the students to be particularly illuminating of their process.

In looking at the various sources of data, I wanted to understand the seminar as an activity system so I utilize Engeström's model to think about the relationships between subjects, mediating tools, and outcomes, which becomes an effective framework to understand the nature of participation along with the use and creation of mediating tools and artifacts.[10] Particularly, I wanted to understand not only how students used their critical language and university capital, but also how they used more mundane tools like notebooks and digital cameras in the process of carrying out their community-based research projects. I also wanted to understand the seminar as a site for literacy learning and literacy practices. My concept of literacy is heavily influenced by the new literacy studies, which views literacy as a social practice and understands that literacies are positioned in relation to the social institutions and power relations that sustain them.[11] Although the intent of new literacy studies is to use ethnographic methods to discern literacy practices, the practices themselves are gleaned from locating and analyzing *literacy events*. With respect to the relationship between literacy practices and literacy events, Barton and Hamilton comment:

> Literacy events are activities where literacy has a role. Usually there is a written text, or texts are central to the activity and there may be talk around the text. Events are observable episodes, which arise from practices that are shaped by them. (p. 8)

In the spirit of new literacies and in honor of the relationship between technological changes and changing definitions of literacy,[12] I include interactions involving digital and visual texts as literacy events as well. Drawing upon the schema outlined by Barton and Hamilton, a focus of the ethnographic study concerned the recording of literacy events in order to understand the relationships between literacy practices and cultural production. A thorough but by no means exhaustive list of the literacy events associated with ethnography fieldwork in urban schools include: recording field notes, collecting written artifacts, taking pictures, recording video, recording interviews, reading signs, reading chalkboards, and reading textbooks. Other literacy events associated with the seminar include: reading research articles, having discussions about research articles, transcribing interview data, analyzing written and digital data, writing research reports, writing personal essays, and editing digital movies. In the following section, I describe the major types of literacy events that were associated with textual production during the summer research seminar. Specifically I focus on note taking, electronic journaling, the creation of iMovies, and research papers and presentations. I conclude by considering the implications of student-oriented ethnographic work for methodologies of educational research and for practices in literacy education.

Critical Ethnography and Textual Production

Note Taking

There were multiple uses for the composition notebooks that were issued to the students at the beginning of the seminars. During the general class sessions, students took notes on lectures and small breakout group discussions. Early during the seminar, teachers check the notes to see that students are learning the level of detail that is appropriate. Students were also encouraged to look at the notebooks of their peers to see how they had annotated similar conversations.

In small group sessions, students were also asked to annotate the conversations; but there were other uses of the notebooks during these segments. For example, students were assigned texts to read and either produced reading notes, summaries, or short answer essays for group discussion. Later, during the seminar when groups were preparing the literature review portion of their research reports, the students would often refer back to their reading notes.

Students also used notebooks to produce research instruments such as surveys and interview protocols. Prior to entering the field, the students would need to generate interview questions for various research subjects as well as survey questions. For example, in a recent seminar a group investigating urban schools' technological learning resources needed to produce interview questions for students, teachers, and administrators, in addition to an observation protocol to be used on school-site visits.

When in the field, students were encouraged to take ample field notes. They would record their observations and perceptions of the various locales in the composition notebooks. For example, during the summer of 2000, students took public transportation to downtown Los Angeles where the Democratic National Convention was being held. While downtown, students had the opportunity to walk around through impoverished neighborhoods, through the official headquarters, and through the headquarters where activist groups were centered. Even though students were equipped with cameras, teachers foregrounded the necessity of capturing the environment with field notes while helping students to develop this capacity.

Students also conducted many informal interviews while in the field. Again, the students might have tape recorders or digital cameras, but their primary source of data collection included the scratch notes they took. During the seminar of 2003, students collected oral histories of citizens who were involved in public schooling during the 50 years following the Brown decision. Occasionally, a subject would agree to speak, but not in front of the camera; so the only source of data collection was the composition notebooks. Students would also happen upon interviews when no cameras or tape recorders were around. Two young women who were collecting oral histories of students who attended schools during the decade from 1954 to 1963 ran into a gentleman in a grocery store who provided an amazing interview. Given that no cameras or recorders were around, they took turns asking questions and transcribing the answers. They were able to refer back to their notes to reconstruct the interview.

There were numerous other field-related tasks requiring students to use their notebooks. For example, during one summer seminar, students visited historical archives where they were not allowed to remove any items from the facility. Any information to be extracted would come only through the recorded notes. Similarly, another group chose to analyze yearbook data from 1950s yearbooks to determine school demographics. As the yearbooks could not be removed from the school archives, students recorded demographic information from a decade of school annuals in their composition notebooks.

During the final portion of the seminar the focus turned toward data analysis. In groups, students focused on generating analytic memos and data spreads in addition to selective transcriptions of recorded interviews and annotations of digital video footage. All of these activities were recorded in the students' notebooks. I should add that the students numbered their notebook pages and created a table of contents page at the beginning of the notebooks to ensure easier navigation. That also made it easier for teacher–researchers to examine the content of the books as well. By the end of the seminar, students averaged over 100 pages of recorded notes in these composition books. It is also important to note that, as teachers and researchers, we made a conscious decision to return these notebooks to the students who had become attached to them over the course of the seminar, rather than keep them for research purposes. Each year, a few volunteers would allow their notebooks to be photocopied to allow us to understand how they were learning to annotate and how the notebooks were being used.

Electronic Journaling and Critical Memoirs

Each morning the seminar would begin with the same activity. For approximately thirty minutes, students would respond on their laptop computers to a journal prompt. These prompts would then be e-mailed to a writing specialist who would then provide e-mail feedback, thereby continuing the conversation.

The electronic journals served several purposes. First, the journals provided material that the students could draw upon in writing their critical memoirs, 1500–2000 word reflexive piece on the process of learning to conduct critical, community-based research. In our most recent seminar, students had these four options to choose from:

> *A Critical Memoir:* Write a critical memoir that recounts a portion of your educational experience. Explain the event in as much detail as possible. Use theory to make sense of the event. Use your knowledge of critical research to discuss what could have been done differently.
>
> *On Being a Critical Researcher:* Talk about your journey as a critical researcher. What have you learned? What advice would you offer to others (students, teachers, parents, community activists) who may be considering such an enterprise?
>
> *A Personal Letter:* Write a personal letter to an author, an artist, ancestor, or other activist who has influenced your journey as a critical researcher. Explain to this person (or people) how they have shaped your image of yourself as a critical researcher.
>
> *An Issue Piece:* Write a brief essay to a policymaker or an elected official, in which you combine experience and theory to discuss an issue related to equity and access. This topic does not have to relate to your group's research project.

To this end, prompts would occasionally encourage students to reflect on various stages of the research process. For example, after their first day in the field collecting data, a prompt would ask then to share their feelings about the process of thinking both about what they liked and what they might do differently if given the chance.

The journals also encouraged students to reflect on their own personal experiences as they related to the research process. During the summers where students were investigating conditions in schools, prompts often asked them to consider their own educational experiences. During the summer spent at the Democratic National Convention, students were encouraged to reflect on their knowledge of politics, their political participation, and their sense of political agency.

Finally, journals asked students to make connections between their changing identities as critical researchers and their plans for the future. Common prompts, especially during the final week, might ask the students to define what it means to be a critical researcher, to consider how they have changed as a result of acquiring the tools of critical research, or to consider how they might live differently in the future. The following journal response was written near the end of the students' experiences at the Democratic National Convention during the summer of 2000:

N's Journal Reflections 8–17–2000

Today was a day of reflections. This week has been filled with many learning experiences and at times that can be overwhelming. There is always a need to take time to reflect and analyze, to learn and to grow. I found myself learning so much just from sitting in the circle today.

Everyone had something of value to say. Hearing everyone's experiences and opinions has enriched my own experience here. I was not at every site all the time, but hearing the account of others has helped me live vicariously every part of the DNC. I have gone through mixed feelings here this week. It began (I hate to admit), with cynicism. The Democracy Live 2000 seemed like a complete farce, a joke. But maybe that is the way TV is done. Then I experienced frustration at not being able to get into other parts of the Convention Center. I wanted to witness democracy inside those large halls.

But I was not disappointed completely because I found democracy elsewhere. The speakers that visited us this week were all fighting for equality in one way or another. They each had their way of approaching the issues that most concerned them. I discovered that there are people in this world who are really passionate and devoted to making this place better for everyone.

Now I leave cynicism behind but not the anger of the first day. I will take that anger with me everywhere I go from now on, where ever that place may be. It is anger that leads to action, and action to changes. This place needs changes, and someone has to help achieve them.

On this road which is my life, I continue to walk ahead, going through doors and hoping to someday make positive changes. Someone I really admire said (something like this) "You go through doors in your life, and through some doors you just can't go back." I think this seminar as a whole has been one giant door, and I know, I can never go back.

This student response captures all of the purposes of the journal writing activity in that she is able to reflect on her own experiences, the process of research, and her changing relationship to the conditions that she has been researching. It also conveys the incredible emotions that accompany this type of work for young people. Finally, it shows the tremendous talent and passion that our students have; talent and passion that often go undiscovered during their traditional educational experiences.

iMovies

During the most recent summer seminar students added iMovies to their list of "textual products." As researchers and teachers, we wanted to expand notions of text and literacy to encompass more new media. In previous seminars students had used laptop computers; they had performed Internet research; and they had created PowerPoint presentations of their research. The summer of 2003 was the first to focus on digital video production as a form of textual production.

The students, who were accumulating oral histories of participants in Los Angeles public schools, used digital videos to record as many interviews as possible. Each research team was issued a digital video camera, a tripod, and a supply of mini-dv tapes. Additionally, a professional filmmaker offered a workshop to help the students become acquainted with the cameras. The workshop also provided students with techniques for composing shots and keeping the camera steady. The filmmaker then sent students on assignment to capture images around the campus. Each group's footage was critiqued and students were given a short list of reminders concerning camera care and operation.

For three weeks student groups traveled around Greater Los Angeles interviewing students, parents, teachers, administrators, ministers, activists, university researchers, and politicians who had some measure of involvement with Los Angeles public schools during the period of 1954–2003. During the final week and a half students reviewed their digital footage for clips they could use to create their iMovies. Then, with the assistance of the filmmaker and university staff, student research teams put together five-minute iMovies. Each team created iMovies complete with music, transitions, and graphics. Copies of the interviews were also transferred from digital masters to VHS tapes and donated to a community-run historical archive.

Research Papers and Presentations

The culminating products of the seminars consisted of a final research paper and accompanying research presentation. Though the format changes slightly with each seminar, the papers and presentations have included: an introduction, a review of literature, a methods section, a reporting of findings, and implications for policy and political activism. The PowerPoint presentations average twenty minutes and the reports 30 pages, with the longest being a 77-page report study of the social and physical ecology of urban schools produced in the summer of 2002.

The papers and presentations have as their primary audience a panel of university faculty and community advocates who have expertise either in the research topics or the research methods. The members of these panels listen and then respond to the presentations as if they were at a traditional academic conference on education or the social sciences. Secondary audiences for the presentations and papers include the parents, teachers, administrators, and policymakers who are also in attendance at the final day's activity.

After the presentations, students' papers, PowerPoints, and iMovies are published on a web site that is accessed primarily by teachers in the Los Angeles area. Papers are also passed on to principals, school board members, state representatives, legal advocates, and community-based organizations. The research from the 2001 summer seminar concerning the composition of an educational bill of rights played a key role in influencing proposed state legislation. Students who researched the potential of hip hop music and culture to motivate academic literacy development presented to a department meeting at a nearby school and later to a local affiliate of the National Writing Project. Students also lectured to undergraduate and graduate seminars at seven major universities on the west coast. Students have presented their research at the last five annual meetings of the American Educational Research Association as well as the 2001 meeting of the Sociology of Education Association. Two students have co-authored an article in a peer-reviewed research journal and at least one student has expressed her desire to write a book.

Implications for Educational Research and Literacy Education in Urban Contexts

There are important implications from the research on the five summer seminars for methods of educational research and for practices in literacy education. Critical poststructural ethnography challenges the who, why, and how of ethnographic work in education. Where traditionally the work of educational ethnography was solely the domain of university research, the summer seminar encouraged students, parents, and teachers to participate as ethnographers. I have argued elsewhere and I continue to advocate that our critical epistemology challenges us as educational researchers to democratize the tools of research; tools that determine ultimately who in our society has the right to speak truth.[13, 14] By opening spaces for young people to conduct educational ethnographies, we can fundamentally change the nature of the practice and the knowledge that is produced and distributed in ways that are enabling for these young people, their schools, and their neighborhoods.

Critical poststructural ethnography also challenges the *how* of ethnographic research. The work conducted by students and adults was intimate, personal, messy work engaged in by interested parties. I call the work unapologetically intimate. Rather than apologize or retreat from the insider perspective, I argue that the benefits for the students of working in schools and neighborhoods close to their own outweigh the supposed challenges of proximity. The nature of the relationships between the students, their subjects, and their communities allowed them to gain access to data that would have been impossible for outsiders to collect. Similarly, my close relationship with the students affected, in positive ways, my access to the data I have collected and interpreted from these summer seminars. In both instances, the research has looked differently than traditional work, but has been powerful and important work nonetheless.

Finally, the why of critical poststructural ethnography has to be tied to personal and social transformation. Rather than seeking to understand the "other" like Margaret Mead, Bronislaw Malinowski, Franz Boas, and other architects of the discipline, this method of ethnographic research ideally helps us to better understand ourselves and our world, in the hope of enabling us to intervene in transformation our relationship to our world and those material conditions we find most unconscionable. Given the present challenges we confront in urban schools, this presents a powerful tool for students, teachers, parents, community advocates, and university researchers who would like to see themselves as agents of change.

I have also argued that any reforms in curriculum and pedagogy targeted at urban populations need to be focused on increasing academic achievement.[15] Toward this end, I believe that the work of the seminar stands on its own merit as an example of the kind of academic work students are capable of. In a five-week seminar, urban high school students read and wrote in large volumes and produced work that was deemed high quality even by university standards. These students attended schools that were identified as underperforming, yet their textual production in many instances belies their academic records.

I would like to see more opportunities for students to engage in local community-based research as part of secondary literacy courses. The idea of allowing students to draw upon personal interests and expertise in order to develop academic competencies and an empowered relationship to their social world is certainly an appealing one for literacy education. The seminar concentrated on personal essays and research reports, but we also toyed with the idea of having students represent their findings through drama, through fiction, through poetry, or even through film.

I am reminded of Denzin's comments that critical, poststructuralist ethnography is personal and emotional in making sense of the new meanings produced for me as a teacher and as a researcher. I cannot write about these students, the research seminar, or the material conditions confronted in these urban schools without emotion. Nor should I. As an ethnographer of literacy, I continue to learn about the acquisition and usage of language and literacies of power in the service of self and social emancipation; I learn more about how researchers can and should position themselves in relation to the communities and subjects with whom they work. I learn more about what I mean when I use the adjective critical as a modifier for nouns like ethnography, literacy, and pedagogy. As a teacher, I learn about the power of stepping lightly, of opening spaces for meaning-making, for authentic praxis as a site for dialogue, reading, writing, and most importantly, for the manifestation of existential freedom, individual, and collective agency. And I share my story as a teacher and learner, not to demonstrate or convince; but I share my text in the hopes of generating new ideas and entering into your conversations pertaining to the democratization of research tools, the liberation of research methods, and ultimately, the potential of schools, pedagogies, and curricula that socialize and constrain the young to be otherwise.

NOTES

1   N. Denzin, *Interpretive Ethnography: Ethnographic Practices for the 21st Century* (Thousand Oaks: Sage, 1997).

2   J. Kincheloe and P. McLaren, "Rethinking critical theory and qualitative research" in N. Denzin and Y. Lincoln, eds. *The Landscape of Qualitative Research* (Thousand Oaks: Sage, 1998), pp. 260–299.

3   Y. Engeström, "Activity theory and individual and social transformation," *Activity Theory,* 7/8 (1991): 6–17.

4   D. Barton and M. Hamilton, "Literacy practices," in D. Barton, M. Hamilton, and R. Ivanic, eds. *Situated Literacies: Reading and Writing in Context* (London: Routledge), pp. 7–16.

5   N. Denzin, *Interpretive Ethnography*, p. 27.

6   N. Denzin, p. 27.

7   C. Geertz, *Local Knowledge* (New York: Basic Books, 2000).

8   J. Kincheloe and P. McLaren, "Rethinking critical theory and qualitative research."

9   E. Morrell, *Becoming Critical Researchers: Literacy and Empowerment for Urban Youth* (New York: Peter Lang, 2001).

10   Y. Engeström, "Activity theory and individual and social transformation."

11   D. Barton and M. Hamilton, "Literacy practices."

12   E.Cushman, E. Kingten, B. Kroll, and M. Rose, *Literacy: A Critical Sourcebook* (Boston: Bedford-St.Martin's, 2001).

13   E. Morrell, *Becoming Critical Researchers*.

14   M. Foucault, *The Archaeology of Knowledge and The Discourse on Language* (New York: Pantheon, 1972).

15   E. Morrell and J. Duncan-Andrade, "Toward a critical classroom discourse: promoting academic literacy through engaging hip hop culture with urban youth," *English Journal,* 91 (2002): 88–94.

20. Unplugged

Releasing the Creative Potentials of Urban Students

WINTHROP R. HOLDER

The Crucible

(It) was the first time that a student organization was conducting a workshop at this important teachers' conference. This was the opportunity that most students hope to have; the chance to tell teachers what works best for us, a chance for them to listen and let us speak. . . . This was not a day (that) the teachers, my colleagues, nor I will forget. On this day, the student became the teacher.

> *The stories, the worldviews, the music, the politics, the humor,*
> *the art of the black community become central parts of every-*
> *day school life, never viewed in isolation or as supplements to*
> *the "real work" of the school but always viewed in the context*
> *of the general curriculum.*
>
> Denicha Ingram

This chapter reports on the 17-year Critical Analysis Project that gave rise to two extracurricular groups, the Society for Social Analysis, and its journals Crossing Swords (1988–2000) in a Brooklyn high school, and the Society for Independent Thought and CounterCurrents (2001-present) in the Bronx—in two urban settings awash with all the pathologies of social breakdown: governmental malfeasance, crime, poverty, and failure. Rather than allowing administrative incompetence coupled with the restrictive curriculum and the prison-like maximum security setting of the school to constrain our thoughts and actions, students contextualized their lived experiences against the backdrop of the crucible of schooling.[1] Toward this end, we unsilenced students' discourse by capturing and preserving their impressions and critical reflections of their engagements with education and contentious facets of life.

Joe Kincheloe

It was students' very own resistance to disengaging learning environments decontextualized from their sense of being which pushed the classroom to explore linkages between the curriculum and their lived realities. The classroom, then, became a site for exploring continuities and discontinuities in life and the curriculum. Toward this end, popular culture, students' multifaceted home discourses and the verve of their everyday social intercourse were integrated into the general curriculum.

Central then to our approach to the classroom was the desire to "open up historical discourse to the possibility of alternative futures" so that students—who although sometimes viewing themselves as conscripts of schooling—would nevertheless discover their distinctive voices by critically engaging and challenging the curriculum and one another's views.[2] This, then, was the orientation that informed the discourse community which was unwittingly invented, and made it possible for Denicha Ingram and two other students to conduct a lively and stimulating workshop on "One Mic: Engaging Hip Hop and Popular Culture in the Social Studies Classroom" at the 2004 Greater Metropolitan New York Social Studies Conference. Explaining how their poetry of everyday life—lunchroom discourses—can be integrated into the classroom, Samantha Leyro explained: "The same passion we put into our gossiping we take and put into our class discussions."[3] Here we see urban students willing to transform and refashion themselves and their classroom by creating one that recognizes and values their voices and alternative modes of discourse.

This helped to release students' formerly suppressed creativity and their hidden registers. To be sure, in order for students to become lifelong autonomous self-learners, education must not be seen as merely instrumental—providing training for a job—but must be embraced as life affirming—providing opportunities for students to view themselves as part of a larger community engaged in imagining and constructing a space for self—and, ultimately, all of us—to be more fully human. How did this all begin?

Reclaiming the Past

When I started formal teaching in the mid-1980s, the system of apartheid was under severe attack and since it was part of the official school curriculum, I was excited about the prospects of teaching. After all, the abhorrent nature of apartheid, or so I thought, would have been sufficient to energize my group of critical, yet idealistic, freshmen. However, as I reflected on the lukewarm response—no doubt a reaction to my initial disengaging approach—I decided to change the focus slightly.

The following day I transcribed a calypso, the Might Sparrow's "Isolate South Africa," and used it as the springboard for discussions. It worked. After a sustained discussion for three quarters of the period, someone in the class asked me to play the song. The following day we listened to the calypso and students decided to bring in more conscious music reflecting the various music of the oppressed—rap, reggae, salsa, meringue, and calypso. Thus, music was continuously sampled in the classroom as a counterpoint to the often disengaging classroom texts. Suddenly, the classroom was alive not only with the beats of various songs of redemption but more and more students were developing a deep interest in and a passion for learning, not just about apartheid but about social issues, especially when they were refracted through the *critical* lens of popular culture. In short, their inherent and developing sense of civic consciousness and internationalism began coming to the fore, replacing what I, before then, misconstrued as civic apathy or resistance to learning.[4]

Students began employing music not only to enhance understanding of the curriculum but also to make sure that their distinctive voices would be heard in the classroom. It was as if students were demonstrating and anticipating the view that:

> It is through their engagement with/in popular culture, and especially with/in music, that children can learn to weave together personal and school knowledge in creative ways, and in the process learn to operate within the rules of negotiation, elaborated inside and outside the school context.[5]
>
> Using popular music as her background sounds, Vernette Olive weaved personal and school knowledge in her exposition. She wrote . . .
>
> Sparrow's song "Isolate South Africa" is . . . saying that discrimination against Blacks must stop and that America and other countries should do something to help end apartheid in South Africa.
>
> Another song that has a positive meaning is ("Get Up, Stand Up") by Peter Tosh. . . . In Global History the term used to refer to . . . feeling(s) of superiority is ethnocentric. Ethnocentrism is opinionated, not factual. . . . I have learned so much in Global History that I can even teach a class on the topics which I've learned.[6]

Thus, by using popular culture and other extracurricular resources to challenge and contest the authoritative (authenticating) voice of the text, students embraced a critical stance which allowed them to unearth and expose biases embedded in the texts. Moreover, by circulating student writings in the classroom we were also fashioning a community of researchers and independent thinkers who would leave imprints of their times for future students to engage. Since 1988, I have often used student writings not only to foster intra- and inter-generational debates, but also to enhance, supplement, and contest the authorized texts.

Writing in the same 1987 classroom, Rosemarie Dunbar sampled reggae to express her detestation for apartheid. She wrote:

"War" by the late Bob Marley has a powerful message.

This song, I think describes what should be done to end apartheid in South Africa:

Until the philosophy which holds one race superior And another inferior is finally and permanently discredited And abandoned. . . . There'll be war. . . .

"War" was one of the many Reggae songs which was heard not only in Africa, but in Europe and Asia. This song and the popularity of Reggae music is a perfect example of cultural diffusion. . . . Today many American musicians are using the reggae beat to get their thoughts and messages across. Music has now become an international telephone.[7]

Thus, by an explication of concepts introduced in class-cultural diffusion, and ethnocentrism, we see students demonstrating knowledge-in-action. By engaging such powerful and progressive lyrics, students developed a deeper interest in learning and in the intersection between popular culture, non-school knowledge or their indigenous knowledge, and the general curriculum.

Discovering Hidden Truths

(T)he words African Americans did write were not valued by libraries, museums, archives, or institutions charged with the responsibility of preserving literary and cultural material.
                                                            Elizabeth McHenry

There was a certain magic to that first year when we discussed Apartheid. Students began realizing that through systematic, independent, inquiry they could discover knowledge and then use the classroom as an arena for the contestation of ideas. Then one day, sophomore Ann M. Green read her self-initiated essay. . . .

We live in a world in which Africans are surrounded by myths. Our task is to destroy them. . . . As an African living in a foreign land it is easy to get lost. One can be easily brainwashed by living each day—reading about, and watching and studying Europeans.

(T)he textbooks are devoted to European history. African history is only squeezed in as an unfortunate mistake that is tolerated. One interpretation of this act is that Africa does not have as much history as Europe. They would want us believe this.

History is often taught in pieces, leaving out the important contributions which Africans made. . . . While claiming to be civilizing Africa, European nations robbed Africa of its riches. It did not stop there. Europe went on to rob Africa of its rightful and complete place in history.

Until we take a stand, reach back and grab our history, the Europeans will keep building on the myth behind which they are trying to hide our history.[8]

When she completed reading and the thunderous applause subsided, her classmates raised a slew of questions. The interest in the essay forced me to release it to a wider audience. I shared it with Dawad Phillip, editor of the *Daily Challenge*, New York's only Black daily newspaper, and within a few days the article was carried in the paper. I also reproduced Ann's article and circulated it in my Black History class. Many students used the article as a source text to interrogate related issues. Keysha Hall responded:

> Not enough Black History is being taught in schools. Unlike English and Math, Black History is not mandatory. . . . It is only an elective, which many students are not even aware of. . . .
>
> Black History is not taught in the in-depth way in which it should be taught in regular social studies classes. That is why Black History courses should be offered to give students a broader and more in-depth view of this neglected area.[9]

Keysha's essay was also carried in the *Daily Challenge* as the guest editorial for its February 1, 1989 issue! By problematizing the gaps in the curriculum, students laid down the gauntlet for their generation and future ones. Self-initiated student discourse such as revealed here often helped to propel discussion into previously uncharted territory. Indeed, Ann's essay also unwittingly initiated the multicultural debate.

The 1990s media debates about the merits of an inclusive curriculum seeped into our classroom. Students pillowed the "system" for its failure to present a holistic curriculum that critically evaluates yet celebrates the true diversity that obtains in the world. Then one day, eight years after "Grab Your History" was written, Quiotta Hooks submitted the following article, which was also carried in the Daily Challenge. . . .

Many people complain about what is missing from the school curriculum. They say (that) it's unfair that schools do not teach as much Black History as they should. Although I agree with this view, there is another question that should be raised: Why should students rely totally on the schools to teach Black History?

There are school libraries as well as public libraries that any individual can visit and find a book about any subject. There are no police officers and security guards in front of libraries preventing black people from entering. During the month of February 1996, I had the privilege of viewing the controversial movie "Malcolm X." . . . This brings to mind an episode of "Street Soldiers"—a call—in current affairs program on 97.1 F.M., Sundays at 9:00 P.M. that I listened to last year. On that particular show the guest, Sister Souljah, expressed the importance of learning our history on our own. A listener called in and stated that although he dropped out of high school, he took it upon himself to learn all he needed to know.

This discussion brought to mind the experience of Frederick Douglass. It was not in a slave's place to learn how to read and write but Frederick Douglass educated himself. He realized that in order to learn to read and write he would have to teach himself. Too many people use the lack of Black History and black people in the school curriculum as an excuse for ignorance. If students are really serious about real education we should take it upon ourselves just as Frederick Douglass did. For, in order to know where you are going, you need to know where you came from.[10]

Here again we see a student writing not in reaction to a classroom assignment but in response to her entry into a thinking and writing community, one that facilitates ongoing longitudinal dialogs. For it was a close reading of previous student views on the multicultural debate, which prompted Quiotta to enter the fray. And what a large canvas did she draw from and on!

Students' courage and commitment to continuously engage all aspects of imperialism and its legacy persist. Drawing on the writings from the Brooklyn classroom, Fitzroy Whyte, one of my current students in the Bronx, commented on Rudyard Kipling's "White Mann's Burden" thus:

> We do not wish to cause you burden
> Nor send forth our children in exile
> Since you are so civilized,
> You should consider the glory of difference for a while
> You only see the façade of our culture and term us as wild
> Because of our original beliefs you consider us devilish children
> We do not wish to cause you burden
> Your rewards are slavery and fraud
> You envision yourself better
> It's only your longevity you guard. . . .
> We do not wish to cause you burden
> Your generosity is too great
> We do not wish to lose our freedom
> Our gods shall protect us from your people and your god.[11]

By speaking out so powerfully and contesting the thin disguises, which were used to rationalize imperialism and its handmaiden, ethnocentrism, and oppression, Fitzroy extended Ann Green's notion of contesting and grabbing history. Thus, students of today, standing on the shoulders of the pioneers from Brooklyn, have entered into the discourse community—one that fashions a space wherein students participate not only in a literary pilgrimage to self-knowledge but also in an exploration of the importance of knowing one's history as a precondition for social activism. At every turn, then, they were pushing the envelope by contesting the dogmas of those who would stigmatize urban students as disengaged youth only concerned with "miscellaneous bling bling."

Unearthing the Poetry of Everyday Life

If in 1988 students used the logic of essay writing to attack and inform each other of the stain of imperialism and apartheid, then since 1989 they have begun working on the emotional level. Learning from popular culture they employed literary devices—skits, poems, raps, graffiti and so on—to spread their message. Imagining a brighter day for South Africa, Ann M. Green offered:

> A man without freedom/A man jailed for his wisdom.
> They jailed one man's footsteps. . . . /
> And still yet the giant leap is on the move/With no doubt they are upset.
> A man, a captive, in his own land/
> The spirit is free, so free Mandela's hands.[12]

By encapsulating the spirit of resistance and resilience, writers highlighted how much the march to freedom in South Africa was at the hub of students' existence in a Brooklyn classroom. Indeed, during the later stage of apartheid, students were like researchers chronicling every facet of that blight on the human conscience. Poetry, then, became for them a mode through which to attack and raise psyche.

Writing as if she were in South Africa witnessing Mandela's release, Sharon Sang captured the scene for posterity:

> On February 14, we felt their fear
> And when I saw his face I shed a tear!
> We couldn't believe they saw the light
> Releasing our leader was only right.
> His eyes so bright, his face so tender
> No sign of hate or of surrender.[13]

Indeed, many of the critical socio-political events of the early 1980s to the present—the fall of the Soviet Union; political turmoil in Haiti; the United States invasions of Grenada and Panama; ethnic cleansing in Bosnia, Rwanda; the Arab Israeli conflict; police brutality and so on—have been chronicled and evaluated by students writing more than 2300 pages in 17 published journals at two different urban sites.[14] And more than 50 adults—parents, community activists and university professors—have offered critical, though supportive, commentaries on students' writings, thereby underscoring our notion of a classroom without borders.

Writing in the midst of the Bush administration's "shock and awe" war against Iraq, Angela Cherry noted: ". . . . In a new song by Jay Z, I'm not sure of his exact words, he says, "Love conquers war/When will they learn?" I agree. But I guess (president) Bush didn't get the message."[15] Thus, students envisioned themselves more as active researchers rather than as passive learners. We were able to facilitate this thrust by allowing students a say in many aspects of the running of the classroom and of the Society and its journal.

One of the final tasks involved with the production process requires student editors to arrange articles into sections in addition to proofreading the writings. When arranging and reviewing each section, editors are free to comment on any article or poem in the firm knowledge that it's only for the ears and eyes of the editorial collective. However, sometimes some notes are revealed. Once we received Ade Nicholson's note which read:

> I enjoyed this essay. I like the way how (the student) "broke down" the song by explaining each part. This piece should be shown around to other writers to encourage them to explain a song of their choice. (Not Me!) *sic*.[16]

We quickly realized its historical significance so we decided to include it in order to highlight how intellectual integrity and humility thrive when students discover and assert their voice in a democratic classroom.

Embracing Ade's suggestion, many students—ironically including Ade—herself incorporated popular lyrics into their classroom expositions, both to give their analysis more punch and urgency, and also to help authenticate self. Thus, by integrating popular culture into the classroom they were subverting the system by asserting their right to be participants in the educational discourse about creating more student-centered arenas.

Perhaps a minor segue to *witness* students' critical interrogation of the popular is necessary here. Chsauna Jenkins, writing in 1990, set the stage for a symposium on the role of the artist in society. She opined:

> . . . . It is not an artist's duty to give positive messages. It is purely the artist's choice. . . . If an artist looks at what's going on in the world and decides to make an album speaking out on social problems . . . that's fine; more power to the artist.

Music is a universal language that can be used to send positive or socially conscious messages. Music can also be just good fun as dancing tunes with lyrics that have nothing to do with racism, governmental corruption or the plight of the homeless. Both approaches are fine.

"Big Daddy Kane," the rapper. . . . is just a personality. . . . But when he visits schools and tells kids not to do drugs, he's not performing. People respect (him) for this because they know that this 22 year old Brooklynite has sound values. If he didn't go around to schools . . . it wouldn't make him any less a person . . . because (he) does not always send "positive" or "progressive" messages (in his lyrics).[17]

This essay spawned a 14-page section in the 1990 edition of *Crossing Swords* and reverberates till today. Writing, in quick response to Chsauna's take, Mauricia O'Keeffe noted:

> . . . . When Chsauna says that "Artists shouldn't feel that it's their duty as role models to send socially conscious messages because they didn't ask to be role models" she misses the point. These artists may not have asked to become role models but that's what they are. Their fans don't only dance to their music but they listen to the artists. Saying that "I didn't ask to be a role model" is copping out.[18]

The above dialog suggests how students may have stumbled upon and practiced "accountable talk" long before it became one of today's educational buzzwords. Indeed, Rosemarie Dunbar on a live radio interview explained the process as follows: "Mr. H. pushed us to talk

. . . That's what we are doing; we are talking in the journal."[19]

And Tricia Parris spoke to the positive role that hip hop, the strain that Cornel West refers to as "prophetic hip hop (that) remains true to the righteous indignation and political resistance of deep democratic energies"—plays, sometimes away from the public eye. . . .[20]

> . . . . In "Dedicated to Smooth" another rap group exclaims: "To be with the smooth nation violence needs to cease/Quiet the wilding and turn a new leaf on life" . . . This song is encouraging people to live in harmony and stop the violence. The artists conclude their message. . . . "To be smooth is to be crime free and drug free/Life is lovely." This song clearly indicates that music is not just a bunch of noise.[21]

Judy Forbin went beyond hip hop to call for music appreciation and tolerance that transcends the popular imagination. Intuitively, she recognized and understood the power of the autobiographical to contextualize and ground one's writings while "keeping it real". She wrote. . . .

> . . . . To some people "Rap" is useless banging noises. That's what my mother called it until I encouraged her to really listen to the lyrics. She had the same feeling about modern reggae (but) changed her opinion after listening carefully to both music forms.

> Older people have a way of condemning modern music especially in the case of reggae, heavy metal and rap. They label these music forms as noise but in their own unique way, these new musical expressions give a message and most of the time they do give good messages. . . .

Rejecting the binary opposites in which the discussion is most often cast by media talk-heads, students often deconstructed music lyrics. Again and again, as they do in their private spaces and informal registers, students contested and rejected the lot in which they were often cast as lovers of violent, homophobic, misogynous anti-social rap. Judy continues. . . .

> . . . . In "Paradise" Phil Collins identifies homelessness as a serious problem. He sings about the homeless crying out for help while the comfortable people enjoy "days in paradise" and ignore the plight of the homeless. . . . In "One Blood" Junior Reed, a reggae artist, gives the message that no matter what a person's color, race or class, we are all of "one blood."[22]

Can we envision more ennobling ways of engaging students in a manner that allows them to connect schooling and life to their developing consciousness of self? These conversations dramatize how by collaborating and reflecting on each other's work, members of the classroom community were able to extend on their classmates' ideas. And by so doing they were able to delve deeper into many areas which individually each student may not have normally considered. Moreover, it was as if students were situating themselves in a "story bigger than themselves and locat(ing self) in a narrative grander than themselves."[23]

Over the years, did students' continuous battling and assertion of "their right to write" substantiate self through a critical engagement of their stories? And, could this have contributed to a more enhanced humanity?

By 1999 they were, to use Kenesha Vassell's title, ready to "break down the barriers" and walls that were erected to tarnish and *contain* hip hop. Drawing on the 1990 symposium as her source text, Kenesha wrote . . .

. . . . The late Tupac Shakur is an example of an artist with positive lyrics. In "Changes" he sings . . .

> "It's time to fight back/That's what Huey said/Two shots in the back now Huey's dead . . . /we got to start making changes."

This verse shows what happens when someone "steps up to the plate" and says no more. He is put in the darkness either physically or mentally. I think that the reason that the powers-that-be try to put down or give black music a bad name is because they are still fearful of our past. . . . During slavery . . . music was also used to plot rebellions. . . . .[24]

These powerful and heartfelt commentaries created an alternative curriculum or information base which other students often used as a source text rather than always relying on the "official" view promoted by the media and others who engage in, to use Joe Kincheloe's apt term, "aesthetic policing"—attempts by the educational elite to exterminate any *forms* (mis)perceived as a challenge to the canon. By listening and engaging hip hop so intensely, students were both documenting their times while at the same time making sure that their scribbles would not be erased once they were recorded in their publication—one that challenged the stereotypical view that the majority of urban teens cannot and do not write.

To be sure, students' writings in this chapter underscored how "popular culture has become an increasingly important pedagogical site" and that when students' voices are valued they become a transformative agent.[25] Indeed, once we, as teachers, also envision ourselves as learners and allow students the freedom to infuse their very own interests and self-activity, we may well discover new possibilities for holding students' interest in traditional schooling.

The Mind at Work

No topic was taboo or inconsequential. Sometimes it was students' very engagement with their lived realities which added spark to otherwise drab lessons. As such, students discovered a voice not just for engaging the core curriculum but for their own critical engagement with the central issues of life. In a sense then, the refashioned classroom allowed students to unsilence their voices by creating a new frame of reference counter to the prevailing teacher-dominated one.[26]

Speaking out very boldly Anicia Dalhouse provides greater insight into certain facets of urban education which is in stark contrast to the volumes written by some of the most competent urban educators and ethnographers. By reflecting critically on her classroom interactions and contextualizing her experiences, Anicia raises central issues about the nature of the teaching-learning continuum. She writes:

> . . . . What is the purpose of education? This is the question I must now ask myself after getting . . . 86 on the U. S. History Regents Exam . . . yet still I was given a failing grade of 55 in the course. . . .

Day in and day out I went to the class and scribbled a note here and a note there to my friends. Many times rather than fall asleep in the class I (left). . . . However, whenever we had tests I never failed. . . . Perhaps my teacher was insulted that I never copied his notes and yet still I knew so much of the material.

. . . Throughout the school all teachers proclaimed that . . . the Regents Exam would be counted as the final exam. That's why I am outraged that my teacher failed me after I passed all of his exams and scored (the) highe(st) . . . on the Regents. . . .

How could he fail me when consistently I scored higher than any of the kids who sat everyday in his boring and uninspiring classroom and took his notes? On contemplation, I've realized that I have answered my own question. *It seems as if the teacher's arrogance led him to believe that because I failed to learn from him, my knowledge was not valid . . .*

I wonder if the true purpose of this school system is more to pull students down than to build (us) up. The history that I know is history I learned from reading on my own. . . . *Too many teachers today are failing to realize that the history they teach is what the City or Board (of Education) tells them to teach for forty-five minutes. I am one of the students who went out and got a thousand years of history, on my own!*[27]

Welcome to education in an urban setting wherein self-directed students take responsibility for learning by challenging and contesting classroom malpractices, in this case that of an educational leader—an assistant principal. Sometimes literature conveys larger truths than facts. Writing in her immensely insightful and popular novel, Sista Souljah captured an image of urban education thus:

> School was like a hustle. Teachers wanted me to come to school so they could get paid to *control* me. What do I get out of the deal? Enough said, I just wasn't having it.[28]

Indeed, "students who analyze and understand" their own marginality and invisibility both in the classroom and in the wider society end up understanding schooling, their inner lives and the stresses and strains that inhibit and constrain learning, "at a level not understood by most educational leaders."[29] It was as if Anicia, too, "just wasn't having'" the teacher continuously break her will with disengaging lessons that sought to castrate her curiosity. And this is what led her to—even as the teacher spoke and wrote on the board—engage in the pastime of writing notes to her classmates, a disposition of resistance that has been acknowledged by Prettyman.[30] Not even the prospects of official school censure and possible vindictiveness when taking the course again tempered the student's desire to document her experiences.

To be sure, no attempt is being made here to join the bandwagon of those who make a name for themselves by thrashing teachers. Rather, like Goodson, we believe that "the life story individualizes and personalizes; the life history contextualizes and politicizes."[31] Anicia's narrative helps us come to terms with the story not just of students' perceptions of what is wrong with urban education, but provides an avenue through which we ponder the larger question: how can we refashion the delivery of urban education so that students' interests, lived experiences and commitment to learning are critically engaged in a manner that does not silence and marginalize the community of learners? Thus, by telling her story it became a public matter for exploration.

There appear to be five key themes flowing through Anicia's missive:

- Respect for students and their pre-existing (even nontraditional) knowledge base or self-knowledge.
- Refashioning the classroom into learning centers that would devise ways of accentuating students interests and strengths.
- Continuous rethinking of the "lines" of authority to include more student voices to help temper the classroom and its mode of engagement.
- Creating ways of intersecting school knowledge with students' everyday lived experiences.
- Fashioning ways for building on students' inherent and intuitive sense of self-reflection.

Here in one swipe a student, in an urban school that would be closed as a failure in 2001, challenged conventional wisdom by foregrounding a host of issues that still engage us today. It's mind-boggling to think that students without the benefit or burden of a few graduate degrees and immersion in all the fuzzy educational theories can stay within their hoods and imagine livelier and more engaging possibilities for nurturing and "creating classrooms that matter" charged, not merely to prepare them to pass tests, but for participation in the dialog about *living*.

Students knew intuitively that no one had to give them permission to critique "what was dispensed to them as knowledge (or) take control over the conditions of the production of knowledge or engage the classroom texts critically in light of their own experiences, histories, and concerns."[32] Their very social self-activity as practiced in their everyday encounters in the lunchroom, ballpark, hallways and wherever they meet, dictate a desire and urge to resist objectification. It is also the space where by critically engaging their environment, students begin "putting their impress on the world."[33]

Forging New Identities

Very early in the process students realized that the journal served not only as repository to preserve their impressions, thereby allowing future students on the literary pilgrimage to self-knowledge to be able to connect with today's pilgrims, but it also helped in the affirmation of self while expanding their discourse community. Moreover, unlike Farrell who contends that "(b)eing an athlete brings peer respect; joining clubs does not . . . except from fellow club members and teachers,"[34] seventeen year Kenesha Vassell was one of many students who unknowingly contested this view. Commenting on her involvement in non-athletic activities, she notes:

. . . . Writing gave me a new identity. As I walked through the hallways many teachers, security officers, and even students who[m] I did not know told me that they read something I wrote.[35]

By recognizing the community of readers who are normally forgotten, Kenesha demonstrates an intuitive appreciation of how print media influence readers and how writers are in turn affected by readers' feedback. Thus, by engaging and highlighting the reading public now, Kenesha makes sure that neither writer nor reader is forgotten.[36]

While at the Brooklyn School, we hosted a yearly symposium wherein students read their poems and performed their raps, students in the Bronx started One Mic! Spectacular Vernaculars: A Monthly Lunchroom Symposium. Commenting on the event Beverly Duckworth, a parent, notes:

> I . . . read *CounterCurrents*, cover-to-cover, and I am extremely impressed with the poems and essays. . . . I attended "One Mic!" in March (2003) and I was tremendously shocked and delighted by the brilliance of the presentations. There were talented students expressing their creativity in poems and raps. As I recall, there were also teachers who were sharing their talents. . . . I also realized that One Mic! . . . caused an interaction among the students, their peers, and their teachers and I believe that this is a very good way of bringing them together."[37]

This bird's eye view of the narrowing of the gap between the classroom and the lunchroom on the one hand, and today's students, those of the past and the wider community on the other, highlights anew our vision of creating a classroom without borders in which parents also play a central role.

Just as the timbre of the classroom was energized by the theatrics and flair of the lunch-room, then in its turn, the lunchroom was now being recalibrated by students injecting some of the very critical forms and ideas from the classroom into the lunchroom. The dialectic was at work. Capturing this dynamic, Jeremy Forbes declared: "One Mic is a verbal repro-duction of CounterCurrents,"[38] in that all of the creative and critical thought in the jour-nal was now being inserted into the lunchroom.

Conclusion

A richer vein enters the educational literature (discourse) when students take the lead and demonstrate how their insights, life stories, familiarity and embrace of popular culture can transform the classroom into an enlightened arena of critical discourse. By "decentering power" within the classroom, the general curriculum is no longer reified but is instead viewed as problematic. If as Gramsci asserts that "all men are intellectuals . . . but not all men have in society the function of intellectuals" then there is an inherent paradox in student writ-ings encapsulated within the body of this chapter.[39] Namely, that by envisioning settings in which students examine the curriculum, popular culture and their life stories in a mean-ingful problem-posing mode, these organic intellectuals-in-formation put themselves on the cusp of discovering that their very everyday social activity may well be consistent and/or con-sonant with critical pedagogy.

In the foregoing we employed the multifaceted and multitalented voices of urban youth to capture and tell a bittersweet tale of classroom life/lore in two democratic and truly student-centered classrooms. Hopefully, by listening to students' lunchroom talk—their poetry of everyday life—and their oft hidden registers, teacher educators and practitioners may build upon this exegesis and explore ways to more critically engage the multiple intelligences of our youth who have been marginalized and silenced for too long, both in the classroom and in the profusion of *studies* in which they have been rendered mere *objects* of research. By unleashing students' resonant voices, it is our hope that committed educators would envision structures that would facilitate the release of students' creative potentials while welcoming their voices into the dialog about schooling.

NOTES

1   J. Devine, *Maximum Security: The Culture of Violence in Inner City Schools* (Chicago: University of Chicago Press, 1996).

2   D. Scott, *Conscripts of Modernity: The Tragedy of Colonial Enlightenment* (Durham & London: Duke University Press, 2004), p. 49.

3   D. Ingram, "When the Student Becomes the Teacher," *CounterCurrents: Journal of the Society for Independent Thought, Walton High School*, 3(1) (2004): pp. 13–14.

4   H. Kohl, *I Won't Learn From You* (New York: New Press, 1994).

5   C. McCarthy et al., "Anxiety and celebration: popular music and youth identities at the end of the century" in C. McCarthy, G. Hudak, S. Miklaucic and P. Saukko, eds. *Sound Identities: Popular Music and the Cultural Politics of Education* (New York: Peter Lang Publishing, 1999), pp. 1–16.

6   V. Olive, "Music against Apartheid," *Crossing Swords, Journal of the Society for Social Analysis, Sarah J. Hale High School*, 1(1) (1988): 11.

7   R. Dunbar, "A Call for Freedom: The Bob Marley Legacy," ibid., p. 10.

8   A. Green, "Grab Your History," *Crossing Swords*, 1(2) (1989): 47–48.

9   K. Hall, "A Call for More Black History," ibid., p. 49.

10   Q. Hooks, "Elevating Oneself Through Self-Discovery," *Crossing Swords*, 6(1) (1997): 10.

11   F. Whyte, "Sorry Master," *Taboo*, 8(1) (2004): 5.

12   A. Green, "Open the Chains," *Crossing Swords*, 1(2) (1989): 53.

13   S. Sang, "The Release," *Crossing Swords*, 2(1) (1991): 55.

14   For a more extensive treatment of students engaging world issues, see W. Holder, "How Can Urban Students Become Writers?" in S. Steinberg and J. Kincheloe, eds. *19 Urban Questions: Teaching in the City* (New York: Peter Lang, 2004), pp. 173–208.

15   A. Cherry, "Desperate Times," *CounterCurrents*, 1(2) (2003): 25.

16   A. Nicholson, "Reactions," *Crossing Swords*, 7(1) (1999): 97.

17   C. Jenkins, "Rappers Delight: Message or Money?" *Crossing Swords*, 1(3) (1990): 126–127.

18   M. O'Kieffe, "Artists Do Have a Responsibility," ibid., pp. 127–128.

19   R. Dunbar, Quoted in "Excerpts from A Radio Interview," *Crossing Swords*, 1(2) (1989): 104.

20   C. West, *Democracy Matters: Winning the Fight Against Imperialism* (New York: The Penguin Press, 2004),

p. 182.

21   T. Parris, "Beyond the Melody," *Crossing Swords, 1(3)* (1990): 128–129.

22   J. Forbin, "The Language of Music" *Crossing Swords, 1(3)* (1990): 129–130.

23   West, p. 177.

24   K. Vassell, "Breaking Down the Barriers," *Crossing Swords, 7(1)* (1999): 68–69.

25   G. Dimitriadis, "Hip Hop and Cultural Pedagogy: From Tupac to Master P and Beyond" in S. Steinberg and J. Kincheloe, eds. *Kinderculture: The Corporate Construction of Childhood* (Colorado: Westview Press, 2004), pp. 284–300.

26   S. L. Bosacki, *The Culture of Classroom Silence*, (New York: Peter Lang , 2005).

27   A Dalhouse, "A thousand years of history," *Crossing Swords, 8(1)* (2000): 3–4.

28   S. Souljah, *The Coldest Winter Ever* (New York: Pocket Books, 1999), p. 9.

29   J.L. Kincheloe and S.R. Steinberg, "Making meaning and analyzing experience-student researchers as transformative agents," in S.R. Steinberg and J.L. Kincheloe, eds. *Students as Researchers: Creating Classrooms That Matter* (London: Falmer Press, 1998), pp. 238–246.

30   S. Prettyman, "Writing and passing notes: resistance, identity and pleasure in the lives of teenage girls," in *Students as Researchers*, : pp. 64–76.

31   I. F. Goodson, "Storying the self: life politics and the study of the teacher's life and work," in William Pinar, ed. *Curriculum: Toward New Identities* (New York: Garland Publishing Inc., 1998), pp. 3–20.

32   H.A. Giroux, *Pedagogy and the Politics of Hope: Theory, Culture, and Schooling* (Boulder: Westview Press, 1997), p. 170.

33   M. Rose, *The Mind at Work: Valuing the Intelligence of the American Worker* (New York: Viking Books, 2004), p. 97.

34   E. Farrell, *Self and School Success: Voices and Lore of Inner-City Students* (New York: State University of New York Press, 1994), p. 103.

35   K. Vassell, "Classroom melodies: giving voice to the voiceless," *Crossing Swords, 8(1)* (2000): 31.

36   E. McHenry, *Forgotten Readers: Recovering the Lost History of African American Literary Societies* (Durham and London: Duke University Press, 2002).

37   B. Duckworth, "Releasing hidden potentials," *CounterCurrents, 2 (1)* (2003): ix.

38   J. Forbes, Quoted in *CounterCurrents*, p. 75.

39   D. Coben, *Radical Heroes: Gramsci, Freire and the Politics of Adult Education* (New York: Garland Publishing, 1998), p. 118.

Contributors

SIDONIA ALENUMA was born in Jirapa, a small town in Ghana, Africa. She has her BA degree from the University of Ghana, Legon, and Honors in Sociology and Russian. She left Ghana in 1989 and has since then pursued further studies. She has an MA degree in International Development Studies from St. Mary's University, Halifax, Canada. She has been living in the United States since 1992 and has graduated from the University of Tennessee, Knoxville, with a PhD in Education. She is currently seeking a permanent faculty position in Education. Her academic interests and specialties include cultural studies in education, multicultural education theory and pedagogy, social justice and social difference, social foundations of education, international development studies, as well as sociology.

NOEL ANDERSON has been an educator for over ten years, teaching in both public and private schools in Philadelphia and New York. He served in senior administrative and consulting roles for several educational non-profits in New York City, working closely with school district administrators, teachers and community members to develop college preparation and after-school programs in under-resourced communities of color. Noel graduated *cum laude* from Brooklyn College with a BA in Political Science. He earned his MS in

Education from the University of Pennsylvania and his PhD in Education Policy from New York University. He is an Assistant Professor in the Political Science Department at Brooklyn College (CUNY). Noel's research interests are urban education policy, equity and education, school de-segregation, community power and politics, and South African education (Apartheid/post-Apartheid). He has presented nationally and internationally, and published several articles on issues ranging from zero tolerance and students of color, to educational equity and school financing. He is currently turning his dissertation, which focuses on the experiences of African American and Latino males in an urban college preparation program, into a book and is working on a monograph tracing the influences of American educational policy on the development of Bantu (Apartheid) education in South Africa. Noel is an avid painter and photographer, citing such diverse artists as African American artist, Jacob Lawrence and Iranian feminist artist, Shirin Neshat as inspirations. "My art work is my balance and my rebellion." Noel lives with his wife, Shan Browning, a television producer/documentarian, and son, Avery, in Ft. Greene, Brooklyn.

BRYONN BAIN, is a poet, artist, and educator, who while completing a master's degree at New York University, organized the group of pioneering activists who founded the *Blackout Arts Collective* in 1997 to empower communities of color through the arts, education, and activism. For the past three years BAC's *Lyrics on Lockdown* campaign has worked with community-based organizations such as *The Malcolm X Grassroots Movement, The Prison Moratorium Project, The Ella Baker Center for Human Rights, Critical Resistance*, and *Drop the Rock* in using hip hop, spoken word, theater, dance, and visual art to raise awareness and mobilize action to abolish the prison crisis in America. He has been featured on *60 Minutes* and in the *Village Voice*. During his first year at Harvard Law School, Bain was crowned Boston's 1999 Slam Poetry Champion, and then went on to win the 2000 Grand Slam Poetry Championship at the world renowned *Nuyorican Poet's Café.'* Bryonn's poetry is featured on the album *NYC Slams: 13 Hottest Poets in New York City*.

ROCHELLE BROCK is an Assistant Professor of Education in the Early Childhood Education Department at Georgia State University in Atlanta Georgia. Her current theoretical interests include Afrowomanist pedagogy, race and gender studies, and Black women's spirituality as a vehicle for academic transformation.

JOSEPH CARROLL-MIRANDA was born and raised in San Juan, Puerto Rico. He was and is seriously involved in student movements and student government for over a decade in Puerto Rico, Latin America and Global Youth. Joseph obtained his BA from the University of Puerto Rico in 1998. In addition, he obtained his MA in Curriculum and Instruction from New Mexico State University. Currently he is a semester shy to be ABD in his Doctorate in Curriculum and Instruction focusing in Learning Technologies and a minor in Critical Pedagogy.

ROSALINA DIAZ is a Latina, born in Arecibo, Puerto Rico and raised in Brooklyn, New York. She was trained as a Cultural Anthropologist at the American Museum of Natural

History where she served as Supervising Anthropology Instructor, and later educational consultant, specializing in Latin American and Caribbean cultures. In addition to being the mother of four girls, she presently teaches Graduate Education courses at the City College of New York. Prior to that she taught High School English/Social Studies for fifteen years with New York City's Department of Education, and Anthropology and Human Geography courses with the City University of New York. Her greatest challenge and inspiration has been raising four Latina daughters in New York City.

GARRETT ALBERT DUNCAN is an Associate Professor of Education, of African and Afro-American Studies, and of American Culture Studies at Washington University in St. Louis. He previously taught in public middle and high schools in southern California where he also briefly taught GED classes for incarcerated young men in the California Youth Authority. Prof. Duncan's research focuses broadly on race, culture, and education. He has presented his research on the school-to-prison nexus at the 1998 "Critical Resistance" conference held at the University of California, Berkeley, at the 2003 "School to Prison Pipeline" conference sponsored by the Harvard University Civil Rights Project, and at the 2004 "Education or Incarceration? Schools and Prisons in a Punishing Democracy" conference sponsored by the Center on Democracy in a Multiracial Society at the University of Illinois at Urbana-Champaign. Prof. Duncan's current project, "Schooling as a Moral Enterprise," is also concerned with questions of race, citizenship and democracy in the contexts of postindustrialism and globalization. He addresses these questions in his forthcoming book *School to Prison: Education and the Celling of Black Youth in Postindustrial America* (Peter Lang Publishing, Inc.).

VENUS E. EVANS-WINTERS is an Assistant Professor at Illinois Wesleyan University in the Departments of Educational Studies and Sociology, where she teaches courses on the foundations of education, sociology of education, urban girls, and qualitative research methodology. Her recent work explores the potential and significance of the merge between Black feminism and postmodernism as a lens to study the schooling experiences of African American female adolescents. Her current areas of research interest are the interactions of race, class, and gender on educational resilience, urban education, and the role of community organizations in the lives of African American female children. She received her Doctorate degree from the University of Illinois at Urbana-Champaign in the Department of Educational Policy Studies.

L. A. GABAY ran for president of his high school class and lost. He has been teaching in New York City for ten years, is attending CUNY Graduate Center for two years and has been a Knicks season ticket holder for fifteen years. For public appearances and contact information please log onto http://www.lagabay.com.

REBECCA A. GOLDSTEIN is an Assistant Professor in Curriculum and Teaching at Montclair State University in New Jersey. Her research interests include student and teacher identity construction, issues of democracy and social justice in urban schools, urban school reform and teacher preparation, and the impact of No Child Left Behind. Please address correspondence to Dr. Goldstein via email at Goldsteinr@mail.montclair.edu.

VICTOR GOODE is an Attorney with Advocates for Basic Legal Equality, Inc., a Toledo-based public interest law firm representing low-income clients in Northwest Ohio. Victor has done pro bono work with the NAACP in Texas and Ohio. Having published numerous scholarly and popular articles about race and civil rights, a recent project has been to encourage legal services for the poor programs to do more race-based advocacy, for example, V. Goode, Race, Racism and Legal Services Training, *Management Information Exchange Journal*, 43 (Spring 2003); V. Goode and P. Flowers, Invisibility of Clients of Color: The Intersection of Language, Culture and Race in Legal Services Practice, *Clearinghouse Review: Journal of Poverty Law and Policy*, 109 (May–June 2002).

JENNIFER D. GOODE is a fourth-year doctoral student (ABD) at Bowling Green State University in Ohio. She is a 2002 recipient of a Minority Fellowship from the American Sociological Association, primarily funded through a grant from the National Institute of Mental Health. Her current research focuses on examining the roles of various agents of socialization on adolescents' developmental outcomes.

ROB HAWORTH grew up in Southern California. He taught in public schools working in special education, alternative secondary schools and secondary social studies classrooms. Currently, he is a doctoral student and teaches social studies pedagogy courses within the teacher education program (TEP) of his institution. His current research involves youth culture, pedagogy and how youth make meaning of the world outside of the classroom.

kecia hayes recently finished her Ph.D. in Urban Education at the CUNY Graduate Center. Her research focuses on how social policies and practices impact the educational experiences of children and parents of color in urban communities. Kecia's dissertation examines the educational experiences of court-involved youth. She has taught graduate courses at the International Center for Cooperation and Conflict Resolution of Teachers College, Columbia University, and was an educational consultant with the NYU School of Education Metropolitan Center, as well as the Center for Social and Emotional Education. She is a founding Trustee of Harlem Episcopal School. Kecia has provided research assistance for *The Colors of Excellence: Hiring and Keeping Teachers of Color in Independent Schools* by Pearl Rock Kane and Alfonso J. Orsini (Eds.); co-authored a chapter in *19 Urban Questions: Teaching in the City* by Shirley Steinberg and Joe Kincheloe (Eds.); and is an editor of *Urban Education: An Encyclopedia* from Greenwood Press, and *Metropedagogy: Power, Justice, and the Urban Classroom* from Sense Publishers.

THOMAS P. HÉBERT is a Professor at the College of Education at the University of Georgia and has conducted research about culturally diverse youth and social emotional issues facing students of color.

WINTHROP R. HOLDER is a teacher of social studies at the Bronx Engineering and Technology Academy and has written on facilitating the writing process for 19 Urban Questions: Teaching in the City (Lang, 2004). His research interests focus on exploring connections between students' lunchroom (talk) symposiums, popular culture, and the general curriculum. He is the author of Classroom Calypso: Giving Voice to the Voiceless (Lang, 2007).

RYONNEL JACKSON is a graduate student at Washington University in St. Louis. He is currently working on his Master of Arts degree in American Culture Studies. His thesis focuses on the post-civil rights, post-desegregation education of African American males at an elementary school in the St. Louis metropolis.

KORINA M. JOCSON is a postdoctoral research fellow at the University of California, Berkeley. Her research focus is on literacies and urban multicultural education, particularly the use of poetry and (multi)media arts in learning.

JOE L. KINCHELOE is the Canada Research Chair at the McGill University Faculty of Education. He is the author of numerous books and articles about pedagogy, education and social justice, racism, class bias, and sexism, issues of cognition and cultural context, and educational reform. His books include: *Teachers as Researchers*, *Classroom Teaching: An Introduction*, *Getting Beyond the Facts: Teaching Social Studies/Social Sciences in the Twenty-first Century*, *The Sign of the Burger: McDonald's and the Culture of Power*, *City Kids: Understanding Them, Appreciating Them, and Teaching Them*, and *Changing Multiculturalism* (with Shirley Steinberg). His co-edited works include *White Reign: Deploying Whiteness in America* (with Shirley Steinberg et al) and the Gustavus Myers Human Rights award winner: *Measured Lies: The Bell Curve Examined (with Shirley Steinberg)*. Along with his partner, Shirley Steinberg, Kincheloe is an international speaker and lead singer/keyboard player of *Tony and the Hegemones*.

RICHARD D. LAKES is an Associate Professor and Program Coordinator of the Social Foundations of Education at Georgia State University, Atlanta. His most recent book (co-edited with Patricia Carter) is *Globalizing Education for Work: Comparative Perspectives on Gender in the New Economy*, published by Lawrence Erlbaum Associates. Lakes can be reached at rlakes@gsu.edu.

PEPI LEISTYNA is an Associate Professor in the Applied Linguistics Graduate Studies Program at the University of Massachusetts, Boston. He coordinates the research program and teaches courses in cultural studies, media analysis, critical pedagogy, and language acquisition. His books include *Breaking Free: The Transformative Power of Critical Pedagogy*, *Presence of Mind: Education and the Politics of Deception*, *Defining and Designing Multiculturalism: One School Sysytem's Efforts*, *Cultural Studies: From Theory to Action*, and *Corpus Analysis: Language Structure and Language Use*.

ERNEST MORRELL is an assistant professor in the Urban Schooling division of the

Graduate School of Education and Information Studies at the University of California at Los Angeles. Prior to this appointment, Morrell served on the Teacher Education faculty at Michigan State University. His work examines the possible intersections between indigenous urban adolescent literacies and the "sanctioned" literacies of dominant institutions such as schools. Particularly, he is interested in the discourse of popular culture; adolescent literacy practices in non-school settings; critical research methodologies; critical literacy education; and urban teacher development. Morrell teaches courses on literacy theory and research, critical pedagogy, cultural studies, urban education, and critical research methods in addition to his methods courses for prospective English teachers.

Morrell is the author of two books, *Linking Literacy and Popular Culture: Finding Connections for Lifelong Learning* (Christopher-Gordon) and *Becoming Critical Researchers: Literacy and Empowerment for Urban Youth* (Peter Lang). Morrell is also the author of two books in press, *Critical Literacy and Urban Youth* (Lawrence Earlbaum) and *Critical Pedagogy in Urban Contexts: Toward a Grounded Theory of Praxis* (Peter Lang). Morrell completed his doctoral study in language, literacy, and culture from the University of California, at Berkeley and taught English in Oakland and Los Angeles, California.

PRIYA PARMAR is currently an Assistant Professor of Adolescence Education at Brooklyn College—CUNY. Prof. Parmar's scholarly interests include critical and multiple literacies, multicultural education, youth culture, and other contemporary issues in the field of cultural studies in which economic, political, and social justice issues are addressed. Prof. Parmar's published scholarly works include "Critical Thinking and Rap Music: The Critical Pedagogy of KRS-One" in *The Encyclopedia of Critical Thinking* (Greenwood Press, 2004) as well as her forthcoming book, "*Rapping Against the Grain: The Pedagogy of an Urban Griot: KRS-One*" (2005).

ELIZABETH P. QUINTERO is an Associate Professor of Early Childhood and Childhood Education, at New York University. Dr. Quintero's research, teaching, and service involve critical literacy in multilingual, multicultural communities. She has particular interest in families of young children, and refugee families in the Middle East, the United Kingdom, and the Americas. She is the author of *Problem Posing with Multicultural Children's Literature: Developing Critical Early Childhood Curricula* (2004, Peter Lang), co-author of *Becoming a Teacher in the New Society: Bringing Communities and Classrooms Together.* (2003, Peter Lang), co-author of *American Voices: Webs of Diversity* (1998, Merrill Education/Prentice Hall), and co-author of *Teachers' reading/teachers' lives.* Albany, NY: State University of New York Press (1997). Before joining the faculty in the Steinhardt School of Education at NYU, she was a faculty member at University of Minnesota, Duluth, and prior to that, director of a federally funded bilingual family literacy project in El Paso, Texas.

SALLY M. REIS is a Professor and Department Head in the Educational Psychology Department at the University of Connecticut who is interested in academically talented students who underachieve in school.

HANDEL KASHOPE WRIGHT is a Canada Research Chair in Comparative Cultural Studies, Director of the Centre for Culture, Identity and Education, and an Associate Professor at the University of British Columbia. His research and teaching interests include multicultural and anti-racist education, cultural studies, continental and diasporic African studies, curriculum theorizing and qualitative research. His recent publications include *A Prescience of African Cultural Studies* (Peter Lang, 2004).

MARGUERITE VANDEN WYNGAARD is a third generation professional musician and began her career in secondary choral education. After fourteen years in the secondary classroom, "Dr. V." earned a PhD in curriculum and instruction, and has begun to establish herself in the understanding, practice, and curriculum alignment that supports culturally responsive pedagogy. Currently she is an Assistant Superintendent at Washtenaw Intermediate School District in Ann Arbor, Michigan, where she provides leadership in secondary reform, urban education and culturally responsive pedagogy, as well as providing technical assistance with district curriculum alignment.

Index

Studies in the Postmodern Theory of Education

General Editors
Joe L. Kincheloe & Shirley R. Steinberg

Counterpoints publishes the most compelling and imaginative books being written in education today. Grounded on the theoretical advances in criticalism, feminism, and postmodernism in the last two decades of the twentieth century, Counterpoints engages the meaning of these innovations in various forms of educational expression. Committed to the proposition that theoretical literature should be accessible to a variety of audiences, the series insists that its authors avoid esoteric and jargonistic languages that transform educational scholarship into an elite discourse for the initiated. Scholarly work matters only to the degree it affects consciousness and practice at multiple sites. Counterpoints' editorial policy is based on these principles and the ability of scholars to break new ground, to open new conversations, to go where educators have never gone before.

For additional information about this series or for the submission of manuscripts, please contact:

Joe L. Kincheloe & Shirley R. Steinberg
c/o Peter Lang Publishing, Inc.
29 Broadway, 18th floor
New York, New York 10006

To order other books in this series, please contact our Customer Service Department:

(800) 770-LANG (within the U.S.)
(212) 647-7706 (outside the U.S.)
(212) 647-7707 FAX

Or browse online by series:
www.peterlang.com